M000187851

600 plants chosen
by the world's greatest
plantspeople

What

Gardeners

Grow

Illustration Melanie Gandyra

First published in 2023 by Frances Lincoln
an imprint of The Quarto Group.
One Triptych Place, London,
SE1 9SH, United Kingdom
www.Quarto.com

bloom
gardening · nature · inspiration

A Bloom book for Frances Lincoln
Bloom is an independent publisher for gardeners, plant admirers,
nature lovers and outdoor adventurers. Alongside books and stationery,
we publish a seasonal print magazine that brings together expert
gardening advice and creative explorations of the natural world.
Bloom celebrates all green spaces, from wilderness to windowsills,
and inspires everyone to bring more nature into their lives.
www.bloommag.co.uk | @bloom_the_magazine

Text © 2023 Bloom / Frances Lincoln
Illustration © 2023 Melanie Gandyra

Commissioning editor Zena Alkayat
Art director Sarah Pyke
Illustrator Melanie Gandyra
Gardener list compiled by Matthew Biggs and Zena Alkayat
Editors Nick Funnell, Sarah Smith, Ellen Hardy
Proofreader Lesley Malkin
Indexer Hilary Bird

Every effort has been made to accurately represent each gardener and
their selection, together with any material quoted. We would be glad to
make good in future editions any omissions or errors if application is made
to the publisher.

A catalogue record for this book is available from the British Library.
ISBN 978-0-7112-72903
Ebook ISBN 978-0-7112-7291-0

Printed in China
10 9 8 7 6 5 4 3 2 1

Contents

Foreword

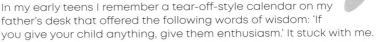

In my early teens I remember a tear-off-style calendar on my father's desk that offered the following words of wisdom: 'If you give your child anything, give them enthusiasm.' It stuck with me.

Finding enthusiasm is one key to a lifetime of happiness. It allows you to radiate an energy that can awaken a new interest in others – it's contagious. It doesn't matter what someone's day-to-day demeanour is like: bring up the subject of their personal passion and an enthusiast is transformed. Even the quietest characters become lively and eager, sharing their joy with anyone who's willing to listen – and often those who aren't. And when that joy is plants and gardening, enthusiasm and passion can transform lives.

This book is filled with personal recommendations from discerning enthusiasts who appreciate exactly what it takes to make a 'good plant'. They have seen it, grown it and understand its nuances. Now they want to share the pleasure. The breadth of experience within these pages is astonishing. *What Gardeners Grow* embraces an unparalleled diversity of expertise, from specialist nursery owners and plant breeders to award-winning designers, plant explorers and broadcasters, and it gathers this expertise into one place through recommendations for you. It is a unique and personal insight into their love of plants and their very favourite selections, and it is a priceless opportunity to benefit from their sage advice so you can make discerning choices in your own garden.

Each entry offers a brief glimpse into the mind of the contributor and their tastes and approach to plants. Some gardeners have been reflective and personal, others lyrically extol the virtues of their chosen plants, offer proven plant associations or simply provide a detailed visual description. Cultivation details ensure that you too can make an informed choice, so you can confidently put 'the right plant in the right place', then proudly name-drop the source of your inspiration, as gardeners are wont to do.

One of the unique features of this book is that it turns the spotlight on a vast treasure trove of knowledge from a hidden gardening world. Among them, unheralded head gardeners at private gardens, with their vast and wide-ranging practical experience, experts at august organisations like the Royal Botanic Gardens, Kew and the Royal Horticultural Society, as well as those in charge of the planting at attractions such as Keukenhof and Giverny – you'll be privy to their personal plant preferences, often revealed for the very first time. The addition of websites means this book also doubles up as an international directory of consultants, designers and gorgeous gardens to visit, while the contemporary yet informative illustrations will be a source of inspiration when painting with plants in your own garden.

Featuring hundreds of plants of all kinds, think of this book as a glorious chocolate box full of treats and surprises. You'll find yourself dipping into its pages again and again, tapping into its energy to fuel your own burgeoning enthusiasm for gardening and plants.

Matthew Biggs, gardener and broadcaster

Publisher's note

One thing you learn very quickly when working with gardeners is that they are a truly generous bunch. They're not only willing and keen to share their discoveries and their experience, they actively seek to excite and encourage anyone with even a passing interest in gardening.

There are those that want to tell you very specific details about a plant they know and love – the exact temperature it's hardy to or whether its leaves are serrated or acutely lobed. Then there are those that paint with much broader strokes, preferring to highlight the way a grass catches the evening light or the delicious scent of a salvia. It's something you'll notice time and again as gardeners divulge the plants that have captured their hearts. The motley collection of plant descriptions – all written especially for this book and listed in no particular order – offers a fantastic mix of both approaches and everything in between. But for me, what was most captivating were the stories of discovery: of falling for a plant on holiday, being gifted a cutting by a relative or remembering some magical moment from childhood. On occasion, more than one gardener has selected the same plant and this is where you see personal experience and individual tales really shine through – no two plants grow the same and no two stories are identical.

Corralling this much information from plantspeople living around the world was a challenge, but that moment of discovering what the next gardener had to say, and the next and the next, was the greatest thrill throughout this project. Each one was like a little gift, opening my eyes to a new way of looking at a plant or simply a new plant. The advice and tips from each contributor were as unique as they are, but in fitting them all to a uniform format I hope we've made a useful book while allowing the personality of each gardener to shine through, unfiltered. I'd love this to be an evolving project with more gardeners and more plants added to each new edition. I look forward to plantspeople getting in touch with this in mind.

I hope the genuine effort we – myself and a small but dedicated Bloom team – have put in to showcase the knowledge and passion of gardeners around the world is apparent, and this rich book encourages you to return to old favourites and unearth your own new discoveries.

Zena Alkayat, publisher

5

MARYLYN ABBOTT
Garden designer and writer,
UK and Australia

Marylyn Abbott is an Australian gardener known for two gardens – Kennerton Green in New South Wales and West Green House in Hampshire, UK. For 15 years she moved between the two, but now gardens in West Green House, a ten-acre garden around a 1720s manor house. *westgreenhouse.co.uk*

Erythronium 'Pagoda' →
Dog's tooth violet 'Pagoda'

I like polite plants and the small 'Pagoda' has very good manners. Over the years it forms larger and more luscious clumps with leaves that are polished and hold their deep green form perfectly. The flowers recall the roof line of an oriental pagoda, or the hats of dancing figures in chinoiserie illustrations, and are held on deceptively strong, needle-thin stems with just a gracious droop. The plants do not invade and are tough – mine live in deep, dry shade beneath a mixture of hornbeam and oak trees, returning each season after total neglect. After flowering, the leaves yellow and the plant disappears before coming back in early spring. This erythronium grows well alongside other clump-forming plants, particularly silvered leaves of *Pulmonaria* 'Diana Clare' with deep blue flowers, and the spotted leaves of *P.* 'Smoky Blue'. I think I first saw erythronium flowering on a stand in the great tent at the RHS Chelsea Flower Show. I lived in Australia in those days and was so cross that I couldn't take the bulbs home. It was just one of many episodes of frustration that eventually led me to move continents. I know it sounds far-fetched, but the desire to grow plants and garden in another climate was overwhelming. It's a challenge I'm still trying to overcome.

GROW Left to naturalise, it clumps up when grown in well-drained soil in dappled shade.

Type
Perennial
Flowering
Spring
**Height/
spread**
50cm x 10cm
Position
Part shade
Soil
Moist, well-
drained
Hardiness
USDA 7b/8a
/ RHS H5

CLAIRE RATINON
Food grower,
East Sussex, UK

Claire Ratinon is an organic food grower and writer. Her work has included growing produce for the Ottolenghi restaurant Rovi, delivering workshops and talks at schools and writing for publications including *Gardens Illustrated* and the *Guardian*. She is the author of *Unearthed: On Race and Roots: How the Soil Taught Me I Belong* and *How to Grow Your Dinner Without Leaving the House*. *claireratinon.com*

Brassica oleracea Acephala Group
Kale

I'm a devotee of the *Brassica* genus in all its forms, but it's kale that I adore the most. Whether it's the dusky reptilian leaves of 'Cavolo Nero' or the soft purple curls of 'Red Russian', kale is a generous plant that I have growing in the ground almost year round (if I'm organised enough). While kale is most often served as a cooked green, it can be eaten raw in salads when its leaves are picked young – although I'd recommend massaging them with olive oil and lemon. I've had the most generous harvests from kale grown in a sunny spot, but they can tolerate some shade and with its striking and varied foliage, I can't think of a kale variety that would be out of place in an ornamental planting plan. It's a plant that is fairly frost tolerant so overwinters well (with a little protection from fleece if it gets especially cold) and will crop again come the following spring. I've taken to leaving my kale plants to bolt so they produce bursts of lemon-yellow flowers in pleasingly geometric patterns that also offer forage for nearby pollinators.

GROW Sow kale from early spring to early summer into small pots or modular trays, one seed per module. When the young plants are sturdy and have six true leaves, transplant to the ground or into a large container. Keep well watered and consider a mesh cover if cabbage white butterflies and pigeons are part of your garden's ecosystem.

Type
Annual,
biennial,
perennial
Flowering
Times vary
**Height/
spread**
1m x 1m
depending
on variety
Position
Full sun, part
shade
Soil
Moist, well-
drained
Hardiness
USDA 8b/9a
/ RHS H4

ELLIOTT FORSYTH
Head gardener, Aldourie
Castle, Inverness, Scotland

Elliott Forsyth specialises in naturalistic planting design, biointensive
vegetable production and gardener training. He trained at RHS Wisley
and the Royal Botanic Garden Edinburgh. For 18 years he was head
gardener at Cambo Gardens in Fife. *aldouriecastle.co.uk*

Selinum wallichianum
Wallich milk parsley

Type
Perennial
Flowering
Summer,
autumn
**Height/
spread**
1.2m x 60cm
Position
Full sun, part
shade
Soil
Well-
drained
Hardiness
USDA 6b/7a
/ RHS H6

This is a very versatile plant from the Himalayas. It looks equally at home at
woodland edges or in late-season naturalistic plantings. Stunning both at a
distance and close up, its architectural, white umbel flowers conjure images of
cow parsley. It has ferny foliage with attractive reddish-tinged stems, and an
additional bonus is that it has good seedheads, which provide interest in winter.
Most umbels are biennials or short-lived perennials, but selinum is a reliable
perennial, making it a low-maintenance alternative. I really like plants that look
good through all stages of growth from emergence to cutback, and this is one.

GROW Easy to grow and adaptable. It looks good from flower to base, so it can be brought
forward in a border to break up predictable heights at the front. Try to avoid disturbing the
tap roots, but if you have to move it, it's best to do so in spring. Like most tap-rooted plants
it is clump-forming, reducing the need to manage lateral spread. It doesn't require staking.

Type
Deciduous
grass
Flowering
Summer
**Height/
spread**
1.2m x 1m
Position
Full sun,
sheltered
Soil
Well-
drained
Hardiness
USDA 9b/10a
/ RHS H3

Pennisetum orientale 'Karley Rose'
Oriental fountain grass 'Karley Rose'

I love this plant – it is one of the most attractive grasses around in my opinion.
I enjoy the curved shape of the flower plume, which is soft and fluffy with pinkish
tones. Some pennisetums do not flower in colder regions, however *P. orientale* and
its cultivars can be relied on. It is clump-forming and I find it looks great at the
foot of mid-sized perennials like monarda or mingling with smaller perennials such
as salvias or liatris. It works in late-season naturalistic borders and Mediterranean
plantings, and associates well with annuals and tender perennials. Its pinkish
tones mean it looks at home with cool pastels or a hot palette.

GROW While reliable, in wetter climates in the northern hemisphere it can benefit from
being placed near a south-facing wall with good drainage. Divide or plant in spring
when in active growth. Unlike many grasses, it does not seed much.

Disporum longistylum 'Night Heron'
Long-styled disporum 'Night Heron'

Type
Rhizomatous
perennial
Flowering
Spring,
summer
**Height/
spread**
2.5m x 50cm
Position
Part shade,
sheltered
Soil
Moist, rich,
well-drained
Hardiness
USDA 6b/7a
/ RHS H6

This exotic-looking woodlander (known also as Chinese fairy bells) is one of the
most beautiful woodland plants around and visitors always ask for its name.
It has especially lovely stems and elegantly pointed, pleated leaves that I love
when they unfurl in spring. The stems also retain their structure through the
winter. The yellow-green bell-like flowers are produced from early summer and
they contrast beautifully with the purple stems and leaves, which turn green
as the season progresses. The flowers are followed by attractive reddish-black
berries. It is clump-forming at the base, with elegant, arching stems above.

GROW Great with ferns or low woodland plants such as tiarellas, which can nestle under
its arching leaves to produce a multi-layered effect. It may sometimes get hit by late
frosts in colder regions but recovers well. Best with an organic mulch and benefits from
a topping of leaf mould to increase moisture retention.

LAURI KRANZ
Owner and founder, Edible
Gardens LA, California, USA

Lauri Kranz is the owner and founder of Edible Gardens LA, where she creates edible landscapes and vegetable gardens for chefs, museums, schools and anyone interested in growing their own food. She is the co-author of *A Garden Can Be Anywhere*. Her work has been featured in magazines such as *Elle Decor* and *Architectural Digest* and she has been featured on NBC's *Today Show*. ediblegardensla.com

Vicia faba ↘
Broad bean

Type
Annual
Flowering
Spring, summer
Height/spread
1m x 50cm
Position
Full sun,
sheltered
Soil
Moist, well-
drained
Hardiness
USDA 8b/9a
/ RHS H4

Growing fava (broad) beans is an extraordinary experience, from the first bean planted to the last bean harvested. The seeds are quite large, easy to handle and quick to sprout and grow. They are also fairly resistant to wildlife and can grow abundantly where other plants are eaten by critters. Fava beans are beautiful in the garden, with tall stems, lush leaves and wonderful flowers that produce the succulent pods and beans. They are incredibly healthy and delicious – I like using them to make bean hummus as well as in pastas and salads. The pods themselves are extraordinary. When you open the bean pod, the inner pod is one of the softest surfaces I have ever felt, gently holding each bean inside its tender grasp.

These beans are a hardy annual crop and exciting to grow! There are several varieties, including green and purple ones. A word of warning, a small number of people have a hereditary allergic-like reaction to fava beans, known as favism.

GROW Fava beans are a cool-season crop. Instead of planting in rows, I like to sow seeds 10–15cm apart in a circular grouping. I prefer not to stake them, letting them grow wild and lean on one another as they mature. I grow them in the open as a standout feature of the garden. I have found that with adequate water, they grow nicely in most soils, but prefer a neutral to slightly acid and well-drained soil. They are nitrogen fixers – they add nitrogen to the soil rather than taking it away.

ULA MARIA
Garden designer,
London, UK

Ula Maria is an award-winning garden designer and landscape architect. She worked for a number of landscape practices before winning the RHS Young Designer of the Year competition. Since then she has established her own practice, Ula Maria Landscape and Garden Design. She is the author of *Green: Simple Ideas for Small Outdoor Spaces*. ulamaria.com

Foeniculum vulgare 'Purpureum'
Bronze fennel

Type
Short-lived
perennial
Flowering
Summer
Height/spread
2m x 1m
Position
Full sun, part shade
Soil
Fertile, well-drained
Hardiness
USDA 7b/8a / RHS H5

Hazy clouds of *F. vulgare* 'Purpureum' foliage gently floating among flowers can add a touch of magic to any planting scheme. It's such a versatile plant – decorative, seasonal, medicinal and culinary all in one. I love its transformation throughout the seasons, so subtle and soft early in the year and providing structural and architectural form as it matures. Late in the summer, small golden flowers crown slender stems, making it irresistible to bees and hoverflies.

GROW Cut the stems back to ground level in early spring and leave them to act as mulch. Can self-seed.

NEIL MILLER

Head gardener, Hever Castle and Gardens, Kent, UK

Neil Miller is a former Lloyd's of London insurance broker who, after being made redundant in the 1990s, followed his passion and retrained as a horticulturist. He joined Hever Castle in 2001 and has been head gardener there for more than 15 years. He is also a judge for Britain in Bloom. *hevercastle.co.uk*

← *Acca sellowiana*
Pineapple guava

I love exotic and tropical plants and this is the nearest you're going to get to growing these in the UK. The plant has beautiful, orchid-style, edible, cherry-red and white flowers with silver green leaves, and delicious fruits that taste of pineapples, apples, strawberries and mint! It is ideal for a small garden. The flowers attract bees and other pollinating insects, while the fruits provide food for the birds.

GROW Easy to grow, low maintenance and no pests or diseases. The plant is self-fertile, but will fruit better if grown with a different cultivar.

Type
Evergreen shrub
Flowering
Summer
Height/spread
2.5m x 2.5m
Position
Full sun, sheltered
Soil
Well-drained, alkaline, neutral
Hardiness
USDA 9b/10a / RHS H3

Strelitzia reginae
Bird of paradise

Perhaps the best known of all tropical plants. A striking addition to your conservatory, it has glaucous banana-like leaves and spectacular orange and midnight-blue flowers in the shape of the head of a colourful crane.

GROW Loves humidity, so mist the leaves regularly and feed every two weeks from spring to autumn with a general-purpose houseplant food. Keep in a sheltered spot outside during the summer, bring inside to the greenhouse or conservatory as first frosts appear. Technically hardy to $-3°C$, but it takes a while to recover from frost damage, so ideal minimum temperature is $10°C–12°C$. Water regularly during spring and summer. From winter allow the soil to dry out between waterings. No pruning required – tatty leaves can be cut back to the base in spring. Prone to red spider mite and mealybug when grown indoors, so check regularly.

Type
Perennial
Flowering
Winter, spring
Height/spread
1.5m x 1m
Position
Full sun, part shade, sheltered
Soil
Moist, well-drained, use John Innes No.3 with added grit if growing in a container
Hardiness
USDA 12 / RHS H1b

Type
Deciduous shrub, small tree
Flowering
Summer
Height/spread
2.5m x 2.5m
Position
Full sun, sheltered
Soil
Well-drained, fertile
Hardiness
USDA 9b/10a / RHS H3

Punica granatum
Pomegranate

I loved seeing pomegranates in Morocco and Israel during my travels, so was excited to know that they would grow in the UK. They have beautiful showy orange-red flowers and exotic fruits – a great talking point!

GROW Overall an easy shrub to grow, it's low maintenance and pest/disease free. Minimal pruning required – prune wayward or crossing branches to maintain a healthy framework in late winter or early spring.

ALISON JENKINS
Designer and ecological
gardener, Somerset, UK

Alison Jenkins has worked as a garden designer for over 20 years. She
manages Damson Farm, a two-acre, organic smallholding and edible
garden, where she practises regenerative gardening and living in
balance with nature. *alisonjenkins.co.uk*

Rubus phoenicolasius
Wineberry

When I planted my first wineberry I was really only thinking of the fruit; I had
no idea it was such an attractive plant. Its bright red, fuzzy stems are striking
and look great through the winter, particularly if trained on a wall. When the
red berries start to develop in late summer they are surrounded by calyxes
that are also covered in fine red hairs. The fruit is delicious, shiny and sticky,
like raspberries dipped in honey. They don't tend to get as far as the kitchen
as they are too tempting to eat straight from the bush, but they are tasty
scattered on yoghurt or ice cream, and freeze well. You may need to net the
plant against birds once it is fruiting as they find the berries just as delicious
as we do!

GROW This is a really easy plant to grow. Once established it grows vigorously, so you
need enough space to let it scramble or be prepared to spend some time pruning and
training it in early winter. It's pretty tough, so can take an exposed site, but if you have
a wall or fence to train it against it may be easier to manage. Alternatively you could
grow it against a frame or wires in a kitchen garden. A mulch of garden compost or
woodchip in the spring will help retain moisture and maintain soil health. It fruits best
on the previous year's growth, so remove all of the current year's fruited stems to the
ground and train in the fresh new growth. I have to confine it to quite a small section
of wall, so I like to train it in loops as you would a rambling rose. Like a bramble, its
tips form roots when they hit the ground, so it is super-easy to propagate. You could
encourage it by tip-layering, but I find it does this all by itself and I have plenty of new
plants to pot up and give away to friends each winter. It doesn't seem susceptible to
disease and its fruit doesn't suffer botrytis as raspberries often do.

Type
Deciduous
shrub
Flowering
Summer
**Height/
spread**
2m x 4m
Position
Fruits best
in full sun,
but grows
happily in
part shade
Soil
Not too
fussy but
doesn't like
to dry out
Hardiness
USDA 7b/8a
/ RHS H5

Type
Rhizomatous perennial
Flowering
Summer, autumn
Height/spread
50cm x 25cm
Position
Full sun, protected
from frost
Soil
Well-drained
Hardiness
USDA 9b/10a / RHS H3

Tulbaghia violacea
Society garlic

I love this plant for its elegance but also for the fact that it
flowers for such a long time – well into the autumn. It's really
useful in containers for this reason. The soft lilac flowering heads
are held high on tall stems above neat, grassy mounds of grey-
green foliage, so it works well layered with earlier flowering
plants. The stems, leaves and flowers are all edible so can be
added to salads or stir-fries. They have a sweet peppery taste
with a hint of garlic that doesn't linger in the mouth, hence the
common name. In its native South Africa it is sometimes planted
around houses as it is said to ward off snakes.

GROW I prefer to plant it in containers but if planting in the ground,
bear in mind that this clump-forming perennial with tuberous roots likes
plenty of sun and free-draining soil – avoid areas that become heavy
or wet. Ensure that it is watered through the summer to encourage
flowering. It may benefit from a little potash feed then, too. It can only
take a light frost so either mulch the crowns in the winter to protect it
or bring it under cover.

Viola tricolor →
Heart's ease

Old-fashioned and unassuming, *V. tricolor*'s dainty appearance belies its resilience and generosity. It seeds freely in my edible garden, which I encourage, particularly in late summer as it provides useful ground cover, protecting and feeding the soil as a green manure over winter. And from early spring right through to autumn, it produces the prettiest of edible flowers, high in antioxidants. It provides nectar for bumblebees and is long lasting as a cut flower. It has been used for its medicinal properties and as a dye plant since the Middle Ages.

Type
Annual, short-lived perennial
Flowering
Spring, summer, autumn
Height/spread
20cm x 30cm
Position
Full sun, part shade
Soil
Tolerant of most conditions except waterlogged
Hardiness
USDA 6a–1 / RHS H7

GROW Sow seed direct any time in spring or summer. Thereafter allow some of the flowers to go to seed and it will put itself about naturally. Make sure you recognise the young seedlings so that you don't accidentally hoe them off. As they have naturally trailing stems, they work well growing through other plants. By late spring, you may need to clear some of them to plant out new crops, but keep a few plants around the edges of the beds. Once they have become leggy, chop them back. I tend to pull them out once they have set seed as there are always younger, fresher plants nearby to take their place.

GWYNEDD ROBERTS
Head gardener and maintenance manager, Portmeirion Gardens, Wales

Gwynedd Roberts is head gardener at Portmeirion Gardens, which could be described as coastal, perched on a rock facing the Dwyryd Estuary, however they also feature a 70-acre woodland that is home to ornamental rhododendrons, camellias and champion trees, as well as beautiful herbaceous borders. *portmeirion.wales*

Astilbe 'Feuer' (× *arendsii*)
Astilbe 'Feuer'

Shade-loving astilbe, commonly known as false goat's beard, also thrive in full sun if regularly watered, and the rich colour of their flowers throughout summer are a joy to behold. They can be planted at the front edge of borders, in containers and beside ponds. It is 'Feuer', with its deep pink-red flowers, that I personally adore.

GROW It can be planted in full sun or part shade, in exposed or sheltered gardens – a combination of attributes that make it a great plant to have in any collection.

Type
Herbaceous perennial
Flowering
Summer, autumn, winter
Height/spread
1m x 50cm
Position
Full sun, part shade
Soil
Moist, well-drained, bog
Hardiness
USDA 6a–1 / RHS H7

Type
Herbaceous perennial
Flowering
Spring, summer
Height/spread
1m x 1m
Position
Full sun, part shade
Soil
Moist, well-drained
Hardiness
USDA 6b/7a / RHS H6

Paeonia lactiflora 'Sarah Bernhardt'
Peony 'Sarah Bernhardt'

Famed for their attractive colours in spring and early summer, peonies are renowned for their longevity and enrich any garden. My go-to peony is 'Sarah Bernhardt'. With its pale pink flower, this plant is slightly taller than other varieties and will require a support in early spring, however the additional work is very worthwhile when it flowers.

GROW Peonies particularly like deep and well-drained soil and if mulched or manured regularly in winter, they will provide colour and interest from spring into summer. They do take up to three years to fully mature, but once established they will produce several flowering stems each year.

ADVOLLY RICHMOND
Garden, landscape, plant
and social historian,
Shropshire, UK

Advolly Richmond is a researcher and lecturer in garden history, ranging
from the sixteenth century to the mid-twentieth century. She is a garden
history broadcaster and the author and producer of *The Garden History
Podcast: An A to Z of Garden History. advolly.co.uk*

Kirengeshoma palmata
Yellow wax-bells

I first came across this very unusual plant in a woodland setting while
volunteering at a beautiful garden in Shropshire many years ago. It was
underplanted with *Aegopodium podagraria* 'Variegatum', which is less
invasive than variegated ground elder – the combination had the most
striking effect. *K. palmata* has been in cultivation in the UK for over a
century. It is a rhizomatous, clump-forming herbaceous perennial with
eye-catching, maple-like foliage, which emerges in late spring and is
marbled grey-green. The waxy, butter-yellow, tubular-shaped flowers
are suspended on arching, dark reddish-purple stems. The flowers are
followed by very peculiar horned seeds.

Type
Rhizomatous
perennial
Flowering
Late summer,
autumn
Height/spread
1.2m x 1m
Position
Dappled shade,
sheltered
Soil
Rich, moist
Hardiness
USDA 6a–1 / RHS H7

GROW Goes well with hostas and ferns. It doesn't like to dry out and must be
protected from cold winds.

Type
Herbaceous
perennial
Flowering
Summer
Height/spread
2.5m x 1.5m
Position
Full sun, part shade,
avoid strong winds
Soil
Deep, moist,
fertile to
accommodate the
thick fleshy roots
Hardiness
USDA 7b/8a / RHS H5

Crambe cordifolia
Greater sea kale

This plant has such an impact in the garden. It is delightfully enormous
and architectural – it is not for the faint-hearted. Whether planted in the
back of the border or as a statement plant, it provides large, airy clouds
of thousands of tiny, white, honey-scented flowers, just like a snow storm
in mid-summer. It is a relative of the common cabbage, which grows in
the wild in the Caucasus. The huge, deeply cut, dark green leaves are a
delight in themselves. The flowers arrive in summer and are followed by
little green, bead-like seeds which are just as attractive. The clouds of
flowers held above thick stems are excellent for pollinators.

GROW Give it plenty of room to reach its full potential. Precautionary staking
is a good idea.

Alstroemeria 'Flaming Star'
Peruvian lily 'Flaming Star'

'Flaming Star' produces such joyful and exotic flowers that are long
lasting in the border and make excellent cut flowers, which can easily
last up to three weeks in the vase. The flowers start as red buds which
open to a glorious, almost fluorescent tangerine flower with bold
maroon splashes on the inner petals. Alstroemerias are native to parts of
South America and the first alstroemeria arrived in England in 1753 when
seeds of *A. pelegrina* were sent by Baron Claes Alströemer of Sweden via
Spain; the plant was subsequently named after him. It has fleshy tubers
which slowly form clumps, and flowers from summer to early winter.

Type
Perennial
Flowering
Summer
Height/spread
75cm x 50cm
Position
Part shade, full sun
Soil
Moist, well-drained
Hardiness
USDA 8b/9a / RHS H4

GROW Rather than cutting them for an indoor display, pull the stems out with a
yank, which can encourage more flowering stems. Pull them after flowering, too.
The fascinating thing about alstroemerias is that a twist in their leaves means
that they 'wear' their leaves upside down, this is known as 'resupination'.

Type
Rhizomatous perennial
Flowering
Summer
Height/ spread
2m x 1m
Position
Part shade, full shade, sheltered
Soil
Moist, rich, fertile
Hardiness
USDA 6a–1 / RHS 7

Veratrum album →
White false hellebore

This plant was given to me by the formidable Shropshire plantswoman Margaret Owen (1930–2014). She held four National Plant Collections including *Veratrum*. I helped out at her renowned garden, the Patch, and the veratrums were wonderful to see. The plant was described in English herbalist John Gerard's *Grete Herball* of 1529 as having 'little starlike flowers of the herbie greene colour tending to whitenesse' with leaves 'folded into pleates like a garment'. Its leaves are poisonous, but are particularly attractive in early spring. The equally appealing *V. nigrum* has brown flowers.

GROW Veratrums make excellent woodland plants. It's advisable to wear gloves when in contact with this plant. I've heard that if you grow both veratrums together, slugs will eat *V. nigrum* as it is less bitter than *V. album*.

MARY REYNOLDS
Founder, We Are The Ark, Ireland

Mary Reynolds is a reformed landscape designer, author and founder of We Are The Ark (Acts of Restorative Kindness to the Earth), a global movement that asks people to give half of their gardens (or as much as they can spare) back to nature and advocates for solutions to the climate and biodiversity crisis. *marymary.ie*

Quercus petraea
Sessile oak (SEE ILLUSTRATION PAGE 112)

Type
Deciduous tree
Flowering
Spring, summer
Height/ spread
30m x 20m
Position
Any
Soil
Moist, well-drained
Hardiness
USDA 6a–1 / RHS H7

This is the king of the woods! Oak is one big living wildlife pantry and oxygen-making machine. Sessile oaks have evolved partnerships with over 240 species of insects, which in turn provide food for many species of birds and mammals. Oak is home to many types of fungi, mammals, lichens, mosses and other plants. Standing dead oak also provides food for thousands more species.

In Ireland, it is said the oaks spend 300 years growing, 300 years living and 300 years dying. According to the fair and advanced native Irish Brehon laws of old, oak was one of the nobles of the woods and so its importance was legally recognised. The fine imposed for cutting one down was two and a half cows.

Ireland used to be covered with 80 per cent native tree cover. Now we have destroyed almost all of that. Only two per cent of Ireland's woodlands consist of native tree cover and most of that is newly planted, so hasn't got the complex diversity of old growth woods. Only 0.02 per cent of our land is covered with the remaining shreds of ancient woodlands. This is where all the diversity lies, where all the hope lies for nature's recovery, once we have woken up to the fact that we are driving ourselves over the edge of an ecological cliff. These old growth woods need serious protection and expansion at all costs.

GROW Locally sourced native acorns are best grown in a box, a pot or directly in the ground, with some of the parent leaf litter. This supports the acorns with the necessary bacterial and fungal partnerships. If you feel they are too big for your garden then consider planting one with a plan to coppice it in the future. Can grow well on soils of poor or medium nutrient status. Doesn't like wet or compacted soil. Tolerates drier soils.

ALICE VINCENT
Writer, UK

Alice Vincent is a journalist and the author of *Rootbound: Rewilding a Life* and *Why Women Grow: Stories of Soil, Sisterhood and Survival*. *instagram.com/noughticulture*

Adiantum capillus-veneris
Southern maidenhair

I'm more of an outdoor than an indoor gardener, but I've probably loved maidenhair ferns the longest. I encountered their delicate, arching foliage when I was still new in my gardening journey and continue to be as struck by the beauty of mine now, as it tumbles over the mantelpiece. A few years back I got the leaves of one tattooed on my arm. I suppose they remind me of the beginning of that journey and where I've come since. Now, I grow their hardier sisters, *A. raddianum*, outside in chimney pots, where they are similarly gorgeous.

When they are established and large, maidenhair ferns are majestic – a softer, more ethereal form of the bouncier, more Sideshow Bob-style ferns you often see inside.

GROW Maidenhair ferns are fussy, and people often complain that they are too easily killed. But the trick is good light, snipping off the brown bits, and a good, deep water every couple of weeks.

Type
Semi-evergreen fern
Height/spread
50cm x 50cm
Position
Full shade, part shade, sheltered
Soil
Moist, well-drained
Hardiness
USDA 9b/10a / RHS H3

DENISE JONES
Co-founder, Petals of the Valley, Monmouth, Wales

Denise Jones and Desdemona Freeman founded Petals of the Valley with the aim of making pure Welsh rose otto essential oil. Along the way they found themselves reinvigorating traditions such as natural potpourri with flowers and herbs. *petalsofthevalley.co.uk*

Rosa × damascena 'Kazanlik'
Damask rose 'Kazanlik'

Of the three roses we grow to produce our rosewaters – *R. × damascena* 'Kazanlik', *R. gallica* var. *officinalis* (apothecary's rose) and *R. alba* 'Maxima' – it is *R. × damascena*, with its deep and exotic scent, that is the one most people are familiar with. As its name implies, the apothecary's rose is the one revered throughout history for its healing properties. 'Maxima', meanwhile, is a beautiful white rose that produces exceptional rosewater during long hot summers – it has a slightly citrus scent, which gives a pleasant cooling spritz on the hottest of days.

Outside of these three exceptional roses, a border edged with *Alchemilla mollis* (lady's mantle) and *Geranium × johnsonii* 'Johnson's blue' takes some beating – not only for the colour combination, but also the way the alchemilla leaves capture the raindrops, making it look as though they are decorated with sparkling diamonds. That its leaves in a bowl of warm water make for a soothing hand wash is an added bonus.

GROW We grow garlic among the roses as it is said to deter black and green fly, but it is also alleged to enhance the scent of the rose. *Calendula officinalis* is another favourite companion plant. Egg shells, banana skins and well-rotted manure are our only other additions to the rose beds.

Type
Shrub rose
Flowering
Summer
Height/spread
1.5m x 1.5m
Position
Full sun, part shade
Soil
Moist, well-drained
Hardiness
USDA 6a–1 / RHS H7

JOHN GREENLEE
Owner, Greenlee &
Associates, California, USA

John Greenlee is a horticulturist and landscape designer specialising in the cultivation and study of grasses and grass-like plants. A champion of sustainable design, he has created gardens for the Getty Museum and the Norton Simon Museum in Los Angeles, the savannas at Walt Disney's Animal Kingdom in Florida and at De Tuinen van Appeltern in the Netherlands. *greenleeandassociates.com*

Sesleria 'Greenlee'
Moor grass 'Greenlee'

This was one of the first hybrid grasses that came from my old nursery in Pomona, California, and it has become one of the favourite ground-cover grasses of designers in both the United States and Europe. It is an evergreen, clumping, low grass growing roughly 30cm high, with purple-tinged flowers in spring and summer. Always tidy, never messy, this grass makes excellent meadow grass and is useful in plantings large and small. It is my personal favourite as it makes a perfect backdrop for bulbs, perennials and annuals. It never steals the show, but always provides a solid foundation of beautiful green foliage. Well-behaved, it never naturalises and always stays where you put it. For the record, the grass was named after me, not by me, but I have to say, the name does have a nice ring to it.

GROW It is a long-lived perennial, best in full sun to part shade. It is adaptable to most climates, safe for those in hot and humid situations. It is moderately drought-tolerant and thrives in a wide variety of soil types. We generally plant plants 30cm apart (from the centre of each plant).

Type
Evergreen grass
Flowering
Spring, summer
Height/ spread
30cm x 50cm
Position
Full sun, part shade
Soil
Moist, well-drained
Hardiness
USDA 6a–1 / RHS H7

OLIVER KEENE
Landscape designer,
Urquhart & Hunt, UK

Oliver Keene is a landscape designer at Urquhart & Hunt, a studio based in Somerset that specialises in contemporary garden restorations with a focus on ecology and nature. *urquharthunt.com*

Nicotiana langsdorffii
Langsdorff's tobacco plant

With its slender stems and a mass of elegant lime-green flowers, this plant has a lovely airy feel to it. To some, its small trumpet flowers may seem like they get lost in a herbaceous border, but I think it provides the necessary foil to make bolder plants really sing. It is an understated 'doer', a plant I often turn to in order to give continuity to a planting scheme. Though when it's given the chance to show off in a container or as a cut flower, you can really appreciate its beauty. It will flower from early summer until the first frost, and it isn't picky about where it grows. It's a fantastic wildlife plant providing night-time nectar for moths, which in turn keeps bats well fed.

GROW This can really grow anywhere in your garden and requires little care. Even though they can self-seed if the conditions are right, for a strong plant, grow them from seed each year under glass or indoors. I have directly sown seed to great effect too, especially in gravel gardens. May need staking if in an exposed, windy site.

Type
Annual
Flowering
Summer, autumn
Height/ spread
1.5m x 45cm
Position
Full sun, part shade
Soil
Any
Hardiness
USDA 10b / RHS H2

DAVID GLENN
Owner, Lambley Gardens
and Nursery, Victoria,
Australia

David Glenn has been a nurseryman for most of his 70-plus years. He gardens with his wife, artist Criss Canning. One of his most important jobs is to fill the house with flowers. His first passion is for herbaceous perennials, having been brought up in England. But from his experience of gardening in central Victoria, he has finally learned not to fight the climate. *lambley.com.au*

Euphorbia rigida
Upright myrtle spurge

This acquisition of *E. rigida* at Lambley was collected more than 20 years ago in the Peloponnese region of southern Greece. There isn't a day in the year when this spurge isn't a delight. It would be worth growing as a foliage plant alone, but during winter, the stems are topped by large showy heads of lime green bracts. The bracts age to crimson during the early spring months, and the foliage is handsome year-round, with waxy blue leaves spiralling around the upright Medusa-like stems. The plants are long lived for a spurge, some have flourished for ten years or more.

GROW I generally cut the spent flower stems to the ground at the end of spring, by which time new growth is well underway. This terrific plant is easily grown as long as it is planted in a sunny, well-drained position. Once established it needs little or no extra summer irrigation.

Type
Perennial
Flowering
Summer
Height/spread
60m x 80cm
Position
Full sun, part shade, any aspect
Soil
Moist, well-drained, most soil types
Hardiness
USDA 6b/7a / RHS H6

Type
Evergreen shrub
Flowering
Summer, autumn
Height/spread
1.2m x 1.2m
Position
Full sun, part shade
Soil
Moist, well-drained
Hardiness
USDA 8b/9a / RHS H4

Salvia leucantha 'Harry's Red'
Mexican bush sage 'Harry's Red'

S. leucantha, in all its forms, is the most important salvia species in our garden during late summer and autumn. 'Harry's Red' is our working title for this variety of Mexican bush sage. It was found growing in my son Harry Glenn's garden in an old Melbourne suburb and is distinguished by its bright purple-red flowers held in mauve calyxes. In our climate, it flowers abundantly from mid-summer until deep into autumn, longer in milder climates.

GROW The shrubby growth eventually reaches over 1m in height and spread, so it's best suited to larger gardens, and is best cut to the ground during late winter. Plant out after the risk of frost has passed in cold areas.

Chionochloa flavicans
Broad-leaved snow tussock

A friend gave me this plant, a native of the North Island of New Zealand, where it grows on rocky outcrops from the Coromandel Peninsula to Hawkes Bay. An evergreen grass with attractive foliage, it produces a clump of arching deep green leaves. In our garden it makes a nice contrast with a neighbouring winter-flowering, silver-leaved phlomis. From mid-spring until well into summer the lime-green, dangling flower tassels are extraordinarily beautiful, as beautiful as any grass I've ever grown. The flowerheads are held symmetrically around the clump on 1m-tall stems.

GROW This grass does need a bit of space, as it will grow over 1m wide and tall.

Type
Evergreen grass
Flowering
Spring, summer
Height/spread
1.2m x 1m
Position
Full sun, part shade
Soil
Well-drained
Hardiness
USDA 7b/8a / RHS H5

HELMUT WAHLER
Master gardener, Austrian
Federal Gardens, Austria

Helmut Wahler has worked for the Austrian Federal Gardens since 1980 and became a master gardener in 1986. Since 1987, he has been chief of cultivation of the Palm House in Hofgarten in Innsbruck, where he works to preserve the Austrian Federal Gardens' botanical collection. *bundesgaerten.at*

Victoria amazonica ↘
Giant water lily

Ever since I was a young gardener this plant has fascinated me with its rapid growth and its leaves measuring around 2m in diameter. English botanist John Lindley named it in honour of Queen Victoria, although it was the Austrian botanist Thaddäus Haenke who first discovered it between 1800 and 1801 on the Mamoré River, a tributary of the Amazon River.

The Hofgarten in Innsbruck was first mentioned in documents in 1396. At that time, the Austrian imperial family used it as a hunting ground. The first palm house was built in 1858 and consisted of a warm and a cold house. It was demolished in 1960 and replaced by the current palm house, which is divided into three climate zones: the cold house, the temperate house and the warm house. In 1964, a basin for Victorias was installed in the temperate house and the first *V. amazonica* was put in a year later.

V. amazonica is a perennial, usually cultivated as an annual due to its fast growth. The genus *Victoria* consists of two species and belongs to the family *Nymphaeaceae*: the *V. amazonica* from the Amazon River and the *V. cruziana* from the Paraná River.

Beginning at the end of spring, a new bud opens up at dusk every three to four days, and on the first night emits a sweet scent to attract beetles. If a beetle crawls inside, the blossom closes and traps it for 24 hours. The calyx begins to warm up, causing the blossom to turn from white to red. The next evening, the blossom opens up again, now red-coloured, letting the beetle escape from its prison. Completely covered with pollen, it carries it to the next fragrant water lily and pollinates it. After pollination, the flower disappears below the water where the pea-sized seeds ripen.

Since there are no beetles for pollination in the palm house, as soon as a white blossom blooms we tie it to a bamboo stick to keep it on the surface and wait for the next flower bud to open. I then carry the pollen from one blossom to the next one. Afterwards I untie it and cover it with a thin net to catch the seeds under water.

Type
Short-lived perennial
Flowering
Spring
Height/spread
3m x 2m
Position
Full sun, 32°C water temperature
Soil
A substrate of field soil, cow manure and lime-free sand in a larch box
Hardiness
USDA 13 / RHS H1a

GROW The seeds are sown into small clay pots filled with soil in winter. I put those 4cm under water in a small, water-filled basin, which is illuminated with a growth lamp from 7am to 7pm. In late winter, as soon as they are well rooted, I transplant into larger pots. The giant water lily is planted out in the palm house in spring in the pool, in a planter made of larch wood. From this point on, a new leaf develops every second to third day. As the plant grows, the water level in the tank also has to increase. To control water snails and lice, we keep Shubunkin fish. From mid-summer onwards, I fertilise with homemade fertiliser dumplings: a 50:50 mixture of field soil and horn shavings, adding enough water to form a solid mass. I leave them in the shade for several days to dry out, and then press three to four fertiliser dumplings into the substrate.

RACHEL SIEGFRIED
Flower farmer and florist,
Oxfordshire, UK

Rachel Siegfried grows hundreds of varieties of plants for cutting on her four-acre flower farm, Green and Gorgeous. Her cut-flower business is also a resource for learning about growing flowers for pleasure or profit, offering courses and workshops. *greenandgorgeousflowers.co.uk*

← *Ranunculus acris* 'Citrinus'
Meadow buttercup 'Citrinus'

Type
Perennial
Flowering
Spring, early summer
Height/ spread
30cm x 30cm
Position
Full sun, part shade
Soil
Moist, boggy
Hardiness
USDA 6a–1 / RHS H7

This is a striking cultivar of the native meadow buttercup, which grows with lush abundance in the water meadows next to the flower farm. The plants produce clouds of shimmering flowers of the palest moonlit yellow that appear to be floating on their fine, branching stems. I was given a clump by a fellow flower grower who recommended it as a useful late spring perennial for cutting. It has certainly proved its worth as an enlivening supporting flower in floral designs – its shiny petals create little flecks of light through arrangements. Flowering at the same time as geums, it does a similar job as a cut flower, but with longer stem length and more abundance. I tend to arrange these buttermilk buttercups with other meadow-style flowers, including early summer hardy annuals such as orlaya, corncockle, briza, cornflowers and Icelandic poppies.

GROW Cut back after flowering to encourage a second flush and to avoid self-seeding. The quickest way to propagate is by summer 'micro' division or from fresh seed sown when it is still green.

Type
Perennial
Flowering
Summer
Height/ spread
1m x 1m
Position
Full sun, part shade
Soil
Moist, well-drained
Hardiness
USDA 6a–1 / RHS H7

Campanula takesimana
Korean bellflower

I am always on the hunt for plants that produce an elegant, arching shape. It is the weight of the large, tubular, bell-shaped flowers of this species that bows the stem into a pleasing curved line. The colour is lilac-white flushed with plum, which seems to blend well with any other colour and its unique shape always looks natural and effortless in an arrangement. Admittedly it's not the tallest, most prolific or weather-resistant campanula, but in my opinion it is the best one to arrange with. I like to pair it with other mid-summer favourites such as foxgloves, roses and clematis.

GROW Easy to grow from seed and, once established, can be divided in spring.

SUSIE PASLEY-TYLER
Garden owner,
Coton Manor,
Northamptonshire, UK

Susie Pasley-Tyler and her husband Ian are the third generation to live and garden at Coton Manor, which they have done for more than 30 years. The original garden was designed by Ian's grandparents in the 1920s. In 2019 it was voted the 'nation's favourite garden' in a competition run by the National Garden Scheme. *cotonmanor.co.uk*

Salvia involucrata →
Rosy-leaf sage

This invaluable plant makes quite a statement in the border and it can be planted singly. Its typical sage flowers are a strong bluish-pink, a colour that works well with many roses and herbaceous perennials. I use a lot of repetition in my borders and this is one of my staple plants for creating that effect. They are hardy in our garden and don't need supporting.

GROW Cut back by half in autumn to avoid wind rock, then cut right down in spring. It's sometimes slow to start growing.

Type
Herbaceous
perennial
Flowering
Summer, autumn
Height/spread
1.5m x 1m
Position
Full sun, sheltered
Soil
Moist, well-drained
Hardiness
USDA 9b/10a / RHS H3

Type
Deciduous shrub
Flowering
Spring
Height/spread
8m x 4m
Position
Full sun, part shade
Soil
Moist, well-drained
Hardiness
USDA 7b/8a / RHS H5

Cornus **'Eddie's White Wonder'**
Dogwood 'Eddie's White Wonder'

One of the most glorious sights in spring. The creamy-white flower bracts with their green centres stand out in spectacular fashion, especially against a green background. The flowers last for a considerable time. In autumn the foliage turns a rich red.

GROW Generally an easy and undemanding shrub to look after.

Cercidiphyllum japonicum
Katsura tree

This is one of the most beautiful trees in the garden, with stunning foliage and an elegant outline. It has distinctive rounded, heart-shaped leaves, similar to *Cercis siliquastrum*. It has small, barely visible flowers in spring and in autumn the leaves develop yellow and pink tones with a delicious scent of caramel. Our tree is multi-stemmed and often our Barbu d'Uccle bantam chickens can be found roosting in its branches.

GROW Give it some shelter to protect from late frosts. And note that acid soil produces the most vibrant displays.

Type
Deciduous tree
Flowering
Spring
Height/spread
12m x 8m
Position
Full sun, part shade
Soil
Moist, well-drained,
acid
Hardiness
USDA 7b/8a / RHS H5

Type
Tuberous perennial
Flowering
Summer, autumn
Height/spread
1m x 50cm
Position
Full sun, sheltered
Soil
Any
Hardiness
USDA 9b/10a / RHS H3

Dahlia **'Labyrinth'**
Dahlia 'Labyrinth'

A spectacularly beautiful giant dahlia with shades of peach and pink. It's a reliable performer and long-flowering. A great contribution to the border with its unusual and subtle colouring.

GROW Benefits from support as it can get quite big. Giving it a 'Chelsea chop' may help to keep it more stable. It can survive the winter outside if conditions are not too cold or wet. However, we lift them, drying out the tubers and storing them in a dark place in the shed, then potting them up in early spring.

Rosa multiflora 'Grevillei'
Seven Sisters' rose

This beautiful rose is planted in four positions on the front of the old part of our house and in three places on the terrace wall. We believe it possibly pre-dates the purchase of the house in the 1920s. The plants are very old and very much part of what visitors to Coton Manor recall as a major feature in the garden.

Seven Sisters' is a once-flowering, tall, rambler rose. Its name reflects the seven shades that are on display at any one time. The big clusters of double, typical multiflora flowers gradually develop from deep cerise to mauve. It has a fruity fragrance and, if the season is not too hot, flowers for a good month in summer.

GROW It responds to having its branches trained horizontally, which prompts it to produce many more flowers. Needs hard pruning when grown on a wall and watering in sunny conditions. We do not spray or feed, but do give it a good covering of cow muck in spring.

Type
Rambler rose
Flowering
Summer
Height/spread
8m x 4m
Position
Full sun, part shade
Soil
Moist, well-drained
Hardiness
USDA 6b/7a / RHS H6

Paeonia 'Sonoma Blessing'
Intersectional peony 'Sonoma Blessing'

This exquisite peony is a cross between a tree peony and a herbaceous peony. Its flowers are more like those of a tree peony, but it lacks the same height and spread and, unlike a herbaceous peony, it is self-supporting. It produces masses of flowers, which are large, beautiful and usually have a darker centre. We have 11 different varieties of intersectional peony in the garden and it is difficult to name a favourite, but I have chosen 'Sonoma Blessing', which is a blush shade of pink with a darker pink centre and is utterly stunning. If the weather isn't too hot, it flowers for about three weeks from late spring. 'Kopper Kettle' ran a very close second.

GROW Very straightforward to grow but it does need two or three years before you get multiple blooms.

Type
Herbaceous perennial
Flowering
Summer
Height/spread
1.5 x 1.5m
Position
Sun, part shade, reasonably sheltered
Soil
Any, grows here on clay
Hardiness
USDA 8b/9a / RHS H4

Polystichum setiferum 'Pulcherrimum Bevis'
Soft shield fern 'Pulcherrimum Bevis' (SEE ILLUSTRATION PAGE 319)

Green is a restful colour and this fern's architectural shape stands out in the woodland garden. It is happy in dry shade, which not all ferns are, and has a delicacy about its foliage that is immensely appealing.

GROW You need patience for these ferns to gain a good size. Generally they are the last of the ferns that need cutting back at the end of winter; it is important to do this in order to see the new leaves unfurling, which is one of the great pleasures of spring.

Type
Evergreen fern
Height/spread
1m x 1m
Position
Full shade, part shade
Soil
Moist, well-drained
Hardiness
USDA 6b/7a / RHS H6

Agastache 'Blue Fortune'
Giant hyssop 'Blue Fortune'

I find this plant an invaluable component of the border. It is understated and somewhat underrated in my opinion. It contributes a very vertical accent and its flowers are a good deep blue. It lasts in flower from the middle of summer to autumn and the insects love it.

GROW Worth planting in decent numbers to get the best effect. Can be slow to show in the spring. Best to leave the previous year's growth standing until spring, as the stems provide protection over winter. It grows best in alkaline soils but tolerates acid ones.

Type
Herbaceous perennial
Flowering
Summer, autumn
Height/spread
1m x 50cm
Position
Full sun
Soil
Moist, well-drained
Hardiness
USDA 6b/7a / RHS H6

FRANCES TOPHILL
Gardener and
conservationist, Devon, UK

Frances Tophill is a gardener, botanist and conservationist. She is
a presenter on *Gardeners' World*, ITV's *Love Your Garden* and *Grow
Your Own*. She has written several books, works with community
gardens and collaborates with the RHS Campaign for School Gardening.
instagram.com/francestophill

Type
Short-lived
perennial
Flowering
Summer
**Height/
spread**
1.5m x 1m
Position
Not fussy,
prefers
sun or part
shade
Soil
Moist, well-
drained
Hardiness
USDA 7b/8a
/ RHS H5

Foeniculum vulgare
Common fennel

I love any plant that interacts with us and with the natural world. In many of
the projects I have worked on and in my own, modest space that I grow in,
which is so hampered by strong and salty winds that blow in off the English
Channel, fennel has been a stalwart and a faithful companion to me and to
the many insects that visit its zingy, yellow flowers.

This is a statuesque perennial, robust in form and tall in height. Its
translucence and delicate foliage provide a screening and a privacy without
being too dominant, very much in the same way a tall ornamental grass might,
but with infinitely more uses. The stems and leaves are edible, with a strong
taste of aniseed – they are great for pickling, adding to salads, fish dishes and
stir-fries. The flowers attract hoverflies in their droves and continue for months
if you deadhead them regularly. Once the flowers are pollinated, the seeds
they form are delicious in curries but also great for drying and hanging as an
air freshener, giving off a spicy, heavy aroma.

GROW The roots do not like to be disturbed so either sow into modules or direct into the
ground once the soil warms up in spring. Once the plants have established, seedlings
appear around the plants. For easy propagation, dig these up carefully, plant straight
away and water well to avoid wilt. Cut the stems back during winter or early spring, or in
summer if you are harvesting. The plant will reshoot from the base each spring.

KENNETH COX
Director, Glendoick
Gardens,
Perthshire, Scotland

Kenneth Cox has run his family's nursery for the last 30 years. He
is the author of 13 books on plants and gardening, a hybridiser of
rhododendrons and azaleas, and has led numerous plant-hunting
expeditions including to China and India. *glendoick.com*

Rhododendron **Glendoick**
Glendoick rhododendron

I was born into rhododendrons. My grandfather, Euan Cox, was a plant
hunter, garden writer and nurseryman and founded Glendoick Gardens
with my father Peter Cox, himself an author, plant hunter, hybridiser and
the world's leading rhododendron expert of his day. The bird series of
dwarf rhododendrons was bred at Glendoick by my father and myself.
These are compact hardy plants suitable for smaller gardens. The first,
'Chikor', was named in the 1960s, and there are now over 30 of them. Some
of the most popular include: 'Wren', which is very low and slow growing,
smothering itself in yellow flowers in spring; 'Egret', with tiny white bells;
and 'Tinkerbird', with scented white flowers.

Type
Evergreen shrub
Flowering
Spring
Height/spread
There is no such
thing... they just
grow
Position
Full sun, part shade
Soil
Moist, well-drained
Hardiness
USDA 8b/9a / RHS H4

GROW Rhododendrons need well-drained, but not dry, acid soil. They can be
grown in pots. In the north, plant them in full light. In more southern latitudes they
grow best in part shade, but don't like being planted under trees.

BEN CONWAY
Head gardener, Ayrlies
Garden & Wetlands,
Auckland, New Zealand

Ben Conway has been at acclaimed private garden Ayrlies in Whitford since 2006, under the guidance of the owner Beverly McConnell. Having previously worked at Government House in Wellington, he now oversees a garden that includes perennial borders, rockeries, woodlands and ponds, as well as a native forest. The focus is on soil and plant health. *ayrlies.co.nz*

Thunbergia coccinea →
Scarlet clock vine

Type
Perennial climber
Flowering
Spring, summer
Height/spread
10m x 5m
Position
Full sun, part shade, sheltered
Soil
Moist, well-drained, pH 5.5–7
Hardiness
USDA 9b/10a / RHS H3

I have chosen this plant as it is such a stunning sight in full flower. Its long-hanging racemes of red and orange flowers extend 1.5m and dangle down to resemble a beaded curtain. You can make quite the statement with this sassy plant. We display it along the front of the gazebo at Ayrlies. Visitors are guided through a narrow entrance, which then opens out onto a view of the swimming pool surrounded by subtropical planting. All the while, you are peering through a curtain of these amazing hanging clusters. It's such a great experience for the garden visitor. Both bees and nectar-feeding birds are also attracted to these flowers. In New Zealand, one of these birds is the tūī, which swoops in and hangs off the pendulous flowers.

GROW Prefers subtropical climates with the warmth of a wall or building to take the edge off cooler nights. The main stem can be in quite a lot of shade if foliage is out in the sun. Growing along a wire or along a building is the best way to show this plant off, so that the flowers can dangle down freely. It dies back by about a third each season, so you must cut out the dead material and train the new growth once the vine begins to grow again in early spring. Training it along a wire as it continues to grow will ensure the flowers are displayed where you want them. Pruning out dead wood and careful training of the new growth will ensure you get a good display in a confined area. Other ways to grow are letting it cover a trellis on a wall or a pergola. If you feel like trying something a bit different, grow it up a tree or another climber such as bougainvillea, so the thunbergia grows up and intermingles.

Type
Deciduous tree
Flowering
Summer
Height/spread
8m x 8m
Position
Full sun, open, sheltered
Soil
Moist, well-drained
Hardiness
USDA 9b/10a / RHS H3

Lagerstroemia fauriei
Japanese crêpe myrtle

As people's gardens and spaces become smaller and smaller, I'm often asked about trees for small spaces. Quite often a very fast-growing tree is selected in new urban developments to give some instant gratification, but they are always planted too close to a building or utilities, and outgrow their place in about five years. This slower-growing small tree is a favourite of mine, with year-round interest. It has a beautiful multi-branched habit, resulting in a vase shape, and stunning autumn leaf colouring. Bees and pollinators flock to the summer clusters of small white flowers. The bark and trunks of all lagerstroemia are a reason to use them in your plant repertoire, but the particular rich warm cinnamon notes of *L. fauriei* are the closest we can get to the *Arbutus menziesii* (madrone), which being native to the west coast of North America doesn't thrive in northern New Zealand. In our warmer humid climate, lagerstroemias come out on top. Still, if you have ever seen *A. menziesii* in among the greens of the rainforests of the Pacific Northwest, your eyes will have been opened to the beauty of such a warm colour and the possibilities to use tree trunks and bark as a statement in landscapes.

GROW Best planted where the late winter sun can show off the rich cinnamon tones of the coloured bark. Prune to shape and remove dead wood, but it's very well behaved.

NICK HAMILTON
Owner, Barnsdale Gardens,
Rutland, UK

After training at Writtle University College and working at Raveningham Gardens, Nick Hamilton helped his father (former *Gardeners' World* presenter Geoff Hamilton) set up Barnsdale Gardens. The gardens have been run organically and peat-free for over 30 years, inspiring visitors to create their own idyllic garden spaces. *barnsdalegardens.co.uk*

Penstemon 'Geoff Hamilton'
Penstemon 'Geoff Hamilton'

How could I not choose this plant? I've been keen on penstemons for many years, because they are such great value for money, and I have built up quite a collection. It was during this period that I came across Clive and Kathy Gandley who, at the time, held one of the National Collections of *Penstemon*. They became good friends and named this fantastic variety, which they bred themselves, in memory of my dad. It's a long-flowering plant, starting early summer and going on into autumn.

GROW Remove spent flower spikes down to a good pair of leaves to encourage more spikes to appear. Once it finishes flowering completely, don't cut it back. If you feel the need to tidy it a bit, only remove the spent flower spikes, as the old stems create a microclimate that protects the new young shoots in the spring. Cut the plant back hard to the new basal clump of young shoots in mid-spring. This will reinvigorate your plant, making it long-lived, as well as keeping it compact. It grows best in full sun, but also tolerates semi-shade admirably. Hardy when treated properly, it needs to be planted in soil with good drainage. Penstemons don't like their roots getting too wet, particularly in winter, so if, like me, you grow on a heavy soil, improve it with organic matter and/or coarse grit. It isn't a big feeder and needs moderate watering in dry spells.

Type
Perennial
Flowering
Summer, autumn
Height/ spread
1m x 1m
Position
Full sun, part shade
Soil
Well-drained
Hardiness
USDA 8b/9a / RHS H4

LAETITIA MAKLOUF
Gardener and author,
London, UK

Laetitia Maklouf is the author of books including *The Virgin Gardener*, *Sweet Peas for Summer* and *The Five Minute Garden*. *laetitiamaklouf.com*

Lathyrus odoratus
Sweet pea (SEE ILLUSTRATION PAGE 49)

Sweet peas were the first plant I ever grew. They inspired me to keep on gardening and, most importantly, to keep on picking! What I love most about them is that the more you pick, the more they give. It's a total reversal of the received wisdom around other precious things, like orchids or fine china, that you shouldn't touch them in case they ruin or break. The scent of a sweet pea is out of this world, and has never, to my knowledge, been successfully bottled. That's why this plant is so special – you only get the joy of its perfect scent once a year and each year that scent attaches itself to a different memory. It is the most nostalgic of plants.

GROW I sow my sweet peas in autumn and keep them out all winter (protected from hard rain and snow) to grow all beefy and strong by spring time. It's best to sow into compost cut half and half with well-rotted manure; these plants are hungry and like a deep root run. I pinch out the tips once they start to flop, and that can happen any time from early winter to late winter, depending on the weather. In summer, water daily and copiously, feed weekly with tomato fertiliser, and pick flowers as soon as they appear.

Type
Annual climber
Flowering
Summer
Height/ spread
2.5m x 50cm
Position
Full sun, part shade, sheltered
Soil
Moist, well drained
Hardiness
USDA 9b/10a / RHS H3

30

PIET OUDOLF
Landscape and garden designer, Hummelo, Netherlands

Piet Oudolf is known for his award-winning garden designs. He started his landscape and design practice with his wife Anja in 1976 in Haarlem. They moved to Hummelo in 1982 to start a nursery growing hard-to-find, garden-worthy perennials. His work includes planting design for the High Line in New York. *oudolf.com*

Filipendula rubra '**Venusta Magnifica**' →
Meadowsweet 'Venusta Magnifica'

Tall and robust, *F. rubra* flowers in early summer, which is a good time as it's before the main flowering period of most perennials. Its pink flowers have a sweet scent and it colours to a chestnut brown in the autumn. The plant skeleton is attractive until deep into the winter. The leaves are large and deeply lobed on zig zag stems. The roots are rhizomatous and will spread, which makes it a great plant for naturalising in moist meadows, but be aware of its semi-aggressive nature in small garden settings.

GROW Best grown in full sun (although they can take some shade), and prefers moist to wet soils. Cut back in late winter.

Type
Rhizomatous herbaceous perennial
Flowering
Summer
Height/spread
1.5m x 1m
Position
Full sun, part shade
Soil
Moist, well-drained, poorly drained
Hardiness
USDA 7b/8a / RHS H5

URSULA BUCHAN
Journalist and author, UK

Ursula Buchan is an award-winning speaker and writer. She studied horticulture at Royal Botanic Gardens, Kew and is the author of many books including *The English Garden* and *The Garden Anthology*. *ursula-buchan.co.uk*

Aster × frikartii '**Mönch**'
Aster 'Mönch'

We should all be grateful to 'Mönch': at a time of year when most roses have lost their vim, hardy chrysanthemums are still in tight green bud and the summer-flowering grasses need a foil to show them off to best advantage, this hardy perennial has become precious for all gardeners wishing to paint seasonal pictures in their borders.

My plant has thin but reasonably sturdy stems, from each of which arises a number of side shoots that sprout single flowers 6cm in diameter. The ray florets are thin, and a cool, refined lavender-blue. They begin to curl and twist as they age, while the disc florets in the centre of the flowers are bright yellow. Now the clumps are well established, they're a wonderful sight, beckoning to me from across the garden.

GROW The elegant daisy starts to flower in mid- to late summer, and keeps going until mid-autumn, when the baton finally passes to the true Michaelmas daisies.

Type
Herbaceous perennial
Flowering
Summer, autumn
Height/spread
1m x 50cm
Position
Full sun
Soil
Well-drained
Hardiness
USDA 6a–1 / RHS H7

REBECCA BEVAN
Senior national consultant for cultivated plants, National Trust, Gloucestershire, UK

Having trained at RHS Wisley and worked for the RHS and *Gardeners' World*, Rebecca Bevan now helps to care for one of the largest collections of cultivated plants in the world that grows across nearly 300 National Trust gardens. *nationaltrust.org.uk*

Paeonia rockii
Rock's tree peony

I love all tree peonies but this one is especially dazzling with its huge but fragile-looking white flowers, which are flushed slightly pink and almost black in the centre. The first one I ever saw was at RHS Wisley, but since then I have met many fine specimens in National Trust gardens, including Benthall Hall in Shropshire and Tintinhull House in Somerset.

GROW It needs a warm sheltered spot on free-draining soil. I'm not sure mine (raised from seed and given to me by plantsman Bob Wallis) will ever be so happy as the one at Wisley, since my garden can be buffeted by cold winds. Best planted in autumn while the soil is still warm. Keep free from weeds and don't underplant with anything vigorous. Pruning is not needed, except to cut out dead branches.

Type
Deciduous shrub
Flowering
Spring, summer
Height/spread
2.5m x 2.5m
Position
Full sun, part shade, sheltered
Soil
Well-drained
Hardiness
USDA 6b/7a / RHS H6

Allium sphaerocephalon
Round-headed leek

Just when all the showy purple alliums have died back in the border, these little beauties come into their own. Delightful in bud, in full flower and gone over, they make a show from mid-summer to autumn. The small bulbs are easy to plant in drifts weaving between established perennials and have such narrow leaves and stems that they take up no room at all. Yet they provide a mass of spherical burgundy pompoms that look great against foliage, grasses or setting off the flowers of complementary-coloured perennials. Absolutely loved by bees and other pollinating insects.

GROW Although small, these bulbs are quite tall so don't plant them at the front of the border. They need to be woven in around the middle. They're too small to be dotted about on their own so be generous with them and they will knit a border together. Plant 8cm deep and 8cm apart, spaced unevenly for a natural effect. They need minimal care, but as the bulbs form clumps you can divide them when dormant in late summer. They also seed about and produce aerial bulbils.

Type
Bulbous perennial
Flowering
Summer
Height/spread
1m x 50cm
Position
Full sun, sheltered
Soil
Moist, well-drained
Hardiness
USDA 6b/7a / RHS H6

Type
Deciduous shrub
Flowering
Spring
Height/spread
4m x 4m
Position
Full sun, part shade, open, not exposed to strong winds
Soil
Moist, well-drained
Hardiness
USDA 6b/7a / RHS H6

Viburnum plicatum f. *tomentosum* →
Japanese snowball

There are a handful of trees and shrubs that naturally produce wide, flat branches, tiered one on top of the other. *V. plicatum* is probably the most reliable among them and I love the way it can reach across a lawn or bed, breaking up the view with its horizontal lines. It's small enough for many domestic gardens and fits into a wide range of styles, modern and architectural or soft and romantic. In late spring the layered branches are decorated with a mass of pure white, lacecap flowers; in autumn the pleated leaves turn rich purple.

GROW To get the best shape, it needs to grow steadily. Start with a young plant and choose the right place allowing room for it to get wide; this is not a shrub you can rein in without ruining it. Avoid cold winds that can scorch off growing points. Water only in droughts while it establishes, then leave it be. Young specimens shouldn't need pruning, except to remove very vertical stems or clear the bottom for under planting with perennials.

NEIL LUCAS
Director, Knoll Gardens,
Dorset, UK

Neil Lucas is the UK's leading ornamental grass specialist. An RHS Council member and judge, he is the holder of ten consecutive RHS Chelsea Flower Show gold medals. His first book, *Designing with Grasses*, aims to encourage others to share his passion for the beauty and utility of grasses. *knollgardens.co.uk*

Miscanthus sinensis 'Cindy'
Eulalia 'Cindy'

This is a selection named and introduced by Knoll Gardens. It produces mounds of fine green foliage topped by many delicately pendulous heads of pinky-red flowers from high summer onwards. It is a little more compact than many other selections. It arose as a seedling in my own private garden where we watched it grow and develop for a few years before moving it to our trial area to see how it behaved. It has a compact shape and freely produces flowers of a good pink, but we were especially delighted with its habit of producing the flowers clear of the foliage, which creates a light and dainty overall effect. It is named after my dog, a beautiful rough collie who left us about the time the miscanthus was beginning to demonstrate its qualities.

GROW All miscanthus prefer a sunny open position away from the root systems of larger woody plants. Otherwise they are pretty easy to grow, requiring no staking, spraying or deadheading. Little feeding is required in most soils, but a surface mulch is always beneficial. Cut all of last season's old stems to the ground at the end of winter/early spring, to allow the new growth to come through.

Type
Deciduous grass
Flowering
Summer, autumn
Height/spread
1.5m x 1.2m
Position
Full sun
Soil
Not fussy, but not too wet in winter
Hardiness
USDA 6b/7a / RHS H6

LARA HONNOR
Founder, Skool Beanz,
Somerset, UK

Working in harmony with nature is key to Lara Honnor's gardening. This is something she learned working at the nursery Long Acre Plants, for no-dig gardener Charles Dowding and with the Brighton Permaculture Trust. After completing a diploma in social and therapeutic horticulture, she created gardening club Skool Beanz, which inspires children to grow vegetables and flowers. *instagram.com/skoolbeanz*

Cynara cardunculus
Cardoon

If ever there was a plant with a personality as huge as it is tall, it is the cardoon. It is a thistle in the sunflower family, and in my garden it brings me as much joy as a field of sunflowers. The lush silvery leaves provide interest all winter and the stalks can be cooked and eaten – snails and sparrows nibble away, but never do much damage, so there is enough for everyone. It tastes like a mixture of celery and artichoke. As warmer weather approaches, so too do the triffid-like stems and spiky buds. The flowerheads are much smaller than those of artichokes but the bees love them just as much, getting a face full of purple. During the week of the summer solstice, the cardoon seems to recognise the mood, and dances to the sunsets, creating the most beautiful silhouettes. Sparrows love perching on it, especially as autumn sets in, when the silver stems turn brown and camouflage the birds perfectly. The heads make wonderful table decorations, but be warned, they pack a spiky punch. I once knocked headfirst into mine as it was leaning over our steps, and the resulting bump on my head throbbed for days until I discovered the tip of a spike lodged in there!

GROW Each winter I give it a thick mulch of manure or mushroom compost. Sheltered plants always fare better (though mine is incredibly exposed!). Try and plant somewhere low, so you can look through it rather than up at it. Cut back before spring.

Type
Herbaceous perennial
Flowering
Summer, autumn
Height/spread
2.5m x 1.5m
Position
Full sun, sheltered
Soil
Well-drained
Hardiness
USDA 7b/8a / RHS H5

ROSY HARDY
Nursery owner and RHS vice president, Hampshire, UK

An award-winning nurserywoman, Rosy Hardy has been growing herbaceous perennials through Hardy's Cottage Garden Plants for the past 30 years. She has won 24 gold medals at RHS Chelsea Flower Shows, making her the most successful female floral exhibitor. Rosy has introduced many varieties, including *Oenothera* 'Rosyjane' and *Oenothera lindheimeri* 'Freefolk Rosy'. *hardysplants.co.uk*

Anemone 'Frilly Knickers' →
Anemone 'Frilly Knickers'

This anemone was developed at the nursery and I was delighted when it won the Horticultural Trades Association Virtual New Plant Award in 2020 with an amazing 33 per cent of the vote. It's a clump-forming plant that is easy to grow and generous with its flowers. The pretty, delicate and romantically ruffled semi-double blooms create a beautiful display from mid-summer through into autumn, filling borders with colour during a downtime that some gardens can struggle with here in the UK. Each petal is finely frilled and white suffused with pale lilac, with undersides brushed with deeper violet – a gorgeous composition. The plant combines beautifully with contrasting dark-leaved actaeas or ageratinas.

GROW It prefers part shade but can cope with more sun if the soil is sufficiently good, moist and humus-rich.

Type
Herbaceous perennial
Flowering
Summer, autumn
Height/ spread
60cm x 45cm
Position
Full sun, part shade
Soil
Fertile
Hardiness
USDA 8b/9a / RHS H4

LINDSEY JONES
Owner, Wildflower Nursery, Pembrokeshire, Wales

The team at Wildflower Nursery grows native wildflowers. The nursery is part of the Saving Pollinators Assurance Scheme with the National Botanic Garden of Wales, which means the plants are grown without the use of peat or synthetic insecticides and that DNA evidence has proved they are important for pollinators. *thewildflowernursery.co.uk*

Succisa pratensis
Devil's bit scabious (SEE ILLUSTRATION PAGE 117)

These pretty, lilac-blue, pincushion wildflowers on tall stems provide a beautiful display in late summer and autumn, when many flowers are past their best. Hoverflies, bees and butterflies come to take advantage of its valuable late pollen and nectar. Naturally found in a range of situations, from damp meadows to coastal cliffs, they are hardy, flower for a long period and make a lovely addition to the garden.

In Latin, *scabere* means 'to scratch', and historically this medicinal plant has been used to treat a range of skin complaints, including scabies and leprosy. It can also be taken as an infusion for coughs and fevers – it was used to treat tuberculosis before antibiotics. Of course, do your own research or seek advice before consuming any wild plant. According to folklore, the common name comes from the short, stubby roots, which the devil is said to have bitten off after becoming angry about the plant's medicinal properties.

This is also the food plant of the rare and vulnerable narrow-bordered bee hawk-moth and marsh fritillary butterfly – we are growing a large number of plug plants for a local conservation project with the aim of bringing back the locally extinct marsh fritillary.

GROW Sow fresh seeds in peat-free compost in autumn and grow on in late spring for planting out the following autumn. Seedlings are prone to damp off so make sure they are well ventilated. Alternatively, purchase peat-free plug plants. Although naturally found in a wide range of sites, it is best in poor soils (overly rich soil makes it leafy, with few flowers).

Type
Herbaceous perennial
Flowering
Summer, autumn
Height/ spread
60cm x 50cm
Position
Full sun, part shade
Soil
Damp, acid, poor
Hardiness
USDA 6a–1 / RHS H7

GARY J MARTIN
Founder, Global Diversity
Foundation, Marrakech,
Morocco

Dr Gary J Martin is the founder of the Global Diversity Foundation and has been involved in plant conservation and ethnobotanical work for over 30 years. As well as receiving several academic awards, he was a Carson Fellow at the Rachel Carson Center for Environment and Society in Germany. He currently cultivates exotic and native plants in the gardens of hotel Jnane Tamsna in Marrakech. *old.global-diversity.org*

Fabaceae
Legume

Type
Varies
Flowering
Varies
Height/spread
12–15m x continuous spread
Position
Intended for open, flat areas between date palms
Soil
Arid, alkaline
Hardiness
Varies

I have chosen a cohort of plants of an imagined Fab Forest: a fabulous *Fabaceae* family forest. After 20 years of cultivating more than 500 species of plants in the Palmeraie district of Marrakech and witnessing increased temperatures and decreased precipitation over time, I am embarking on a new project to select associations of herbaceous and woody plants that grow well together in arid and alkaline soils. I have been particularly impressed with the ability of exotic and native species of the *Fabaceae* family to be resilient in the face of climate change and weather variability, and decided to put them all together as a multi-storied anthropogenic ecosystem.

The secret to cultivating the Fab Forest in the arid zones of Morocco is to create a modified ecosystem, with a layer of medium-sized (12–20m) trees forming an open canopy over an understory of shrubs and small trees (2–10m) and a seasonal ground cover that comes alive during winter rains. The goal is to achieve an intriguing and luxuriant garden without irrigation.

The emphasis in the Fab Forest is on diversity: flower colour ranges from white through pink, purple and yellow. Some trees retain their leaves year-round and others have a short winter leafless period. The vegetation is dense enough to protect the soil and open enough to allow sunshine to filter through.

For the overstory: *Ceratonia siliqua* (carob), *Cercis siliquastrum* (Judas tree), *Gleditsia triacanthos* (honey locust), *Prosopis juliflora* (mezquite), *Robinia pseudoacacia* (black locust) and *Styphnolobium japonicum* (Japanese pagoda tree).

For the understory: *Albizia julibrissin* (Persian silk tree), *Colutea atlantica* (bladder senna), *Coronilla valentina* (Scorpion vetch), *Erythrostemon exostemma* (gallito), *Erythrostemon gilliesii* (bird of paradise), *Parkinsonia aculeata* (Mexican palo verde) and *Spartium junceum* (Spanish broom).

For ground cover: *Medicago sativa* (alfalfa), *Trigonella foenum-graecum* (fenugreek) and *Vicia faba* (broad bean).

GROW With the exception of the herbaceous ground cover, which is replanted yearly, the shrubs and trees need little care: no fertilisation, pruning or watering. The Fab Forest canopy reaches 12–15m and is designed to achieve a continuous spread that provides light shade. Created in full sun, the modified ecosystem develops its own unique pattern of full exposure to the sun and partial shade. The overstory and understory are drought-resilient shrubs and trees, some deciduous and some evergreen. Ground cover is frost-tolerant annuals.

SARAH WAIN
Former garden supervisor, West Sussex, UK

Together with her husband, Jim Buckland, Sarah Wain led the garden team at West Dean Gardens in West Sussex for more than 25 years. *twitter.com/sarahlwain*

Eucalyptus camaldulensis
Murray red gum

I grew up in a small rural town in Western Victoria, Australia and used to travel an hour each way to school. Peering out the bus window I'd see stately red gums gracing the paddocks, like oaks in an English park. Over the years I would look out for them like friends, recognising them by their individuality. I loved them then and I love them still.

Also commonly called the river red gum or red gum, this is a tree that dominates parts of Western Victoria and the Murray-Darling river system but can be seen throughout Australia. It's often found along waterways or where there is adequate rainfall. It produces clusters of white flowers and curved lance-shaped leaves, and young trees have a creamy-whitish bark with patches of yellows, pinks and brown. As they age, single trees take on astonishing individual shapes of great identifiable character, with peeling bark at their trunk bases. A mature tree can reach over 30m in height.

GROW This red gum is a tree for the great outdoors in Australia and not one to be considered for garden use given its requirement for space and its habit of losing limbs without warning.

Type
Evergreen tree
Flowering
Summer
Height/ spread
30m x 12m
Position
Full sun, shelter from cold winds
Soil
Fertile, neutral to slightly acid
Hardiness
USDA 8b/9a / RHS H4

CLAIRE AUSTIN
Owner, Claire Austin Hardy Plants, Shropshire, UK

Claire Austin established her nursery with her husband, Ric Kenwood, in 2001 after 20 years growing perennials at her father's company, David Austin Roses. They grow more than 1,500 varieties of perennials, including extensive collections of peonies. A recipient of numerous medals, she is also an illustrator and photographer. *claireaustin-hardyplants.co.uk*

Paeonia lactiflora 'Myrtle Gentry' →
Peony 'Myrtle Gentry'

It's difficult for me to put a finger on what my favourite plant is because I have grown so many over my decades as a perennial grower. But if I were forced to choose a plant right now, it would be a peony, and 'Myrtle Gentry' ticks all the boxes. The large, double, soft pink flowers are gorgeous, the scent is blissful and it is great in a vase when picked. The flower stems stay upright even in bad weather and, like all peonies, it is long-lived and easy to grow and maintain once established.

GROW Don't plant too deeply otherwise the plant will not bloom. Remove dead stems and leaves before new shoots emerge in spring to prevent disease such as peony wilt.

Type
Herbaceous perennial
Flowering
Summer
Height/ spread
90cm x 90cm
Position
Full sun, part shade (in hotter climates)
Soil
Well-drained, not waterlogged
Hardiness
USDA 6b/7a / RHS H6

37

TOM HOBLYN
Garden designer,
Suffolk, UK

Tom Hoblyn is a landscape designer and horticulturist who set up his design practice shortly after graduating from the Royal Botanic Gardens, Kew. An established figure at both RHS Chelsea and Hampton Court Flower Shows, he has won three gold medals, as well as a People's Choice Award. *thomashoblyn.co.uk*

Dryopteris wallichiana
Alpine wood fern

I find this to be one of the most noble of ferns, one of those plants that stops you in your tracks. Its upright habit contrasts well with other more sprawly ferns, adding some structure. It has a shuttlecock-type appearance, but the lance-shaped fronds are reflexed at the tips – almost as though sculpted. The fronds have a permanent sap-green colour with a dark brown, almost black midrib. This is a good accent plant to provide structure in the fernery. In time it forms a pretty crown that looks great even in winter. It goes well with wide, spreading ferns such as *Polystichum setiferum* 'Herrenhausen'. I had the pleasure of meeting the great grandson of Nathaniel Wallich (after whom the fern is named) while at Kew and I've been lucky enough to view Wallich's catalogue of the hundreds of plants he collected at Kew's Herbarium on several occasions. As a result I've always had a bit of a soft spot for all things Wallichian.

GROW Suppliers say this is an easy and hardy fern to grow, tolerant of a range of conditions, but to grow a really handsome specimen, it needs partial shade and permanently damp soil – if it dries out at all, it will suffer. It will also suffer if it lies soaking wet all year. Do not plant it in full shade or any direct sunlight. If it's happy, though, very little needs doing. Mulch in spring. Although meant to be semi-evergreen, the fronds become messy in winter so I cut them back to show off the crown. Deer can be a problem, as they like taking a bite out of the crown when the fiddleheads are just unfurling.

Type
Semi-evergreen fern
Height/ spread
1m x 1m
Position
Part shade
Soil
Damp, not heavy
Hardiness
USDA 7b/8a / RHS H5

MARTIN OGLE
Head gardener, Lowther Castle & Gardens, Lake District, UK

Martin Ogle has led the development of the Dan Pearson garden masterplan at Lowther Castle since 2012. He also leads the overall daily operation at Lowther Castle, which is becoming a must-see garden visitor attraction. *lowthercastle.org*

Veronicastrum virginicum 'Spring Dew'
Culver's root 'Spring Dew'

Prior to working on the ongoing project at Lowther Castle, I had never really given veronicastrums much focus. During the early days of the project, while studying planting plans for a new parterre tapestry garden designed by Dan Pearson, I started gathering stock plants from which new plants would be grown. I remember it being one of the plants that was first sourced and having great success from dividing it. I enjoy its structural leaf and pattern, and 'Spring Dew' has the most delicate pure white flowers that stand tall and proud in the garden and are a magnet for insects. This variety will need staking, but given room in the garden it will serve you well and tolerate a range of conditions.

GROW Allow spent stems to stand throughout winter, which will provide you with excellent structural winter interest. New plants can be raised from cuttings or division.

Type
Herbaceous perennial
Flowering
Summer
Height/ spread
1.2m x 75cm
Position
Full sun, part shade, open
Soil
Moist, well-drained
Hardiness
USDA 6a–1 / RHS H7

ALAN STREET

Nursery manager and director of shows, Avon Bulbs, Somerset, UK

Alan Street joined Avon Bulbs in 1979. The nursery has participated in some 40 RHS Chelsea Flower Shows and won 31 gold medals. *avonbulbs.co.uk*

Tropaeolum tricolor
Three-coloured nasturtium

I have grown three-coloured nasturtium for over 35 years – I can't remember where I first got it. Grown for its floral display, it is dormant in summer and starts coming up in early autumn with the finest thread-like shoots, almost as thin as small needles. It needs careful placement and a support of some sort as it is a true climber, hanging on and curling its way through twigs and shrubs in its native Chile. A few tubers can produce hundreds of red, blue and yellow flowers from early spring to the start of summer, each of which will last for many weeks. Some seed is set but the tubers, which are quite an odd shape, increase freely. Another point of interest is that all parts of the plant are edible. A bar in London once contacted us looking for a regular supply of fresh blooms for its cocktails.

GROW This semi-hardy tuberous plant will grow outside perfectly happily. Place it in a large pot under cold glass but make sure the pot itself never freezes – once the roots are damaged, the plant will probably die. If grown in too warm conditions, it gets drawn and soft and will start to flower too early. Give it sufficient support, a sheltered site away from the fiercest winds (a southerly aspect is best) and, most importantly, keep it dry when dormant in the summer. When leaves start turning yellow as soon as the weather gets really warm, do not water. Provide a few liquid feeds during early spring. Avoid thin chalky soils as they can be too dry in spring when the plant is in full growth. No pruning required.

Type
Tuberous perennial climber
Flowering
Spring
Height/ spread
1.5m x 15cm
Position
Full sun, sheltered
Soil
Moist, well-drained
Hardiness
USDA 10b / RHS H2

LAURA AND JACK WILLGOSS

Founders, Wildegoose Nursery, Shropshire, UK

Jack and Laura Willgoss met at RHS Wisley as trainees in 2006. After graduating they worked as gardeners on private estates before realising their dream of running a nursery showcasing herbaceous perennials and grasses. *wildegoosenursery.co.uk*

Actaea 'Queen of Sheba'
Actaea 'Queen of Sheba'

Actaeas make superb garden plants, especially those selected for their dark maroon-flushed foliage. Those saturated leaves make a fabulous backdrop for early summer blooms and earn the plant its place in the garden long before the spectacle of its own flowers and extraordinary scent steals the show in late summer and autumn. 'Queen of Sheba' is our favourite. It is a Piet Oudolf selection, and he certainly seems to know a good plant when he sees one. The plants are an impressive 2m tall in our garden and despite their fine stems are remarkably self-supporting. The flower stems are arched over at the top like a shepherd's crook and have branching arms of tiny star-shaped, creamy-white flowers. Their sweet scent is one of the highlights of autumn. We have ours emerging through a froth of golden *Deschampsia cespitosa* 'Goldtau', their tops mingling with golden and ruby red crab apples above.

GROW In our experience, acteas are generally trouble-free in terms of pests and diseases. They bulk up gradually and never threaten to take over a border. To keep the foliage looking good, they need rich soils that hold some moisture in drier summer spells. Woodland-like conditions with humus-rich soils suit them best, but they can cope with open sunny positions if the soil is sufficiently humus-rich with some moisture retention.

Type
Herbaceous perennial
Flowering
Late summer, autumn
Height/ spread
2m x 40cm
Position
Part shade
Soil
Moist, well-drained
Hardiness
USDA 6b/7a / RHS H6

ANDY STURGEON
Landscape designer and
writer, Brighton, UK

Andy Sturgeon's designs explore the relationship between plants, structure and the wider landscape. He is the winner of three best in shows and nine gold medals at the RHS Chelsea Flower Show. *andysturgeon.com*

Digitalis canariensis 'Bella' →
Canary Island foxglove 'Bella'

I used *D. canariensis* at Chelsea in 2016 and as soon as it came off the lorry from the nursery it was turning heads – I knew it was the star of the garden. I spent the whole week watching people drooling over it and since then I've planted it wherever I can. The sophisticated, apricot-orange flower spikes are like flames erupting from the glossy, slightly serrated leaves carried on reddish stems. This variety is much more compact than the species, making it a great choice for a small garden, and in truth it doesn't need much looking after despite its exotic credentials.

GROW Cutting back branches will rejuvenate a leggy plant and dead branches will need shortening after a cold winter, but otherwise it needs little attention. Give it an occasional feed and an annual mulch. Deadhead to encourage side shoots.

Type
Evergreen shrub
Flowering
Summer
Height/spread
1.5m x 1m
Position
Full sun, but it can stomach some shade, sheltered
Soil
Moist, well-drained, especially in winter
Hardiness
USDA 9b/10a / RHS H3

ANNE WRIGHT
Owner, Dryad Nursery,
North Yorkshire, UK

Anne Wright is a nursery owner who has been breeding miniature daffodils, snowdrops and hepaticas for more than 30 years. *dryad-home.co.uk*

Narcissus 'Little Dryad'
Daffodil 'Little Dryad'

Named after my nursery, this is an early seedling that ticked all the boxes. It is very small, elegant, upright and scented with swept-back, creamy white petals. A perfect miniature.

GROW I grow my miniature daffodils under glass in clay pots plunged to the rim in sand, which dries out completely by the end of spring. They are repotted every year. Many will be happy outside in containers, rock gardens or raised beds where they can be appreciated at close quarters, and given protection from slugs. Do not allow them to become waterlogged and do not overfeed. If grown in containers, don't allow them to freeze through the roots.

Type
Bulbous perennial
Flowering
Spring
Height
12cm
Position
Full sun
Soil
Well-drained
Hardiness
USDA 8b/9a / RHS H4

DERRY WATKINS
Founder, Special Plants,
Wiltshire, UK

Derry Watkins founded plant and seed nursery Special Plants near Bath in the late 1990s and began by specialising in tender perennials. She also grows hardy plants, biennials and unusual plants. *specialplants.net*

Heliopsis helianthoides var. *scabra* 'Bleeding Hearts'
North American ox-eye 'Bleeding Hearts'

The sultry dark leaves of this beautiful plant are topped with deep red flowers, fading to orange and bronze from mid-summer to mid-autumn – a delicious colour combination. It blooms the first year from seed sown in early spring and makes a good cut flower. It's also good for pollinators.

GROW Easily grown from seed or cuttings. Vulnerable to slugs when young. Clump-forming, it does not spread and is upright enough not to need support.

Type
Herbaceous perennial
Flowering
Summer, autumn
Height/spread
1.2m x 50cm
Position
Full sun, open
Soil
Well-drained
Hardiness
USDA 6b/7a / RHS H6

SUE STICKLAND
Gardener and writer,
Wales

Sue Stickland is a gardener, gardening writer and lecturer. Now semi-retired, she works mostly on the Gaia Foundation's Seed Sovereignty Programme, which aims to support the development of an ecologically sustainable seed system in the UK and Ireland. *seedsovereignty.info*

Phaseolus coccineus '**Czar**'
Runner bean 'Czar'

This white-flowered runner bean was bred in Victorian times, but I find the pods are as mild flavoured, stringless and tender as those of any modern variety. It is prolific, cropping well into autumn. I also grow some plants just for their large white seeds, which are good homegrown substitutes for butter beans. I remember when this variety was nearly dropped from seed catalogues when the UK joined the European Union in the 1970s, as it became illegal to sell varieties that had not been officially registered. But it survived this, as well as more recent competition, to remain a useful garden variety.

GROW Add organic matter to the soil before planting out seedlings 20cm apart. These are tall leafy plants, so give them a strong framework. Water in dry spells once flowers appear and pods start to set. Pick the pods every few days to encourage the maximum yield of green beans or leave the seeds inside to swell to use as butter beans. Warm nights can stop the flowers setting, so an open site (not against a wall) is preferable.

Type
Annual
climber
Flowering
Summer
**Height/
spread**
2.5m x 1.5m
Position
Full sun,
semi-
sheltered
Soil
Fertile, well-
drained
Hardiness
USDA 10b
/ RHS H2

Type
Annual
climber
Flowering
Summer
**Height/
spread**
1.8m x 1m
Position
Full sun,
semi-
sheltered
Soil
Fertile, well-
drained
Hardiness
USDA 10b
/ RHS H2

Phaseolus vulgaris '**District Nurse**'
Borlotti bean 'District Nurse'

This variety of the Italian borlotti bean is well suited to the cool, wet climate of Wales. Back in the late 1900s, an old lady in Cardiff gave some seeds to her district nurse, and the variety has been kept alive by local gardeners ever since, gradually adapting to the climate. It is now in seed libraries and is sold by some small seed companies. It's a climbing plant and needs support. The pretty lilac flowers are followed by patterned green and purple pods filled with plump, red-splashed seeds. I often use some of the bean seeds fresh from the plant in late summer – they are quicker to prepare and cook, and less mealy in texture than their dried counterparts. The rest I dry to use in winter soups and casseroles.

GROW I start the seeds off in modules in a greenhouse, then plant them out when the risk of frost has passed, 20cm apart. This gives a longer growing season for the beans to swell and the pods to mature and dry on the plants.

KATHY BROWN
Author and gardener,
Bedfordshire, UK

Kathy Brown writes about cottage gardening, edible flowers, containers and bulbs. She is the owner of Kathy Brown's Garden in Stevington, which is open to the public. *kathybrownsgarden.com*

Lunaria rediviva
Perennial honesty

This is a plant that flowers from spring to mid-summer, is scented and grows in difficult dry, north-facing positions in the UK. It grows in semi-shade as well as shade, is undemanding and totally reliable. A tough perennial with a creeping rhizome, erect stems and elliptical seed pods.

GROW No pests, no need to stake. Cut back in late summer.

Type
Herbaceous
perennial
Flowering
Spring, summer
Height/spread
90cm x 90cm
Position
Any
Soil
Moist, well-drained
Hardiness
USDA 6a–1 / RHS H7

ANNE SWITHINBANK
Horticulturist and writer,
Devon, UK

Anne Swithinbank has been a horticulturist since 1986. Trained at RHS Botanic Gardens, Kew, she worked as glasshouse supervisor at RHS Wisley and now undertakes landscaping, writing and TV and radio projects. *twitter.com/anneswithinbank*

Type
Rhizomatous perennial
Flowering
Early summer
Height/spread
90cm x 45cm
Position
Full sun, in the UK choose a south- or west-facing spot; middle of a border or at the foot of a wall
Soil
Light, well-drained, avoid acid
Hardiness
USDA 6a–1 / RHS H7

Iris 'Poem of Ecstasy'
Iris 'Poem of Ecstasy'

Nominating a favourite plant from the garden is proving an impossible task. Would I choose a tree, an annual, a cultivar of tender *Nerine sarniensis* or clove-scented deciduous shrub *Viburnum carlesii* 'Aurora'? Best then to opt for one not yet planted – and so from the top of the shopping list I pluck tall bearded iris 'Poem of Ecstasy'. For long enough I have imagined watching its lavender buds opening to large, fragrant, ruffled blooms held majestically above blue-green, sword-shaped leaves. Upright standards are a soft, peachy pink and the falls are lavender, lit by orange beards.

I appreciate all irises but the bearded ones in particular, because they fully live up to their namesake, the goddess of the rainbow and messenger of the gods. The beard refers to the fluffy hairs at the base of the fall petals, looking like hairy caterpillars crawling away from the flowers. Often of contrasting colours, they are thought to be attractions or guides to pollinating insects.

True, the show of flowers from one plant is relatively short-lived but between them the shorter dwarf kinds, intermediates and taller cultivars add colour from spring to early summer. Perhaps the flamboyant blooms of iris, oriental poppy and peony are even more special as they are so fleeting.

Our soil – a water-retentive clay with flints – is all wrong for bearded irises, but fortunately there is a low, south-facing section of wall to the front of our house where drier soil is slightly raised and they should thrive. Best of all, 'Poem of Ecstasy' is well known as a 'good doer' and makes a generous clump. I can imagine settling my new plant in place, with rhizomes arranged and firmed to sit with their surfaces showing and facing south to catch the sun. Yet I also like similar but paler 'Celebration Song' and vibrant, splendidly named 'Moustache Rose', which both follow the theme of pink standards and lilac falls. Then there is the fabulous, washy beauty of 'Ciel Gris Sur Poilly'. We had better start building a raised bed.

GROW In my garden the yellow-flowered bearded iris inherited from my aunt, as well as iris 'Kent Pride', whose coppery-orange blooms complement especially handsome foliage, thrive in their own space, untroubled by weeds and other plants. Irises are tough but if they are planted in shade or their rhizomes are smothered by growth, flowering will grind to a halt. After a few years, growth retreats to the outer edge of a clump leaving old, non-flowering rhizomes in the middle. This is the cue to lift the clump after flowering (during summer or into early autumn). Snap or cut healthy sections bearing fans of leaves away from the dead-looking inner rhizomes and replant in groups. Should tall leaves threaten to topple the plants, cut through the flags halfway. Water newly planted bearded irises during dry spells in their first year, while they are establishing. In good soils they may not require feeding. Avoid high nitrogen fertilisers and instead apply a spring boost of bone meal or a proprietary feed high in phosphates and potash.

ANN-MARIE POWELL
Garden designer,
Hampshire, UK

Award-winning gardener Ann-Marie Powell started her practice in 1998 and has built an impressive portfolio of gardens that combines the best of contemporary design with an innovative use of materials in a naturalistic style. *ann-mariepowell.com*

Rosa × odorata 'Mutabilis' →
Tea rose 'Mutabilis'

This effervescent, ever-changing beauty is the plant I most look forward to greeting in the morning when I step into the garden – I am always so pleased to see her. A kaleidoscope of colour-changing blooms dances continuously for a good six months through summer into autumn, always with elegant playfulness. Flowers are honey-yellow, ageing through coppery orange and cerise, and fluttering as if the whole shrub is covered in butterflies. Loose, lax and open, it lends an untameable wildness to a border, container or even to a fence when trained as a wall shrub – she can even be trained as a hedge. Almost thornless (an easy picker for vases), she invites pollinators to enjoy her pollen and nectar with her open blooms. No garden should be without this easy, bountiful plant.

GROW I enjoy growing this low-maintenance rose in pots, so I can move her around the garden where I can enjoy her best. She's happy in a wide range of positions and I've just freed one plant to grow in the open border without root restriction. I'm excited to see it mature into headier heights of up to 2m.

Type
Shrub rose
Flowering
Summer, autumn
Height/spread
2m x 1.5m
Position
Full sun, but will grow in east- or west-facing borders, exposed or sheltered
Soil
Moist, well-drained, but will withstand even poor soil
Hardiness
USDA 7b/8a / RHS H5

VAL BOURNE
Garden writer,
Cotswolds, UK

Val Bourne is a writer, lecturer, podcaster and author. Her third-of-an-acre garden is exposed, but she also trials plants at the much warmer RHS Wisley. She gardens organically and has an allotment where dahlias fight for space among the vegetables. *valbourne.co.uk*

Colchicum autumnale 'Pannonicum'
Meadow saffron 'Nancy Lindsay'

Having a cold garden in the Cotswolds may be a bleak experience at times, but it makes you appreciate the beauty of each season. As a result, I have a soft spot for flowers that signal the end of one and the beginning of another. When this colchicum opens its refined, rose-pink goblets in late summer, it announces the season is fading fast. When the garden is looking dry and fading, I see these magical flowers and I know that cyclamen, nerines, hesperantha and many more colchicums will soon follow and revive everything. The foliage is well-behaved and not nearly as offensive as most colchicums. The goblets emerge without any foliage, held on long, slightly angled stems, like champagne flutes in the hands of guests who really need to head home. I also warm to gardener and plant collector Nancy Lindsay (1896–1973) herself. According to Gloucestershire rumour, she expected to inherit Hidcote Manor from her great friend Lawrence Johnston. Instead, he left her his French estate, Serre de la Madone, when he died in 1958. She was furious and legend has it she burned a lot of his papers in his Hidcote garden when she heard. This Romanian colchicum was collected by Lindsay in 1936 from a plant-hunting expedition to Iran. It was quite something for a woman to travel into the wilderness in the 1930s.

GROW This is an easy bulb to grow, and once planted it should be left to multiply. After a year or so, a clump can produce 100 flowers from nowhere in days. The early spring foliage lasts a long time, though it does brown badly, so tuck this away in a secluded position.

Type
Cormous perennial
Flowering
Late summer, autumn
Height/spread
50cm x 50cm
Position
A bright border edge is perfect, away from full sun; I haven't found this good in grass
Soil
Moist, well-drained
Hardiness
USDA 7b/8a / RHS H5

MIKE MAUNDER
Executive director,
Cambridge Conservation
Initiative, Devon, UK

Dr Mike Maunder is executive director of the Cambridge Conservation Initiative, the world's largest concentration of conservation researchers and practitioners. It is a collaboration between the University of Cambridge and internationally focused biodiversity conservation organisations, and is based in the David Attenborough Building. *cambridgeconservation.org*

Tigridia pavonia
Peacock tiger flower

Type
Bulbous perennial
Flowering
Summer
Height/ spread
1.5m x 10cm
Position
Full sun, sheltered
Soil
Well-drained
Hardiness
USDA 11 / RHS H1c

This plant reminds me of the abundance of the tropics. The flowers are big, bright and brash – the garden equivalent of a pink plastic lawn flamingo – and bring to mind the over-amplified photos of some horticultural catalogues. They flower at that ripe period when dahlias are reigning. *T. pavonia*, like the dahlia, is part of the ancient Mexican botanical heritage of the Aztecs, but in contrast to the dahlia, each flower only lasts a few hours, making every flowering an event to be anticipated and savoured.

GROW I plant the bulbs in a large clay pot in a free-draining compost. During the summer I place the pot in full sun and feed copiously with half-strength tomato liquid feed. They are prone to slugs and snails, so regular picking over is needed. In autumn I dry out the pot and store it in a cold greenhouse. Once the plants have gone dormant I cut away the season's growth. In spring I prepare them for growth by replacing the top 3cm of compost with a fresh mix and water well.

Lychnis flos-cuculi
Ragged robin

Type
Short-lived perennial
Flowering
Spring, summer
Height/ spread
1m x 50cm
Position
Full sun, part shade
Soil
Damp but well-drained
Hardiness
USDA 6a–1 / RHS H7

There are a couple of verges near me that come mid-spring are a mass of ragged robin and cuckoo flower (*Cardamine pratensis*), at their best just before the early purple orchids. Sometimes these damp verges are mashed by tractor tyres or mown before flowering has finished. The ragged robin was not part of my childhood – I was raised on the chalk in Hampshire – so I delight in growing this beautiful plant on my damp Devon lawn. I have raised plants from seed and planted them in my front garden, where they form clusters of stems with a mass of flowers. The lawn is now managed as a mossy damp meadow and the ragged robin has started self-sowing. Ragged robin is a plant of the spring when the carnival of wildflowers seems unending and I wait for the swallows to return.

GROW Naturalise into a damp informal lawn – the seed needs a few gaps in the grass to germinate. Ragged robin likes a damp situation but will not thrive in rank grass or saturated soil. I mow in late summer to allow seed to set, and prior to mowing collect any ripe seed to scatter after I finish.

Type
Deciduous shrub
Flowering
Late winter, early spring
Height/spread
1.5m x 2.5m
Position
Full sun, sheltered
Soil
Well-drained
Hardiness
USDA 6b/7a / RHS H6

Abeliophyllum distichum
White forsythia

This shrub is all about hope. It flowers early in spring and produces drifts of fragrant white flowers. I have happy memories of looking for this plant in the mountains of South Korea where it is threatened with extinction; working with my old friend Professor Yong-Shik Kim we surveyed sites looking for surviving populations. This involved working in snow and in some cases witnessing the first surge of spring flowers. This plant symbolises the beauty of the Korean flora and the monumental rebuilding of the nation's forests after a catastrophic civil war. When this shrub flowers it tells me that winter is approaching its end and that rare species can be saved from extinction. It also reminds me of the extraordinary commitment of South Korea's conservationists and botanists. Perhaps one day Professor Kim and I can look for this lovely shrub in the mountains of North Korea.

GROW A woodland plant, it likes light shade and wants to grow through leaf litter – a mulch of leaf litter is essential. It likes summer moisture and is absolutely bone hardy.

Hesperis matronalis
Dame's violet

After a long period of working in the tropics, I returned to the UK. One of the joys of coming back was getting to know the wild plants. The first spring was a revelation: living in Devon I watched snowdrops and primroses unfold, later, I noticed a purple haze in a nearby garden – it was a large colony of dame's violets. The colour, shifting with the light, varied between punky pink and smoky purple. While not native, this plant has become a long-established part of the cottage garden flora and was popular as a scented flower in the 1600s. Its flowers bring drifts of evening scent and colour, and have the bonus of attracting orange-tip butterflies. I use the drifts to start the season and allow lilies and foxgloves to come up through the plants. Don't bother with the anaemic white form, it's a waste of time.

GROW From a few plants the population has grown into a self-sowing colony. I usually harvest seeds and scatter them in the garden, including in annual flower areas. It does best for me in deep, moist soil – it can become stunted in dry sunny spots. It's a robust and happy plant, so no need to water or feed. Prune after flowering to reduce self-sowing and thin out and transplant seedlings as required.

Type
Biennial, short-lived perennial
Flowering
Spring, summer
Height/ spread
1m x 50cm
Position
Full sun, part shade
Soil
Moist, well-drained, alkaline, neutral
Hardiness
USDA 6b/7a / RHS H6

GEORGINA REID
Founding editor, *The Planthunter*, Sydney, Australia

Georgina Reid is a writer and editor, and founder of *The Planthunter* and *Wonderground* print journals. *The Planthunter* documents, explores and questions the ways humans relate to the natural world. *Wonderground* offers deeper explorations into the relationships between people, plants and place. She is the author of *The Planthunter: Truth, Beauty, Chaos and Plants. theplanthunter.com.au*

Casuarina glauca 'Cousin It'
Desert she-oak 'Cousin It'

I live and work on the banks of the Hawkesbury River. My studio is just metres from the water and is surrounded by a stand of *C. glauca* (in Australia, the common name is swamp oak). Swamp oak tends to sucker, and so in a very small space we have a sort of miniature forest along the foreshore of our property. A swamp oak forest used to blanket the shores of the river, but has now nearly all been removed because it blocks views and access to the water. While the Coastal Swamp Oak Forest ecological community lists it as endangered in New South Wales due to development and over-clearing, a smaller, prostrate form of *C. glauca* has become a favourite garden mainstay. Found growing in the late 1980s on an exposed headland just north of where I live, this form was called 'Cousin It' due to its resemblance to the hirsute Addams Family character.

GROW 'Cousin It' makes brilliant, textural and very sculptural ground cover. It tumbles over retaining walls, forms mounds amid taller vertical plantings and, most importantly for this lazy gardener, it acts as a living mulch. It is a slightly more manageable form of swamp oak than the ones down by the river.

Type
Evergreen shrub
Height/ spread
10cm x 1m
Position
Full sun
Soil
Moist, loam, sand
Hardiness
USDA 9b/10a / RHS H3

ALEC WHITE
Nurseryman and
owner, Primrose Hall,
Bedfordshire, UK

Alec White is a horticulturist with a passion for peonies. He holds
the National Collection for intersectional peonies in the UK,
working to preserve these unique plants for future generations.
primrosehallpeonies.co.uk

Paeonia 'Singing in the Rain'
Intersectional peony 'Singing in the Rain'

Peony 'Singing in the Rain' has masses of delicate semi-double, coral-pink flowers
and is absolutely stunning. The best thing about it is that it flowers for about twice
as long as a tree peony, so you can get flowers for four weeks or more. It is a
wonderful example of an intersectional peony – a cross between a herbaceous
peony and tree peony variety – with strong sturdy stems, which means it doesn't
need staking or support as some traditional varieties do. A great plant in the
flower border, it's also excellent in pots and containers. It is easy to grow, low
maintenance and will live for decades in the garden with minimal care. It also
produces wonderful, strongly coloured autumn foliage, making it a great focal
point in your garden as things start to wind down for the year.

GROW Peonies can take up to five years to flower reliably so cut out the waiting time
by planting a well-established, mature peony plant. Don't plant too deep (ensure the
crown is no more than 2.5cm below the surface), and feed once a year with a good,
well-balanced fertiliser in spring, summer or autumn. Cut back in autumn; they will die
to the ground, making it obvious when to cut them back, and re-emerge the following
spring. Water consistently while buds are forming in spring, but take care not to over
water as peonies don't like having wet roots.

Type
Herbaceous
perennial
Flowering
Summer
**Height/
spread**
75cm x 50cm
Position
Full shade,
part shade,
sheltered
Soil
Free
draining
Hardiness
USDA 6b/7a
/ RHS H6

MARIAN BOSWALL
Landscape architect and
horticulturist, Kent, UK

Marian Boswall is a leading landscape architect and co-founder of
the Sustainable Landscape Foundation. Her projects invest in the land
for the long term and explore how it can heal and connect us on all
levels. She writes and lectures and is author of *Sustainable Garden*.
marianboswall.com

Malus 'Evereste'
Crab apple 'Evereste' (SEE ILLUSTRATION PAGE 179)

The humble crab apple finds a home in nearly every garden I design. In late
winter the birds mob the pretty fruits when all else is gone. In spring, a daily
visit to inhale the scent and listen to the bees is food for the soul. Not too fast
or too slow a grower, it requires no maintenance except a very occasional
prune once it reaches the size you want.

GROW Looks beautiful alone, in a group or in rows to line an avenue. Underplant with
spirea for waves of white in spring. Keep watered for the first few seasons, with a
tree bag to minimise water use, then it should be able to fend for itself in all but the
worst drought. Common advice suggests moist but well-drained soil, although mine is
perfectly happy on Wealden clay.

Type
Deciduous
tree
Flowering
Spring
**Height/
spread**
8m x 8m
Position
Full sun, part
shade
Soil
Moist, well-
drained
Hardiness
USDA 6b/7a
/ RHS H6

ERIN BENZAKEIN
Founder, Floret,
Washington, USA

Erin Benzakein is the founder of flower farm Floret and is considered one of North America's leading 'farmer-florists'. Her first book, *Floret Farm's Cut Flower Garden*, won the American Horticultural Society's Book Award. Her second book, *Floret Farm's A Year in Flowers*, made the *New York Times* bestseller list. Erin conducts extensive field trials on flowers and foliage, including those uncommon in floristry. *floretflowers.com*

Lathyrus odoratus ↘
Sweet pea

When I was a little girl, I spent summers in the countryside visiting my great-grandparents. One of my jobs was to keep fresh flowers by my Grammy's bedside table. She had a number of beautiful bloomers growing in her garden, but the ones that I remember most are the tangle of rainbow-coloured sweet peas climbing up her carport posts. When my husband and I bought our first house, the first thing I planted was a huge tunnel of sweet peas right in the center of the garden. That spring, as the first flowers opened, their scent transported me back in time to summers of my youth and the happy memories of picking flowers in Grammy's garden. I've been growing sweet peas for nearly twenty years now, and each spring as they climb their trellises, it's like seeing my dear old friends once again.

GROW Sweet peas benefit from a technique called pinching. Once plants are 10–15cm tall, pinch out the central growing tip, just above a leaf joint, leaving just two or three leaf nodes. This will encourage the plant to branch vigorously from the base. Extremely productive and highly fragrant, its vines grow rapidly and require a strong structure to climb. Sweet peas are heavy feeders and need a little extra pampering to produce abundantly. Prepare planting beds by applying bone meal, a thick layer of compost or well-rotted manure and a generous dose of natural fertiliser. Sweet peas love water and without consistent moisture they'll fail to thrive. Keeping their thirst quenched during warm weather is crucial, so set up soaker hoses as soon as you plant them to keep their lush growth unchecked. In warmer regions where winter weather is relatively mild, sweet peas can be sown in autumn. Everywhere else, sow in late winter/early spring.

Type
Annual climber
Flowering
Summer, autumn
Height/spread
2.5m x 50cm
Position
Full sun, part shade
Soil
Moist, well-drained
Hardiness
USDA 9b/10a
/ RHS H3

RICHARD BAINES
Curator, Logan Botanic
Garden, Dumfries and
Galloway, Scotland

Richard Baines is responsible for the management and development of
Scotland's most exotic garden, which is part of the Royal Botanic Garden
Edinburgh. He is a TV and radio broadcaster and author of *Plant Explorer*,
which is about plant exploration in northern Vietnam. *rbge.org.uk/logan*

Schefflera macrophylla
Large-leaved umbrella plant

One of the major highlights of our 2014 expedition to northern Vietnam was *S. macrophylla* with its massive leaves, architectural features and sheer exoticness. This species dwarfs every other species of schefflera I have ever seen. I've heard it described as 'the daddy of all schef023fleras'. Eventually growing up to 15m, it has long petioles that support hovering hands of leaflets. The attractive new growth and leaf undersides are covered in a layer of rust-coloured hairs. On Phan Xi Păng Mountain, specimens vary considerably from mature, sparse, multi-branched plants to younger, more compact, floriferous ones. My immediate thoughts on seeing it was how good it would look growing back at Logan underplanted with exotic gingers. It's a plant that takes some beating for impact.

GROW Grow in dappled shade in woodland conditions. Add organic matter when planting. If you can, plant it on a slope so that you have a vantage point at the top – the results can be spectacular. Do not be disheartened if the plant loses its leaves during a cold winter; it is tough and will likely shoot again from the trunk. Feed young plants fortnightly and keep watered during drought.

Type
Evergreen
tree
Flowering
Late
summer,
winter
**Height/
spread**
15m x 5m
Position
Part shade,
sheltered
Soil
Moist, with
added
organic
matter
Hardiness
USDA 8b/9a
/ RHS H4

Rehderodendron macrocarpum
Rehderodendron macrocarpum

This is a true giant of the Vietnamese forest, growing up to 25m tall, and often first identified by the plethora of davidia-like seeds scattered around its base. First observed on Mount Emei, China, and rarely cultivated in Britain, it is a delightful member of the *Styracaceae* famil. The enormous seeds, up to 7cm long, are slow to germinate and exhibit double dormancy. Each fruit hangs pendulously along the branches, starting off green then maturing to a pinky-red. As the leaves emerge, it produces clusters of showy white flowers in spring.

GROW Rehderodendrons thrive in warm, moist, acid soils in a sheltered woodland and in a mild, temperate climate. Once established, this tree grows quickly and flowers at a young age. Incorporate a wheelbarrow-full of farmyard manure while planting, and just watch it grow! Keep well watered during drought and provide an annual mulch.

Type
Deciduous
tree
Flowering
Late spring,
early summer
**Height/
spread**
25m x 4m
Position
Full sun,
part shade,
sheltered
Soil
Well-drained,
fertile, acid
Hardiness
USDA 8b/9a
/ RHS H4

Type
Evergreen
tree
Flowering
Spring
**Height/
spread**
15m x 5m
Position
Part shade,
sheltered
Soil
Moist, acid
Hardiness
USDA 8b/9a
/ RHS H4

Rhododendron suoilenhense
Giant-leaved rhododendron

R. suoilenhense is named after the mountain district Suoi Lenh in Vietnam. It was first recorded in 1991, growing between altitudes of 2,100m and 3,100m. In the wild it grows up to 15m with bold, broadly oblong leaves up to 40cm long. Young plants have enormous leaves and resemble something you might find in a tropical rather than a rhododendron forest! It flowers relatively early in its life, often at around seven-years old, whereas *R. protistum* can take up to 50 years to produce its first flowers. It's a late-blooming species, so its flowers are much less likely to be affected by late frosts. A great plant for creating an exotic feeling.

GROW Best planted under the canopy of mature trees and associates well with *Magnolia wilsonii*. It does not like being pruned so plant it where it has lots of space.

Lilium primulinum var. *burmanicum*
Oriental lily

The day that we discovered this lily was one of the most memorable mornings of my life. After climbing Y Ty Mountain in northern Vietnam, we were awoken at 5am by the chatter of monkeys passing over the camp. Although I had never heard this sound before, I immediately recognised it and felt incredibly privileged to hear this wonderful dawn chorus.

The plant is an exotic, oriental-looking lily that grows almost at the rugged summit of the mountain in full exposure. It's a highly scented species that freely produces many large butter-yellow trumpet-shaped flowers, stained burgundy at the base. Growing alongside it was *Allium wallichii*, which we collected as a new record for the *Flora of Cambodia, Laos and Vietnam*. All in all one amazing day!

GROW In Scotland this is a fantastic plant for a cool, north-facing border. It appreciates ample amounts of organic matter. Best grown in shelter as the flowering stem can be snapped off. When planting put a layer of sharp sand below the bulbs to aid drainage. When grown from seed it will easily flower in year three.

Type
Bulbous perennial
Flowering
Summer
Height/ spread
1.5m x 20cm
Position
Full sun, part shade, sheltered
Soil
Moist, well-drained
Hardiness
USDA 9b/10a / RHS 3

MARTIN CRAWFORD
Founder, Agroforestry Research Trust, Devon, UK

Martin is the founder and director of the Agroforestry Research Trust, a non-profit making charity that researches and educates around edible forest gardens (or food forests), which mimic a forest-like structure but use mainly edible plants. *agroforestry.co.uk*

Elaeagnus umbellata
Autumn olive

A superb plant: deciduous but not out of leaf for very long, ideal for bees and useful in hedges and windbreaks. It bears large crops of edible red fruits about 1cm in diameter in autumn. Also a great nitrogen-fixing shrub, which aids the growth and cropping of other nearby plants.

GROW For fruit production, it is best to grow named cultivars from the UK, USA or Europe. Easy to grow, it tolerates exposure. Grow two different selections for cross-pollination for good fruiting. Tolerant of trimming, but will fruit much less if trimmed regularly.

Type
Deciduous shrub
Flowering
Spring, summer
Height/spread
5m x 5m
Position
Full sun, part shade
Soil
Moist, well-drained
Hardiness
USDA 7b/8a / RHS H5

Type
Deciduous fern
Height/spread
1.5m x 2.5m
Position
Part shade
Soil
Moist, well-drained
Hardiness
USDA 7b/8a / RHS H5

Matteuccia struthiopteris
Shuttlecock fern

This is the first fresh edible we pick from our forest gardens in late winter and early spring. It has excellent flavoured shoots (known as 'fiddleheads'), lush green fronds in spring (which is why it has been used ornamentally for a long time), and is early into growth (mid-March in Devon). It spreads slowly via rhizomes, but not if you harvest lots for cooking.

GROW Easy to grow given the right conditions of moist soil and some shade. Sheltered beneath deciduous trees or shrubs is best, but will grow in the sun if the soil stays moist.

ULF NORDFJELL
Landscape architect,
Stockholm, Sweden

Ulf Nordfjell is a landscape architect. He has won three gold medals at RHS Chelsea Flower Show. City parks in Malmö, Lund, Gothenburg and Stockholm are prime examples of his work; he also designs private gardens. He works to unite architecture and design with horticulture and nature. *nordfjellcollection.se*

Asarum europaeum →
Asarabacca

I used this plant (also known as European wild ginger) at RHS Chelsea Flower Show in 2007, the year that marked the tercentenary of Carl von Linnaeus. I used it both to celebrate the 'father of modern taxonomy', who named many plants, but also because it is such a graphic ground-cover plant with its glossy, kidney-shaped, dark evergreen leaves. It creates the perfect backdrop for plants such as *Anticlea elegans* and lilies. After a long winter it develops its rounded green leaves to create the most elegant carpet.

GROW A long-lived plant, it only needs to be split when you need more plants. Cultivated for the leaves as a ground cover, not for the invisible flowers. It is self-sowing. Can be grown to the polar circle. Prefers an occasional feed and an annual mulch.

Type
Rhizomatous perennial
Flowering
Spring
Height/ spread
10cm x 50cm
Position
Full shade, part shade, sheltered
Soil
Moist, well-drained
Hardiness
USDA 6b/7a / RHS H6

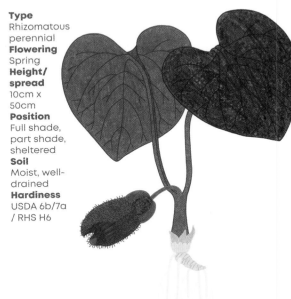

LULU URQUHART
Landscape designer,
Urquhart & Hunt,
Somerset, UK

Lulu Urquhart is passionate about rewilding and ecological restoration. Urquhart & Hunt is a landscape design studio dedicated to nature and specialising in contemporary restorations of gardens and their wider landscapes. In 2022, Lulu and Adam Hunt won an RHS Chelsea Flower Show gold medal and best in show. *urquharthunt.com*

Lobelia × speciosa 'Hadspen Purple'
Lobelia 'Hadspen Purple'

I am a Somerset romantic and this plant has been bred by two people I very much admire from the walled garden at Hadspen House – Sandra Pope and her late husband Nori – when it was owned by garden writer Penelope Hobhouse. For me it is part of the land and garden history of this area, and it feels so precious that I can use this plant in honour of them. I have used it in schemes throughout the UK, and especially enjoy planting it in Somerset, its home. Its flowers arrive once you've had your thrill out of your roses – it's a time when I'm looking around with expectant eyes at what will be the next crescendo. Tall, sturdy, vertical, sentinel and bright, this clump-forming perennial has dark green leaves flushed with purple and tall stems with deep purple flowers. I get excited by its plum colours, as I love hot flower combinations. It's loved by bees and butterflies.

GROW Generally simple to care for, this plant will grow in a mix of ground conditions so is good for clay soils and wetter areas in either sun or shade. I've planted it in my own garden among *Stachys officinalis* 'Rosea', *Artemisia vulgaris*, *Panicum virgatum* and *Iris chrysographes*.

Type
Perennial
Flowering
Summer, autumn
Height/ spread
70cm x 45cm
Position
Full sun, part shade
Soil
In sun it likes moist ground, and in light shade it can tolerate drier soil
Hardiness
USDA 7b/8a / RHS H5

GRACE ALEXANDER
Founder of Gather
with Grace Alexander,
Somerset, UK

Grace Alexander is a consultant clinical psychologist, seed-monger and founder of Gather with Grace Alexander, a monthly membership for people who adore plants, gardens, colour and beauty. *gracealexanderflowers.co.uk*

Daucus carota
Wild carrot

Confusingly, there are lots of common names for this beautiful plant (including Bishop's lace) and they seem to be used interchangeably with that of *Ammi majus*, despite being very different. Queen Anne's Lace is one of these common names – the legend is that Queen Anne was challenged to create a piece of lace as beautiful as the flower. In doing so, she pricked her finger and a drop of blood fell on the daucus, leaving a red spot in the middle of the flower forever. This helps sweep away any confusion; if the lacey flower has a spot of red in the centre, then you know what you have is a true *D. carota*.

The thing I adore about *D. carota* is that it is so ubiquitous and yet so unique. If you walk along clifftops in Cornwall it is everywhere, clinging to rocks and mossy banks, stunted to a few inches tall by the ferocity of the conditions. When they put up a hoarding when rebuilding a local railway station, a perfect row of *D. carota* appeared from beneath, running the length of the road. I grow it in my flower field, both the white wild one and the dappled chocolates of 'Dara'. In my rich, fertile clay it grows until it reaches my ears. I rarely cut it as a flower; it is the seedheads that I adore – I let it flower and go over. Once each tiny floret sets seed, they turn unerringly in towards each other until the whole flower resembles a bird's nest. With a collar of forked bracts around the top of the stem, the silhouette is utterly distinctive.

D. carota is the wild form of what is now the cultivated carrot and, given the staple that it has become, I think humanity should give thanks. However, *D. carota* is also an invaluable foodstuff for pollinating insects; mine are rarely without bees, wasps, lacewings and hoverflies in the summer. The only downside? The seeds are very successful in spreading by latching onto passing animals using hooked teeth. Throughout autumn I am constantly picking them off my jumpers and my dogs.

GROW Tough as boots, these will grow almost anywhere, although will be shorter if your soil is poor. I cannot recommend you grow this for eating, but knowing that *D. carota* has a tap root like a domesticated carrot helps in growing it successfully. Sow seed directly, rather than attempting to transplant seedlings or plants. Also, like domesticated carrots, you need fresh seed. Keep cutting if you wish to prolong flowering, although I am all about the seedheads. Technically it is a biennial, but I grow them as hardy annuals. They need cold to trigger germination. Be aware that in some areas of the US, it is considered to be so invasive that it is illegal to cultivate. If that's the case, try *Ammi majus* instead.

Type
Biennial
Flowering
Summer
Height/spread
1m x 50cm
Position
Full sun, part shade
Soil
Any, preferably well-drained
Hardiness
USDA 6a–1 / RHS H7

PENNY REDMAN
Gardener, Old-Lands,
Monmouthshire, Wales

Penny Redman is a gardener in charge of the Old-Lands estate where she runs the wildlife-friendly walled garden, growing produce for the onsite farm shop without pesticides. She worked at RHS Wisley and became interested in organic and biodynamic gardening while working with Camphill Communities in the US, Brazil and the UK. *old-lands.co.uk*

Helianthus annuus
Common sunflower (SEE ILLUSTRATION PAGE 259)

Type
Annual
Flowering
Summer, autumn
Height/spread
Varies depending on variety
Position
Full sun, sheltered
Soil
Moist, well-drained
Hardiness
USDA 8b/9a / RHS H4

Sunflowers are so striking and help to frame the planting in the walled garden. We grow many different cultivars as the colour range is so wide and varied. I like to grow the branching varieties, which look more elegant than the straight-up tall ones. We use them for cutting and putting in vases for the holiday cottages. With careful cutting and deadheading, we can have these flowering for months, right up until the first frost. We leave the seedheads for the birds at the end of the season. The flowers also attract many pollinators, especially leaf cutter and furrow bees. They are perfect summer flowers, with lots of colour variations, and mix so well with vegetables.

GROW I start the seeds in small pots, usually two in a pot in mid-spring. I plant them out at the end of spring. We use a no-dig approach; these grow well after spreading well-rotted compost on to the ground. I make sure they have enough water at the beginning of the season, watering well on initial planting and then only watering again if it is particularly dry. I make my own compost and find that this is all the feed they need – although, very occasionally, I give an extra feed of diluted homemade comfrey liquid.

Type
Annual climber
Flowering
Summer, autumn
Height/spread
1.5m x 50cm
Position
Full sun, sheltered
Soil
Moist, well-drained
Hardiness
USDA 10b / RHS H2

Pisum sativum 'Carouby de Maussane'
Pea (mangetout)

I love growing peas. There is nothing nicer than picking and eating them straight from the plant. Mangetout is great for the impatient. We introduced a pick-your-own experience in the walled garden, and it has proved a real success among our holidaymakers. They have so enjoyed the magic of eating with the seasons. Mangetout are climbing plants with pretty flowers, especially 'Carouby de Maussane', an heirloom variety from France.

GROW Sow in modules, then plant out close together when the soil has warmed up in spring. They seem to grow much better with less of a gap between them, clinging on to each other. Water well on planting, and again when in flower.

Brassica oleracea Acephala Group
Kale

Type
Annual, biennial, perennial
Flowering
Summer, autumn
Height/spread
1m x 1m
Position
Full sun
Soil
Moist, well-drained
Hardiness
USDA 6a–1 / RHS H7

Kale is such a popular leafy green with our holidaymakers and another one we have introduced into our pick-your-own experience. We grow many different varieties, including 'Cavolo Nero', green curly kale and 'Red Russian'. But scarlet kale stands out as a beautiful ornamental plant as well as a really tasty one. Kale is so wonderfully easy to grow, and you can make successional sowings all through the season.

GROW I usually start seed off in trays, then prick out into modules. Once the plants have grown to a good size with decent root systems, I plant them into the ground. I cover them with mesh for the first month. The cover is removed once the plants grow to touch it, after that they are usually strong enough to make it on their own. Keep taking the old leaves off the plant to help reduce slug habitat.

Nicotiana
Tobacco plant

Type
Annual
Flowering
Summer,
autumn
**Height/
spread**
Varies
Position
Full sun, but
N. sylvestris
prefers part
shade
Soil
Moist, well-
drained
Hardiness
USDA 9b/10a
/ RHS H3

These are such good value plants in the garden. They look great in an annual flower border, but equally good at the ends of vegetable beds. There is such a variety of species to choose from and they are fun to grow from seed. I grow N. langsdorffii, N. mutabilis, N. sylvestris and N. glutinosa. They flower endlessly, are brilliant for cutting and are super-attractive to pollinators. It's great fun to watch a large bumblebee find its way into an N. mutabilis flower. Sam, the owner of the estate, often comes through the garden by torchlight in the evenings to watch the moths and has seen many hawk-moths drinking nectar from these flowers. They are wonderful flowers that create a lightness in the garden.

GROW As with most half-hardy annuals, the secret is not to sow too early. Look at six weeks from sowing to planting out, so don't sow before mid–spring, however tempting it might be. The final height and spread varies between species but they make good mid- to back-of-border plants, or use on the end of veg beds. Dislikes very wet or very dry soils.

Type
Annual
Flowering
Summer
**Height/
spread**
1.5m x 4m
Position
Full sun
Soil
Fertile, rich,
moist, well-
drained
Hardiness
USDA 9b/10a
/ RHS H3

Cucurbita maxima 'Candy Roaster'
Squash 'Candy Roaster'

I grow lots of different squash, each year trying out new ones. Some work well and others not so well. One successful variety has been 'Candy Roaster', an heirloom squash from the USA. It grew fantastically, producing the most lovely, long, pink fruits. It stores well and is quite a sweet squash. I believe it was used in the first pumpkin pies, though it's also excellent in soups, roasted whole or in curries. It's good to have a few recipes up your sleeve because it's a prolific squash, so you'll be eating it through to spring.

Squash plants make perfect ground cover. You need space for them to spread unless they are being trained up a trellis (which would need to be very strong). I always grow them on the ground and, to be honest, just let them get on with it.

GROW Sow in late spring and plant out in the first week of summer (June in the UK). It doesn't like to start out too early and loves some warmth to get going. I usually sow two seeds in a pot and keep them in an unheated greenhouse. Give them lots of water when they are planted but after that leave them to it. 'Candy Roaster' doesn't mind a dry spell.

CAMILLA JØRVAD
Gardener and
photographer, Ærø,
Denmark

Following a career as a wedding photographer and a downward spiral of stress and depression, Camilla Jørvad found gardening to be an undeniable factor in her healing journey. Creating a space where both nature and her family can thrive is now her life's work. *sigridsminde.com*

Agastache 'Blackadder'
Giant hyssop 'Blackadder'

Type
Herbaceous perennial
Flowering
Summer, autumn
Height/spread
1m x 50cm
Position
Full sun, open
Soil
Well-drained
Hardiness
USDA 8b/9a / RHS H4

Year after year this has been one of the plants most loved by insects in my garden. Its flowers are always full of life. Agastache, with its tall spires, looks amazing in company with the plateau-like blooms of another insect favourite, *Achillea millefolium*, especially the 'Terracotta' variety.

GROW It needs a light, well-drained soil to help it get through winter.

CHRISTINE WALKDEN
Horticulturist and
broadcaster,
Hertfordshire, UK

Christine Walkden is a horticulturist who carries out consultations, leads garden tours and lectures internationally. She is also an author, resident gardening expert for BBC's *The One Show* and a panel member on *Gardeners' Question Time. christinewalkden.com*

Soldanella alpina
Alpine snowbell

This is my favourite plant as it grows and flowers in the Alps at the edge of snow melt. I have even seen it coming up and flowering through snow, so all you can see are the tiny flowers peeping out, with no sight of the foliage. I admire its tenacity to be able to grow beneath a snow blanket and push its delicate flowers up and out – it's charming to see such a small plant in such a massive, wild and hard landscape.

It produces a rosette of dark green, leathery and rounded leaves around 2.5cm across with very prominent veins and umbels of flowers. Each nodding, lavender-purple flower is about 1.5cm in length and fringed halfway up.

GROW I use sieved leaf mould and up to 50 per cent grit when growing this plant in a pan-style planter. In a garden situation, plant in humus-rich, well-drained soil. In my experience it does not do well in John Innes compost, however much grit you use. As a snow-melt plant, it needs to be damp when running up to flower. Do not allow it to dry out. In warmer parts of the UK plant or grow in a shadier position so it doesn't dry out in summer.

Some people find it easier to grow in an alpine house than outside in open ground. Be aware that slugs and snails love this plant. Ensure slug protection is in place very early on in the growing season or the slugs will graze the newly emerging leaves before they have a chance to grow.

Type
Perennial
Flowering
Spring
Height/spread
15cm x 15cm
Position
Full sun, part shade, sheltered
Soil
Humus-rich, well-drained gritty soil, I have seen it growing on both acid and calcareous soils in the Alps
Hardiness
USDA 6b/7a / RHS H6

Abeliophyllum distichum
White forsythia

A plant that is seldom seen, but in my opinion should be much more widely planted. I grow it cheek-by-jowl with a physocarpus to give it some protection. It's my favourite winter-flowering plant as I just love the fruity fragrance of the small white flowers that are flushed with pink and produced on bare stems.

GROW This plant is not always fully hardy, so grow in a protected site among other shrubs or up against a wall to help defend the lovely flowers from frost. To keep the plant flowering well, prune back flowered shoots by half immediately after the flowers start to fade each year.

Type
Deciduous shrub
Flowering
Late winter, early spring
Height/spread
2m x 2m
Position
Full sun, sheltered
Soil
Well-drained, mineral-based
Hardiness
USDA 6b/7a / RHS H6

TOM MASSEY
Garden designer,
London, UK

Tom Massey has won multiple awards and recognition for his work since founding Tom Massey Studio in 2015. Known for his bold, daring and thought-provoking show gardens, he focuses on sustainability, ecology and site context in private and commercial landscapes. *tommassey.co.uk*

← *Crataegus monogyna*
Common hawthorn

Hawthorn trees are massively underrated. They are tough and resilient – you see them growing out of craggy cracks in cliff faces or on windswept hillsides. They are also characterful and have abundant blossom and provide berries. Not many people know that the berries and leaves are edible, and these are sometimes referred to as 'bread and cheese' (although they taste nothing like it).

For a garden setting, look for multi-stem specimens. Hawthorn makes a great alternative to amelanchier, which is more widely used but can be susceptible to fungal diseases. A British native, hawthorn is a small bushy tree or large shrub and is tolerant of coastal, exposed, polluted and damp sites. It's also a good tree for wildlife. The plant offers four seasons of interest. The deeply lobed foliage emerges in spring, followed by highly fragrant single white/cream flowers. Small dark red haws (berries) appear in late summer and provide food for birds. The leaves turn yellow and bronze in autumn before falling to reveal the plant's branch structure.

GROW It's a useful specimen tree for town, coastal or exposed gardens. It can also be used for hedging and can be clipped to reduce its size. As the common name suggests, hawthorn has sharp thorns that help provide a safe nesting place for birds. It's a great tree for a small garden, but do watch out for those thorns, which are pretty brutal. Plant away from pathways or in raised planters to lift the thorns out of harm's way.

Type
Deciduous tree
Flowering
Spring
Height/spread
6m x 5m
Position
Full sun, part shade, will grow in exposed conditions
Soil
Moist, well-drained
Hardiness
USDA 6a–1 / RHS H7

KATIE CAMPBELL
Writer, lecturer and garden historian, London, UK

Dr Katie Campbell lectures widely, writes for various publications and leads garden tours. Her garden books include *Icons of Twentieth Century Landscape Design* and *British Gardens in Time: The Greatest Gardens and the People Who Shaped Them.*

Citrus sinensis
Sweet orange

On a whim I put some pips from a particularly delicious orange on to some wet tissue, wrapped it in cling film and left it on a windowsill; several of the pips sprouted and now I have a mini grove of orange treelings. I have no idea what sort of orange it is, but my five little trees, all about a foot high, are thriving on a sunny windowsill. *C. sinensis* has a lovely scent, shiny evergreen leaves, and I am anticipating delicate white blossoms and hopefully delicious fruit. I hope they will grow large enough that I can train them as espaliers across a sunny wall.

GROW When they get bigger I'll tap the pot to find out when they need water; gnarled gardeners in Italy claim they can tell by the timbre of the sound how dry the roots are. I've noticed that potted orange trees are often left to get very dry in Italy, but I have been quite diligent about watering my treelings and they seem to appreciate it. I haven't yet tried citrus feed on them, but I will when they get bigger.

Type
Evergreen tree
Flowering
Spring, summer
Height/spread
4m x 1.5m
Position
Full sun, sheltered
Soil
Loam
Hardiness
USDA 10b / RHS H2

ROSIE BINES
Garden designer and
plantswoman, London, UK

Rosie Bines's designs for gardens and public spaces celebrate seasonality and promote biodiversity. She was head gardener at Petersham Nurseries for more than a decade (co-creating its School of Garden Inspiration) and is also a TV presenter. *instagram.com/rosiegardens*

Tropaeolum majus 'Salmon Gleam'
Nasturtium 'Salmon Gleam'

I love growing nasturtiums – they epitomise summer for me. Even the shapes of the leaves and how the rain beads beautifully on the surface make me happy. They are cheap, accessible, easy to grow, pretty and edible to boot! Whether they are trailing from raised planters and pots, romping through beds, clambering up fences, colourful and abundant, it's non-stop joy from the simple nasturtium. I have happy childhood memories of pushing the fat seeds into warm soil around the greenhouse and watching the vigorous blooms spread until the path was half covered over the summer. I first planted 'Salmon Gleam' in the beautiful cutting garden at Petersham Nurseries. It romped under the dahlias, roses and sunflowers, tumbling on to the hoggin paths and kept our florists furnished with trailing foliage for months on end. The apricot flushed petals with deep crimson throats sat wonderfully alongside so many colours, from the primrose yellows of cephalaria and the smudgy reds of helianthus to the rich zinnias and dahlias.

Nasturtiums are one of the quickest and easiest hardy annual flowers to grow, producing masses of blooms throughout summer and autumn. They attract beneficial insects, repel pests and increase crop productivity, so are excellent companion plants in any veg patch or cutting garden. Their perpetual blooms, saucer-shaped leaves and long stems are wonderful for cutting. Lovely in bouquets or tumbling out of vases, the foliage lasts an extremely long time, adding interest and movement to large-scale arrangements. Like dahlias, one of my other favourites, they can give you flowers from late spring to the first frosts, so are excellent value if you're short on space and big on joy.

Not only are they beautiful, they're edible. Every bit of them: buds, flowers, leaves and seeds. Adding loveliness to anything you garnish them with, they're especially pretty in salads, and delicious finely chopped into smoky fishcakes or melted on to anything savoury as nasturtium butter. You can freeze them in ice cubes, decorate cakes and biscuits with them and even use the leaves for wrapping up dolmas. The seed pods are known as poor man's capers. I love growing beautiful edibles that blur the lines between kitchen and garden.

Nasturtiums are ideal for lots of different sunny spots. They're pretty drought tolerant. Since they trail and spread so prolifically, many people use nasturtiums as a ground cover. They're especially useful for suppressing weeds in newly planted borders, cutting gardens and veg patches.

GROW If you have space to start them off indoors in mid-spring, you can extend the flowering season. Start the seeds in pots four to six weeks before the last frost using free-draining, peat-free compost. Press the seeds in 2cm deep and cover them. Keep just moist but do not over water. Transplant after all danger of frost has passed. You will probably see any self-sown seedlings from the previous year popping up about the same time. Alternatively, direct sow in summer. Loosen the soil and plant 2cm deep. Bear in mind some varieties need space (a couple of metres), whereas others are more contained. All nasturtiums do best in poorer soils. If the soil is too nutritious, you get a profusion of leaves but not so many flowers. In containers, mix two parts peat-free multipurpose compost with one part grit to ensure good drainage. Once established, nasturtiums need little attention – just a good amount of sunshine and some water once a week or so.

Harvest as many seeds as you can, share seeds with fellow gardeners and spread the nasturtium love! If you want to use them as cut flowers, harvest the blooms just as they are opening for the longest vase life. If using the foliage, pick individual leaves or full vines once they become leathery or firm to the touch.

Type
Annual climber
Flowering
Summer, autumn
Height/ spread
40cm x 1.8m
Position
Full sun, part shade in very hot climates, sheltered
Soil
Poor, well-drained
Hardiness
USDA 9b/10a / RHS H3

CAROLINE AND IAN BOND
Creators, Upton Wold, Gloucestershire, UK

Over five decades, Caroline and Ian Bond have overseen the development of the extensive garden Upton Wold in the Cotswolds. The garden is home to the National Collection of both *Juglans* (walnut) and *Pterocarya* (wingnut). *uptonwold.co.uk*

Rosa 'Climbing Étoile de Hollande'
Rose 'Climbing Étoile de Hollande'

When we first began to develop the garden we planted many roses. They are as close to instant impact as we got. Over the years, the trees, shrubs and perennials have filled out and provided structure and colour, but the roses remain a firm favourite. This one has beautiful deep red double flowers and a wonderful, old-fashioned scent.

GROW One of the first roses to bloom in the garden each year, this rose is repeat flowering, often until late in the season. It can grow very tall and spread generously, so ensure you have a lot of wall space for it to climb.

Type
Climbing rose
Flowering
Summer, autumn
Height
6m x 6m
Position
Full sun
Soil
Fertile, well-drained
Hardiness
USDA 7b/8a / RHS H5

Juglans regia
Common walnut

The arboretum at Upton Wold is home to many walnut trees. We hold a National Collection comprising some 170 cultivars, which reflect Ian's passion for trees from around the world. Walnut trees are of course beautiful, but there are so many delicious or useful things you can do with the nuts and wood.

GROW Generally free of diseases and unfussy about aspect and shelter, but it does need to be planted in full sun.

Type
Deciduous tree
Flowering
Spring
Height/ spread
12m x 8m
Position
Full sun
Soil
Moist, well-drained
Hardiness
USDA 6b/7a / RHS H6

MARTIN GEE
Head gardener, Weston Park, Shropshire, UK

Martin Gee has worked at Weston Park, the ancestral home of the Earls of Bradford, for 50 years. *weston-park.com*

Heuchera
Coral bells

Heucheras are good all-round plants that provide colour year-round. They can be used in pots, as ground cover, in parterres and even in bedding displays. They are much loved by bees.

GROW We use heucheras in all sorts of locations. Vine weevil can be a problem, though we have never experienced it. Doesn't like to get wet. Provide mulch and a general fertiliser in spring.

Type
Perennial
Flowering
Summer
Height/ spread
Varies, but up to around 50cm x 50cm
Position
Part shade
Soil
Moist, well-drained, fertile
Hardiness
USDA 6b/7a / RHS H6

Pelargonium zonale
Horseshoe geranium

An excellent pot plant for a conservatory, *P. zonale* gives colour all summer, and even into winter if given some warmth. It has a good collection of varieties with coloured leaves, such as 'Mrs Pollock', 'Caroline Schmidt', 'Dolly Varden', 'Mr Henry Cox', 'Frank Headley' and 'Apple Blossom Rosebud', to name a few.

GROW Feed weekly with a liquid feed and deadhead. It is very easy to grow. Excellent plant for a conservatory, a patio or even in a border for the summer. Only water when needed – it will tolerate drought for a short period.

Type
Perennial
Flowering
Summer
Height/ spread
1.5m x 1m, though this varies depending on variety
Position
Full sun
Soil
A good, loam-based compost
Hardiness
USDA 11 / RHS H1c

RAYMOND J EVISON
Founder and chairman.
Guernsey Clematis Nursery,
Guernsey, UK

Raymond Evison has been growing and breeding clematis plants for over 60 years and has introduced more than 200 cultivars. He is vice president of the RHS and honorary fellow of the Kew Guild. His nursery produces more than two million clematis plants a year. He has been awarded 30 RHS Chelsea Flower Show gold medals. *raymondevisonclematis.com*

Clematis 'Guernsey Cream' →
Clematis 'Guernsey Cream'

It is difficult to select just one clematis, but this one has an interesting background and is a fine garden plant. 'Guernsey Cream' was selected by me during the late 1980s from a batch of seed sent from China by Professor Long Yayi. It is a very good form of the creamy yellow Chinese species *Clematis patens*. Prof. Long recently explained that she collected the seed from a clematis plant that grew from the root system of a pine tree that had been dug up in northeastern China and brought to grow in Beijing Botanical Garden. It was a big surprise to everyone when this clematis suddenly appeared and flowered. It had obviously been dug up with the tree and was growing in the tree's root system! I raised several seedlings from the original seed, and named the best form. It is extremely winter hardy and has done well in trials carried out by Chicago Botanical Garden, which evaluated clematis in its harsh climate. It was listed as one of its top ten clematis varieties. Its rounded flowers are creamy yellow with cream anthers and appear in late spring and early summer, producing a great show. The flowers are followed by amazing and attractive seedheads.

GROW Can be grown in containers, but I prefer to grow it in a garden where it can be planted with other shrubs or wall-trained plants. If planted in a north-facing position (in the northern hemisphere), flowers will be green – a certain amount of sunshine is required to bring out the true colour. Feeding is beneficial: use rose or tomato feed in early spring before flowering and again after flowering. It flowers on the previous season's stems and so only needs light pruning at the end of winter to remove weak/damaged stems down to a pair of strong leaf axil buds.

Type
Perennial
climber
Flowering
Summer
**Height/
spread**
1.5m x 90cm
Position
Part shade,
sheltered
Soil
Moist, well-
drained,
alkaline,
neutral
Hardiness
USDA 8b/9a
/ RHS H4

TOM BROWN
Head gardener, West Dean
Gardens, West Sussex, UK

Tom Brown is head gardener at West Dean Gardens, where he oversees around 100 acres, including glasshouses, herbaceous borders, a kitchen garden, arboretum and a landscape full of shrubs and trees. He writes for garden magazines, offers gardening advice on BBC radio and judges at the RHS Chelsea and Hampton Court Flower Shows. *westdean.org.uk*

Phlox paniculata 'Blue Paradise'
Perennial phlox 'Blue Paradise'

There are so many garden phlox to choose from, but 'Blue Paradise' is a cracker and has never let me down. It has rich, blue panicles of flowers on dark stems that cover slightly bronzed foliage in mid-summer. The blue flowers associate so well with roses and other perennials, and optimise the cottage style that many of us strive to achieve. At dusk, blues in the garden become enhanced and almost magical, making 'Blue Paradise' perfect for those of us who appreciate their gardens in the softer light.

GROW Plant in an open border. Phlox appreciate good garden soil enriched with well-rotted compost or manure. The plants also like being top dressed with mulch and can be 'Chelsea chopped' to avoid staking and delay flowering. Try to plant in groups of three or five to achieve impact.

Type
Herbaceous
perennial
Flowering
Summer
**Height/
spread**
1.5m x 50cm
Position
Full sun, part
shade
Soil
Moist, well-
drained
Hardiness
USDA 6a–1
/ RHS H7

60

MICHAEL MARRIOTT
Rose expert, Shropshire, UK

Michael Marriott worked for David Austin Roses for 35 years, starting as nursery manager and finishing as head rosarian. He retired in 2020 and now lectures and consults on all matters relating to roses and rose-garden design. With his partner, Rosie, he gardens organically on three-quarters of an acre in Shropshire plus two allotments. *michaelmarriottrosarian.org*

Rosa 'Adélaïde d'Orléans'
Rose 'Adélaïde d'Orléans'

'Adélaïde d'Orléans' is a beautiful rambling rose. Normally, if I'm looking for a rambler, I want more than just a generous crop of flowers – perhaps a superb fragrance or a good crop of long-lasting hips. But this has neither of these. There is a fragrance, but it's of medium strength at best, and the few hips that form are small and stay green. The flowers, however, are so beautiful – medium-sized, semi-double and pure white, although the buds start pink. They are produced freely in large heads, which hang down so gracefully that there is hardly a leaf to be seen when it's in full flower. We have it growing over three arches going up a cobbled path to a little picket gate that leads on to a lane. It was meant to stay as three arches but they soon joined up to make a fairly solid tunnel. To make up for no flowers later in summer, we have three or four clematis growing through them, providing blue blooms. If grown into a tree, the flowerheads hang down in long festoons. It is also healthy and, in the UK, more or less evergreen.

GROW An easy rose to grow and very healthy. With its lax growth it is perfect for a pergola, large arch or for growing through a tree. It could also be allowed to hang down a high wall. Needs at least five or six hours of sun a day. Water if very dry. Feed in spring. Little pruning is required, unless to keep it within bounds.

Type
Rambler rose
Flowering
Summer
Height/ spread
8m x 4m
Position
Full sun
Soil
Moist, well-drained
Hardiness
USDA 6b/7a / RHS H6

Rosa Lady of Shalott ('Ausnyson')
Rose [Lady of Shalott]

Type
Shrub rose
Flowering
Summer, autumn
Height/ spread
1.5m x 1m
Position
Full sun, part shade (at least five hours of sun a day), sheltered
Soil
Moist, well-drained
Hardiness
USDA 6b/7a / RHS H6

Lady of Shalott is one of David Austin's best English roses. It starts flowering early in the season, often a week or two before most other roses, then carries on almost continuously until late in the year. Even in bad wintry weather, it is still trying to flower. The flowers are not fully double like those of many English roses, but the arrangement of petals, in the form of a loose rosette, is still lovely. The unopened buds are a strong shade of apricot, in contrast to a softer but still rich apricot when fully open. The fragrance is variable, but is strong and truly delicious when at its best. As a shrub in a mixed border, it associates beautifully with perennials in a whole range of colours, but especially those with purple flowers, such as some salvias and geraniums. In our garden we have planted a couple either side of some steps and have some more mixed up with hollyhocks and lilies close to a seat where we often sit.

GROW Very easy to grow. It is a healthy and versatile variety and, according to how it is pruned, makes either a vigorous 1–1.5m tall shrub or, for training against a wall or fence, a climber up to 3–4m in height. As a shrub it should be pruned down about halfway in mid-winter; as a climber, simply reduce the length of the side shoots to about 10cm. Planting it in a mixed border helps to keep it healthy. Water if dry. Feed in spring and mid-summer.

Phacelia tanacetifolia
Fiddleneck (SEE ILLUSTRATION PAGE 153)

I first saw this growing in Germany as a cover crop in a field; it looked superb and was covered in a mass of bees. I managed to find out the name and started growing it at home. It is an excellent plant for protecting bare ground from the elements and improves the soil if dug in. Bees and other insects love it, so it's a great way of encouraging them into the garden. From a purely aesthetic point of view, it is lovely to look at and associates beautifully with other plants. It also makes a good cut flower and is scented.

GROW Phacelia is an annual and easy to grow from seed sown at just about any time of year. It overwinters if not too cold (above −5°C or so). It's a wonderful plant for protecting the ground after harvesting vegetables such as potatoes or for scattering among mixed borders. It is also the easiest plant to pull up.

Type
Annual
Flowering
Summer, autumn
Height/ spread
1m x 50cm
Position
Full sun
Soil
Well-drained
Hardiness
USDA 8b/9a / RHS H4

Rosa Partridge ('Korweirim')
Rose [Partridge]

This is different to most roses, which like to grow upwards either as shrubs or climbers. With no support, this grows absolutely flat on the ground. It is closely related to a species rose, probably *R. wichurana*, which is the parent of many ramblers, including 'Paul Noël' and 'François Juranville'. The small, white flowers start a little later than most roses, in mid-summer, but then carry on into autumn. They are strongly scented – clove-like at close quarters – and much loved by bees. The flowers are followed by red hips that the birds don't seem to like as they are still there the following spring. We grow it for hanging down a retaining wall and for growing through other shrubs such as *Cotoneaster horizontalis* and small trees such as *Elaeagnus umbellata*. Having such lax growth, it could simply be grown as a ground-cover plant. It is healthy and wonderful in all situations.

GROW Water if very dry. Feed in spring and summer. Prune mid-winter.

Type
Ground cover rose
Flowering
Summer, early autumn
Height/ spread
60cm x 5m
Position
Full sun
Soil
Moist, well-drained
Hardiness
USDA 7b/8a / RHS H5

Type
Perennial climber
Flowering
Autumn
Height/ spread
1m x 1m
Position
Full sun, sheltered
Soil
Well-drained
Hardiness
USDA 11 / RHS H1c

Dioscorea elephantipes
Elephant's foot

I've always had a passion for plants with a big base, or caudex as it should be called, such as *Nolina recurvata* and *Cissus tuberosa*. One of my favourites is *D. elephantipes* or, as it used to be known, *Testudinaria elephantipes*. I can't remember where I first came across it, perhaps at Kew or at the Huntington Library in California, which has a wonderful six-acre cactus garden. I bought some seeds that germinated readily and now, around 20 years later, I have one rather magnificent plant. It is native to South Africa, where it grows with the winter rains. In the UK, I leave it unwatered and completely dormant all summer, and it will suddenly start sending out shoots that grow incredibly quickly around late summer. This is the time to start watering it and continue doing so until late spring of the following year, when it begins to go dormant again. The mass of stems can get about 1m in length and would, in the wild, scramble through other shrubs to reach the light – in the greenhouse it ideally needs something to grow over. The leaves are rounded and about 1cm across. The flowers are minute but, for me, its swollen base is the main attraction. The base of mine is about 20cm across now and deeply fissured and cracked with a thick outer layer of bark.

GROW Keep in a frost-free greenhouse. Water only during the growing season. Feed during the growing season. Although healthy, it is occasionally subject to aphids. Produces long stems that need support.

Malus 'Comtesse de Paris'
Crab apple 'Comtesse de Paris'

Type
Deciduous
tree
Flowering
Spring,
summer
**Height/
spread**
8m x 4m
Position
Full sun, part
shade
Soil
Moist, well-
drained
Hardiness
USDA 6b/7a
/ RHS H6

There are many wonderful species and varieties of crab apple and we have three excellent ones in our garden – *M. transitoria* with blush-pink flowers and small yellow fruit, 'Evereste' with soft pink flowers and medium-sized red fruit and, perhaps my favourite, 'Comtesse de Paris', which makes a tidy small tree and is incredibly free-flowering. The flowers are white or a soft blush-pink and are followed by yellow fruit, each about 3cm across, that last well into winter – until the birds decide they are at the right stage for eating. We have it growing in a prominent position in the corner of a mixed border, not far from a rowan and a guelder rose. It is a little higher than the house, making it easy to admire.

GROW We leave it alone. Prune only when necessary if it gets too big.

Type
Deciduous
tree
Flowering
Spring
**Height/
spread**
8m x 8m
Position
Full sun,
sheltered
Soil
Moist, well-
drained,
neutral
Hardiness
USDA 6b/7a
/ RHS H6

Malus domestica 'Bramley's Seedling'
Apple 'Bramley's Seedling'

When we moved into our house about six years ago there were a number of large trees in the garden, most of them Leyland cypresses that became a good supply of logs for our stove and posts for our fruit cage. But one tree we definitely wanted to keep was a magnificent Bramley apple tree. We think it might be as old as the house, so late Victorian. It is a beautiful shape with a large trunk around which we have put a curved seat to create a shady spot. We've planted a number of wildflowers beneath it, including campion, knapweed and cornflower. We have also planted the rose 'Kew Gardens', which does very well considering how shady a spot it is. There is a fair bit of mistletoe growing in it, as well as a strawberry coming out from one of the holes. Another hole is home to a wren's nest. In flower it is the most beautiful sight and it fruits prolifically. The windfalls are a great delight for birds, especially blackbirds, fieldfares and redwings.

GROW Apart from some occasional pruning to stop it getting too big, we leave it alone.

Type
Species rose
Flowering
Early
summer
**Height/
spread**
2m x 2m
Position
Full sun, part
shade
Soil
Any good
garden soil,
neutral
Hardiness
USDA 6a–1 /
RHS H7

Rosa villosa
Apple rose

I love the species roses – the wild roses that originated in all areas north of the equator to beyond the Arctic Circle and all the way from North America to Japan. It is difficult to know exactly how many species there as they tend to hybridise rather easily and some are very similar, but the estimate is around 150. *R. villosa* is native to most of Europe and introduced into the UK. It is distinctive with its silvery-grey leaves, especially in spring and early summer. The common name is apple rose because of the size of its bright red fruit. These are not quite the size of normal eating apples – they're more like crab apples. The flowers are like those of many other species – pink and with five petals – but no less beautiful. The pink is bright and contrasts beautifully against the silvery leaves. It makes a large shrub with arching growth, which shouldn't be pruned at all, as it spoils the shape and discourages flowers. We have it in an informal part of the garden surrounded by wild-ish perennials and not far from a field maple. As a species rose, it has one season of flowering with hips in the autumn. To bridge the gap we have one of the *Clematis viticella* hybrids growing through it, which flowers in late summer.

GROW We leave it alone. No pruning needed.

STEPHANIE HAFFERTY
No-dig gardening expert
and writer, Wales

Stephanie Hafferty is a garden and food writer specialising in small-scale homesteading, as well as a teacher and leading authority on no-dig gardening. Her gardening experience includes running market gardens and kitchen gardens for restaurants, art galleries and private estates. She is the author of *No Dig Organic Home and Garden*. stephaniehafferty.co.uk

Aloysia citrodora
Lemon verbena

Type
Deciduous
subshrub
Flowering
Summer
**Height/
spread**
2.5m x 2.5m
Position
Full sun,
sheltered
Soil
Well-
drained
Hardiness
USDA 9b/10a
/ RHS H3

The first time I crushed the leaves of a lemon verbena plant and inhaled the intense lemon sherbet fragrance, I was smitten. This sensational herb is worth growing just for the sheer pleasure of its scent and its delicate white flowers that attract and feed a wide range of insects. But I love it because it is easy to grow and look after, and so versatile. If I could only have one herb in my garden, it would be lemon verbena.

The herb is a natural aid to digestion and has many beneficial properties, reducing inflammation, boosting immunity and aiding relaxation. Lemon verbena tea helps to soothe winter colds: simply add hot water to fresh or dried leaves. You can use the leaves to stuff meat, fish and vegetables and they are delicious infused in vinegar and olive oil. Finely chopped, they also add a lemon flavour to salad dressings, sauces and marinades. Mix dried leaves with sugar for a zingy addition to baking. Lemon verbena syrup is refreshing with sparkling water, drizzled over ice cream or as a base for cocktails. The leaves can also be infused with gin or vodka to create liqueurs.

A handful of fresh leaves (or half dried) added to a bowl of warm water with half a cup of Epsom salts makes a wonderfully refreshing herbal foot soak, ideal after a day's gardening. It also makes a zingy herbal kitchen and bathroom cleaner when infused in white vinegar for three to four weeks.

To dry the leaves, simply cut off the green stems and hang them in bunches in a dry, airy space out of direct sunlight, until they feel crunchy and brittle. Store in dry, clean glass jars in the cupboard.

GROW I grow my lemon verbena plants in pots of multipurpose compost. Once the last spring frost has passed, they are put out on the patio close to my kitchen door for ease of harvest. Keep the soil moist. Mulch in the autumn with compost (this also feeds the plant). As the weather cools in autumn, I cut off the green stems, hanging them in bunches in the kitchen to dry for winter teas. The pots then go into the greenhouse or polytunnel during winter. They can also be overwintered on a sunny windowsill indoors. Lemon verbena is an ideal herb for growing indoors if you do not have an outdoor space. Regular picking during the growing season ensures a continuous crop of leaves, but it is good to allow some stems to flower for the marvellous scent and to feed foraging insects. Lemon verbena is easy to propagate by softwood cuttings.

TOM COWARD
Head gardener, Gravetye
Manor, Sussex, UK

Tom Coward started at Gravetye in 2010. It was at Great Dixter, as Fergus Garrett's assistant, that he honed his horticultural skills and style. Since starting at Gravetye, he has been working on the restoration of the garden, which was originally created by visionary gardener William Robinson in 1885. *gravetyemanor.co.uk*

Type
Deciduous
tree
Flowering
'Spring
**Height/
spread**
8m x 8m
Position
Full sun
Soil
Moist, well-
drained
Hardiness
USDA 6b/7a
/ RHS H6

← *Malus domestica* **'Howgate Wonder'**
Apple 'Howgate Wonder'

Growing plants is very rewarding, but growing food is even more so. The results are instantly tangible, engaging all of the senses. Fruit crops are especially important to Gravetye – you just can't compare the quality of the fruit from the garden with that of fruit from the supermarket. 'Howgate Wonder' is an amazing apple that grows to incredible sizes. The sight of this giant fruit ripening on the tree is reason enough to grow it alone, but it also has an excellent flavour and multiple uses in the kitchen. It's a vigorous, reliable cropper that cooks well and makes one of the best juices. It is also tasty as a dessert apple and popular with young children, who are amazed by its size. This is one of our most important apples at Gravetye as our head chef is so fond of working with it and it's an essential element of our fruit-juice blend. We have about 50 varieties of apple tree here, but if we could only grow one, this would be it.

GROW Prefers a sheltered position with good air circulation, drainage and fertile soil. I think it works well as an espalier, allowing its magnificent fruit to be admired. Careful pruning, fruit thinning and weed control make a massive difference. Regular watering in dry periods makes the fruit grow even bigger. Harvest time is generally mid-autumn, but for the best flavour leave the fruit on the tree for as long as possible. The sweetness of the apples increases after storage.

JAMES BASSON
Landscape gardener, Alpes
Maritimes, France

Since 2000, James Basson has been creating timeless sustainable gardens with his wife in the south of France. He is a four-time gold medal winner at the RHS Chelsea Flower Show and won best in show in 2017. He has won multiple gold medals in a variety of international garden shows including in Japan, Singapore, China and America. *scapedesign.com*

Origanum majorana **var.** *tenuifolium*
Slender-leaved sweet marjoram

Living and working in the Mediterranean climate, I find the hardest time of year is the summer. Spring's profusion has dried to a crisp and it is the moment for form and foliage. It is also the time for intense aromatics, and there is none more desirable than sweet marjoram, which is both subtle and powerful – it is hard to draw away from the nose. Its light and airy form, together with summer flowers, powders the landscape, and it has a softness that is irresistible along a garden path. This sweet marjoram is a wild selection from Cyprus: a dense, compact, bushy, half-hardy subshrub. It has evergreen velvety leaves that are grey-green becoming grey-silver in the hottest months. Its flowers are small and dusty white, arranged in spikelets.

GROW A very versatile plant, it accepts hard pruning back to its base to refresh a taller airy shape or regular pruning to form a dense, soft mass of leaves. It can deal with five months of drought. Do not feed it, do not water it, prune it if you like.

Type
Evergreen
subshrub
Flowering
Summer
**Height/
spread**
60cm x
60cm
Position
Full sun,
open
shrubland,
steppe
Soil
Poor, stony,
well-drained
Hardiness
USDA 8b/9a
/ RHS H4

67

SALLY GREGSON
Retired owner, Mill Cottage
Plants, Somerset, UK

Sally Gregson ran a nursery specialising in rare Japanese hydrangeas,
new hybrid epimediums and species collected in Szechuan and Yunnan,
China. She now lectures and writes, and is the author of the books
Practical Propagation, Ornamental Vegetable Gardening and *The Plant
Lover's Guide to Epimediums. millcottageplants.co.uk*

Epimedium 'Kaguyahime'
Barrenwort 'Kaguyahime'

This hybrid form was bred by Mr S. Yamaguichi in Japan. In spring it bears
two-tone pink and purple flowers held above evergreen leaves. The new young
foliage is brilliantly splashed red-purple over green. Another wonderful option is
E. 'Wildside Ruby'. The pillar-box red of the new foliage is visible across the garden,
with small yellow and pink flowers like sparks from a bonfire. The Chinese hybrid
epimediums are suited to the shade of later-flowering shrubs and perennials.
They bring subtle colour into the late spring garden with flowers that would stop
anyone in their tracks. They are easy and should be more widely grown.

GROW I always deadhead the faded flowers to prevent their seeds falling into the crown
of the plant. As they are self-sterile, seedlings will always be different and may take over
the original. Tidy up winter leaves in spring but not right down to the ground. Leave a few
to protect the flower buds from late frosts. May need additional watering during dry spells.

Type
Perennial
Flowering
Spring
**Height/
spread**
60cm x
30cm
Position
Part shade
Soil
Rich, moist,
well-drained
Hardiness
USDA 8b/9a
/ RHS H4

Hydrangea serrata 'Shōjō'
Hydrangea 'Shojo'

This beautiful hydrangea bears pastel pink lacecaps with a white eye at the
centre of each sterile floret. As the flowers are pollinated and mature, they turn
ruby red, as do the leaves. It is a presence in the garden from mid-summer until
winter. *H. serrata* is a relative of the mopheads and lacecaps, but needs to be
grown in shade. It is shorter than *H. macrophylla* and in flower a month earlier. The
flowers are smaller – more in proportion to the size of the plant – and very pretty.

GROW *H. serrata* flowers better if the spent flowerheads are removed as late as mid-
spring; they protect the emerging flower buds from any damage from late spring frosts.
May need additional watering during dry spells.

Type
Deciduous
shrub
Flowering
Summer,
autumn
**Height/
spread**
1m x 1m
Position
Part shade
Soil
Rich, moist,
well-drained
Hardiness
USDA 8b/9a
/ RHS H4

Type
Rhizomatous
perennial
Flowering
Late spring,
early
summer
**Height/
spread**
90cm
Position
Full sun
Soil
Well-drained,
alkaline,
neutral
Hardiness
USDA 6b/7a
/ RHS H6

Iris 'Benton Olive'
Tall bearded iris 'Benton Olive'

My favourite of the Benton irises. The gentle mixture of olive-green standards
over soft buff-coloured falls with a central violet band and darker veining has
to be examined closely. The Benton tall bearded irises were bred by Sir Cedric
Morris in the mid-twentieth century. Not only was he a remarkable plantsman,
but also an artist. The flowers are in subtle shades of translucent colour, a
world away from the big modern hybrids, and were bred to be painted in
watercolours. Together with his partner, Arthur Lett-Haines, he started the
East Anglian School of Painting and Drawing. Some of the great artists of the
twentieth century – Lucian Freud, Maggie Hambling – trained with them, while
Vita Sackville-West, Beth Chatto and many iconoclastic movers and shakers of
gardening also socialised with them.

GROW Benton irises should be lifted after flowering every three to four years to clean the
rhizomes of weeds that have seeded into the tight angles. Discard the central rhizome
furthest from the leaves; replant into free-draining soil.

ISABELLE PALMER
Founder, The Balcony
Gardener, London, UK

Isabelle Palmer is a renowned city garden designer and the founder of the Balcony Gardener, earning attention for her innovative and fresh approach to small spaces and container garden design. She is the author of *Modern Container Gardening*, *The Balcony Gardener* and *The House Gardener*. *thebalconygardener.com*

Nigella damascena
Love-in-a-mist (SEE ILLUSTRATION PAGE 74)

These are my go-to gem-like flowers for planting combinations. I am always in wonder at their beauty. In either pink, purple, blue or white (my favourite) they are magical and majestic with their frothy leaves and delicate petals. I am incredibly excited when they appear at the start of the summer from their forgotten seeding in April. Flowering through to early autumn if sown in successions, they are lovely for the front of a sunny border or dotted around the front and sides of pot combinations.

GROW Easy to cultivate from seeds. I sprinkle these in abundance in my pots, ground and borders so they peek up among the spaces of my perennials or stand on their own. The seedlings are easy to recognise among weeds because of their lacy foliage. As nigella only blooms for a few weeks, it is best to sow seeds two or three times from late spring to early summer and it usually grows better from direct-sown seeds than from transplanted seedlings. Fertilise throughout the growing period and keep well watered. Nigella is virtually problem-free once established, probably because the plants don't live long enough to be bothered by pests or disease. Collecting seeds for next year is easy and it also self sows. The seed pods are good in dried flower arrangements, too – an added benefit.

Type
Annual
Flowering
Summer
Height/spread
50cm x 50cm
Position
Full sun, part shade
Soil
Fertile, well-drained
Hardiness
USDA 9b/10a / RHS H3

MADELINE MCKEEVER
Farmer and seed grower,
Brown Envelope Seeds,
County Cork, Ireland

Madeline McKeever grew up on a farm in County Meath. She studied botany at Trinity College Dublin and completed an MSc in vegetation history. She began farming in West Cork in 1986. The first Brown Envelope Seed catalogue was produced in 2004 and contained 25 varieties. Since then the number of varieties has increased and all are certified organic. *brownenvelopeseeds.com*

Solanum tuberosum
Potato

This is such a satisfying plant to grow, whether it is in a field or a grow bag, it comes up quickly and enjoys all kinds of weather, except frost. Unearthing the potatoes is like finding jewels underground. Per square meter, they are great value in food production and need very little maintenance. They leave the ground nice and clean and ready for another quick autumn crop.

Potatoes are grown from tubers as an annual, but of course are herbaceous perennials. They have beautiful white to pink to purple flowers with striking golden anthers. The flowers are followed by small, green, tomato-like berries in late summer. These contain seeds that can also be sown. When they are grown from seed they only produce a tiny tuber in the first year, but it is a new potato variety. In subsequent years the potatoes get bigger.

GROW I like to grow potatoes directly in the ground with as much homemade compost as I can. They need to be 'rowed up' – that is, earth needs to be pulled up around the stems to stop light getting to the tubers. Light causes them to go green, which makes them taste bitter and makes them mildly poisonous.

Type
Herbaceous perennial
Flowering
Spring, summer
Height/spread
1m x 50cm
Position
Full sun, part shade
Soil
Moist, well-drained, slightly acidic
Hardiness
USDA 10b / RHS H2

HELENA DOVE
Kitchen gardener, Royal
Botanic Gardens, Kew, UK

Helena Dove manages the kitchen garden at the Royal Botanic Gardens, Kew, and some of the crops she grows have a slant towards future foods and the scientific research that takes place on site. She has a passion for heritage cultivars and adores edible flowers and unusual crops that may not immediately be thought of as food. *helenadove.com*

Solanum lycopersicum 'Black Opal' →
Tomato 'Black Opal'

A cordon tomato with dark chocolate cherry fruits, this is one of my favourites. I grow it every year and love to munch on the fruits as I work through the day, especially when they are warmed by the sun and super sweet. The dark tomatoes are higher in antioxidant anthocyanins than the regular red tomatoes, and the cherry size means 'Black Opal' produces masses of fruits in a good summer. It produces well outdoors as well as under glass.

GROW Start off sowing seeds inside in spring, to plant out strong plants once the frosts have been and gone. Make sure to give them a strong support, as they get heavy once laden with fruits.

Remove side-shoots weekly to ensure the plant puts more energy into the juicy fruits. In early autumn, I pinch the plant out to stop it producing new trusses, ensuring existing tomatoes ripen before the inevitable autumn cold. Give a good water once a week, aiming the hose at the roots to avoid water splashing on the plant and potentially encouraging blight. Remove lower leaves for the same reason.

Type
Annual
Flowering
Summer
Height/spread
1.5m x 50cm
Position
Full sun, sheltered
Soil
Well-drained
Hardiness
USDA 11 / RHS H1C

Malus domestica 'Egremont Russet'
Apple 'Egremont Russet'

I love an apple and 'Egremont Russet' just happens to be both one of my favourites and an easy one to grow – a hardy tree with pink blossoms and delicious fruits that have brown russeting patches and a good depth of flavour. I grow mine on dwarfing rootstocks in restricted forms such as espaliers or step-overs, as I don't have a lot of space for an orchard. I think apple trees are beautiful, they give wonderful blossoms in spring, shade in summer, harvest in autumn and structure in winter.

GROW For smaller gardens, buy apples on dwarfing rootstocks such as M27, M9 or M26. Plant a maiden whip in autumn for best establishment. You should be able to pick fruits after a year or so.

Type
Deciduous tree
Flowering
Spring
Height/spread
8m x 8m (non-dwarfing rootstock)
3m x 3m (on M26 rootstock)
Position
Full sun, sheltered
Soil
Well-drained, moisture-retentive
Hardiness
USDA 6b/7a / RHS H6

Prunus persica 'Crimson Bonfire'
Peach 'Crimson Bonfire'

I have had the absolute joy of managing a peach house at Kew and nothing beats the sun-warmed fruits and the dribble of juice down the chin. But at home, I stand little chance of having a peach house, and this is how I discovered the 'Crimson Bonfire'. A peach bred for a pot, it has stunning red leaves so adds joy to my small garden, even when it isn't laden with fruit. It is also self-fertile.

GROW Peaches need to come indoors when they are in flower around late winter, as the frosts will destroy the flowers, although fleece will also do the job. When growing plants in pots, make sure to water well once a week. The aim is to get the soil wet all the way down to the base, which is made easier if you don't fill the pot right to the brim. Try using a watering collar to fill up and soak away before refilling.

Type
Deciduous tree
Flowering
Late winter, spring
Height/spread
1.5m x 1m
Position
Full sun, sheltered
Soil
Well-drained
Hardiness
USDA 8b/9a / RHS H4

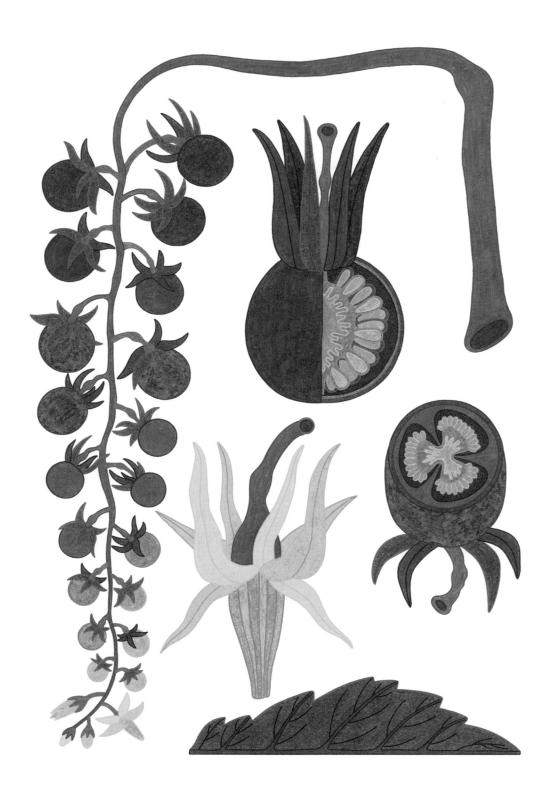

Lactuca sativa var. *angustana* 'Purple Sword'
Celtuce 'Purple Sword'

Lettuce is such a fantastic early crop in the kitchen garden and the backbone of so many dishes, but celtuce gives a twist to this common vegetable. Also known as stem lettuce, this lettuce towers upwards in the salad bed and, once I have finished harvesting its lower leaves, it gives me an amazingly thick and nutty stem to stir-fry. 'Purple Sword' has a purple tinge to its leaves and it really does look like the blades of a sword. It makes a stunning combination in the salad bowl with the fresh green leaves of other lettuce.

GROW Start from seed and water well once temperatures rise. Do not try to grow these during the heat of summer as they go straight to seed, giving you a very slim stem. To avoid this, they can be grown in shade. Once flowering, the stem will taste very bitter and is best added to the compost heap.

Type
Annual
Flowering
Summer
Height/ spread
35cm x 35cm
Position
Full sun, part shade, sheltered
Soil
Well- drained
Hardiness
USDA 7b/8a / RHS H5

Phaseolus coccineus 'White Lady'
Runner bean 'White Lady'

I used not to enjoy growing runner beans, as they need a large and robust structure to help them stay upright, drop all their flowers when it's too hot, then take a fair amount of preparation in the kitchen to remove the string. But 'White Lady' changed all that. She still needs a fair amount of support and will shed her beautiful white flowers, but the beans are so delicious. They have virtually no string and I pick them when they are immature and snack on them raw. Since I started my love affair with 'White Lady', I've come to discover the delicious taste of the flowers, leaves and tendrils. I think I'm a convert! Her beautiful white beans also store well for winter casseroles.

GROW Start from seed under glass in spring and plant out once the risk of frost has passed. Give the vines a sturdy support and water well throughout the season, especially when flowering. Always dig out the roots, as they will come back next year if the winter is mild, but the resulting vines will be less productive.

Type
Annual climber
Flowering
Summer, autumn
Height/ spread
3m x 1m
Position
Full sun, sheltered
Soil
Well- drained, moist
Hardiness
USDA 10b / RHS H2

Tropaeolum majus 'Orange Troika'
Nasturtium 'Orange Troika'

Nasturtiums are such good doers in the kitchen garden. As well as supplying delicious leaves, flowers and seeds for the plate, they attract beneficial insects and pollinators, smother the ground to reduce weed growth and, in times of need, can be used as a sacrificial plant (attracting pests away from your main crop). 'Orange Troika' has a variegated leaf which looks like an artist has flicked bleach at a canvas. When I worked at Myddelton House Gardens we had a border called Tom Tiddler's Ground, where the plantsman E. A. Bowles grew only plants with silver and gold variegation or red leaves. I wasn't a big fan – it was all a little much for my kitchen gardener eyes, which quite like order – but 'Orange Troika' has made me fall back in love with variegation. The leaves brighten up the understories of the plot and look smashing in a salad.

GROW I start from seed and plant out where I want them. They will self sow, but as very vigorous plants they can smother young veg crops, so make sure you show them who's boss early on. Harvest flowers often to keep production strong. They will also grow up and over an arch or through a fruit tree, which can be incredibly beautiful. They will produce flowers from the beginning of summer through to autumn, but are not frost tolerant. They need some heat to break dormancy, but can be sown directly once the soil has warmed up.

Type
Annual climber
Flowering
Summer, autumn
Height/ spread
2.5m x 1.5m
Position
Full sun
Soil
Well- drained, poor
Hardiness
USDA 9b/10a / RHS H3

Beta vulgaris 'Barbabietola di Chioggia'
Beetroot 'Barbabietola di Chioggia'

Type
Annual
Height/spread
15cm x 10cm
Position
Full sun, part shade, sheltered
Soil
Well-drained
Hardiness
USDA 9b/10a / RHS H3

Beetroot is one of the first crops I grew in a pot when I was renting and I realised I wanted to grow food as a career. It is one of the easiest crops to grow and possibly one of the most delicious, though often hard to come by in the supermarket unless they are covered in vinegar. Fresh beetroot is so versatile in the kitchen, from an ingredient in chocolate cake to being roasted with honey. The tops are equally yummy and can be used as a spinach replacement.

'Barbabietola di Chioggia' has a stunning root with alternate red and white moon rings (which are actually just vascular tissue). Beetroot can be grown throughout most of the year and stores well in root clamps (a traditional storage method) over the winter. A relatively quick-maturing crop, it can be planted in containers, flower borders and among large crops such as cabbage and globe artichokes.

GROW Start from seed and succession sow throughout the year. I start mine in modules and keep sowing, so I can replace the rows as soon as I harvest them. Beetroot has cluster seeds, meaning you will get several plants in each module. There is no need to thin these out, just grow them in a cluster and you will get a quantity of smaller beets, which are delicious and sweet.

Type
Annual, biennial
Height/spread
1.2m x 60cm
Position
Full sun, sheltered
Soil
Moist, well-drained
Hardiness
USDA 7b/8a / RHS H5

Brassica oleracea Acephala Group 'Nero di Toscana'
Kale 'Nero di Toscana'

I love, love, love kale, and this dark green, blistered leaf, which looks a bit like dinosaur skin, is up there with my favourites. I ignore its 'superfood' status and give it a 'superplant' status. It looks stunning in a mixed border and there is nothing more beautiful on a sunny winter's morning when white frost is highlighting the kale's veins and edges. From a harvest point of view, it produces all year round, which means more production from one space, and 'Nero di Toscana' suffers much less from white fly than some other kales. There will always be a place for this dinosaur in my plot.

GROW Sow in late spring and establish well. Keep watered throughout the summer, otherwise it will bolt. If bolting occurs, a late-summer sowing should produce large enough plants to see you through winter, when the frosts will make the harvests sweeter. Tear off the lowest leaves when harvesting to keep the plant heading for the skies. If pigeons and white fly are issues, net the plants and, in more open aspects, stake them to avoid the winds rocking the roots.

TRACEY SPOKES
Head gardener and florist,
Northamptonshire, UK

Tracey Spokes is head gardener at Kelmarsh Hall, which she describes as a gorgeously dishevelled garden. She is also a consultant at Rolleston Hall, a private garden in Leicestershire, where she was head gardener for 11 years. *onceupon-atime.co.uk*

Type
Annual
Flowering
Summer
**Height/
spread**
50cm x 50cm
Position
Full sun,
part shade
Soil
Well-drained
Hardiness
USDA 9b/10a
/ RHS H3

Nigella damascena →
Love-in-a-mist

Nigella is so often overlooked. It's a cottage-garden staple with its feathery foliage and delicate pastel blooms, followed by fabulous, almost alien-like seedheads. A prolific self-seeder, it pops up every year. Admittedly it can get a little carried away, but that's not a problem in my book. For me, nigella is perfect. It requires little maintenance, holds its own next to more boisterous neighbours and lends itself to cutting magnificently. The plant is pretty much trouble-free – all it needs is a little water during dry spells. I grow it with foxgloves and lady's mantle or among the veg.

GROW Scatter seed at the front of borders in late spring. It may need a little watering to get going. Keep an eye on the seedlings as they come up as they can be overgrown by more vigorous neighbouring plants.

Lathyrus odoratus 'High Scent'
Sweet pea 'High Scent'

No country garden should be without these flowers. In the height of summer, their scent takes you back to childhood, when life was simpler and the sun always shone. These annual climbers come in many different colours and are perfect for cut-flower growers. I love all sweet peas, but particularly 'High Scent', which has a delicate cream with lavender hue and the most magnificent scent of all. A big sniff is all you need for a big smile.

Type
Annual
climber
Flowering
Summer,
autumn
**Height/
spread**
2m x 50cm
Position
Full sun, part
shade
Soil
Well-drained,
fertile
Hardiness
USDA 9b/10a
/ RHS H3

GROW Sow in January in the UK (I never sow in November as the chances of keeping them alive is slim – too many mice and slugs). Soak the seeds on a damp paper towel for a couple of days to aid germination. Sow two or three seeds in a 9cm pot filled with peat-free compost. Water. When seedlings are 8cm, pinch out the growing tips for bushier plants. Ideally, they should be planted out after the last frost, but I find I need the space in the greenhouse so, after hardening them off, I plant them out and keep my fingers crossed. Grow in soil enriched with well-rotted manure. At the beginning of the growing season, feed weekly with a weak nitrogen feed to stimulate growth, then swap to a weak potash feed to encourage flowers. Keep them watered and fed and they will repay you tenfold.

Alchemilla mollis
Lady's mantle (SEE ILLUSTRATION PAGE 190)

Lady's mantle is a fairly low-growing perennial that is beautiful, but never the bride. Much maligned, it's often overlooked as just 'alchemilla'. Everyone talks about how the leaves collect raindrops, which sit on the foliage like jewels, but for me you can't beat the fluffy lime-green flowers creating a flowing underskirt beneath taller perennials. It's as much at home in the garden as in the vase. A perfect companion to poppies, foxgloves, delphiniums and roses. So easy to look after and so easy to love.

GROW Easy to grow, it self-seeds quite happily in paths and borders alike. Cut the plant back hard after flowering to get a fresh crown of lush leaves and maybe a second flush of flowers. Keep watered in dry spells.

Type
Herbaceous
perennial
Flowering
Summer,
autumn
**Height/
spread**
50cm x 50cm
Position
Full sun, part
shade, full
shade
Soil
Moist, well-
drained
Hardiness
USDA 6a–1
/ RHS H7

JULIA SNOWBALL
Head gardener, Yorkshire
Lavender, Yorkshire, UK

Julia Snowball is head gardener at Yorkshire Lavender, a 60-acre hillside farm featuring lavender gardens, a specialist plant nursery and panoramic views of the surrounding countryside. *yorkshirelavender.com*

Lavandula angustifolia **'Folgate'**
English lavender 'Folgate'

Why have I chosen lavender out of all the herbs and plants I love? It just seemed the most natural choice after 20 years of learning, working and discovering the different species and cultivars. I have always loved herbs, even as a girl. I was fortunate to grow up on a farm with wildflowers growing in hedge backs, double dykes and grassland meadows. Years later, newly married, I had the thrill of tripping out of the backdoor into the garden while preparing lunch or supper and accidentally-on-purpose standing on the chamomile, bruising it so that it gave off that gorgeous pungent aroma. When I reached for a few cuttings of oregano or lemon thyme to add to the food I was cooking, I couldn't help cutting a bunch of lavender from along the row of *L. angustifolia* 'Folgate', to hang in the kitchen. It helps deter flies and, once dry, can be scrunched up to make lavender bags to place in the 'woolly' drawer.

Lavender not only gives beauty and scent to a garden, it is also essential for many insects, especially all members of the bee family, and for humans too. Working and handling lavender most days, I have realised how important it is for relieving stress. It gives off such calming properties, and the extracted lavender oil is beneficial for mental health.

I feel there is a lavender cultivar out there for everyone. Lavender fits into most gardens, even if it has to live in a container placed in the right position and be potted on most years. The cultivar I've chosen (a difficult decision), is 'Folgate', because of its strong blue open flowers that bees find easy to home in on. The subtle fragrance makes the extracted oil superior to that of some stronger lavenders. And a four-year-old 'Folgate' hedge in full flower with the hum of bees around it takes some beating!

GROW Lavender is a hardy shrub with a woody stem. It is one of the easiest plants to grow and thrives on neglect – up to a point. Plant your lavender in full sun, in dry, well-drained sandy soil. Think of the poor, stony Mediterranean soil that lavender loves. It is easy to over water lavender so if you plant it in the ground, I advise only watering it once a week for three weeks after planting, then no more. If in a pot, once a week in hot weather is enough. The pot is better stood on feet or gravel to let the water drain through easily, especially in winter.

Lavender in a container is better potted on once a year, as it does like space of its own. All lavender species need to be cut back after flowering. Cut this one back 1.25cm above the hard wood, leaving 1.25cm of green wood. This gives the plant time to green up before the autumn, which will protect it in cold weather. Lavender does not suffer from diseases, so it is an excellent companion plant for roses. It's also brilliant for the vegetable patch, as it helps to ward off most 'nasties', especially aphids.

Type
Evergreen shrub
Flowering
Summer
Height/spread
60cm x 60cm
Position
Full sun, sheltered
Soil
Moist, well-drained
Hardiness
USDA 7b/8a / RHS H5

ROSEMARY ALEXANDER
Principal, The English
Gardening School,
Hampshire, UK

Rosemary Alexander is founder and principal of the English Gardening School. A well-respected garden designer, she is also an RHS judge, author of the *Essential Garden Design Workbook* and opens her own garden under the National Gardens Scheme. *englishgardeningschool.co.uk*

Brunnera macrophylla 'Jack Frost'
Siberian bugloss 'Jack Frost'

This is an invaluable and low-maintenance thick ground cover for light shade and under deciduous trees. It lightens up my woodland area with its illuminating silvered foliage and sprays of blue forget-me-not flowers for several months. Good among ferns and comes into foliage and flower before hostas.

GROW Beware of the more ordinary *B. macrophylla* as it can become rather invasive. Cut back after first flowering to freshen foliage rosette and extend the season of interest. If conditions are too dry, it can lead to scorched foliage; too wet and it could lead to root damage or rot. Resistant to deer and rabbits, but can be slug prone. Clumps spread by creeping rhizomes. It's easy to split; divide in spring every three to five years.

Type
Rhizomatous herbaceous perennial
Flowering
Late spring, early summer
Height/spread
50cm x 1m
Position
Full shade, part shade, sheltered
Soil
Humus-rich, moist, well-drained
Hardiness
USDA 6b/7a / RHS H6

TOM HART DYKE
Horticulturist and plant hunter, UK

Tom Hart Dyke is founder of the World Garden at Lullingstone Castle. In 2000 he was kidnapped by a Colombian guerrilla group during a plant-hunting trip and held for nine months. During his captivity he made plans for a dream garden. The garden features rare and unusual plants and the National Plant Collection of *Eucalyptus*. *lullingstonecastle.co.uk*

Salvia 'Dad's Brown Trousers'
Salvia 'Dad's Brown Trousers'

This joyous botanical wonder has brought me so much spine-tingling, plant-filled joy. The name is inspired by my late father, who could often be found wandering around the garden in his beloved light brown-pink trousers. I first discovered this robust cultivar in 2011 as a fluke seedling in the Mexican section of the World Garden. We grow many different varieties of sub-shrubby Mexican salvias and the bees had done their work. This cultivar is set apart by its strongly branching habit, which spreads nicely without becoming straggly. The fresh green foliage has a delicious oily fragrance when crushed. Charming large flowers with peachy pink tones take on an almost light brown hue in full bloom.

GROW This cultivar is reliably hardy given a sunny aspect and any soil with good drainage. If growing in a container, I'd recommend applying a slow-release fertiliser in spring. Personally, I don't bother with deadheading throughout its long flowering season, but mid-spring I cut back hard to encourage vigorous new growth and increase the longevity of the plant.

Type
Perennial
Flowering
Late spring, summer, autumn
Height/spread
60cm x 60cm
Position
Full sun
Soil
Well-drained
Hardiness
USDA 7b/8a / RHS H5

JIM BUCKLAND
Former garden supervisor,
West Sussex, UK

Together with his wife, Sarah Wain, Jim Buckland led the garden team at West Dean Gardens in West Sussex for over 25 years.

Asarum europaeum
Asarabacca (SEE ILLUSTRATION PAGE 52)

I first became aware of this modest-but-enchanting (at least to me!) plant beneath the deep shade of the four hornbeams that 'anchor' the corners of the terraced formal gardens at Castle Drogo on the edge of Dartmoor and that are surrounded by 3m-tall yew hedges. That location tells you a lot about the plant's cultivation: its tolerance of deep shade and a wide range of soils, its love of a moist environment, and the fact that it's fully hardy in the UK. All in all, it's an excellent garden plant. It forms low, slow-growing, creeping clumps with evergreen, glossy green, kidney-shaped leaves that make a perfect foil weaving beneath other showier subjects. The only downside is that it's slow to propagate, so isn't always easy to source and is also a bit pricey. But worth it!

GROW I am fond of woodland gardens in which an appropriate selection of herbaceous plants knit together to form a dense, ecologically balanced and relatively stable green tapestry. *A. europaeum* has a native range that extends from Finland to Bulgaria, where it forms dense sheets of ground cover under deciduous or coniferous woodland (a bit like ivy in the UK), which makes it a natural component of this type of planting. However, I have planted it in lots of alternative situations and it always seems to perform in its own understated way.

Type
Rhizomatous
perennial
Flowering
Spring
Height/
spread
10cm x 50cm
Position
Full shade,
part shade,
sheltered
Soil
Moist, well-
drained,
acid, neutral
Hardiness
USDA 6b/7a
/ RHS H6

KATIE RUSHWORTH
Garden maker and TV
presenter, Yorkshire, UK

Katie Rushworth is a garden designer and presenter on ITV's *Love Your Garden*. She runs an online and in-person consultancy guiding people on how to create the garden of their dreams. *katierushworth.com*

Type
Herbaceous
perennial
Flowering
Summer
Height/spread
1m x 50cm
Position
Full sun, part shade
Soil
Moist,
well-drained, loam
Hardiness
USDA 8b/9a /
RHS H4

Monarda
Bergamot

I remember the first time I saw this plant – it looked like nothing else I'd ever seen. The flowers make me think of a jester's hat and I adore the scent of the aromatic foliage. Its unusual flower shape makes it great for contrasting with other flower forms, such as spires and daisies. It is loved by bees, hence its alternative common name of bee balm, and anything that attracts more pollinators to the garden is a must for me. It comes in a vast array of reds, pinks and purples, but it's the deep violet ones such as 'Scorpion' that I'm particularly drawn to. It also has good winter structure.

GROW Several varieties of monarda are susceptible to mildew – I find a good deep mulch in early spring helps keep the clump healthy. They are also shallow rooting and like conditions to be slightly on the moist side – the mulch helps lock in moisture.

THE LAND GARDENERS
Garden designers,
Oxfordshire and London, UK

Henrietta Courtauld and Bridget Elworthy established The Land Gardeners to research plant and soil health through growing, cutting and designing. Their mission is to work with growers to improve the health of our land. They design productive gardens and restore walled and historic gardens. *thelandgardeners.com*

Rosa
Rose

We are in love with all roses, but particularly English shrub roses as they are velvety, abundant and glamorous, and they flower throughout the summer. We pick armfuls of varieties such as *Rosa* 'Royal Jubilee' and 'Heritage', and put them in silver jugs or Constance Spry-style vases. We also love hybrid tea roses. These are often seen as stiff or static, but we enjoy picking them because they have such vibrant colours and a long vase life. A particular favourite is the bright orange-red hybrid 'Alexander', which was growing at Wardington Manor (where we grow our cut flowers) when we first arrived. We grow roses in rows in our cutting garden, making them easy to pick. Although roses are mainly grown for their summer flowers, there are many that have hips in autumn – for example, we pick long boughs of the rambler *R. filipes* 'Kiftsgate' for its beautiful hips.

GROW Most roses like sun, but you can find some expectations – the wonderful climber *R.* 'Madame Alfred Carrière' is happy growing trained against a north wall in our garden. Plant them in loamy soil with lots of good compost. A little wind is good for roses to prevent them from getting black spot. We prune in early spring, taking care to remove any dead, damaged or crossing stems. We make our own compost teas and use them as a foliar feed, watering them regularly throughout the growing season.

Type
Perennial
Flowering
Summer,
autumn
**Height/
spread**
Varies
depending
on variety
Position
Full sun,
part shade
Soil
Fertile,
moist, well-
drained
Hardiness
USDA 6b/7a
/ RHS H6

WENDY KIANG-SPRAY
Writer and speaker,
Maryland, USA

Wendy Kiang-Spray gardens in Rockville, Maryland. Her articles about gardening and food have appeared in national and local print publications and her book, *The Chinese Kitchen Garden*, is about growing and cooking Chinese vegetables. *wendykiangspray.com*

Momordica charantia
Balsam pear

Commonly known as bitter gourd or bitter melon in the US, my Cantonese-speaking family knows this fruit as *fu gwaa*, meaning 'bitter'. I grew up eating it in stir-fries my mother would make with sliced beef and garlic. I probably spent the first couple of decades of my life carefully selecting *just* the beef to top my rice, before I learned to appreciate the flavour of this fruit, which is often described as 'coolingly bitter'. It's a taste that, once acquired, you begin to crave.

Recognised by its bumpy green appearance, it's a really interesting fruit. To prepare it, you slice it lengthwise, scoop out the pith with a spoon, then cut the outer into pieces. The texture is similar to green pepper and the key to balancing the bitterness is to cook it with other strong flavours such as garlic and spices. One of the craziest things about bitter melon is, if left to mature, the fruits become yellow and then split, revealing that the once white pith inside has turned red.

GROW This is a climbing vine so needs something to climb up. The trickiest part is the seed germination. Seeds have a thick coat so it's helpful to nick or soak them before germination. I sow mine indoors and transplant when the soil warms. Water well until established. Harvest about 60 days after planting out when the fruits are green and shiny and there's a slight smoothing out of the ridges. They should be about 15–30cm long.

Type
Annual
climber
Flowering
Summer
**Height/
spread**
2m x 2m
Position
Full sun
Soil
Rich, moist
Hardiness
USDA 12 /
RHS H1b

78

Type
Annual climber
Flowering
Summer, autumn
Height/ spread
2m x 50cm
Position
Full sun, sheltered
Soil
Moist, well-drained
Hardiness
USDA 11 / RHS H1c

Luffa acutangula ⬊
Angled loofah

This is also called loofah gourd in the US and sometimes silk squash or Chinese okra. It is super easy to grow and is not only tasty, but useful. Loofah is a large and vigorous vining plant guaranteed to make anyone feel like a successful gardener. The gourds can grow pretty long, but for eating should be harvested at an immature stage (about 12cm). They are a bit soft inside, with a mild taste and can be used in the same way you would use summer squash. The plants produce many fruits and are also very fast-growing. Don't worry if you miss harvesting some, just let them grow and grow, and by the end of the season they'll have turned into the long, scrubby, lightweight sponges that you buy in stores! If growing for sponges (and eating), choose *L. cylindrica* (known as smooth or sponge gourd). If growing just for eating, stick with the thinner and longer angled loofah, which has a better taste. Angled loofah has ridges that need to be pared before cooking.

For sponges, I wait until the end of the growing season and bring the plant in before the first frosts. The outer skin is brownish and it's fun to peel it off, revealing a fibrous skeleton. Run it under water, squeezing until it's totally clean, then shake the seeds out and use as is.

GROW It is helpful to get a head start by sowing seeds indoors and planting out when the soil warms. Before long, the vigorous vines will be dotted with yellow flowers.

STEVE LANNIN
Head gardener, Iford Manor, Wiltshire, UK

Steve Lannin is head gardener at the Grade I*-listed gardens of Iford Manor, having previously worked as head gardener at Mapperton House, Sudeley Castle, Lowther Castle and Allt-y-bela. *instagram.com/stevelannin*

Rosa 'Tuscany Superb'
Rose 'Tuscany Superb'

I first encountered 'Tuscany Superb' in the rose garden at Sudeley Castle in the Cotswolds. The garden is sheltered and warm, which traps the scent of the roses in summer. The scent was intoxicating and a decade later the fragrance of roses on a warm, calm day transports me back to Sudeley. For several years I was lucky enough to look after Arne Maynard's garden at Allt-y-bela in Wales. The gardens are romantic and informal. 'Tuscany Superb' was one of the roses that Maynard grew in the cottage garden where he trained them on hazel domes. The extra support allowed the roses to grow to eye level where the scent and semi-double flowers could be properly appreciated. I grow 'Tuscany Superb' at home now, both because of its lovely deep magenta flowers, thornless nature and scent, but also because of the associations it has with those wonderful gardens.

Type
Shrub rose
Flowering
Summer
Height/ spread
1m x 1m
Position
Full sun, but can tolerate part shade, sheltered
Soil
Adaptable
Hardiness
USDA 6a–1 / RHS H7

GROW At Sudeley Castle the rose garden was surrounded by a deep box hedge that provided shelter for overwintering ladybirds. The key to the roses surviving an early aphid attack was to wait for the ladybirds who, given the opportunity, would clear the aphids. Black spot was managed by clearing fallen leaves and by applying a heavy mulch in winter, which prevented any spores overwintering in the soil from being spread by spring rain. Roses are hungry plants, so feed them after the first flush of flowers. Deadhead regularly. The plant appreciates a humus-rich mulch in late winter followed by a feed after flowering. Prune mainly in winter and do so lightly, to create a goblet-like shape.

DARREN DICKEY
Head gardener, Trebah
Garden, Cornwall, UK

Darren Dickey started working at subtropical garden Trebah in 1991
and became head gardener in 2002. He studied at Duchy College,
Camborne, while working as an apprentice at Glendurgan Garden.
trebahgarden.co.uk

Phyllostachys edulis
Moso bamboo

When I first started at Trebah I helped the team move bamboos from various
locations around the garden into one central area to create our 'Bamboozle'.
P. edulis was planted as a small clump within this area and had canes of no
more than 2cm in diameter. Since then, several stands of have been established
and attained a form, stature and size similar to those in China and Japan. The
plant grows larger in areas of the UK with milder winters, such as Cornwall. It is
testament to the conditions at Trebah that many plants like *P. edulis* do so well.

GROW *P. edulis* is a running bamboo that continues to expand unless a root barrier
is installed, so spread is only limited by the space you want it to fill. Bamboos are not
for everyone and choice selection is key, but they can add a dramatic effect in the
garden. At Trebah, *P. edulis* has attained a height of over 15m with a diameter of up
to 15cm. 'Edulis' means edible and these are the shoots we commonly use in stir-fries.
Squirrels are also rather partial to them and we protect the emerging shoots with
tree guards that help prevent them from being nibbled off at ground level. If you are
looking to grow *P. edulis* to a similar size, you need mild winters, cool moist springs and
summers in which the soil does not dry out too much. Prune in early spring and remove
dead or weak canes. Mulch to help retain moisture and, if required, feed in spring with
a high-nitrogen fertiliser.

Type
Evergreen
bamboo
Flowering
Rare
**Height/
spread**
15m x 8m
Position
Full sun,
part shade,
requires
shelter from
strong winds
Soil
Humus-rich,
moist, well-
drained
Hardiness
USDA 7b/8a
/ RHS H5

Wollemia nobilis
Wollemi pine

Wollemi pine grows well at
Trebah and we have several
fine specimens. Its slender form
takes up little space, allowing for
several plants in a small area.
Its attractive needles persist
in two or four ranks and male
and female cones can appear
on the same tree. It also has
unusual bumps on its bark that
resemble puffed rice cereal.

GROW Grows best in a sheltered
spot with good sunlight levels and
humus-rich soil. Protect plants
when young from rabbits, deer
and other animals with a mesh
guard. Mulch to retain moisture.

Type
Evergreen
tree
**Height/
spread**
12m x 4m
Position
Full sun,
part shade,
sheltered
Soil
Humus-rich,
moist, well-
drained,
neutral, acid
Hardiness
USDA 8b/9a
/ RHS H4

Davidia involucrata var. vilmoriniana
De Vilmorin handkerchief tree

This has attractive flowers with
white bracts in spring, lime-
green foliage in summer, good
autumn colour and seed pods
through winter when the tree has
lost its leaves.

GROW Protect young plants from
rabbits, deer and other animals
with a mesh tree guard. Mulch
when young.

Type
Deciduous
tree
Flowering
Spring
**Height/
spread**
12m x 8m
Position
Full sun,
part shade,
sheltered
Soil
Cool,
humus-rich
soil that
doesn't
dry out too
much in
summer
Hardiness
USDA 7b/8a
/ RHS H5

Gunnera manicata
Giant rhubarb

This must be the most spectacular plant at Trebah. It was planted in the 1950s in what was a puddled moor, and the conditions couldn't be more perfect. In the clay-rich, moisture-retentive soil, the large, ribbed rhubarb-like leaves and spiky green leaf stalks reach their full potential, towering above you as you walk beneath them. It bears pink flower spikes in early summer and dies back to ground level in the winter.

Type Herbaceous perennial
Flowering Summer
Height/ spread 2.5m x 4m
Position Full sun, part shade, sheltered
Soil Moisture-retentive
Hardiness USDA 7b/8a / RHS H5

GROW Moisture is the key to getting the size of plants seen at Trebah. They need lots of it when they are developing in spring and to maintain their supporting strength in summer. They do not need to be in water but do benefit from moisture-retentive soil. Tidy the leaves in autumn and cover the crown to protect from frost.

Echium pininana
Giant viper's bugloss

This is another spectacular plant that naturalises well at Trebah. It is a biennial and also frost tender, so needs protection in severe cold to get it through the first winter. But, wow, is it worth it. It puts on a growth spurt in the second year, sending up a single spier up to 4m high. Then, gradually through the summer, a succession of mauve flowers open and become instantly covered in bees feeding off the copious nectar.

Type Biennial
Flowering Spring, summer
Height/ spread 4m x 1m
Position Full sun, sheltered
Soil Well-drained, dry
Hardiness USDA 9b/10a / RHS H3

GROW Raise from seed and do not disturb the tap root once planted. Needs a sheltered, sunny position protected from wind and frost. Good compact soil around the root is required to minimise wind rock.

Cyathea medullaris
Black tree fern

This slender, fibrous fern is one of the more challenging trunked ferns to grow. It is probably the least hardy and requires protection in even the most sheltered garden. But it is worth the effort as it has the most spectacular new fronds. Large and lush and lime-green, these can be anywhere up to 5m long, while the jet-black trunks, covered in black hairs, can tower up to 20m above you.

Type Evergreen tree fern
Height/ spread 20m x 5m
Position Full sun, part shade, sheltered in a frost-free position
Soil Humus-rich, moisture-retentive
Hardiness USDA 9b/10a / RHS H3

GROW The key is to give it as much surrounding shelter as possible and a serious amount of protection in winter. They can grow fast but one bad cold snap can take them out and you lose all your effort. We use layers of horticultural fleece around the stem and tucked in the top to cover what will be next year's fronds. Remove dead fronds after the risk of frost has passed and water from the top down in dry conditions.

Dicksonia antarctica
Soft tree fern (SEE ILLUSTRATION PAGE 155)

This thrives at Trebah and has naturalised in many locations. It forms a fibrous 'trunk' made up of roots with evergreen fronds at the top. New frond crosiers are impressive as they emerge in late spring/early summer. The first plants introduced into the UK arrived in Falmouth docks in 1880. Of those 3,000 cut trunks, 300 were planted at Trebah.

Type Evergreen tree fern
Height/ spread 4m x 4m
Position Full sun, part shade, sheltered
Soil Humus-rich, moisture-retentive
Hardiness USDA 9b/10a / RHS H3

GROW Tree ferns do best in moist, semi-shaded positions protected from strong winds and frosts. If bought as trunks, support them with a stake for the first 12 months to help the roots establish and water well from the top down. Protect the crown from frost with horticultural fleece during the winter and remove it when the frond crosiers start to emerge. Remove dead fronds after all risk of frost has passed and water from the top down in dry conditions.

GREG OVENDEN
Head gardener, Pashley Manor Gardens, East Sussex, UK

Greg Ovenden undertook work experience at Great Dixter Gardens and worked at RHS Wisley for 11 years in the propagation department and the display glasshouse before becoming a head gardener. He has a keen interest in subtropical planting and cacti. *pashleymanorgardens.com*

Podophyllum versipelle **'Spotty Dotty'** →
Mayapple 'Spotty Dotty'

'Spotty Dotty' has unusual hexagonal leaves (green in colour with dark spotty markings) and understated, dark red, bell-shaped flowers. It is a brilliant ground cover for very shaded areas. It can also be added to a border as an understory foliage plant. At Pashley we grow ours on the border of one of the lakes in full shade, where I have found that the marking and colouration on the leaf is much more prominent.

GROW Apply a generous layer of mulch during spring and remove previous year's growth after the risk of frost has passed.

Type
Rhizomatous herbaceous perennial
Flowering
Summer
Height/spread
50cm x 50cm
Position
Part shade, full shade
Soil
Moist, well-drained
Hardiness
USDA 8b/9a / RHS H4

Type
Evergreen shrub
Height/ spread
2m x 1m
Position
Full sun, part shade
Soil
Well-drained
Hardiness
USDA 9b/10a / RHS H3

Pseudopanax **'Moa's Toes'**
Lancewood 'Moa's Toes'

Native to New Zealand, many plants in the *Pseudopanax* genus are perfect for adding a tall contrasting form to any border. Their leaf shapes interest me – *P. ferox* is particularly striking, with its almost saw-blade-like leaves. I think I grew to love them after growing *P. ferox* as a child – it has now grown to about four metres tall and is currently in my parent's garden, known by my Dad as 'the dead-looking tree'. 'Moa's Toes' is a great variety – a tall, upright, evergreen shrub with unusual three-lobed leaves with red veins. They are particularly good in subtropical plantings but can also be used with more traditional shrubs and perennials, and contrast nicely with plants such as kniphofias or astelias.

GROW Prefers free-draining soil, and can tolerate exposed positions due to its slender form – wind passes through without causing too much damage. When establishing young plants I find it best to grow them on in pots for a few years until a good rootball has been established, before planting out.

Tulipa **'Queen of Night'**
Tulip 'Queen of Night'

One of the darkest tulips available, 'Queen of Night' complements most other tulips, and works particularly well with orange varieties such as 'Ballerina'. At Pashley we have grown it in several mixes throughout the garden, such as with 'Night Club', a multi-headed, dark pink tulip. You can see it at Pashley's annual Tulip Festival, where we show thousands of tulips. Recently we planted almost 45,000 tulip bulbs ready for the spring display.

GROW We replace our bulbs annually to make sure we have a good display of flowers but they can be used for a couple of years if deadheaded and fed after flowering.

Type
Bulbous perennial
Flowering
Spring
Height/ spread
50cm x 10cm
Position
Full sun
Soil
Well-drained
Hardiness
USDA 6b/7a / RHS H6

Rosa 'Geranium' (Moyesii Hybrid)
Rose 'Geranium'

One of my favourite roses. A scrambling, climbing shrub rose with single red flowers, it's perfect for pollinators. Although it only has a short flowering period, it does produce beautiful orange-red hips during the autumn months. I use it as a large specimen plant in the hot-coloured herbaceous borders to add arching height and interest.

GROW Apply a thick layer of mulch in spring and feed with a granular rose feed. Compared to other roses it requires minimal pruning (pruning group 21). Top tip: do not prune after flowering to allow the hips to appear.

Type
Shrub rose
Flowering
Spring
Height/spread
2.5m x 1.5m
Position
Full sun
Soil
Moist, well-drained
Hardiness
USDA 6b/7a / RHS H6

Type
Succulent perennial
Flowering
Spring
Height/spread
1.5m x 1.5m
Position
Full sun
Soil
Free-draining compost, ideally part potting grit and part peat-free compost
Hardiness
USDA 11 / RHS H1C

Aeonium 'Zwartkop'
Aeonium 'Zwartkop'

One of the first plants I bought as a child, this is an evergreen succulent producing rosettes of glossy black leaves that eventually produces a large flower bract with small, yellow, aster-like flowers. It's the perfect plant for adding a tropical look to an area or to be used as a large specimen for a container. At Pashley we have planted some in beds by the swimming pool and also used them as larger specimens in containers with *Persicaria runcinata* 'Purple Fantasy'.

GROW Grow in full sun for the best colouration of leaves, however it will tolerate part shade. Requires protection over winter and should be moved into a frost-free glasshouse. It is easy to propagate: simply remove a rosette, allow it to callus over and insert into free-draining compost. Water regularly during the summer and sparingly during winter.

STEPHEN HACKETT
Head gardener, Horatio's Garden South West, UK

Stephen Hackett has been head gardener at Horatio's Garden in Salisbury since 2016. He trained in horticulture after a 25-year career in further and adult education. *instagram.com/gardener_the*

Artemisia abrotanum
Southernwood

This aromatic, shrubby herb is closely associated in my mind with my favourite poet, Edward Thomas, who wrote the poem *Old Man* about it. In the poem he describes his young daughter Myfanwy picking leaves from a plant growing beside the front door and rolling them between her fingers, releasing their unusual scent, which in turn sets off a sequence of memories and thoughts.

I have always grown it by my front door, and often do the same with the leaves, as do my children. Southernwood was traditionally grown as an insect and moth repellent – sprigs could be placed in wardrobes and drawers for this purpose (its French name is *garderobe*). In summer, spikes of (not very exciting) white-yellow flowers appear. The leaves have a bitter, lemony flavour and can be used in teas and to flavour cakes and puddings. It is also a medicinal herb for a range of ailments, although it should not be taken by pregnant women.

GROW Propagates easily by cuttings taken with a heel in spring or autumn and grown in sandy/gritty soil. Needs to be pruned hard to 30cm or so in spring on a regular basis to avoid the plant becoming too lanky and woody (similar to lavender).

Type
Semi-evergreen subshrub
Flowering
Summer
Height/spread
1m x 1m
Position
Full sun, part shade
Soil
Well-drained
Hardiness
USDA 6b/7a / RHS H6

AMANDA PATTON
Garden designer,
Sussex, UK

Amanda Patton is a designer with more than 20 years experience. Her work has appeared in *Gardens Illustrated* and *Garden Design Journal* and she has received prizes from RHS Chelsea and Hampton Court Flower Shows, as well as the Society of Garden Designers. *amandapatton.co.uk*

Anthriscus sylvestris 'Ravenswing'
Cow parsley 'Ravenswing'

Many of the flowers I like to grow are late-summer bloomers, meaning late spring and early summer can be a potentially sparse time in the garden. The purple-leafed form of the native cow parsley fills this gap with a froth of delicate see-through flowers that provides a diaphanous layer throughout my herbaceous plantings. The pretty purple leaves give a good tonal contrast with the emerging greens and, as it's a short-lived perennial, also add spontaneity as the plants seed around – I'm never quite sure where they are going to emerge next. This means my otherwise static herbaceous plantings get a fresh lift and subtly different feel each spring. This plant looks wonderful against alliums – I grow two tones of the same size, *Allium hollandicum* and *A. h.* 'Purple Sensation' – and also against the leaves of the ornamental grasses.

GROW As this plant is short-lived, I plant it from 9cm pots; you don't need that many to start off with as they will seed around – just pull up where not required. I plant them randomly between herbaceous plants and grasses and just leave them to it.

Type
Short-lived perennial
Flowering
Spring, summer
Height/spread
1m x 30cm
Position
Sun, part shade
Soil
Moist, well-drained
Hardiness
USDA 6b/7a / RHS H6

Hakonechloa macra ↘
Japanese forest grass

This graceful grass is wonderful for those awkward dry shade areas. The leaves are gently arched and a lovely bright green, forming a billowing mass of texture that associates especially well with the small leaves of box or sarcococca. It is one of the first grasses to emerge in spring with dramatic new growth almost as soon as the previous season's leaves have been cut back, though there is room to plant bulbs such as the white-flowering *Narcissus* 'Thalia' between clumps as they bulk up. While it does flower, blooms come in the form of fine, light sprays and, while pretty, are not the reason to grow this grass. The main reason is the movement that it brings to a space. As the weather begins to cool in autumn, the grass takes on rich yellows and oranges, much like beech leaves, before settling to a soft brown for winter.

GROW It can be a little slow to get started and resent being moved, so plant in its ultimate position as large as you can. In times of drought the leaves can shrink to the size of a needle but don't worry, a quick and ample watering will bring it back quickly. Leave the dried leaves over winter and cut back in early spring as the new growth appears.

Type
Deciduous grass
Flowering
Summer
Height/spread
40cm x 40cm, but can spread more when happy
Position
Full sun, part shade, full shade
Soil
Moist, well-drained
Hardiness
USDA 6a–1 / RHS H7

Deschampsia cespitosa
Tufted hair grass

Type
Evergreen grass
Flowering
Summer
Height/spread
1m x 80cm
Position
Part shade, full sun
Soil
Moist, well-drained
Hardiness
USDA 6b/7a / RHS H6

Why do I love grasses so much? They bring movement and light into a garden, with every delicate seedhead capturing the slightest breeze and every drop of sunlight, especially if you place them where they will be backlit. They give varied interest through ten months of the year; they allow you to create horizontal layers in your planting, as you can see through them; and they create a unity between otherwise diverse plants within a pseudo-naturalistic plant setting.

If I could only have one grass, it would be this one. Early in the year, bright green growth emerges in a neat, vase-shaped mound that looks wonderful with spring bulbs and alliums. As the season progresses, translucent clouds of inflorescences rise up before the whole plant gradually loses its colour, associating well with late flowers such as Japanese anemones. In winter it becomes the palest of all the grasses, bringing greater interest to dark seedheads, like those of echinaceas, veronicastrums and phlomis.

GROW Easy to grow and tolerant of a range of conditions. They are evergreen, but I usually cut mine back as I would deciduous grasses in early spring to allow fresh foliage to emerge and to prevent the plant from becoming tatty.

Type
Perennial
Flowering
Summer, autumn
Height/spread
80cm x 70cm
Position
Full sun, part shade (flowering may be reduced)
Soil
Enriched, light
Hardiness
USDA 8b/9a / RHS H4

Kniphofia thomsonii var. thomsonii
Thomson's red-hot poker

Forget the rather gaudy pokers with solid flowerheads that look a bit moth-eaten as the flowers progress, this is an utterly different plant. I saw it first at Marchants Hardy Plants, a nursery in Sussex, where I immediately bought as many as I could fit in the car (not as many as I'd have liked). Once in place, it was always the plant that drew the most 'wows'. Unlike other pokers, which have a single solid head at the top of the stalk, the tube-shaped flowers of this are arranged singly at intervals along the metre-long stems, creating a much more delicate, see-through look. And the colour! A rich, warm and very soft orange that positively glows. The flowers last for months and look especially wonderful with the blue-purples of nepetas and salvias.

GROW Give it a bit of space, especially while it's establishing, and protect from winter frosts. Adding grit into planting pockets helps provide the good drainage it needs. Once happy it will romp away, but needs protection from slugs.

Sporobolus heterolepis
Prairie dropseed

Type
Deciduous grass
Flowering
Summer, autumn
Height/spread
90cm x 90cm
Position
Full sun, exposed
Soil
Grows in any soil other than heavy clay and can withstand both drought and damp
Hardiness
USDA 6a–1 / RHS H7

The scent (very unusual for a grass) struck me before I even saw this plant: heady notes of vanilla that stopped me in my tracks. I was in the Millennium Garden at Pensthorpe Natural Park designed by Piet Oudolf, it was autumn, and it didn't take long to track down the source. But scent is not its only virtue. It is one of those useful grasses with masses of airy seedheads in a warm orange that fades to pale buff in winter, creating a good foil to dark seedheads. It also has a fine texture, stays green through spring and summer and remains through winter if not cut back.

GROW It can be slow to establish but once settled it is usually long lived and trouble-free. Looks good with late-season perennials and winter seedheads – add spring bulbs to extend the season. Cut back annually in early spring.

Persicaria amplexicaulis 'Blackfield'
Red bistort 'Blackfield'

Slender wands of dark pink flowers sit high above a neat clump of large pointed leaves a little bit like dock leaves – though don't let that put you off! It generally flowers continuously from early summer to the first frosts, meaning you can always pick plenty of blooms without any noticeable effect on the plant. As the wands sit proud of the leaves, it has a delicate impression and its habit of movement, catching the light and creating layers through which other plants can be seen, allow garden designers to use it similarly to grasses. Bees absolutely love it, too.

GROW It's a bit of a thug, so give it space and be prepared to cut off chunks of root (but as these spares root easily they can be planted elsewhere). Most sources say it needs sun and moist soil but it copes well on my heavy clay, which is shady and prone to drying out. I leave mine over winter when the leaves have gone but the dark stems look like giant spiders among the borders. Cut back in early spring.

Type
Herbaceous perennial
Flowering
Summer, autumn
Height/spread
90cm x 90cm
Position
Full sun, part shade
Soil
Moist, well-drained, poorly drained
Hardiness
USDA 6a–1 / RHS H7

Phlomis russeliana
Turkish sage (SEE ILLUSTRATION PAGE 302)

I'm far more interested in the year-long effect of a plant than just its flowers. I want plants that create varied green tapestries when not in flower, plus winter interest when they have finished flowering. I'm interested in how they will work within a scheme, relating to other plants, to create something that is greater than the sum of its parts. For me, *P. russeliana* scores highly on all of these points. Large, rough-textured leaves start the season, associating well with grasses and fine-leaved plants such as box or salvias, before tall flower stems emerge with yellow-hooded flowers held in whorled clusters dotted along their length. As the flowers drop, the calyxes that held them change from green to brown, retaining their strongly architectural form right through the winter.

GROW If you find the leaves too heavy-looking, plant them further back within your borders allowing something soft such as deschampsia or crocosmias – especially the warm yellow ones – to grow in front. Do plant with grasses as the winter effect is magical. It doesn't like winter wet, so improve drainage before planting if your soil is heavy.

Type
Herbaceous perennial
Flowering
Summer, autumn
Height/spread
70cm x 40cm
Position
Full sun, though tolerates some shade
Soil
Moist, well-drained
Hardiness
USDA 6b/7a / RHS H6

Pittosporum tenuifolium 'Tom Thumb'
Tawhiwhi 'Tom Thumb'

I'm interested in creating gardens with an emphasis on tonal contrasts, and dark-leafed plants are very useful in this respect. 'Tom Thumb' is naturally small and rounded, so I sometimes use it in place of box ball to underplant a tree or larger shrub and infill around with grasses. It looks especially good with the warm colour of *Anemanthele lessoniana* – the two make a good winter combination as both are evergreen. While 'Tom Thumb' generally doesn't flower, in spring the textured small leaves emerge a bright green before darkening as the season progresses, giving the bush a vibrancy and change of appearance not often seen in evergreen shrubs. It's a lovely plant to drift among see-through perennials and grasses to give rhythm and structure to a meadow or prairie-style planting.

GROW It's slow growing and naturally mounded so doesn't require any pruning, unless to remove damaged branches, though this is rare as it has a dense, self-supporting habit. A low-maintenance plant.

Type
Evergreen shrub
Flowering
Spring, summer
Height/spread
70cm x 70cm
Position
The leaves colour best in full sun but can take some shade, needs protection from cold, drying winds
Soil
Any, other than heavy clay
Hardiness
USDA 8b/9a / RHS H4

SEAN HARKIN
Head gardener, Inner
Temple, London, UK

Sean Harkin previously ran the gardens at Kensington Palace, where he created a white garden in memory of Diana, Princess of Wales. He has also managed the Herbaceous Ornamental Team at RHS Wisley. He is head gardener of the historic Inner Temple, which has been gardened since 1307. *innertemple.org.uk*

Erigeron karvinskianus
Mexican fleabane

E. karvinskianus is unassuming compared to the more flamboyant stars of the garden, though I love its carefree ability to self-seed in any sunny cracks or walls and its soft, low billows of dainty daisy flowers in shades of white to blush-pink. I first came across it when working as a seasonal gardener at Hestercombe in Somerset where it was the perfect companion, dressing the magnificent Edwin Lutyens stonework. Since then I have enjoyed it at Wisley, where it softens the Arts and Crafts-style Laboratory Building.

Mexican fleabane flowers for nine months of the year or longer and I enjoy how the small flowers take on hues of pinks with the heat. At Inner Temple we are encouraging the colonies to spread to soften the grand buildings and stone features of the garden. Thankfully it does not harm any stonework and gives the garden a spontaneity alongside our other favoured self-seeders.

GROW I find it totally pest free and beneficial to lots of pollinators, including the small blue butterfly – they're the perfect partners. It is good for softening garden features such as walls or steps. It's also useful as a ground cover in poor soils in full sun with bulbs and other drought-tolerant plants emerging. Self-seeded plants are generally more resilient than planted ones.

The plant enjoys the heat of walls, so grow it in cracks of stonework or buildings. To achieve this, rather than sprinkling seed into areas, I plant some near where I want them to colonise, either in the ground or in pots. Make sure not to weed out or spray herbicides so the seedlings can emerge where they have found their home.

It can take some shade, but will not colour pink or thrive as it does in full sun. We generally cut back in late winter to get a fresh flush but the plant doesn't necessarily need anything – in some areas we just leave it alone.

Type
Perennial
Flowering
Spring,
summer,
autumn
**Height/
spread**
50cm x 1m
Position
Full sun
Soil
Doesn't
need much
soil once
self-seeded
Hardiness
USDA 7b/8a
/ RHS H5

ALAN GREY
Gardener and
broadcaster, Norfolk, UK

Alan Grey presented gardening show *Take A Leaf*, and hosts a gardening programme for BBC Radio Norfolk, as well as writing for various gardening publications.

Brugmansia
Angel's trumpet

My granny grew this as a pot plant, but I wanted it to be a tree, so I now grow it in very large containers. In summer, each plant is covered in up to 250 blooms.

GROW Feed, feed, feed! They are very greedy, so feed with a fertiliser diluted to half the strength at every watering.

Type
Evergreen shrub
Flowering
Summer, autumn
Height/spread
4m x 2.5m
Position
Full sun, sheltered
Soil
Loam-based
compost, neutral pH
Hardiness
USDA 11 / RHS H1c

ROBERT VERNON
Co-owner, Bluebell
Arboretum & Nursery,
Derbyshire, UK

Robert Vernon and his wife Suzette started Bluebell Arboretum & Nursery after meeting as students in 1969. The nursery is now managed by their son Bob and daughter-in-law Rachel, who continue to develop the arboretum. *bluebellnursery.com*

Cornus kousa 'Miss Satomi'
Kousa 'Miss Satomi'

There are lots of (arguably too many) fine, white-flowered cultivars of the Asiatic *C. kousa* worth growing but the sensational 'Miss Satomi' is special. Established plants are covered in fabulous rich pink flower bracts in mid-summer. These are followed by lychee-like fruits and in autumn the foliage colours well, especially in lime-free soil. *C. kousa* is native to China, Korea and Japan. This variety is a Japanese selection and was named after the granddaughter of the nurseryman who raised it.

GROW Like all flowering dogwoods, 'Miss Satomi' does best in full sun – hot summers stimulate free-flowering the following year. It does well in containers planted in an equal parts mixture of John Innes No.3 and ericaceous compost.

Type
Deciduous shrub
Flowering
Summer
Height/spread
6m x 6m
Position
Full sun, part shade
Soil
Moist, well drained, suitable for most reasonable soils but won't flourish on chalk
Hardiness
USDA 6b/7a / RHS H6

Type
Deciduous tree
Flowering
Spring
Height/spread
4m x 3m
Position
Full sun, part shade, sheltered
Soil
Moist, well-drained, slightly acid
Hardiness
USDA 9b/10a / RHS H3

Magnolia 'Vairano'
Magnolia 'Vairano'

A stunning, recently introduced magnolia raised in New Zealand, but named by Reto Eisenhut in Switzerland. The clear pink, dinner-plate-sized flowers are borne on relatively young plants in spring.

GROW After flowering, the dead flowers conveniently drop off rather than hanging on like unsightly used tea bags.

Prunus 'Jacqueline'
Flowering cherry 'Jacqueline'

Among the 400 plus cultivars of Japanese cherries in cultivation in the UK, 'Jacqueline' is top rank. She was raised as a seedling from various parent plants growing at Kalmthout Arboretum in Belgium and collected by the famous dendrologists Robert and Jelena de Belder. The flowers are a vibrant pink and it has excellent autumn colours.

GROW Choose a sheltered spot in full sun.

Type
Deciduous tree
Flowering
Spring
Height/spread
3m x 5m
Position
Full sun
Soil
Moist, well-drained
Hardiness
USDA 6b/7a / RHS H6

Type
Evergreen tree
Height/spread
80m x 10m
Position
Full sun, part shade
Soil
Well-drained
Hardiness
USDA 6b/7a / RHS H6

Sequoiadendron giganteum
Giant redwood

Who can't wonder at the beauty and magnificence of these venerable natural giants from western North America? There are now over 60 established in our arboretum. The first one, planted on March 11 1992, when only 15cm high, now stands over 18m tall but, of course, in tree terms it's still barely adolescent.

GROW It can take 50 years to reach full maturity.

Frangula alnus
Alder buckthorn

The native alder buckthorn is superb for conservation areas and good for mixed native hedgerows. Although it's not the most ornamental plant in our arboretum, it does have pretty mustard-yellow autumn tints that show as its red berries turn black. But what's important about this plant is that it's one of only two shrub species (the other is *Rhamnus cathartica*) on which our lovely, sulphur-yellow brimstone butterflies can breed.

GROW It can be grown as a large shrub or, with little trouble, can be made into a handsome small tree with a single trunk.

Type
Deciduous shrub
Flowering
Spring, summer
Height/spread
4m x 4m
Position
Full sun, part shade
Soil
Moist, well-drained
Hardiness
USDA 6a–1 / RHS H7

Wisteria brachybotrys 'Okayama'
Silky wisteria 'Okayama'

This wisteria is from Japan (Okayama is a city and prefecture west of Kyoto) and stands out when its fragrant, violet flowers contrast with the coppery, young foliage. Splendid when grown on a wall, pergola or through a tree.

GROW Wisterias are members of the *Leguminosae* family, which have nitrogen-fixing bacteria in their roots. Creating their own fertility, they dislike artificial fertilisers and can prefer poor soils. Responds well to pruning in late summer.

Type
Perennial climber
Flowering
Summer
Height/spread
18m x 8m
Position
Full sun, part shade, sheltered
Soil
Moist, well-drained
Hardiness
USDA 6b/7a / RHS H6

GABRIELA SALAZAR
Florist and gardener, Valle de Bravo, Mexico

Gabriela Salazar is the founder of world-renowned floral design studio La Musa de las Flores. High in the Mexican mountains, she grows cut flowers to create romantic arrangements that echo the relationship between design and nature. *lamusadelasflores.com*

Type
Tuberous perennial
Flowering
Summer, autumn
Height/spread
2.5m x 30cm
Position
Full sun
Soil
Moist, well-drained, rich in organic matter
Hardiness
USDA 9b/10a / RHS H3

Dahlia ⬊
Dahlia

I live in Valle de Bravo, a small town two hours from Mexico City, but my fascination with flowers started in the UK, where I lived for five years. When I moved back to Mexico, I began my own garden. In Mexico we grow a lot of vibrant plants, but they don't have the soft colours and romantic charm of those I had fallen for in England. Dahlias and cosmos were already growing wild around here (dahlia is the national flower of Mexico), so I knew then that dahlias were going to thrive. I decided to grow all the varieties I loved the most, like 'Cafe au Lait' and the pompon types, and to use these in my arrangements to bring together the soft aesthetic I fell for with the vibrancy of my home country.

GROW I grow dahlias as annuals because my garden is small and I need to grow other flowers while my dahlias are sleeping. I fertilise with rich humus when I plant and apply a mulch two months later. I also apply horticultural oil every week and cut the lower leaves for ventilation to protect the plant from powdery mildew.

DAVID LAUGHLIN
Curator manager, Royal Botanic Garden Sydney, Australia

David Laughlin started life in rural Ireland surrounded by woodland and has had a fascination with the natural world ever since. In his current role at the Royal Botanic Garden Sydney, he works with world-leading plant collections. *rbgsyd.nsw.gov.au*

Bismarckia nobilis →
Bismarck palm

The Royal Botanic Garden Sydney is known for its palm collection, including 18 of the 30 rarest palms in the world. My favourite palm is not rare, but it is majestic and rewarding to grow. *B. nobilis* is the only species in the genus *Bismarckia*. I love these solitary trunked palms for their huge silver fronds and stunning form that make a statement in the landscape.

GROW These stately palms grow slowly at first, taking years to develop a trunk. Mature palms do not like to be transplanted and will sulk for many years after transplanting, so when planting a young palm try to ensure it is in its final position. You need a male and female to produce viable seed for propagation. It is adaptable to a range of soil, but if you live in temperate regions, unfortunately this is not the palm for you as they don't like frost. They do have a very high tolerance for heat. Generally easy to grow given adequate drainage and a sunny position.

Type
Palm tree
Flowering
Spring, summer
Height/ spread
15m x 6m
Position
Full sun
Soil
Well-drained
Hardiness
USDA 12 / RHS H1b

Anigozanthos rufus 'Kings Park Federation Flame'
Kangaroo paw 'Kings Park Federation Flame'

The kangaroo paw is an iconic Australian plant and, with its spectacular and unusual flowers, one of my favourites. This fantastic cultivar was developed to celebrate the Centenary of Federation of Australia in 2001 and after many years of trials, it was finally released in 2009. It has proven to be one of the best-performing and adaptable Australian plants and I always try to include it in borders where its height adds structure. It is also attractive to birds and insects. The strappy foliage is grey-green, creating a beautiful contrast to the bright orange flowers, which also make excellent, long-lasting cut flowers.

GROW Drought-resistant and tolerant of light frosts, kangaroo paws are often grown as annuals due to their susceptibility to fungal disease ink spot. The wonderful thing about 'Kings Park Federation Flame' is that it has minimal disease issues. These are low-maintenance plants requiring only that the spent flowers be cut back to ground level. Apply a slow-release plant fertiliser annually in autumn. After establishment, water only in extended dry periods. Adaptable to a range of zones from subtropical to cool temperate.

Type
Perennial
Flowering
Spring, summer
Height/ spread
1.5m x 1m
Position
Full sun
Soil
Well-drained, acid
Hardiness
USDA 9b/10a / RHS H3

Type
Herbaceous perennial
Flowering
Spring
Height/ spread
1m x 50cm
Position
Full sun
Soil
Well-drained, slightly acid pH of 5.5
Hardiness
USDA 11 / RHS H1c

Actinotus helianthi
Flannel flower

The seeds of flannel flowers germinate rapidly after fire – their regrowth is one of the signs of recovery after wildfires. Seeing wild groups of the velvety silver flowers on a bush walk is such a joy. It can be found growing in southeast Australia and is becoming a popular garden plant with wonderful cultivars such as 'Federation Star' and 'Starbright' developed. It has beautiful and unusual star-shaped flowers with delicate, lobed, grey foliage.

GROW Grows best in a spot with protection from wind as the delicate stems break easily. Surprisingly for a plant from the poor soils around Sydney, it has relatively high fertiliser needs. The most important requirement is good drainage as it will not tolerate wet feet. A light prune after flowering will help keep the plant more compact. Keep an eye out for pests such as aphids, scale insects and mealybugs during spring and summer.

Type
Evergreen tree
Flowering
Summer
Height/ spread
20m x 15m
Position
Full sun
Soil
Tolerant, but prefers a sandy soil
Hardiness
USDA 11 / RHS H1c

Angophora costata
Smooth-barked apple

This is an iconic tree around Sydney harbour. With its gnarled trunk, pink bark and pretty white flowers, it is stunning to see in the landscape. The mature bark of smooth-barked apple trees sheds in late spring, revealing a magnificent fresh salmon-pink colour underneath, but they look their best in early summer with the morning or late afternoon sun reflecting off their bark, which makes them glow. This tree is a true icon of the Sydney region.

GROW Best grown from seed, this is a very drought-tolerant tree with few problems once established. They are large trees with extensive root systems and a majestic spreading canopy, so it's best not to plant close to buildings or underground services. The main problem this tree encounters is the root-rot fungus *Phytophthora cinnamomi*, which is prevalent around Sydney and has killed many of these iconic trees.

Millettia grandis
Umzimbeet

One of my first memories of the Royal Botanic Garden Sydney was the spectacular sight of *M. grandis* in flower. Shortly after starting my apprenticeship I came across this southern African beauty and it's been a highlight of late spring ever since. Often known as tree wisteria, this tree in its full glory when covered in purple flowers; it is a wonder of nature. These flowers are followed by decorative velvety brown seed pods.

GROW When grown in fertile deep soil with ample water it makes a fine small-to medium-sized tree. It will also tolerate sandy soils and some shade but will grow taller and flower more prolifically in full sun. Young trees are fast growing and need careful training to form a balanced canopy. In the *Fabaceae* family, these trees have nitrogen-fixing bacteria on their roots, which adds nutrients to the surrounding soil. After initial establishment it only needs good drainage and regular watering. It benefits from an application of compost or well-rotted leaf and wood chip mulch annually in spring.

Type
Semi-deciduous tree
Flowering
Spring, summer
Height/spread
25m x 6m
Position
Full sun, part shade
Soil
Rich, loamy, well-drained with a slightly acidic pH
Hardiness
USDA 11 / RHS H1c

Type
Epiphytic cactus
Flowering
Spring
Height/ spread
Trailing to 1m
Position
Part shade, some direct sun
Soil
Free-draining container media such as orchid mix
Hardiness
USDA 12 / RHS H1b

Rhipsalis campos-portoana
Jungle cactus

There are about 39 species of rhipsalis and they are all either epiphytic (living their lives in trees) or lithophytes (living on rocks). I could have picked any number of these great plants, which I love for their versatility and the tropical look they provide. I use them everywhere, from indoors to hanging baskets and in my vertical wall garden. They are great for people who live in apartments and don't have a lot of space, but want a beautiful cascading green plant to soften an urban environment. Mostly grown for their foliage, they also produce small white flowers in spring followed by red-orange berry-like fruit.

GROW These plants are very easy to propagate from cuttings. Just shove a few cuttings in some potting mix and they will produce roots in no time. They are incredibly easy to grow and will even forgive you if you occasionally forget to water. The main tip is to make sure their roots are in a well-drained media, as they don't like sitting in water. They enjoy a warm position with morning sun or bright indirect light. I mist my plants daily in summer to raise the humidity level. To keep them growing vigorously and looking their best give them a monthly application of half-strength liquid fertiliser in spring and summer. In subtropical and tropical climates they will grow well outdoors in a semi-shaded position.

Encephalartos horridus
Eastern Cape blue cycad

Type
Cycad
Flowering
Summer
Height/ spread
80cm x 40cm
Position
Full sun, part shade
Soil
Very well-drained with a slightly acidic pH
Hardiness
USDA 9b/10a / RHS H3

At the Royal Botanic Garden Sydney, we have an extensive cycad collection. This cycad has stunning rigid armoured leaves that mean they must be handled with care. These cycads are listed as endangered in the wild, due mostly to over-collecting, which is now not such a problem as there are plentiful supplies in cultivation. In nature they are only found in a few districts of South Africa's Eastern Cape. I love the look of this one – it is an architecturally striking plant that makes a bold statement in the garden. It's also the bluest of all the cycads and is grown for its stunning foliage. There are male and female plants, with the males producing a cylindrical blue-green cone that tapers off at both ends, while the female cone is egg-shaped and produces pale red seeds.

GROW The most important thing to note with cycads is that all parts of the plant are toxic to mammals and they need to be handled with care. The seeds, cones and pollen are particularly toxic and we always wear chemical-resistant gloves and face masks when handling. Eastern Cape blue cycad also has vicious teeth on its leaves, making it unsuitable for gardens with pets or young children. I guess I'm not really selling this cycad to you, but now for the good parts!

These are easy-to-grow plants with few pests and diseases. They will tolerate mild frosts and take extreme heat. They make excellent potted plants for a sunny courtyard and will certainly become a talking point in the garden. They do require perfect drainage and will benefit from occasional watering during dry periods. Potted plants will dry out faster than in-ground plants, so it's best to water potted plants weekly in summer. During winter the cycads reduce their growth and require much less water, and often natural rainfall is sufficient. They will benefit from a light application of fertiliser during the growing season. Ideal for temperate and subtropical climates.

Type
Evergreen tree
Flowering
Spring, summer
Height/ spread
15m x 4m
Position
Full sun
Soil
Sandy, pH 5.5–7.5
Hardiness
USDA 10b / RHS H2

Banksia serrata
Saw banksia

One of my first experiences in Australia was watching rainbow lorikeets drinking nectar from the flowers of this plant on a fine summer's day. In the heat of summer the nectar ferments and becomes alcoholic – the birds became drunk, staggering around and falling out of the tree having a great old time! Parrots seem to behave similarly to humans when drunk but hopefully don't suffer similar side effects the next day. This was one of the funniest things I had ever seen and I have loved the plant ever since. It is a small, gnarly tree with attractive cream cylindrical flowers. The bark of mature plants is corky and is a distinctive feature.

GROW These plants are members of the *Proteaceae* family, with proteoid roots meaning they have evolved to be efficient at mining nutrients such as phosphorus from infertile soils. Care must be taken when fertilising banksias, as too much phosphorus will be toxic due to their ability to extract it so efficiently. Fertilise with low-phosphorus fertilisers only, such as blood and bone. Mature plants are fire-tolerant and reshoot from epicormic shoots that lie dormant under the thick protective bark until stimulated into regrowth by fire. These small trees require a well-drained sandy soil and a sunny position. Extra water during drought periods will be required.

CONRAD MCCORMICK
Garden designer, Antrim Coast, Northern Ireland

A garden designer and journalist, Conrad McCormick features on TV show *Gardening Together* and contributes to BBC Radio Ulster's *Gardeners' Corner*. He has a passion for exotic plants. *instagram.com/thatbotanicguy*

Pseudopanax crassifolius
Lancewood

This is a fantastic small tree, though not everyone appreciates its otherworldly appearance. I often think that if Dr Seuss were to draw a tree, this is how it would look. It grows as a single, slender trunk with stiff, leathery, dark brown leaves that are 1cm wide and 90cm long. These are toothed, though not as fierce as they may initially appear. It keeps this juvenile form for ten to 15 years, after which it begins to branch at the top and assume a more tree-like shape with shorter leaves. It's thought that it may have adopted this unusual appearance to avoid being eaten by the giant moa, a now extinct flightless bird from New Zealand. Once safely above the moa's height, it was able to transform into a slightly more 'normal' tree.

GROW *P. crassifolius* is fantastic among lower shrubs and perennials, provides vertical exclamations but is light in structure and form, so casts little shade on the companions around its feet. Several planted in a grove can give an exotic look to the garden. They can live happily for many years in a pot and are tolerant of infrequent watering.

Type
Evergreen tree
Flowering
Summer, autumn
Height/ spread
12m x 2.5m
Position
Full sun, part shade, sheltered
Soil
Well-drained
Hardiness
USDA 8b/9a / RHS H4

Type
Herbaceous rhizomatous perennial
Flowering
Spring, summer
Height/spread
1.5m x 1.5m
Position
Full sun, part shade, sheltered
Soil
Fertile, moist
Hardiness
USDA 9b/10a / RHS H3

Hedychium densiflorum 'Stephen'
Dense ginger lily 'Stephen'

Evocative of steamy jungles, the delicately scented, creamy, butterscotch-yellow flower spikes of this ginger lily appear reliably over leafy stems in late summer each year. Many hedychiums don't bloom in northerly latitudes as the growing season isn't long enough, but despite its delicate looks this one's tough, growing and thriving outdoors even in chilly climes.

GROW While it will survive in leaner conditions, it needs rich living to give its best, so ensure the soil is beefed up with plenty of compost and well-rotted manure. It can be grown in a large container which is overwintered and put outdoors in summer. Mulch in spring and in cold areas over winter, and feed with slow-release fertiliser. Propagate by division in late spring, just as it's coming into growth.

Schefflera taiwaniana
Taiwanese schefflera

Many of us know the ubiquitous indoor umbrella plant, *Schefflera arboricola*, having either grown it or seen it in a dentist's waiting room. *S. taiwaniana* comes from mountainous areas and is its hardy and classy cousin. Elegant and incredibly unusual, it lends a pseudo-tropical vibe to the garden. New leaves appear in late spring, covered in a fine down-like coating of white hairs, like little hands reaching for the sky. As they mature, the deep green leaflets are delicately arranged like the spokes of a wheel, balanced with poise on long petioles.

GROW I've grown it in dense, dry shade under the canopy of a large *Acer pseudoplatanus*, where it flourished despite the adverse conditions. In my new garden it is thriving in improved clay, where it has already grown 2.5m tall by 2m wide. It's best to keep it sheltered from cold, drying winds, but it is surprisingly tolerant of cold. Mulch with well-rotted compost in spring. Pruning is unnecessary unless required to keep it within bounds. Do not mulch scheffleras with manure of any form – it can spell disaster, as I've learned to my cost.

Type
Evergreen tree or shrub
Flowering
Summer
Height/spread
4m x 2.5m
Position
Part shade, full shade, though can take more sun at northerly latitudes
Soil
Moist, well-drained, though surprisingly tolerant of dry conditions
Hardiness
USDA 8b/9a / RHS H4

94

JULIET SARGEANT
Garden designer and founder, Sussex Garden School, East Sussex, UK

Juliet Sargeant's previous career in medicine and psychology informs her people-orientated approach to design. She is on the RHS Show Garden selection panel and a judge. She won an RHS Chelsea Flower Show gold medal for her ground-breaking Modern Slavery Garden in 2017 and has featured on the BBC 100 Women list. *julietsargeant.com*

Hebe parviflora var. *angustifolia*
Narrow-leaved hebe

Much of my work is about problem-solving – in particular, trying to find the right plants for tricky garden spots where nothing else will grow. This plant is one of my secret weapons; it is really tough but has a delicacy that belies its bullet-proof nature. As its common name suggests, it has narrow, willow-like leaves. Unlike most evergreens, its leaf colour is a fresh green, so it looks almost like bamboo. It won't flower in shade, but for me that is not a problem because its appeal is not in its white flowers, but in what you can do with it. If left alone, the plant will grow over 2m tall, but you can clip it into box-like balls or even use it as a clipped hedge. The more light it has, the bushier it will be. If you want a freshness and lightness for the evergreen structure of your garden, this is the plant for you.

GROW *H. parviflora* sprouts from almost anywhere on its stem but try to clip it little and often, rather than stressing it by cutting into thick branches. Not to be confused with *H. stenophylla*, which looks similar but has been found to have different chromosomes.

Type
Evergreen shrub
Flowering
Summer
Height/spread
1.5m x 2m
Position
Full sun, part shade, full shade
Soil
Moist, well-drained
Hardiness
USDA 7b/8a / RHS H5

Type
Aquatic perennial
Flowering
Summer
Height/spread
20cm x 30cm
Position
Full sun, part shade
Soil
In water at least 50cm deep
Hardiness
USDA 6b/7a / RHS H6

Stratiotes aloides
Water soldier

We often think native UK plants are uninteresting, but I love the weirdness of the water soldier. As a child, I used to look out for it in my mother's pond in spring. It has the strange habit of bobbing to the surface, where it is a favourite of dragonfly nymphs. They like to climb on to its erect, sword-like leaves, where they undergo their larval moult and fly away as adults. As the weather turns at the end of summer, the water soldier sinks below the surface to rest over winter, before popping up again the next year.

GROW Very easy to grow. Spreads easily, sometimes too easily (it is considered invasive in Northern Ireland). Can be brittle and difficult to handle at certain times of year, so wait until it is large and strong enough if you are dividing or moving.

Coprosma repens 'Pina Colada'
Looking-glass plant 'Pina Colada'

As a horticulturist I wince a little when I see plastic plants, but I love *C. repens*, because it is a real shrub disguising itself as plastic and gives wonderful autumnal tones all through the year. The small, colourful leaves are so shiny that they could easily fool, and the variety names alone are reason enough to have them in your garden: 'Pina Colada', 'Tequila Sunrise', 'Rainbow Surprise'! There are very few colourful evergreens, but this brings the bling to the plant world. I particularly like to pair 'Pina Colada' with bright orange and yellow flowers or to combine it with autumnal grasses; it picks up on the sienna and umber tones.

GROW It does not like to be overshadowed by other plants and loses its leaves on one side if placed too close to a neighbour. Responds well to feeding. Needs little pruning. Prefers neutral to slightly acid soil, but mine do well in chalk, as long as they are fed well and kept moist enough.

Type
Evergreen shrub
Height/spread
1.5m x 1.5m
Position
Full sun
Soil
Moist, well-drained
Hardiness
USDA 9b/10a / RHS H3

MIRANDA JANATKA
Garden writer,
Bedfordshire, UK

Miranda Janatka is a staff writer for *Gardeners' World* magazine.
Prior to that she trained and worked as a botanical horticulturist at the
Royal Botanic Gardens, Kew, caring for rare and endangered plants.
instagram.com/miranda.janatka

Davidia involucrata
Handkerchief tree (SEE ILLUSTRATION PAGE 313)

This is a gorgeous medium-sized tree, often found in botanic gardens but for some reason less seen elsewhere. Called the handkerchief or dove tree, it's covered with white handkerchief-like blooms in spring that flutter in the breeze – an incredible sight to behold.

While studying and working at Kew I fell in love with more than just the plants. My now partner was working in the arboretum nursery when I met him and he taught me the magic of grafting plants. You make delicate but powerful surgical incisions into the stems of two plants, one chosen for its strong roots, the other a shoot from a mother plant you want to grow on. You then bind these together and use wax to cover the wound. If you do your work well, the two plants merge and grow on as one. Family apple trees, which produce several different varieties of fruit simultaneously on the same plant, are made this way. We chose the handkerchief tree to graft because, much like wisteria, it won't flower until mature, so grafting allows you to have blooms on a small tree just a couple of years old. I practised my cuts endlessly before I was finally trusted to work with live material. It worked first time. The handkerchief tree I grafted now grows and blooms proudly in our front garden, reminding us fondly of our magical days at Kew.

GROW Plant in a sheltered spot with plenty of woodland flowers and spring bulbs underneath. When planting work lots of well-rotted garden compost into the ground first and stake for the first few years. Prune in autumn to remove any broken, diseased or crossing branches.

Type
Deciduous tree
Flowering
Spring
Height/ spread
15m x 10m
Position
Full sun, part shade, sheltered
Soil
Moist, well-drained
Hardiness
USDA 7b/8a / RHS H5

Rosa banksiae 'Lutea'
Double yellow banksia rose

A rose without thorns! While the flowering period is only a few weeks, the sight of this rambling rose smothered in double yellow flowers is glorious. Lightly scented, it can be grown along a fence, up a wall, through a tree or used to cover an arch or pergola. At the Alhambra in Spain, it's grown to great effect below a layer of hanging wisteria, and at Waterperry Gardens in Oxford it's been allowed to take over a yew tree. This is an easy plant to grow that provides a lot of colour and delight in the garden, but doesn't require as much feeding and care as other roses to create a magnificent and wonderfully wild-looking display.

GROW Prune well to keep from taking over. Once mature, cut one in three of the oldest stems back to the base of the plant each year and tie in new stems for best flowering. Also ensure it has a structure or plant to grow against for support. Top-dress the soil with compost or general-purpose fertiliser to encourage blooms after planting. Water generously until established and mulch in spring, keeping mulch away from the base of the plant to prevent rotting.

Type
Rambler rose
Flowering
Spring, summer
Height/ spread
12m x 4m
Position
Full sun, sheltered
Soil
Moist, well-drained, humus-rich
Hardiness
USDA 7b/8a / RHS H5

SIMON BAGNALL
Head of gardens and grounds, Worcester College, Oxford, UK

Simon Bagnall leads a team of eight gardeners and is responsible for the development and maintenance of the 26-acre, Grade II*-listed garden at Worcester College, Oxford. He also works as a consultant and mentor. *instagram.com/worcestercollegegardener*

Pelargonium tomentosum ↘

Peppermint geranium

This incredible plant is top of my favourites list because of its wonderful apple-green leaves. It is easy to grow and has a willing rambling habit. Unlike its showier cousins, it has small, rather understated white flowers, which are produced abundantly. But what it lacks in flower power it makes up for in gorgeous leaf form, texture and scent. The leaves are roughly heart-shaped, velvety to touch and produce a gorgeous rich peppermint scent when crushed.

P. tomentosum looks wonderful planted alone in big pots or can be used as a foil for other plants. I grow it in the front of borders or near seating where students, fellows and visitors can touch its wonderful downy leaves and enjoy its scent. I have plants that go back 20 generations or more, which is a joy as they have followed me on my botanical journey. I love to grow it with *Plectranthus ciliatus* 'Nico' – the two plants are great bed buddies and the leaf types work brilliantly together.

GROW I propagate it from softwood cuttings in early autumn – three cuttings, each approximately 10cm long, to a 9cm pot. Place in gritty seed compost and mist very occasionally. The cuttings root quickly and are potted on in spring ready for planting out once the risk of frost has passed.

I've found it to be an unfussy plant, growing well in most soil types or good-quality composts. Water weekly through the summer, but allow the compost to dry out between watering. Feed weekly with high potash feed.

Type
Perennial
Flowering
Summer
Height/spread
1m x 1m
Position
Full sun, part shade
Soil
Well-drained, alkaline, neutral
Hardiness
USDA 11 / RHS H1c

FIONA EDMOND
Owner and designer, Green Island Gardens, Essex, UK

Formerly an international golfer, Fiona Edmond now runs Green Island Gardens, works as a freelance garden designer, and gives talks and runs courses. In 2019 she was awarded National Plant Collection status for her collections of *Hamamelis* and *Camellia*. *greenislandgardens.co.uk*

Trachelospermum jasminoides
Star jasmine

This ticks all the boxes for me: it is evergreen, a self-clinging climber, produces a profusion of white flowers with a heavenly scent all summer, and the leaves turn orange-red in autumn. It is low maintenance, disease- and pest-resistant, and will happily grow in a pot. Despite all the books saying it should be grown on a south-facing wall, for me it grows equally well against south- and north-facing walls. It flowers a week or so later on the north face, prolonging the weeks of enjoyment I have of its heady scent.

GROW If it gets too big or outgrows its space I just take a pair of shears to it in spring. Best in acid soil that is moist but well-drained.

Type
Evergreen climber
Flowering
Summer
Height/spread
12m x 7m
Position
Full sun, part shade
Soil
Well-drained, acid
Hardiness
USDA 8b/9a / RHS H4

Daphne bholua 'Jaqueline Postill'
Daphne 'Jaqueline Postill'

An upright evergreen shrub that flowers from around Christmas until well into spring, this produces clusters of tubular, pale lilac flowers with an intoxicating scent that is readily released around the garden. Daphnes can be temperamental plants to get going, often flowering themselves to death, and they have a propensity to just keel over and die for no apparent reason. *D. bholua* 'Jaqueline Postill' is the easiest and most reliable in my opinion. It is disease- and pest-resistant, needs little to no maintenance, and in my humus-rich soil readily throws up suckers that can be cut off to make new plants. In fact, in some areas of the garden it is putting in a takeover bid, but I love it so much that I just let it get on with it.

GROW Books would have you believe it doesn't like to be pruned, but I cut huge branches off to bring inside so I can enjoy the scent in the house during the winter months.

Type
Evergreen shrub
Flowering
Winter, spring
Height/spread
2.5m x 1.5m
Position
Full sun, part shade, sheltered
Soil
Well-drained
Hardiness
USDA 8b/9a / RHS H4

Type
Evergreen shrub
Flowering
Autumn, winter
Height/spread
4m x 2.5m
Position
Sun or part sun
Soil
Moist, well-drained
Hardiness
USDA 8b/9a / RHS H4

Camellia sasanqua 'Hugh Evans'
Camellia 'Hugh Evans'

Forming an attractive evergreen shrub with pointed green leaves, often red when new, this variety is simply covered in a profusion of single pink flowers with lovely yellow stamens and a delicate scent from late autumn to the end of winter. Unlike their showier spring-flowering camellia relatives, the flowers of autumn-flowering camellias are not spoiled by frosts and are not held on the shrub when past their best. I have selected 'Hugh Evans' as it is such a prolific flowerer, and for so many months. It can also be grown as an informal hedge.

GROW Autumn-flowering camellias are much more tolerant of less acidic soils than the spring-flowering varieties and flower from a young age.

Hamamelis × intermedia 'Pallida'
Witch hazel 'Pallida'

I first fell in love with hamamelis when we lived in London in the late 1980s, where I think in hindsight I was a bit like a caged bird. I found my escape in the Isabella Plantation (a woodland garden) in Richmond Park, which was later to become a great inspiration for my own garden. In the depths of winter, when there was little else flowering in most people's gardens, I was blown away by the magical presence of the witch hazels there, with their curious, spidery, many-petalled flowers in shades of yellow, orange and red, totally unspoiled by whatever the winter weather threw at them. The spicy, fruity scents are an added bonus, as are the autumn colours the leaves turn when grown in sun.

I have learned that, as a general rule of thumb, for scent you need to go for the paler yellow flowers, and if it's autumn colour you're after then choose a red or darker orange variety such as 'Diane'. It's very hard to select just one, but the first one I fell in love with was 'Pallida', which often starts flowering in late autumn before the buttery yellow leaves have fallen, and continues flowering until spring.

GROW Even in the summer when they are not at their showy best, they provide an attractive spreading shrub with rounded hazel-like leaves. For those with small gardens they can easily be grown in pots and pruned to restrict their size without compromising on flowers or leaf colour.

Type
Deciduous shrub
Flowering
Winter
Height/ spread
4m x 4m
Position
Full sun, part shade
Soil
Well-drained
Hardiness
USDA 7b/8a / RHS H5

Acer palmatum 'Chitose-yama'
Japanese maple 'Chitose-yama'

I love acers and have lost count of how many different varieties I have in my garden, but if I had to choose just one then this would be it. Forming an elegant rounded shrub, its architectural presence is valuable even in winter when it has no leaves. In spring the new leaves emerge a pretty dusky pink, which in my garden look lovely against the backdrop of the *Photinia × fraseri* 'Red Robin' hedge. Small green flowers are insignificant but are followed by attractive red-winged seeds in summer. The seven-lobed leaves mature to a greeny-brown before turning the most brilliant crimson in autumn.

GROW Like all acers it is best grown in sun to get the best autumn colour. Also good in pots, acers require little to no maintenance and are a valuable addition to the garden year-round. This one is no exception.

Type
Deciduous shrub
Flowering
Spring
Height/ spread
2.5m x 2.5m
Position
Full sun, part sun
Soil
Moist, well-drained
Hardiness
USDA 6b/7a / RHS H6

Pittosporum tenuifolium 'Tom Thumb'
Tawhiwhi 'Tom Thumb'

This isn't the most obvious choice or the most showy plant, but it is a stalwart in all my gardens. Naturally forming a ball-shaped, purple-leaved evergreen shrub, it is invaluable in design terms for its shape and colour, lending itself to the repeat planting around the curved borders in my gardens. The tiny rounded leaves of the new growth are bright green, maturing slowly to dark purple, making it a firm favourite with flower arrangers. Flowers are insignificant, but as with many plants I grow it is in the leaves and structure of the plant that I see the true value.

GROW It can be clipped to restrict its size or even grown as a hedge, making it a good alternative to box.

Type
Evergreen shrub
Flowering
Spring, summer
Height/spread
1m x 1m
Position
Full sun, part shade
Soil
Well-drained
Hardiness
USDA 8b/9a / RHS H4

JACQUELINE VAN DER KLOET
Garden and landscape designer, Netherlands

Jacqueline van der Kloet is one of the best-known gardening authorities in the Netherlands. In North America, she teamed up with Piet Oudolf for innovative plantings at New York's Battery Park, New York Botanical Garden and Chicago's Lurie Garden. Her work across Europe and Asia ranges from the palace Huis ten Bosch in Japan to the Newport Bay Club at Disneyland, Paris. *jacquelinevanderkloet.nl*

Hakonechloa macra
Japanese forest grass

A structural plant, modest but always clearly present because of the movement of the foliage as soon as there is a little bit of wind. Bright green, but there are also varieties with variegated foliage. It turns golden orange at the end of summer and is therefore stunning in the first months of autumn.

GROW A slow grower which likes full sun or dappled shade in soil that is not too dry. The plants mature after three years and can have a spread of 80cm. Very sturdy. Five plants per square metre if used in groups.

Type
Deciduous grass
Flowering
Summer
Height/ spread
50cm x 80cm
Position
Full sun, part shade
Soil
Moist, well-drained, most soil types
Hardiness
USDA 6a–1 / RHS H7

Helleborus orientalis ↘
Lenten rose

A great plant for winter and early spring: evergreen and with lovely, anemone-type flowers in white, pink or deep red, or variations on that. Very nice as a key plant with spring-flowering bulbs as it flowers for weeks on end.

GROW At its best in rather moist soil in dappled shade. In autumn the foliage tends to turn dull and brownish so it should be removed when the first flower buds appear. This also helps to see the flowers in full splendour. New foliage will start to grow right away. Self-seeding. Plant alone and in groups – if the latter, go for seven plants per square metre. An easy grower, it will appreciate crushed egg shells as food.

Type
Perennial
Flowering
Winter, spring
Height/ spread
50cm x 50cm
Position
Full shade, part shade, full sun
Soil
Moist, well-drained
Hardiness
USDA 6b/7a / RHS H6

Verbena officinalis var. *grandiflora* 'Bampton'
Vervain 'Bampton'

A rather new plant which has proved very eye-catching: deep purple foliage, masses of tiny purple flowers and a very architectural texture. At its best in combination with other, even more massive plants, like grey-leafed artemisia, ornamental grasses or the magenta *Geranium* 'Patricia'. It flowers all summer long.

GROW Grows best in a rather dry soil in full sun. Very easy. Profusely self-seeding. Five plants per square metre if used in groups.

Type
Perennial
Flowering
Summer, autumn
Height/ spread
1m x 1m
Position
Full sun
Soil
Moist, well-drained
Hardiness
USDA 6b/7a / RHS H6

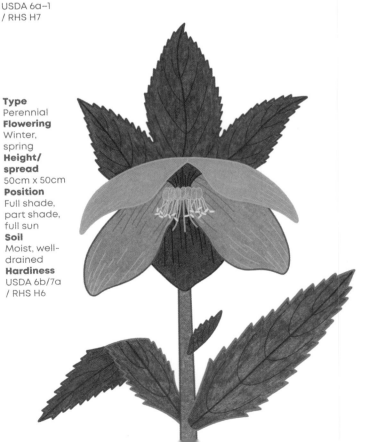

IMOGEN JACKSON
Head gardener and
horticultural therapist,
Shropshire, UK

Imogen Jackson is head gardener at Horatio's Garden Midlands. She studied social and therapeutic horticulture at Coventry University. She is a member of the Chartered Institute of Horticulture and advisor for the Defence Gardens Scheme. *instagram.com/happy_thoughts_ht*

Salvia rosmarinus
Rosemary

Rosemary is an elegant, long-lived plant that is extremely versatile. It has beautiful blue (or white, pink or purple) flowers twice a year that attract bumblebees, providing them with essential early nectar. It can be dense, bushy, upright, arching or prostrate depending on the cultivar. You can grow rosemary in containers or in herb or ornamental borders, and it looks wonderful with a wide range of other plants. Its dark green foliage and the texture of its needle-like leaves make a fabulous contrast to many other plants and, as an evergreen, it provides great ground cover and helps to provide structure and interest to your winter garden.

As a horticultural therapist I find it valuable in a wide range of sessions. Its woody, almost spicy scent is only released on crushing or rubbing the leaves, encouraging tactile contact with the plant. It has been shown to restore memory and help concentration and is a symbol of friendship, loyalty and remembrance. Sprigs of rosemary can be used in cut flower arrangements, tussie mussies and wreath decorations. It is great for cooking, but chop it up finely or add it as sprigs that can be removed. I have fond memories of sniggering with my brother about the pine needles in dad's cooking! It can be made into delicious jelly or steeped in vinegar, wine or olive oil for tasty dressings. It is also strongly antiseptic and anti-inflammatory and can be easily dried or frozen. Drink it as a tea or make it into hair, skin or bath oils. Rosemary is also reputed to repel carrot fly and weevils.

GROW Rosemary is easy to grow from softwood or semi-ripe cuttings in summer. If you are growing in a container use a large pot that's at least 20cm wide and add plenty of grit. Plants grown in containers will usually need replacing after about five years. 'Severn Sea' is a pretty, arching prostrate cultivar that looks great in containers, but is slightly less hardy than the species or other cultivars.

Pinch out the tips to keep the plant looking bushy and prune after flowering. It doesn't grow back from the wood, so don't cut back too hard. Do not prune in the autumn as any new growth will be susceptible to frost. Young plants are particularly susceptible to cold and wet. It generally doesn't need feeding and too much nitrogen feed will prevent it from flowering.

Type
Evergreen shrub
Flowering
Spring, summer
Height/ spread
2m x 2m
Position
Sun, tolerates some shade, sheltered
Soil
Well-drained, dry
Hardiness
USDA 8b/9a / RHS H4

JOHN RIPPIN
Founder, From Thistles And Weeds, Anglesey, Wales

After many years leading teams developing and restoring historic gardens for the National Trust, most recently as head gardener at Bodnant Garden, John Rippin founded design and maintenance service From Thistles and Weeds. *thistlesandweeds.co.uk*

Rhododendron dauricum 'Mid-winter'
Rhododendron 'Mid-winter'

Rhododendrons can be overpowering, gaudy or alien-looking in a garden, but this winter-flowering gem is elegant, delicate and beautiful. For most of the year, this compact, natural-looking shrub just blends in, but when its small pinky purple flowers emerge in mid-winter they provide inspiration whatever the weather, singing out on dark, wet and cold days. Covered in a dusting of snow, the flowers create memories that last a lifetime.

GROW Plant in a sheltered position if you have acid soil. It is equally happy in the open or in light shade, and would also be great on the shadier side of a house or in a narrow border, provided the ground isn't too dry.

Type
Deciduous or semi-evergreen shrub
Flowering
Winter
Height/spread
1.5m x 1.5m
Position
Full sun, part shade
Soil
Moist, well-drained, acid
Hardiness
USDA 6b/7a / RHS H6

Sciadopitys verticillata
Umbrella pine

The range of trees suitable for small gardens often feels restrictive and so a pine tree that remains compact for many years is a great and unusual architectural plant to consider. This one has fabulously long, chunky needles arranged like the spokes of an umbrella. You can even grow them in containers for many years as long as you provide adequate water. Bodnant Garden in Wales has the tallest one in the UK, so I know that even after a lifetime these wonderful trees won't outgrow their welcome.

GROW Umbrella pines grow in most soils and situations, but prefer full sun and soil that doesn't dry out too much.

Type
Evergreen conifer
Flowering
Winter
Height/spread
20m x 8m
Position
Full sun, part shade
Soil
Moist, well-drained
Hardiness
USDA 6b/7a / RHS H6

Cirsium rivulare 'Atropurpureum'
Plume thistle 'Atropurpureum'

This is one of the two plants I based my company name and logo on (the thistle part). I have always loved growing it for its naturalistic look and intense burgundy flowerheads that attract many types of insects. The flowers come early in summer and carry on flowering if deadheaded regularly. I also love the foliage that forms at the base of the tall flower stems, which contrasts well with other perennials. The flowers are held high above the foliage and create a structural accent in borders with a see-through effect, so that other flowers can easily be shown off around it in exciting combinations.

GROW I grow most of my border perennials mean and lean, so they don't need additional support or protection from pests and diseases. I simply use a mulch to preserve moisture and create a healthy, weed-free root zone. Deadhead this plant to encourage more flowers and to tidy it up, although the downside of this is that birds won't get the seedheads. You can leave the flower stems over winter to enjoy that dramatic sunlight-on-frosty-seedhead effect, as well as wonderful cobweb patterns on damp mornings. Cut down all the stems and leaves to ground level in early spring, so that all the overwintering bugs still have a chance to survive and the plant can get on with growing and producing its next stunning seasonal display. An open aspect is best, but it is adaptable.

Type
Herbaceous perennial
Flowering
Summer
Height/spread
1.5m x 50cm
Position
Full sun, part shade, open
Soil
Moist, well-drained
Hardiness
USDA 6a–1 / RHS H7

Phyllostachys nigra 'Henonis'
Henon bamboo

Type
Evergreen bamboo
Height/ spread
8m x 2.5m
Position
Full sun, part shade, open
Soil
Moist, well-drained
Hardiness
USDA 6a–1 / RHS H7

Not for the faint-hearted, this magnificent bamboo has always been my favourite, despite having so many incredible garden-worthy bamboos to compete against. It was the first bamboo I acquired and I have given many offsets away over the years to admiring friends. I love this plant for its incredible vigour (capable of sending up culms – hollow stems – over 5cm in diameter and more than 8m tall), as well as for the beautiful verdant green hues the new culms emerge with. The foliage is also dramatic, delicate and a fresh, vibrant green. I use this as a bold architectural focal point in a design and to block or screen off features and unwanted views.

GROW To induce the impressive timber-sized culms, just supply the plant with ample nourishment and water. Give it a dressing of manure, grass clippings or compost and a good drink as often as you can manage. You will see the plant respond a few days later by producing fresh leaves or shooting up amazing new culms with more vigour than before. Best results come when there is open sky above the plant and adequate moisture is available.

Prune all unwanted culms to the ground annually, including any old, dead, weak or damaged ones (these make excellent canes for the vegetable garden). Prune off lower branches to show the magnificent culms off to their best effect. Cover the base of the plant with a deep mulch, then feed and water to produce the bigger diameter culms (spring and early autumn for the feed).

After the plant is established, sever any runaway shoots on an annual basis once they have had a chance to root. Transplant or pot them up and give them to friends who are adventurous enough to care for this kind of plant.

Selinum wallichianum
Wallich milk parsley

Type
Herbaceous perennial
Flowering
Summer, autumn
Height/ spread
1.5m x 50cm
Position
Full sun, part shade, open
Soil
Moist, well-drained
Hardiness
USDA 6b/7a / RHS H6

This is the other one of two plants that inspired my company name and logo (the weed part). It's like the UK native cow parsley taken to the next level, creating a 'wow' factor in garden borders. I love many umbellifers for their delicate foliage and insect-friendly flowerheads, but this is my firm favourite. It is just the right size to create an accent or focal point in smaller borders but not too large to be overpowering. The combination of beautiful white umbels, perfectly poised on red-tinted stems above gorgeous, finely divided green foliage is a great pleasure. I love to grow cultivated versions of flowers that reflect plants seen around me in the wild spaces of Wales, ones that flower for long periods, are well behaved and retain some of that simple wildflower beauty that can be lost in highly bred cultivated plants. As a plant from the Himalayas, *S. wallichianum* is the perfect example, bringing a touch of wildness and its pure form of beauty into our gardens.

GROW This plant can be grown from seed or allowed to seed itself around a border once established. It is a great plant for combining with other perennials and grasses with contrasting flowers and foliage. Rabbits can be a problem with umbellifers, but this one seems to be more resistant than others. Applying an organic mulch improves the health of the plant as well as keeping weed competition to a minimum.

FIONA DENNIS
Owner, Fi's Yard,
East Sussex, UK

Fiona Dennis has worked as an alpine and herbaceous propagator at Royal Botanic Gardens, Kew and as an advisor for the RHS. She managed the gardener training programme for English Heritage and was head gardener at Charleston, East Sussex. Fi's Yard supplies hardy herbaceous perennials and country garden plants. *facebook.com/fisyardlewes*

Type
Rhizomatous perennial
Flowering
Spring
Height/ spread
45cm x 1.5m
Position
Sun, part shade, sheltered
Soil
Moist, well-drained
Hardiness
USDA 6a–1 / RHS H7

Galium odoratum →
Sweet woodruff

This plant offers a great sense of renewal in spring, a fresh, clean sweep of the garden floor, with clusters of white flowers appearing on soft, bushy growth. I have it flowing out of an old pair of purple Dr. Martens. It's good ground cover for difficult places. It has a light-hearted effect, softening edges and the stems of tall plants and cascading alongside steps like a white-water spring. It's not to be fussed over; you can tear it away when it starts to overstep its place in the overall palette of the garden.

GROW Woodruff needs firm management, so dig out encroaching growth at the end of summer. Note that it is too unruly for rich, moist soils. Can tolerate dry, poor soils.

Dianthus **(Allwoodii group) 'Alice'**
Perpetual-flowering carnation 'Alice'

'Alice' is the variety in one of Duncan Grant's luscious paintings of Charleston's garden. It is so old fashioned, but overdue for a revival. The best pinks will fill a garden with scent. This has silver-grey, grass-like leaves, which start to thrust out long flower stems in late spring. These hold four to six red-pink double flowers each, opening one or two at a time. It's an unexpectedly tall plant, flowering all summer and well into late autumn. A showstopper for edging paths in flouncing, bouncing blooms and a fine cut flower that brings a cottage-garden feel into the house. It retains a thick, silvery, evergreen ruff in the winter months.

GROW This plant really benefits from deadheading. Be tough when cutting to ensure the plants do not get straggly. Cut away as much as a third each autumn.

Type
Perennial
Flowering
Summer, autumn
Height/ spread
40cm x 35cm
Position
Full sun, sheltered
Soil
Well-drained
Hardiness
USDA 10b / RHS H2

Type
Biennial, short-lived perennial
Flowering
Summer
Height/ spread
3m x 1m
Position
Full sun
Soil
Well-drained
Hardiness
USDA 7b/8a / RHS H5

Alcea rosea
Hollyhock

I like plants that dwarf me in the garden and with *A. rosea* I sometimes feel like a tiny Borrower character working away under their tissue-thin petals. They can grow up to 3m high on single stems that taper off to an infinite number of buds. These open successively making their way up the tip, finally showing their last bells in autumn. Choose single varieties if you can get them – nurseries seem to be pushing us towards overstuffed vulgarities that nobody wants!

GROW Plant away from borders as it is too much of a ruffian to be part of a team. Instead, insinuate into cracks and dull corners, creating a spectacle where otherwise there is nothingness. Drop seeds into nooks and crannies and be patient, they only start to flower in their second year, and are infinitely tolerant once established. Don't fuss about rust, just cut away any affected leaves that offend the eye.

DARREN LITTLE
Head gardener, St Michael's
Mount, Cornwall, UK

Darren Little is head gardener at the subtropical gardens on St Michael's Mount, an island surrounded by the Celtic Sea off the coast of Cornwall. He is also a long-time resident of the island. *stmichaelsmount.co.uk*

Aloe polyphylla
Many-leaved aloe

I have been growing these aloes for nearly 10 years here in the gardens on St Michael's Mount and am surprised how hardy they can be. Most of them are either grown in areas with mild temperatures or in controlled environments such as glasshouses. All the ones here are kept outside all year round and thrive. They are baked in the sun and planted against the giant granite rocks, which act like radiators to produce reflected heat. I was also amazed how well they survived in harsh snow and ice, but then they are from the Drakensberg Mountains in South Africa, where temperatures can drop to −15°C. It is a green succulent that produces its leaves in a Fibonacci spiral up to five rows thick and blooms orange-yellow flowers in early summer. It can only be propagated by seed as it does not produce stems. Over the last few years, we have saved the seeds after flowering and have now produced our own stock.

GROW Plant partially vertical to help the rain run off, so they don't dampen off – but don't go too vertical as they can fall out if they don't have much support. Choose a sunny position in free-draining soil, preferably against a stone wall to benefit from radiant heat. Add grit to encourage a free-draining soil and prevent rotting out in damp weather. They are hungry plants and like plenty of feed to keep healthy, especially if grown in a pot. If you get them to flower, save the seed to propagate.

Type
Succulent
perennial
Flowering
Summer
**Height/
spread**
30cm x
60cm
Position
Full sun
Soil
Well-
drained,
sheltered
Hardiness
USDA 9b/10a
/ RHS H3

JANE LIPINGTON
Horticulturist, Emorsgate
Seeds, Cotswolds, UK

Jane Lipington has worked at the Jerusalem Botanical Gardens, as head gardener for Miriam Rothschild and as a researcher for the BBC series *Wild About Your Garden*. She is now part of Emorsgate Seeds, which grows wildflowers for seed production both as row crops and meadows. *wildseed.co.uk*

Crambe maritima
Sea kale

C. maritima is occasionally found in my native county of Dorset and next door in Devon, along some of my favourite wilder and more remote teenage haunts. It is both one of the most handsome plants you can grow in the garden and one of the most delicate early spring vegetables. This has been the downfall of sea kale because, having been successfully introduced to Covent Garden Market as a vegetable in 1795, it is now quite rare in the wild. With its elephant ear, grey-green fleshy leaves and towering, frothy panicles of honey-scented creamy flowers, it is hard to beat even before you start to eat it.

GROW Sea kale is a plant of the seashore and is found around the coast of the UK on shingle banks or on sand over shingle. Please do not pick from the wild – only the forced young leaves are palatable, the older ones are bitter. It is available from nurseries as plants and is easily grown from seed. I have found it grows both in my vegetable garden in full sun and in gravel in an east-facing yard that is a little shady. The important thing is that the soil must be free-draining to prevent the crown from rotting off in winter (although it often appears to regrow again from the roots). The seeds are hard-coated and corky, which aids dispersal by wind and tide. The hard seed pericarp must be removed before sowing. Sea kale also grows well from root cuttings taken when the plant is dormant. The emerging foliage can be eaten in spring if covered with a clay pot and forced as you would rhubarb. Don't be too greedy or you will sacrifice the flowers.

Type
Herbaceous
perennial
Flowering
Summer
**Height/
spread**
1m x 50cm
Position
Full sun
Soil
Well-
drained
Hardiness
USDA 6a–1
/ RHS H7

SUSANNA GRANT
Planting designer,
London, UK

Susanna Grant is a writer and shade plant specialist. She transforms sills, courtyards, side returns and balconies into green, wildlife-friendly oases. She is the co-founder of Linda, an occasional Sunday shop that sells shade-loving plants. She is the author of *Shade*. hellotherelinda.com

Tellima grandiflora
Fringe cups

This is a North American woodland plant and is such a useful perennial for dry shade. Planting under trees is always tricky but this works well and looks great with so many plants. I often use it with *Luzula nivea*, brunnera and lunaria. I saw this plant growing en masse under some trees on the Dartington estate in Devon in the garden of a dilapidated modernist house. They'd obviously self-seeded prolifically and the dainty nodding flowers looked and smelled amazing. The plant produces slender, arching stems that rise out of rosettes of hairy, heart-shaped leaves. The small, bell-shaped flowers are a white-green turning a pinkish-red over summer. The foliage can be evergreen in warm, sheltered spots. It grows naturally by streams or river banks, but I've always grown it easily in London clay.

GROW You can cut it back once it has finished flowering, unless you want to encourage self-seeding. Once established, it is drought tolerant but does need a bit of shelter. Easy to propagate, it can be divided in spring.

Type
Herbaceous
perennial
Flowering
Late spring,
summer
**Height/
spread**
60cm x
30cm
Position
Full shade,
part shade
Soil
Neutral,
well-drained
Hardiness
USDA 6b/7a
/ RHS H6

Silene fimbriata
Fringed-flowered campion

Type
Herbaceous
perennial
Flowering
Late spring, summer
Height/spread
90cm x 30cm
Position
Full sun, part shade
Soil
Well-drained, but
can tolerate dry
Hardiness
USDA 7b/8a
/ RHS H5

I love this plant – its flowers are so unusual with their balloon-shaped bottoms fringed with tiny white petals. I'm partial to lots of campions, but I plant this and *Silene vulgaris* the most. The plant produces flowers in late spring but can go on through summer if it's happy, and it's really versatile in terms of planting schemes. I always feel there's something Victorian about these plants – it might be something about the shape and delicacy of the flowers and maybe because they work so well with ferns. Either way, this is a really useful, pretty plant.

GROW A long-flowering and low-maintenance plant – it just needs cutting back after flowering. You can divide it in autumn or early spring before flowering.

Akebia quinata
Chocolate vine

A lovely, vigorous and easy-to-grow climber – possibly my favourite. It's especially useful for large, shady areas. The bright green foliage is almost as pretty as the scented, maroon flowers, and it happily curls its way around any support. It starts to leaf in late winter and flowers in spring, then looks great for most of the year. In a sheltered garden it can stay green pretty much all year round. Like a lot of my favourite plants, it appears delicate and tender but is very low maintenance. I have two in my garden, one unceremoniously planted behind a shed on a north-facing wall and one in a large planter. Both are very happy.

GROW Doesn't like root disturbance, so plant it where you want it to stay. It's fast growing so I often grow them in large pots to control the size. They don't really need pruning, but you may need to tie in or lightly trim new growth after flowering.

Type
Semi-evergreen
climber
Flowering
Spring
Height/spread
12m x 8m or more
Position
Full sun, part shade
Soil
Well-drained, fertile
but not overly fussy
Hardiness
USDA 6b/7a / RHS H6

ERROL FERNANDES
Head of horticulture,
Horniman Museum and
Gardens, London, UK

Errol Fernandes has a background in fine art and psychotherapy, as well as being botanically trained. He is particularly interested in ecological and sustainable horticulture, and developing planting schemes that sit alongside nature and that have a low impact on the environment. *horniman.ac.uk*

Type
Rhizomatous
perennial
Flowering
Spring
Height/spread
2.5m x 50cm
Position
Part shade,
sheltered
Soil
Moist, rich, well-
drained
Hardiness
USDA 6b/7a
/ RHS H6

↙ *Disporum longistylum* **'Night Heron'**
Long-styled disporum 'Night Heron'

At home I have a small shady garden and I grow a wide range of woodland plants from all over the world. Many of these species are enjoyed fleetingly, lunging forward to have their moment before fading into the background and giving way to a succession of other plants that follow them. But there are a few plants in my collection that look good throughout the year, and this disporum is one of them. The deep purple leaf shoots emerge in early spring, slowly unfurling with grace and elegance and fading to a glossy dark green as they mature, developing into a handsome shrubby, herbaceous perennial. Charming, pale green, bell-shaped flowers cover the plant in spring, a magnet for bees and other pollinators. The flowers develop into clusters of small green berries that gradually darken to a deep purple. These stems hold their form and remain verdant into the winter, with the berries providing a much-needed injection of colour. Later in winter the foliage and stems die back and the whole performance begins once more.

GROW This plant enjoys a moist, free-draining soil with plenty of leaf mould. Having said that, I have found it to be unfussy. It looks great alongside plants such as *Actaea simplex* 'Black Negligée' and dark tulips that share the same deep purple tones in the foliage. Wonderfully exotic when paired with large-leaved foliage plants such as *Persicaria virginiana* 'Brushstrokes' and *Petasites japonicus*. Cut the previous year's growth back to the base when you see the new shoots emerging.

FERGUS GARRETT
Head gardener,
Great Dixter House and
Gardens, East Sussex, UK

Fergus Garrett has previously worked for Rosemary Alexander of the English Gardening School and Beth Chatto at the Unusual Plants Nursery in Essex. In 1992 he became head gardener at Great Dixter, working closely with Christopher Lloyd until his death in 2006. Fergus works full-time, hands-on in the garden, as well as writing and lecturing. *greatdixter.co.uk*

← *Ferula communis*
Giant fennel

I've seen this in the wild, growing out of abandoned walls and disused places in Istanbul. It is strong and architectural yet elegant, and when standing in a colony you get transported to another world. Its dainty, lace-like foliage in late winter and early spring is followed by colossal stems bearing lime-green flowers in summer.

GROW Plant in anything by waterlogged soil and in an open position. Interplant it with hardy hedychiums, so when the fennel goes dormant the hedychiums take over. The two plants are very happy to share the same space.

Type
Herbaceous perennial
Flowering
Summer
Height/spread
3m x 1m
Position
Full sun
Soil
Well-drained
Hardiness
USDA 9b/10a
/ RHS H3

JESS SNOWBALL
Glasshouse manager,
Chelsea Physic Garden,
London, UK

Jess Snowball trained at Chester Zoo and Royal Botanic Gardens, Kew before taking up her current role of glasshouse manager at Chelsea Physic Garden. She has previously been a houseplant columnist for *Gardens Illustrated. chelseaphysicgarden.co.uk*

Echium wildpretii
Tower of jewels

After arriving at the Physic Garden in 2018, I was introduced to a whole load of echiums I'd never set eyes on before that absolutely blew my mind. Two that stood out were *Echium simplex* and *E. wildpretii*, but it's the latter that took the top spot for me and I've been obsessed ever since. I normally prefer textures over flowers so when I first saw this plant, curiosity really started to set in. The glaucous rosette of thin, hairy, silvery-green leaves resembles something like a prehistoric sea creature and makes a good ground cover. Then one on our pond rockery started to flower and the centre started to elongate. When the flowers opened on this super-long spike I'd never seen that particular shade of red before. It was raspberry-like but brighter than burgundy. I then counted around 50 bees on just this one inflorescence. It was love at first sight – colour and texture heaven all in one plant.

GROW Generally pest and disease free. Try to keep drier in the winter, and the more sun it gets the better! Water as you would a succulent (allow it to dry out between watering) and more frequently in summer. It will droop and let you know if left too long without water.

Once seed forms, let it self-seed everywhere as you will have more success growing them where they sow rather than moving them around. To start one off, grow under glass for a year then plant out later for flowering; protect with fleece during winter. It normally flowers after the second year depending on the length of cold treatment. It is monocarpic so dies after flowering.

Type
Biennial
Flowering
Summer
Height/spread
2m x 50cm
Position
Full sun, sheltered
Soil
Well-drained
Hardiness
USDA 10b / RHS H2

SUZY COCKS
Nursery owner,
South Yorkshire, UK

Suzy and Chris Cocks run Taylors Clematis Nursery, which started out growing bedding plants and herbaceous perennials in the 1980s, but now specialises in clematis. They have won numerous RHS gold medals as well as a plant of the year. *taylorsclematis.co.uk*

Clematis urophylla **'Winter Beauty'**
Clematis 'Winter Beauty'

Originally from Japan, this variety is fully evergreen with thick glossy leaves and clusters of small, pure white, campanula-shaped flowers over the winter. It prefers a sunny site, sheltered from strong winds, although I have seen it growing successfully 20m from the sea on the east coast of England with no protection. It survives temperatures down to $-10°C$ and has an eventual height of 4.5m, but you can control this with pruning. You can grow it in a pot or in the ground but not in heavy clay. It will die off if waterlogged at any stage.

GROW Feed once a week with high potash-based feeds between spring and autumn for maximum flower production. You can do a light prune to tidy it up straight after flowering.

Type
Evergreen climber
Flowering
Winter
Height/spread
4.5m x 2.5m
Position
Full sun, part shade
Soil
Moist, well-drained
Hardiness
USDA 8b/9a / RHS H4

Clematis **'Fujimusume'**
Clematis 'Fujimusume'

This clematis was raised in 1952, originally from Japan. The name means 'girl under wisteria bloom'. It has very large, Wedgwood-blue blooms and flowers from mid-spring until early autumn. It was the first clematis I grew, in a pot on the north side of our house, and I was very impressed. It's not the tallest of clematis, but it makes up for it with stunning flowers. It is also ideal for growing as a companion plant alongside low-growing shrubs.

GROW The plant requires deadheading and a light prune towards mid-summer to encourage extra flowers in late summer. Feeding with a high-potash feed is essential at this time to encourage more blooms. It is fully hardy, but like other clematis, won't grow in clay or waterlogged areas.

Type
Perennial climber
Flowering
Summer
Height/spread
1.5m x 1m
Position
Full sun, part shade
Soil
Moist, well-drained
Hardiness
USDA 6b/7a / RHS H6

Type
Perennial climber
Flowering
Summer, autumn
Height/spread
4m x 1.5m
Position
Full shade, full sun, part shade
Soil
Moist, well-drained
Hardiness
USDA 6b/7a / RHS H6

Clematis koreana **Amber**
Clematis [Amber]

This has to be my favourite clematis – it definitely ticks all the boxes, from flowering to ease of growing. We won plant of the year with it at the RHS Chelsea Flower Show in 2016. It was the first time we entered the competition and it was so exciting. Chris had to promote 'Amber' for two minutes in front of about 50 RHS judges competing with 20 other contestants. When we got the result we were over the moon! This clematis was bred by Marco de Wit from Holland. It is fully hardy and can be grown in any aspect of the garden, in a pot, in the ground, trained through an obelisk or up a wall. It has stunning double lemon-coloured flowers in spring with great seedheads after flowering. It also flowers on old growth, so after its second flush requires no more pruning. 'Amber' is extremely hardy and never suffers from clematis wilt or any other diseases.

GROW Feed once a week from spring to autumn with a high-potash liquid feed. After the first flush of flowers, give it a light prune (to about halfway down) and tidy up. It will then give a second flush in mid-summer.

NEIL PORTEOUS
Head gardener and
historic garden consultant,
Northern Ireland

Neil Porteous experiments with new plants and seeks innovative ways
to show them off in gardens. He is head gardener at Mount Stewart in
County Down, and gardens and parks advisor for the National Trust,
Northern Ireland. *neilporteousgardens.com*

Magnolia cathcartii
Cathcart magnolia

M. cathcartii is one of the most unusual magnolias. An evergreen, its white,
highly fragrant flowers open in early summer, borne on long stalks. Initially these
gorgeous flowers open only slightly, resembling a wine glass, before opening
out fully to reveal the beauty of their long and attractively arranged anthers. The
plants were bought from Crug Farm from a collection made in 2003 from north
Vietnam by Dan Hinkley together with Bleddyn and Sue Wynn-Jones.

GROW It's hardy in coastal Ireland and loves to grow under a light canopy in a moist spot.
Anywhere where Juncus reed or creeping buttercup grows would suit. It is not easy from
cuttings – they take a long time to form roots, the whole process typically takes 18 months.

Type
Evergreen
tree
Flowering
Summer
**Height/
spread**
15m x 8m
Position
Full sun,
part shade,
sheltered
Soil
Moist, well-
drained
Hardiness
USDA 9b/10a
/ RHS H3

Type
Bromeliad
Flowering
Summer,
autumn
**Height/
spread**
1m x 60cm
Position
Full sun,
sheltered
Soil
Well-
drained
Hardiness
USDA 10b /
RHS H2

Ochagavia carnea
Tresco rhodostachys

Many bromeliads grow incredibly well in Irish gardens. *O. carnea*, from Chile, can
be grown in well-drained soil at the dry, sunny base of an established large tree
or used as an epiphyte lodged in the branches or in a fissure or join on the bole
of a tree. They need some direct sun, but apart from that, they just like being left
alone, which is lucky as they are all pretty spiny customers. This one flowers late
summer or early autumn in Ireland and brightens up the garden with its huge
pink inflorescence. There are other bromeliads that do equally well: *Fascicularia
bicolor*, *Greigia sphacelata*, *Aechmea recurvata* and *Billbergia nutans*. When
happy these plants form colonies, their rosettes growing on top of each other.

GROW Propagate off-sets cut in autumn and place in free-draining compost.

Type
Evergreen
tree
Flowering
Autumn
**Height/
spread**
15m x 4m
Position
Full sun,
sheltered
Soil
Moist, well-
drained
Hardiness
USDA 6b/7a
/ RHS H6

Schima khasiana →
Schima khasiana

This striking evergreen produces its flowers early.
As dreary autumn descends, *S. khasiana* opens its
buds to reveal marzipan-scented white flowers with
a complex yellow central boss. They contrast with its
long, elegant, glossy leaves with their red petioles
and central midrib. It flowers for a long time and
I think it is one of the most beautiful of all plants. It
was introduced to Irish gardens by the late Patrick
Forde of Seaforde Nurseries, and perhaps the best
form is in the garden at Castlewellan, County Down.

GROW A woodland-edge plant that needs shelter and a good amount of direct
sunshine in which to flower well. It grows into a medium-sized, generally conical
tree, but is shallow rooted and prone to blowing over if not in a sheltered position.
Propagate by semi-ripe cuttings taken in late summer and grow with additional
light and bottom heat of 20°C. Will root in pots of pure perlite.

MAGS COUGHLAN
Head gardener, Ballymaloe
House, County Cork, Ireland

Mags Coughlan is head gardener at Ballymaloe House, a world-famous hotel and cookery school on 300 acres of farmland in East Cork that's internationally recognised as the birthplace of modern Irish cuisine. She grows fruit, vegetables and cut flowers in the two-acre walled garden. *ballymaloe.com*

Crataegus laevigata 'Paul's Scarlet'
Hawthorn 'Paul's Scarlet'

I used this tree the first time I designed a friend's garden. I was nervous about taking on my first project and so researched and researched trees for their windy site, finally settling on 'Paul's Scarlet'. Initially, my friends wanted cherry trees to line their driveway, but given the exposed site, we settled on the hawthorn. They loved it and, years later, the trees are still thriving. They have glossy, dark green leaves and flowers in late spring, with clusters of crimson blossoms yielding red fruits.

Type
Deciduous tree
Flowering
Spring
Height/spread
8m x 8m
Position
Full sun, part shade
Soil
Moist, well-drained
Hardiness
USDA 6a–1 / RHS H7

GROW On an exposed site, the most important thing in my opinion is to stake the newly planted tree to ensure there is no root rock. No pruning necessary but I sometimes remove lower branches to show off the trunk – and to facilitate mowing!

Verbena bonariensis
Purple top

Verbena bonariensis is perhaps the first Latin plant name I learned. I love how this plant bobs and weaves throughout the garden, seeding around when it's happy. In the summer it gives height and colour in the herbaceous borders and can sometimes escape the swivel hoe, ending up in the vegetable beds. The solid, green-leaved clumps produce rigid stems topped with pretty purple flower clusters that dance airily through borders.

Type
Herbaceous perennial
Flowering
Summer, autumn
Height/spread
2.5m x 60cm
Position
Full sun, sheltered
Soil
Moist, well-drained
Hardiness
USDA 8b/9a / RHS H4

GROW Prune back to knee height in autumn, and new shoots will appear in late spring. Prefers a sheltered area as a windy site can knock over tall plants.

Quercus petraea ↓
Sessile oak

Ballymaloe House is a firm favourite with guests who return year after year and generation after generation. Many of them ask to plant a family tree to remember their time there. This idea, along with Fáilte Ireland's Ancient East tourism initiative, led to the opportunity for guests to plant a sessile oak in the grounds to leave their mark on the estate.

The sessile oak is a traditional Irish oak and was once widespread throughout the country, with an average lifespan of 200 years. I love the idea of planting an oak woodland that will be enjoyed by generations to come. It is an iconic shape and always with a story to tell.

Type
Deciduous tree
Flowering
Spring
Height/spread
30m x 20m
Position
Full sun, part shade
Soil
Moist, well-drained
Hardiness
USDA 6a–1 / RHS H7

GROW Planting a two-year-old whip while keeping in mind to the ultimate size of the tree can often blow my mind. Positioning the tree is very important, taking into consideration the trees and shrubs surrounding it. Perhaps encircle young trees with sheep wire to protect against sheep, deer, rabbits and so on.

112

Adiantum capillus-veneris
Southern maidenhair

I don't have my own garden and so have filled my small living space with houseplants. The maidenhair fern is my absolute favourite. Despite the dry, hot atmosphere of the room it lives in, it has survived and thrived mainly due to constant misting with rain water – it truly is a pampered plant! It has dainty, thumbnail-sized fronds on black stems. I love the elegance of the stems and its movement in any breeze through an open window. Everyone admires the feminine, airy shape of the plant.

GROW I occasionally move this plant outdoors on a sunny day but always regret it as even the softest breeze seems to dry out the delicate leaves. If I want to really spoil this fern, I'll pop it into the bathroom while the shower is on. Never let it dry out and keep misting with rainwater to maintain an element of humidity around the plant.

Type
Semi-evergreen fern
Height/ spread
50cm x 50cm
Position
Part shade, full shade
Soil
Moist, well-drained
Hardiness
USDA 9b/10a / RHS H3

INDIA HURST
Floral designer and grower, Worcestershire, UK

India Hurst is a florist and flower grower. She founded floral design studio Vervain in 2014 and grows the majority of flowers the studio uses, including an ever-growing bearded iris collection. *vervainflowers.com*

Type
Rhizomatous perennial
Flowering
Spring, early summer
Height/ spread
1m x 50cm, but varies depending on variety
Position
Full sun, open, sheltered
Soil
Light, well-drained, neutral
Hardiness
USDA 6b/7a / RHS H6

Iris germanica
Bearded iris

Bearded irises have a way of capturing your imagination. I find their endless colour combinations and over-the-top frills such a wonderful source of inspiration. For me, part of the charm is their short flowering season – they seem to put their all into creating the most outrageously beautiful flowers for just a fleeting moment in early summer. They grab your attention with their tall spires covered in anything from three to seven flowerheads, making you stand in awe.

The flower is made up of three upright petals (standards) and three lower petals (falls). Each fall has a beard and inside the centre of the standard you find the crests, stigmas, anthers and style. Often bearded iris standards and falls will be very different in colour or pattern, with a beard in a contrasting vivid colour. The heads can be anything from tiny dainty little things no higher than a few centimetres (dwarf bearded irises) to towering 1m stems with flowers the size of your hands (tall bearded irises). They all draw you in and make you start noticing each little delicate colourful vein or speckled marking. Each one even has a slightly different ruffled beard.

I first fell in love with bearded irises when I attended a floral class at a bearded iris farm in Oregon while on holiday. Since then I've been hooked and my collection has grown and grown. I've even started dabbling in hybridising to create my own wild and wonderful colour combinations.

GROW Bearded irises love a well-drained sunny spot – the more sun the better to bake their rhizomes. I've grown them in pots and they seem to do well, but the ones in the ground produce taller and stronger flower stems. When planting, ensure the rhizomes are exposed and not covered by soil. Be sure to dig them up and split them every three to five years to ensure they stay healthy and don't become overcrowded.

Feed twice a year, with a low nitrogen feed – once in spring before flowering and once in late summer after flowering. Snapping off any dead or gone-over flowers encourages the next bud on the stem to open, so keep on top of deadheading if you want your flowers to open faster. Cut back the leaves into a fan shape after flowering in late summer/early autumn and always remove any dead leaves to help avoid rhizome rot.

SALLIE SILLARS
Head gardener and
horticultural therapist,
Glasgow, Scotland

Sallie Sillars is head gardener at Horatio's Garden Scotland in Glasgow, a green and biodiverse sanctuary that helps to promote healing and encourage rehabilitation and a greater sense of wellbeing for everyone in the National Spinal Injuries Unit. *horatiosgarden.org.uk*

Verbascum thapsus
Great mullein

This is a statuesque plant with attitude. I have fond memories of seeing it as a child during holidays in Devon – one of many plants that inspired a slow realisation that horticulture should be my chosen career. It's a plant that makes its presence felt and certainly catches the eye. Not only because of its size – reaching over 2m when happy – but because of its huge, silver, furry leaves and its ability to pop up in the strangest of places where not much else grows. It's a survivor. Disturbing the ground can be enough to stimulate long-resting seeds (sometimes decades old). Roadways, fields and pathways are hot spots for germination, which means that having poor soil is not such a problem – a sunny gravel garden is ideal. It's a biennial, forming a beautiful rosette of donkey's ears leaves in its first year and a tall flower spike with small, pale yellow, saucer-shaped flowers bursting forth from summer to autumn the following year. It is home to many insects including the voracious mullein moth – look for its yellow- and green-striped caterpillars in late spring to mid-summer.

GROW Save the seeds and re-sow in spring using a free-draining, fine, gritty, soil-based compost with a covering of vermiculite, as the seeds need light to germinate. Seeds can be a little unpredictable so as an insurance policy also sow them in autumn directly where you want them to grow. Watch out for mullein moth caterpillars – they can strip a plant if they have a good year.

Type
Biennial
Flowering
Summer
Height/ spread
2.5m x 50cm
Position
Full sun
Soil
Well-drained, alkaline
Hardiness
USDA 6b/7a / RHS H6

Nicotiana sylvestris
Woodland tobacco plant

This majestic biennial grows from the tiniest seeds, which always amazes me. How does something so huge come from the smallest of things? There must be an enormous amount of information packed into each one and I find that incredible. Its candelabras of white trumpet-shaped flowers are only surpassed by its intense scent, which drifts through the garden, especially on warm, still evenings. It's a delight and always top of my wish list. *N. sylvestris* is a relative of cultivated tobacco, *N. tabacum*, and like that plant shares a rich musky scent if you brush its leaves. *N. sylvestris* leaves are soft and delicate but become quite large.

GROW When you pick a spot to plant it out, choose a sheltered position and allow up to 50cm for them to spread – they will soon fill it. As the weather warms, the flower spike forms. If it is planted late, it can delay flowering until a second year and, after dying back, resurrect itself the following year. Don't rely on that, though: boost your stock with seed-sown plants and you will have a beautiful display from summer to autumn.

I grow it from seed saved from previous years. Sow in late spring as thinly as possible (not easy as seeds are very small, so be prepared for careful pricking out) on to moist, sieved compost and gently press on to the surface, but do not cover as they need light to germinate. Keep warm and moist, and wait. They can be slow starters, so give them up to 28 days. Let the seedlings grow to over 2.5cm before pricking out and potting. Keep them indoors until all risk of frost has passed.

In autumn allow the flower spikes to turn brown and harvest the seeds just as the tiny pods open so you catch them before they fall. There is nothing as rewarding as building up your own seed stock; I am guilty of looking through it constantly when the frosts are hard on the ground and dreaming about all the great things yet to come!

Type
Biennial, short-lived perennial, often grown as an annual
Flowering
Summer
Height/ spread
1.5m x 50cm
Position
Full sun, part shade, sheltered
Soil
Moist, well-drained
Hardiness
USDA 10b / RHS H2

114

TAYLOR JOHNSTON
Nurserywoman, Rhode
Island, USA

Together with business partner Ed Bowen, Taylor Johnston runs Issima, a nursery that specialises in under-cultivated but garden-worthy plants, as well as unusual hardy plants. She formerly worked at the Isabella Stewart Gardner Museum in Boston. *issimaworks.com*

Sanguisorba '**Drama Queen**'
Burnet 'Drama Queen'

Perhaps I'm in the minority, or perhaps by virtue of having a small nursery I truly don't believe I have a favourite plant. When asked, I tend to fall back on whatever plant I'm singing the praises of at that moment. Right now it's a selection that my partner Ed Bowen made when he was operating as a one-man show under the nursery name Opus.

'Drama Queen' was selected here from var. *parviflora*, but with clear *tenuifolia* influence in its taller stature and longer inflorescences. It has an incredibly sturdy, upright habit with many pendulous, white, bottlebrush flowers on up to 2m-long stems in early summer and yellow foliage in autumn. It's easy and floriferous in a range of conditions, but especially where it's not too wet or too dry. The plant is incredibly beautiful and, as luck would have it, stubbornly slow to propagate. Every year when it flowers, it stops me and Ed in our tracks. At various points of the day I find myself standing in front of the planting, admiring its dynamic movement in the breeze and the number of pollinators that seem to hover in its ether.

GROW Best in moist, average soil, in full sun. Stubbornly slow to bulk up, it can be propagated by division. Be sure to water in and tend as you would most other perennials. Once established, the plant is extremely tough (sanguisorbas are in the rose family and have deep, woody roots). Check ahead for extended dry spells in its first year, but then it's hands off. It will only need to be deadheaded if you so desire.

Type
Herbaceous perennial
Flowering
Summer
Height/ spread
2m x 1m
Position
Full sun, part shade
Soil
Moist, well-drained
Hardiness
USDA 6b/7a / RHS H6

WILL PURDOM
Managing director,
Botanico, Suffolk, UK

Will Purdom trained at the Royal Botanic Garden Edinburgh before founding his own nursery Botanico, which specialises in rare, exotic and unusual species from around the world. *thebotanico.com*

Woodwardia unigemmata
Jeweled chain fern

A fern which provides all-year interest, but especially in spring when the new fronds emerge. Unlike more common chain-link ferns, this species has a hidden surprise – the new fronds are bright red and fade to green, and they can grow up to 5ft long! It is also hardy down to –5°C, which means it will take a good frost and come back with a vengeance. This plant works really well in any fernery, bringing colour in the spring.

GROW Needs a sheltered spot, ideally with temperatures between –7°C and 30°C. In the growing season, water every week and feed once a month with a fertiliser high in nitrogen.

Type
Evergreen fern
Height/spread
1.5m x 2.5m
Position
I grow it in full sun, but some recommend part to full shade
Soil
Keep constantly moist, although it will tolerate some dryness
Hardiness
USDA 8b/9a / RHS H4

THOMAS UNTERDORFER
Keeper of the landscape,
Bonnington House and
Jupiter Artland, Edinburgh,
Scotland

Thomas Unterdorfer grew up in rural Austria surrounded by pristine nature. He studied horticulture in Vienna and later at the Royal Botanic Gardens, Kew. He has worked in the private gardens of Daylesford, Appleton Manor and Rockcliffe. *instagram.com/thomasunterdorfer*

Succisa pratensis →
Devil's bit scabious

I remember devil's bit scabious from botanising in wet meadows in Austria, where it formed part of a delicately balanced ecosystem of starved hay meadows cut once a year for animals. Later on I found it in the UK, most recently around Loch Affric growing along the banks of tracks. It flowers in late summer through to the first frosts, its lilac-blue buttons with reddish stamens swaying in the wind. In Bonnington it is used in the parterre, creating a haze of purplish-blue clouds. Seedlings appear in the surrounding beds, but can easily be transplanted. I love the way it appears throughout the gardens, even in paving cracks, without taking over. It is a great example of a plant from the wild being part of a garden and a story, making a connection to memories of friends, travels and good times.

GROW It's an attractive perennial that thrives in damp but not waterlogged environments. Its flowers emerge from late summer until the first harsh frosts, when they look especially precious. It comes quickly into flower if grown from seed. In the garden it generally doesn't need staking, but we usually cut it back to the ground when the stems start to fail. I find it grows best in an open position with lots of sunshine, like in a meadow in the Austrian Alps or along a stream in the Highlands.

Type
Herbaceous perennial
Flowering
Summer, autumn
Height/ spread
1m x 50cm
Position
Full sun, part shade
Soil
Moist, well-drained, poorly drained
Hardiness
USDA 6a–1 / RHS H7

ANNA GREENLAND
Organic grower and writer,
Suffolk, UK

Anna Greenland has grown top-quality organic veg for chefs such as Raymond Blanc. She is now turning her own patch of land in Suffolk into a productive market garden. She is the author of *Grow Easy: Organic Crops for Pots & Small Plots. annagreenland.com*

Calendula officinalis
Common marigold

For me, there is no other plant in the garden that has such myriad uses. I use its sunny, orange blooms for beauty in my plot, to attract beneficial insects, as a cut flower, and for culinary and medicinal use. Completely unfussy, it is a great beginner gardener's plant that keeps on giving. It was the first edible flower I grew to supply Jamie Oliver's restaurant Fifteen Cornwall many moons ago, and I quickly realised how happily it mingled with the vegetables in my plot. The petals have a peppery kick and can be added fresh to salads, pestos or frittatas, and fresh or dried to soups or stews. Traditionally they were added to the stock/stew 'pot', giving rise to one of its other common names, pot marigold. The petals impart an orange dye and the plant was also known as 'poor man's saffron'. I freeze flowerheads in ice cubes for summer drinks and use fresh blooms as a tea infusion to aid digestion. But calendula is perhaps best known for soothing cuts and bruises; I infuse dried flowerheads in oil to make a balm, which we continuously use on my child's scraped knees! I defy you not to be cheered by calendula – it's far more than a pretty flower!

GROW Sow in late summer for blooms in late spring or sow in spring for summer flowers. Plants grow well dotted through a vegetable plot or in pots to lure in pollinators and beneficial insects. If grown in pots, feed every two weeks with seaweed feed. For medicinal use, always pick flowers when half open and keep the green resinous base attached. Ensure you keep deadheading. Once flowering slows, cut back to promote more growth.

Type
Annual, biennial
Flowering
Summer, autumn
Height/ spread
50cm x 50cm
Position
Full sun, part shade
Soil
Unfussy and can grow in nutritionally poor soil
Hardiness
USDA 7b/8a / RHS H5

ADOLFO HARRISON
Director, Adolfo Harrison
Gardens, London, UK

Adolfo Harrison is an award-winning garden designer. He sits on the
selection panel for the RHS Chelsea Flower Show and lectures at the KLC
School of Design. He has twice won the Judges' Award at the Society of
Garden Designers Awards. *adolfoharrison.com*

Cynara cardunculus Scolymus Group
Globe artichoke (SEE ILLUSTRATION PAGE 146)

Has one plant ever given so much throughout a year? In spring, the artichoke's
glaucous architectural leaves dominate a space with a graceful, arching
habit. From here, scaled buds emerge sitting on stems 2m tall. Not only can the
bud's ornate form be enjoyed in its own right, but it is one of the most delicious
vegetables you can eat (the Victorians predominantly grew *C. cardunculus* for
the edible leaves, and it looks and behaves practically the same as *C. scolymus*).

Those who can resist the temptation to eat the bud's petals and heart
dipped into a beurre blanc sauce are rewarded with one of nature's greatest
flowers. Our local wildlife would appear to agree – these large, brilliant blue,
thistle-like flowers are always full of bees getting drunk on nectar. And if that
wasn't enough, the flower dies down to form an enormous seedhead. One tip I
discovered: the seeds can get a bit tatty towards winter. Literally pull these dark
tufts off the front and it reveals the brightly straw-coloured, fluffy choke behind.
The choke radiates light and they stand up like a sunflower in winter. One final
gift: these seedheads harbour all sorts of hibernating insects.

GROW If you have clay soil, grow in a large pot with a large hole in the base so that the
tap root can access the ground moisture without the main rootball getting saturated in
winter. Once the tap root has developed it shouldn't need much watering. Remove tatty
leaves as necessary and cut seedheads at the end of winter. A note of warning: you will
inevitably need to deal with aphids, but there are a number of organic methods to can try.

Type
Perennial
Flowering
Summer,
autumn
**Height/
spread**
2m x 1.5m
Position
Full sun,
sheltered
Soil
Well-
drained
Hardiness
USDA 7b/8a
/ RHS H5

PETRA ULRIK
Associate landscape
architect, Urquhart &
Hunt, UK

Petra Ulrik is part of the team at Urquhart & Hunt, a studio based in Bruton.
She is passionate about beautiful planting schemes, ecological harmony,
authentic craftsmanship and practical horticulture. *urquharthunt.com*

Dahlia 'Bishop's Children'
Dahlia 'Bishop's Children'

This dahlia brings joy to the garden when other plants are fading away into
autumn gold. The flowerheads are light and elegant, almost hovering above
other plants. The stems are strong enough to hold the flowers without staking,
making the whole appearance that bit more natural. I particularly enjoy its deep
aubergine leaf colour and how the flowers come out in slightly different colours,
ranging from apricot to salmon pink.

GROW This dahlia is self-sufficient and shows up year after year. The more it's
deadheaded the more buds it brings. I've grown this in construction rubble mixed with
clay. The soil was improved by letting dandelions and clovers break up the soil with their
deep roots and by adding allotment compost as top dressing. My plants were grown
from seeds. The seeds need to be germinated on a heated bench; pot the little seedlings
on and harden off before planting out.

Type
Perennial
Flowering
Summer,
autumn
**Height/
spread**
70cm x 40cm
Position
Full sun
Soil
Moist, well-
drained
Hardiness
USDA 9b/10a
/ RHS H3

IÑIGO SEGUROLA ARREGUI
Founder, LUR Paisajistak, Basque Country, Spain

Iñigo Segurola Arregui has worked on many public and private projects, most of them in the Basque Country. In 2021 he started the construction of his studio garden, LUR Garden, a 20,000 square metre garden with 16 different spaces that explore the aesthetic potential of plants. The garden is open to the public. *lurpaisajistak.com*

Dicksonia antarctica
Soft tree fern (SEE ILLUSTRATION PAGE 155)

D. antarctica does really well in the region around Donostia and San Sebastian, where the yearly rainfall is around 1,800 litres, with warm humid summers and not very cold winters. I love the size and form of their leaves. They are very similar to the dryopteris ferns, which are native to the region and have leaves of similar colour and form, but what is surprising is the size of their leaves. Once the plant is established, these reach 2m in length, and once decayed they slowly create the thick 'trunk'.

In our humid climate, they produce two layers of leaves per year if planted in the right location. The roots, which emerge through the trunk, do not dehydrate. This helps them to advance their growth and contributes extra thickness to the trunk. They tend to reproduce themselves by spores, and this fact encourages me to go dicksonia hunting every spring. Their majesty, elegance, beauty and impressive adaptation to our site mean they are one of my favourite plants when arranging and designing shaded gardens.

GROW I have found that adding a thick layer of oak and chestnut leaves, gathered in the surrounding woodlands, helps give extra growth to this unique fern.

Type
Evergreen tree fern
Height/ spread
4m x 4m
Position
Full shade, part shade
Soil
Moist, well-drained, sheltered
Hardiness
USDA 9b/10a / RHS H3

MARGARET BARKER
Founder, Larnach Castle, Dunedin, New Zealand

Margaret Barker and her late husband purchased the derelict Larnach Castle in 1967. Her family and their team restored the building and recreated and extended the garden. Larnach Castle Gardens are now rated as six-star by the New Zealand Gardens Trust. Margaret is a former chair of the New Zealand Gardens Trust and is associate of honour of the Royal New Zealand Institute of Horticulture. *larnachcastle.co.nz*

Alsophila dealbata
Silvery tree fern

I am inspired by the silvery tree fern (ponga in Maori, syn. *Cyathea dealbata*) because of its singular beauty and symbolism. It grows naturally throughout most of our country from north to south, including on my own plot of land on the Otago Peninsula near Dunedin. This fern is endemic, native only to New Zealand. It is used as an emblem by the New Zealand army, our sports teams, our farming products and our national airline. The circular shape of the koru, an unfurling frond in Maori carvings, conveys the idea of perpetual movement, while its inward coil suggests a return to the point of origin. This koru is used extensively in traditional Maori art, in modern art and as a symbol. The ponga's fronds, which tend to lie flat and horizontal, can each extend 4m, creating a perfect lace-like green circle when seen from above. These fronds have a silver colouration on the underside: an ethereal circle, etched and delicate in the half light of the forest's interior. I grow this plant because it expresses the very essence of our country.

GROW If in a frosty area, protect the crown with cloth over straw or similar material. Cut off old fronds.

Type
Evergreen tree fern
Height/ spread
10m x 8m
Position
Full shade, part shade, sheltered
Soil
Moist, well-drained
Hardiness
USDA 10b / RHS H2

ROBERT BARKER
Garden designer,
Cambridgeshire, UK

Robert Barker founded his garden design company after a career as a singer-songwriter. He trained with the RHS at Capel Manor College and Royal Botanical Gardens, Kew. He was awarded a gold medal for his first show garden at RHS Hampton Court Flower Show in 2016. *robertbarkerdesign.com*

Gymnocarpium dryopteris
Oak fern

This is a lovely delicate and subtle fern. It is small, but with its bright green leaves it adds an element of sophistication to a sheltered damp area. I have used it in both of my show gardens at Hampton Court and Chelsea Flower Show, and it looks stunning planted under trees. It is not easy to source but is worth the effort.

GROW Plant in a spot that is sheltered from the sun and has moist soil, as the plant can dry out easily. Grow in neutral to acid soil, enriched with compost.

Type
Deciduous fern
Height/spread
50cm x 1m
Position
Full shade, sheltered
Soil
Moist, well-drained
Hardiness
USDA 7b/8a / RHS H5

Iris **'Black Swan'**
Iris 'Black Swan'

Every year it never ceases to amaze me that such an alien-looking rhizome can produce such a magnificent flower. Right from the start of my career I have always loved irises. The fact that they flower for such a brief time always reminds me how important it is to appreciate the seasons and enjoy each moment. Once the flower has faded and is cut back, the sword-like leaves add important architectural contrast in herbaceous borders.

GROW There is always a horticultural debate about whether to bury the rhizome or not, but a very reliable source told me to leave the rhizomes on the surface of the soil facing the sun and that method has never failed me.

Type
Rhizomatous
perennial
Flowering
Summer
Height/spread
1m x 50cm
Position
Full sun
Soil
Well-drained
Hardiness
USDA 6a–1 / RHS H7

Type
Rhizomatous
herbaceous perennial
Flowering
Summer
Height/spread
50cm x 50cm
Position
Part shade, full shade,
sheltered
Soil
Moist, well-drained
Hardiness
USDA 8b/9a / RHS H4

Podophyllum versipelle **'Spotty Dotty'**
Mayapple 'Spotty Dotty' (SEE ILLUSTRATION PAGE 82)

In 2018 I designed a garden called Skin Deep for Harley Street Skin Care at the RHS Chelsea Flower Show. The garden was very sculptural, containing nearly 1,000 concrete blocks of all different sizes representing people with different skin conditions. I wanted to repeat this textural quality within the planting. I did this with plants such as boehmeria, foxgloves and pulmonarias, but the one that really got people talking was 'Spotty Dotty'. Its leaves are very unusual but it sits perfectly within a herbaceous border when grown with the right companion plants.

GROW They do not like to dry out and the leaves can scorch, so a moist, shaded or part-shaded spot is perfect. Grow in well-drained, humus-rich soil sheltered from wind.

EMMA CRAWFORTH
Gardening editor,
*Gardeners' World
Magazine*, London, UK

Emma Crawforth has been gardening for some 30 years, combining working in public gardens (including the Royal Botanic Gardens, Kew and Threave Garden & Estate) with practical training. She is a trustee of gardening charity Plant Heritage. *instagram.com/emma_crawforth*

Nigella damascena
Love-in-a-mist (SEE ILLUSTRATION PAGE 74)

Type
Annual
Flowering
Summer
**Height/
spread**
50cm x 50cm
Position
Full sun
Soil
Well-
drained,
alkaline,
neutral
Hardiness
USDA 9b/10a
/ RHS H3

This flower is one of the easiest to sow and leaves a legacy of new plants by shedding seeds when it finishes blooming. While other plants can go through an unattractive stage as they die off or grow to maturity, nigella stays beautiful throughout its life. It peaks with an intriguing flower shape, consisting of brightly coloured sepals crowned by a ring of erect styles and surrounded by lush green, lacy bracts, giving it its delightful name, love-in-a-mist. Florists gain white, pink or blue blooms that last well in a vase, as well as globe-like papery seedheads if cut for drying. Christopher Lloyd, founder of the gardens at Great Dixter, favoured the blue 'Miss Jekyll' and complemented it with red flax, which showed off the greens that are a significant part of the flowerhead. I like it with sturdy pot marigolds for similar reasons, but I think it looks best of all self-sown into paving cracks.

GROW Be sure to give nigella enough space to grow; it looks best when the plants are far enough apart for you to appreciate the flowers individually, say at 15cm stations. Sow successively so as to have flowers at different stages of maturity throughout the summer and sow a batch in autumn, too, with the hope of seeing first blooms the following spring. Scatter seed into free-draining soil in spring or autumn. Thin out seedlings. Support is not needed. Cut for the vase as required and leave uncut flowers to develop seedheads.

KIM WILKIE
Landscape architect,
Hampshire, UK

After 25 years of running his own practice, Kim Wilkie now juggles working as a strategic and conceptual landscape consultant with the muddy practicalities of operating a small farm. He also writes about land and place, lectures in America and meddles in various national committees on landscape and environmental policy. *kimwilkie.com*

Type
Herbaceous
perennial
Flowering
Summer
**Height/
spread**
50cm x 50cm
Position
Full sun, part
shade
Soil
Moist, well-
drained
Hardiness
USDA 6a–1
/ RHS H7

Plantago major ↘
Cart track plant

When you ask 'what do gardeners grow?', my answer is English longhorn cattle. The fundamental beauty of the English landscape is the relationship between the productive countryside and the thousand-year-old farmsteads that tend it. Wood pasture, hedgerows, coppice woodland and flood and hay meadows are the backbone of that landscape. And so my iconic plant is *P. major* – also known as the cart track plant or more commonly as plantain. It is one of the main power plants of a good herbal ley, driving carbon deep down into the soil and bringing water and minerals up from below. For the cows, it is a key medicinal herb, and actively reduces methane in the rumen.

GROW Works beautifully with yellow rattle.

121

TIM UPSON
RHS director of horticulture, education and communities, UK

Tim Upson is responsible for horticulture across all five RHS Gardens. He trained at the Royal Botanic Gardens, Kew, before obtaining a PhD in plant systematics and later working as curator and deputy director of Cambridge University Botanic Garden. Tim's interests include the mint family (*Lamiaceae*), Mediterranean plants, oceanic islands and plant conservation. *agardenthroughtime.wordpress.com*

Narcissus 'Oxford Gold' →
Daffodil 'Oxford Gold'

Type
Bulbous perennial
Flowering
Early spring
Height/ spread
50cm x 50cm
Position
Full sun, part shade
Soil
Moist, well-drained
Hardiness
USDA 6b/7a / RHS 6

Finding daffodils growing in the wild is always exciting and I've been lucky enough to find several while travelling in Portugal, Spain and Morocco. The hooped daffodil is one I got to know well when taking students on a field course to the hills of the Serra da Arrabida, south of Lisbon. There was always great anticipation as we drove up to spot the first ones of the trip. Most often they would be along the roadside away from the dense natural scrub. One year we came across a site that had been burnt the previous summer and was now a sea of yellow daffodils – with the shading vegetation removed, the previously dormant daffodils had burst into flower.

'Oxford Gold' is a recently (2007) selected form of *Narcissus bulbocodium* that bears many flowering stems of large, butter-yellow blooms with a great scent – sometimes as many as 20 flowers per bulb. Flowering quite early, it makes a superior garden plant for the edges of borders and gravel gardens. Inspired by the famous alpine meadow of wild *N. bulbocodium* at RHS Wisley, I am seeing if it will naturalise in a meadow. I always grow a few in pots as well, either to bring indoors or simply place where they can be more easily admired at closer quarters.

GROW Best in a sunny position. If grown in pots and containers, feed once the flowers fade and allow the narrow leaves to die back naturally.

Type
Short-lived perennial
Flowering
Summer
Height/ spread
1m x 50cm
Position
Part shade
Soil
Moist, well-drained
Hardiness
USDA 12 / RHS H1B

Impatiens niamniamensis
Parrot plant

I first came across this plant in the tropical rainforests of Cameroon in Africa while I was working at the Limbe Botanic Garden. Several species of impatiens are found in the forests there and this one was relatively common, growing on the forest floor, on rotting logs and occasionally among moss on tree branches. The bright red and yellow flowers stood out, their shape and colour suggesting bird pollination, probably by the native sunbirds. The upright stems have a whorl of leaves and the flowers nod below, sometimes borne directly from the stem.

On my return home, I was delighted to find the plant for sale as a houseplant and immediately bought one. I have been growing it for the last 30 years, propagating regularly, taking it from house to house and giving them away. It's still available from specialist suppliers.

GROW Grow as a tender houseplant or in a heated glasshouse. Keep well watered and feed in the growing season. It needs semi-shade and thrives in bathrooms or kitchens where it appreciates the extra moisture. Its slightly succulent stems make it easy to root – just pop a section of stem in a pot or even a jar of water. Older plants do become straggly and top heavy, so propagate every couple of years. If the atmosphere gets too dry (often in winter when radiators are on), it can suffer from red spider mite and aphids in spring. These can easily be rubbed or washed off with a dilute solution of washing-up liquid. If the plant is badly infected, cut back to a shoot and allow it to grow again.

Salvia rosmarinus 'Sissinghurst Blue'
Rosemary 'Sissinghurst Blue'

Rosemary is a naturally variable plant – hence the many cultivars available, from prostrate to mound forming and those with very erect habits. For me, 'Sissinghurst Blue' has always stood out for its upright habit, its graceful stems that arch over, the finesse of its slender leaves and its profuse, rich blue flowers, which immediately draw you to it. As the name implies, it was found as a seedling at Sissinghurst Castle in about 1958. Its slender leaves suggest it may have been a hybrid with *Salvia rosmarinus* var. *angustissimus*, the narrow-leaved rosemary found in Corsica and occasionally cultivated in the UK.

GROW Definitely a plant for hot, sunny positions. Give it space to allow it to display its upright and arching stems. Great for a gravel garden or tucked away at the base of steps or walls. Water to establish, but otherwise it's best grown hard with minimal water and feeding. Can be lightly pruned to control shape and size if needed.

Type
Evergreen shrub
Flowering
Spring, summer
Height/ spread
1.5m x 1m
Position
Full sun
Soil
Dry, well-drained, good on calcareous soils
Hardiness
USDA 8b/9a / RHS H4

Lavandula × intermedia 'Sussex'
Lavender 'Sussex'

Type
Evergreen shrub
Flowering
Summer
Height/ spread
1m x 1m
Position
Full sun
Soil
Dry, well-drained
Hardiness
USDA 7b/8a / RHS H5

Whether I'm growing plants as a gardener or understanding their classification and evolution as a scientist, my interest is in plant diversity. This plant combines both aspects – I have researched lavenders and written a monograph on them with my colleague Susyn Andrews. The diversity of lavenders goes far beyond the varieties that are familiar to us in our gardens, and include species from the Canary Islands and the deserts of North Africa and Arabia. This plant is a naturally occurring hybrid between spike lavender (*Lavandula latifolia*) from Mediterranean Europe and English lavender (*L. angustifolia*), a mountain species from the Alps and familiar in our gardens. Occasionally the two species meet on mountain sides and hybridise to produce natural populations – these are the plants that form the basis of the lavender industry in France. The intermedias grow larger than English lavender, flower a little later in summer and for a longer period.

'Sussex' is a strong-growing cultivar with deep violet-blue flowers in large flower spikes. It blooms over a long period of time, peaking in mid-summer but lasting through to autumn. But the main reason I grow it is because it's loved by pollinators, attracting more than any other lavender I grow. On warm sunny days, the plants are covered with bumblebees, honey bees, hoverflies, butterflies and day-flying moths. From a distance, they look to be crawling with insects. It's most likely that the flowers are flared and so more open, which allows a wide range of insects to gather nectar. Like some hybrids, it is sterile and doesn't set seed, meaning it continues to produce nectar for a prolonged period. The introduction of this plant is a global story. It was first selected in France, then trialled in New Zealand, where it was named, before being imported to the UK and featuring in the RHS Plant Trials ending in 2001.

GROW I grow mine along our gravel driveway with good drainage and plenty of sun. Once established, the plants get their roots deep into the soil and are very drought tolerant. Allowing a few other plants, such as the leaves of grasses or a few self-seeded poppies, to grow through can be effective. But my favourite is to underplant with a few scattered bulbs of *Allium sphaerocephalum* (round-headed garlic) – the rounded purplish flowerheads complement the violet-blue of the lavender spikes. Water to establish and prune annually, ideally after flowering or before active growth starts the following spring. When pruning, remove the flower spikes and a short piece of growth. You can prune harder to control size and shape but always leave some young buds on the stem (you can see these on the older wood as green spikes).

Type
Rambler rose
Flowering
Summer
Height/ spread
3m x 2.5m
Position
Full sun, tolerates some shade
Soil
Well-drained, fertile
Hardiness
USDA 7b/8a / RHS H5

Rosa 'Lauré Davoust'
Rose 'Lauré Davoust'

There are many wonderful roses to grow and I could have picked several. This one is special because I first came across it on a visit to La Mortela, the Hanbury Botanic Garden in northern Italy. The plant in full flower was breathtaking and I immediately knew we needed to find a space for one in our garden. The clusters of small cupped flowers that change from bright to soft pink looked to be dripping from the wall against which it had been trained.

La Mortela is a special garden sited on a rocky promontory stretching into the Mediterranean, creating a microclimate that allows many subtropical plants to be grown alongside more temperate subjects. Just across the bay is Monaco and the hills behind are covered with orange and olive groves. The garden belonged to Thomas Hanbury, a trader and important figure in UK gardening history. It was Hanbury who also bought the garden of George Fergusson Wilson in Surrey and gifted it to the RHS in 1903. The site is now RHS Wisley and my current base. We have planted this rose close to a seating area, allowing it to climb and ramble into a pine tree so it can be admired and enjoyed during mid-summer.

GROW Requires training against a wall of the house, alternatively let it grow into a tree or over a pergola. It's best to give it a little shelter to protect the flowers from damage by wind or rain. Feed once a year and tie into its support as needed. Pruning is required to control size and vigour.

Chionochloa rubra
Red tussock grass

Type
Evergreen grass
Flowering
Summer
Height/ spread
1.5m x 1m
Position
Full sun
Soil
Moist, well-drained
Hardiness
USDA 6a–1 / RHS H7

I love to grow grasses for both the structure and texture they bring to a garden, and their movement in the wind. They provide an excellent foil to other flowering perennials and create rhythm in a planting. I first came across this group of grasses at the Garden House in Devon many years ago. I was inspired by the spectacular use of this New Zealand species dotted in a ribbon through a meadow-style planting of herbaceous perennials. Its bronzed leaves and strong tufted form with outward-arching leaves provided both contrast and structure and, in my eyes, flowed through the planting. The flower spikes are sparse, wispy and attractive enough, but it's the other qualities that make this so special for creating an inspiring display. I use it in my own garden to create a repeated structure (not quite on the same scale as I originally saw) and 20 years after it first inspired me, I am now a trustee of the Garden House.

This plant complements many perennials, such as echinaceas and achilleas, carrot relatives such as *Orlaya grandiflora*, with their plate-like flowers, and or dwarf gladioli with their upright flower stems.

GROW Needs little attention once established.

MIGUEL URQUIJO AND RENATE KASTNER
Landscape and garden designers, Madrid, Spain

Miguel Urquijo and his wife and business partner Renate Kastner founded landscape design studio Urquijo-Kastner in 2001, having trained and worked in horticulture and design since the early 1990s. They carry out their work mainly in Spain and specialise in private gardens in rural settings. *urquijokastner.com*

Arbutus unedo ↘
Strawberry tree

Type
Evergreen tree
Flowering
Autumn
Height/ spread
8m x 8m
Position
Full sun, sheltered
Soil
Well-drained, slightly acidic
Hardiness
USDA 7b/8a / RHS H5

I was once asked: If I had to be reincarnated as a plant, what would it be? It seemed like a childish question, but it ended up forcing me to reflect on some of the characteristics I value in people. I chose my favourite plant, and when I began to justify the choice I was surprised to see that some of the virtues I admired in it were the same as those I would want in a human. They should be adaptable to the varying conditions of life, not get too fussy about things in general and have a decent outlook all year round. Not too small but not too big either, with some flair once in a while (why not?), although not so striking as to arouse envy. Someone you could count on, someone collaborative and not at all greedy. This person should be able to face life's challenges with dignity, courage and sobriety. And finally, be capable of recovering with no apparent loss after a tragedy or major disturbance.

In our gardens, that plant equivalent is the strawberry tree. We would not mind being as good as this little tree. If there is one plant that has repeated in all our gardens this is it. It is a perennial shrub/small tree of the *Ericaceae* family that has a very picturesque shape, with a muscular trunk and sinuous branches that twist and turn giving the illusion of motion. It generally grows to 3–5m in height, although specimens of up to 10m have been found. It can live more than 60 years. It has reddish-brown bark with greyish tones. The finely serrated waxy leaves are a vivid green during spring and summer, turning darker later, but attractive throughout the year. Clusters of pink to white, urn-shaped flowers appear in profusion at the branch tips and persist for weeks in the cooler air of autumn. The fruit is a round berry of an intense orange, later turning red. It takes up to a year to mature, so often you find flowers and berries adorning the tree near Christmas.

It is true that the strawberry tree does not like prolonged intense frosts, and that's why in nature it usually takes refuge in shady areas that offer humidity in summer and shelter in winter. In many of our gardens, where temperatures can drop sporadically below −15°C, these plants hold up well if the ground is well-drained. Not infrequently in nature they appear in areas of great exposure, enduring the scorching heat of summer and the intense cold of winter. At the same time I know that they do well in subtropical places like the Canary Islands and even in totally tropical environments like Cuba.

These plants are capable of recovering after major disturbances such as fires. It is precisely this adaptation that allows us to rejuvenate a strawberry tree if it has aged ungracefully or has overgrown and you want to start again. It would be the equivalent of what can be done with old yews or box plants, but I would say that the recovery of the strawberry tree is even more vigorous.

Finally, its leaves and bark contain tannins that have been used for tanning. In several countries of the Mediterranean basin a liqueur is made with its fruits, which can also be eaten ripe directly or used for jam. Its wood is used in cabinet making. It is an excellent honey plant and bees love it. The Berbers of North Africa even plant strawberry trees to scare away evil spirits.

GROW The only thing I would try to avoid is clay or poorly-drained soil. Dislikes mineral fertiliser but will cherish good garden compost. It tolerates almost any exposure, even being able to grow under the allelopathic hot shade of *Pinus pinea* so common in our latitude. Very importantly in these days of climate uncertainty this plant, once established, is great for drought-tolerant gardens. In nature it survives in areas where water can be absent for more than four months.

From the landscape point of view, it is suited to many gardens if you're looking for a little tree that will not cause trouble due to excessive growth. It is one of the best evergreen multi-stem plants I could think of. With some patience, magnificent free hedges can be formed – by free, I mean those that don't require the commitment of regular pruning to look good. These small trees keep compact, achieving a good screen that does not give the feeling of a formal hedge and therefore of a 'garden end'. With regular trimming (two or three times a year), you can also make topiary of any shape or volume. The trick is to be very disciplined and severe with this in the early years, to promote and increase the number of sprouts from ground level.

It is a very neutral plant that collaborates and mixes well with countless other species. It can be used in groups or as a solitary tree. We combine it with other typical mediterranean evergreens such as *Pistacia lentiscus*, *Myrtus communis* and *Bupleurum fruticosum*.

JOE WHELAN
Head gardener, Nymans, West Sussex, UK

Joe Whelan has worked in horticulture in a variety of disciplines, including garden design, landscaping and food production. He started at Nymans in 2015 and was appointed head gardener three years later. Before that he worked in the northwest of Ireland, restoring a Victorian kitchen garden at a prestigious county house. *nationaltrust.org.uk/nymans*

Magnolia × wieseneri

I've always loved magnolias, but coming to Nymans was my first proper experience of working in a garden with such a vast collection of them. Of all of them, *M. × wieseneri* (which I hadn't heard of before) jumped out as being the most remarkable. It's a hybrid between *M. sieboldii* and *M. obovata*, two very beautiful magnolias in their own right. A small deciduous tree, its flower petals 'are ivory-white, which contrast wonderfully against its large crimson stamens. Up close, the flower can almost appear artificial. The scent is incredible too, with an antiseptic-type aroma. The flowers can be picked and placed in a bowl of water and the scent can fill an entire room.

GROW It's what I call a summer show-off, a tree best grown for its remarkable flowers. It's slow growing but not at all fussy, and although it's at its best in early summer, it will continue to flower sporadically for much of the season if in a sheltered spot. It prefers a wee bit of shade – at Nymans, our best specimen grows on the edge of a grove of larger magnolias. Once established, it looks after itself pretty well and doesn't require any pruning, but if necessary, prune in winter.

Type
Deciduous small tree or shrub
Flowering
Summer
Height/ spread
6m x 6m
Position
Full sun, part shade
Soil
Well-drained, fertile, acid
Hardiness
USDA 7b/8a / RHS H5

STEPHEN GRIFFITH
Curator and head gardener,
Abbotsbury Subtropical
Gardens, Dorset, UK

Stephen Griffith has been responsible for restoring and developing Abbotsbury gardens, a sheltered woodland valley with special microclimates, since 1991. He has taken part in botanical expeditions to Chile, the Himalayas and Borneo to collect seeds and gain ideas for its development. He lectures and leads garden tours around the world. *abbotsburygardens.co.uk*

Type
Rhizomatous
herbaceous perennial
Flowering
Summer, autumn
Height/spread
2.5m x 1m
Position
Full sun
Soil
Moist, well-drained
Hardiness
USDA 9b/10a / RHS H3

Canna × ehemannii
Ehemann's canna

This is a lovely canna with bold, upright leaves and pendant, tubular, carmine red-to-purple flowers late in the season. Grown en masse in the centre of a border the flamboyant blooms make an impressive display. It can also be used to give some height at the back of the border.

Cannas have been used since Victorian times for adding an exotic touch to late summer borders. *C.* × *ehemannii* is one of the hardier forms and can be left in the ground over winter if it is well mulched.

GROW Prefers a warm, sunny site and grows well along a south- or west-facing wall (in the northern hemisphere). In terms of soil, it likes something slightly on the acid side. Add good garden compost, manure or leaf mould, to help with water retention.

Podophyllum versipelle 'Spotty Dotty'
Mayapple 'Spotty Dotty'
(SEE ILLUSTRATION PAGE 82)

This is a superb, large-leaved ground-cover plant for a shady spot. Its unique marbled markings make it really stand out. It has an exotic tropical look, yet is quite hardy. I grow it as an alternative to hostas as slugs and snails don't bother its luscious leaves. It also has a hidden secret, often missed: its beautiful maroon red, bell-shaped flowers that hang down hidden away under the leaves.

GROW Best grown in a shady spot under the canopy of shrubs.

Type
Rhizomatous
herbaceous
perennial
Flowering
Summer
**Height/
spread**
50cm x 50cm
Position
Full shade,
part shade
Soil
Moisture-
retentive,
humus-rich
Hardiness
USDA 8b/9a
/ RHS H4

× Phyllosasa tranquillans 'Shiroshima'
Shiroshima bamboo

This hardy bamboo forms a bold dense block of bright foliage, making it one of the loveliest variegated bamboos for the back of the border or large raised beds. It makes a good evergreen screen and bold landscape plant with an exotic subtropical look. It is generally clump-forming, but can occasionally run if the ground is continually warm and moist.

GROW I find it responds to heavy mulching with organic matter and extra watering by growing more vigorously. In time it makes a large specimen clump, but can look floppy and unkempt when dry at the root. Regular thinning of its canes reduces congestion and makes it stand out better as a specimen plant.

Type
Bamboo
**Height/
spread**
2.5m x 8m
Position
Full sun
Soil
Moisture-
retentive
loamy soil
Hardiness
USDA 8b/9a
/ RHS H4

Woodwardia radicans
European chain fern

Of all the ferns I grow, this one has the largest fronds. They have a luscious sheen to them when they are young and, as they get bigger, they arch over until the tips touch the ground. From the end of the fronds they produce brown, hairy, swollen bulbils that, on touching the ground, send out roots and start to grow a new plant.

I first saw this in the wild, growing in the mountains of the Laurisilva forests in Madeira where large colonies form a giant linking chain of roots and fronds, hence the common name, chain fern. Individual fronds can grow up to 1.6m long and add a touch of the jungle to any planting scheme. It grows best in a sheltered woodland setting in moist shade or by a north-facing wall. A good plant for ground cover with a subtropical appeal.

GROW Easy to propagate from the growing tips – either peg them down to assist rooting or take cuttings and place in sand or vermiculite in a pot on a bench propagator. It doesn't like to dry out, so keep an eye on watering if you have just planted them. Leave the old fronds on the plant over winter for extra protection.

Type
Evergreen fern
Height/spread
1.5m x 2.5m
Position
Part shade
Soil
Moist, well-drained
Hardiness
USDA 9b/10a / RHS H3

Butia capitata
Jelly palm

If you're looking to create a subtropical garden, this is a superb palm tree. Generally hardy in the mildest parts of the country, it is a slow grower but, given time, forms an impressive architectural specimen with its feather-shaped, glaucous grey fronds. The woody trunk is formed of old leaf bases. When the plant is mature it produces large, elongated flower stalks and flowers in a woody sheath, followed by egg-shaped orange fruit in autumn.

GROW A slow grower so plenty of soil preparation is needed to help it establish quicker. Dig as large a hole as possible to break up the soil structure, then add plenty of organic compost and bone meal for slow nitrogen release. Keep well watered and mulch around the crown to help retain moisture. Requires little attention once established.

Type
Palm tree
Flowering
Summer
Height/spread
6m x 5m
Position
Full sun, quite wind tolerant
Soil
Moisture-retentive, loamy
Hardiness
USDA 11 / RHS H1c

Tetrapanax papyrifer 'Rex'
Chinese rice-paper plant 'Rex'

This plant has enormous appeal if you want to use large-leaved shrubs to instil a feel of the tropics in your garden. The giant leaves, held on tall stems, have a covering of rusty brown hairs. Within the stems there is a pith that is used to make a very fine rice paper. It produces panicles of white globular flowers in autumn. There are several variants of leaf form available – 'Rex' is one of the largest and most popular.

GROW Best given some shelter as strong winds shred the leaves. Mulch the ground in winter to protect its running root system. Every couple of years cut the stems back quite hard to 50cm or 1m off the ground to encourage fresh new growth, which makes much larger leaves. It can form a running colony of stems as it has a suckering habit, but this can easily be controlled with a spade in the winter. Prefers a moist, rich soil that does not dry out.

Type
Shrub or small tree
Flowering
Autumn
Height/spread
8m x 8m
Position
Full sun, sheltered
Soil
Moist, well-drained
Hardiness
USDA 8b/9a / RHS H4

EMMA ROBERTSON
Owner, Tor Garden Plants,
Devon, UK

Tor Garden Plants is a specialist nursery for pond, marginal and moisture-loving plants that sits on the edge of Dartmoor. *torgardenplants.co.uk*

← *Iris laevigata* 'Variegata'
Variegated Japanese iris

Of all the water irises for ponds, *I. laevigata* 'Variegata' has to be one of the best. Not only does it have an elegant blue-purple flower with a striking white flash on the petals, it also has the most attractive variegated foliage. Stunning on its own, with stripes of green and white displayed in tidy fans, it adds interest to the pond all year round. It is always my go-to plant when designing planting schemes for ponds as it lights up any dark areas and makes a real focus point.

GROW This iris likes to be planted with its rhizome and roots just below the water surface, either in pots or directly into the soil along pond margins. It loves a heavy clay soil, which is advised over an aquatic compost. In pots the iris would need dividing and repotting every three years after flowering or in early spring. Feed early spring and after flowering – I use blood, fish and bone.

Type
Rhizomatous perennial
Flowering
Summer
Height/spread
90cm x 50cm
Position
Full sun, part shade, ideally with some shelter
Soil
Moist, clay
Hardiness
USDA 6b/7a / RHS H6

FRANS BEIJK
Garden designer,
Keukenhof, Lisse,
Netherlands

Frans Beijk is chief designer at Keukenhof gardens, which is renowned for its spring displays of tulips and other bulbs. Frans draws the designs for the garden before digitising them and each of the millions of bulbs in his designs are planted by hand. *keukenhof.nl*

Narcissus 'Actaea'
Daffodil 'Actaea'

My father worked at Keukenhof for over 34 years as a gardener and I've been visiting the gardens for as long as I can remember. When I came to work here myself, I already knew half of the gardeners and the gardens very well.

N. 'Actaea' is one of the earliest daffodils to be cultivated and it has a very natural appearance that makes it seem at one with nature. It is snowy white with a small but bright yellow eye that's edged in red. They are very beautiful planted in beds that edge alongside water or in forest areas where its white colour can pop out against the green background.

GROW Plant somewhere sheltered or in a group. You only need to water them when there hasn't been any rain for a week. Combine spring-flowering bulbs with other plants and summer bulbs to have a colourful garden for months.

Type
Bulbous perennial
Flowering
Spring
Height/spread
40cm x 1m
Position
Full sun, part shade, sheltered
Soil
Moist, well-drained
Hardiness
USDA 6b/7a / RHS H6

SIMON GOODENOUGH
Estate manager, Folly Farm,
Berkshire, UK

Simon Goodenough manages the estate at Folly Farm, a collaboration between architect Edwin Lutyens and gardener Gertrude Jekyll, with a garden now reimagined and designed by Dan Pearson. Over a 45-year career, he has also been supervisor of the Temperate and Arboretum Nursery at Royal Botanic Gardens, Kew and the curator of the National Botanic Garden of Wales. *twitter.com/simongoodenough*

Astelia chathamica
Silver spear

On a visit to New Zealand in the 1980s, I was struck by the shining silver leaves of this plant when I saw it in both private gardens and public parks. It presented a striking feature among softer green foliage. I had seen the plant in the UK but paid little attention to it until I saw its potential in a garden setting. It was like a shining metallic phormium, almost shimmering in sunlight and looking magical when glistening with raindrops. At the time I was developing a New Zealand garden at Ventnor Botanic Garden on the Isle of Wight and the astelia became an exciting feature that provided me with the exclamation marks I wanted for my borders.

GROW Happiest if given some shelter, it grows in most locations, except those with northerly exposures. Although able to withstand a degree of drought, it prefers regular moisture. I have found it to be happiest in a friable soil with a reasonable clay content. Soil pH does not seem to be a major factor, but very high or low pH does seem to curtail growth. You can divide established clumps in spring. Young plants grow quite successfully in containers, providing they are adequately fed, but do eventually need to be moved on. Older leaves die and a spring spruce-up helps to keep the plant looking its best. This is a moderately tender perennial, best grown in milder climates.

Type
Rhizomatous perennial
Flowering
Summer
Height/spread
1.5m x 1m
Position
Full sun, part shade
Soil
Moist, well-drained, clay, loam
Hardiness
USDA 9b/10a / RHS H3

Impatiens tinctoria
Dyers busy lizzie

In 1985 I took charge of Ventnor Botanic Garden where I first came across this plant. My first impression from afar was of a cloud of butterflies. The flowers were trembling delicately in the breeze. Held on slender stalks, they seemed to hover around the strong fleshy upright plant. As I got closer, I was aware of the sweet fragrance the flowers had. I was smitten and since then this plant has featured in my own gardens.

GROW *I. tinctoria* is frost tender, although I have found that mulching over the roots once I have cut back the foliage (which goes down at the first frost) makes it virtually bomb proof. Applying a good mulch for the winter is prudent.

Type
Tuberous perennial
Flowering
Summer
Height/spread
2.5m x 1m
Position
Part shade, dappled shade
Soil
Moist, well-drained
Hardiness
USDA 9b/10a / RHS H3

Type
Herbaceous perennial
Flowering
Summer, autumn
Height/spread
1m x 50cm
Position
Full sun
Soil
Well-drained, chalk, loam, sandy
Hardiness
USDA 6a–1 / RHS H7

Aster × frikartii 'Mönch'
Aster 'Mönch'

This is a bomb-proof, floriferous perennial at home almost anywhere. It flowers through summer and autumn, is great in beds and borders, and super in informal gardens or traditional cottage gardens. It's also a worthy cut flower – the flowers are a lovely lavender-blue. I have grown this for as long as I can remember. In my personal experience, this cultivar seldom suffers from mildew or mould, as many other asters do. Keeping plants invigorated by regular division is a good policy.

GROW This plant is easily propagated in spring by division or basal cuttings. Cut back in the late autumn. It's generally trouble-free, but may suffer from verticillium wilt, powdery mildew and grey moulds.

Type
Rhizomatous
perennial
Flowering
Spring
**Height/
spread**
50cm x 50cm
Position
Part shade
Soil
Moist, well-
drained,
loam
Hardiness
USDA 7b/8a
/ RHS H5

Arisarum proboscideum
Mouse plant

Early in my career, I visited a private garden that had an extensive woodland garden. In one of the dappled shady beds, a ground cover of glossy green, arrow-shaped leaves caught my eye as I could see a lot of what looked like mouse tails sticking out from between the leaves. Closer examination revealed dozens of purple-brown spathes beneath the extraordinarily long tips that had first drawn my attention. I showed the flowers to some nearby children and their reaction has been ingrained in my memory ever since – squeals of delight at discovering this floral 'nest of mice'. I have since planted the plant in my own garden, where I enjoy recapturing the magic of my first encounter. The grandchildren love it.

GROW Easy to grow, it makes a delightful spreading ground cover that can be contained readily. The curious flowers appear in spring and have to be looked for, but are a source of wonder. It is best planted where it looks good in morning sunlight but gets shade in the afternoon. Winter wet can be a problem if soils become waterlogged. Can be easily divided in autumn or winter. It makes a fun pot plant, where you can enjoy its flowers to their fullest.

Type
Bulbous
perennial
Flowering
Late spring,
summer
**Height/
spread**
1m x 50cm
Position
Full sun,
tolerant of
some shade
Soil
Moist, well-
drained
Hardiness
USDA 8b/9a
/ RHS H4

Camassia quamash →
Camas

This bulbous plant has numerous uses, but I love it in my wild meadow. The intense blue of the flower spikes occurs just after most spring bulbs have finished and before other wildflower species get going. It brings a beautiful wash of blue through the meadow, it seeds freely and has offsets that allow it to multiply surprisingly quickly. Good as a cut flower too.

GROW Intolerant of waterlogging and shallow soils. In very cold areas it may need some protection from frost. Easily propagated from seed, which should be sown as soon as it is ripe and put in pots in a cold frame. Offsets can be taken when the plant is dormant.

Hydrangea seemannii
Seemann's hydrangea

I first saw a mature *H. seemannii* while visiting a friend's garden where it was covering the entire gable end on the west wall of the stone cottage. The sun was setting, the plant was in full flower and the sight took my breath away. I was more familiar with the deciduous *H. petiolaris*, but this evergreen cousin offered new opportunities for wall covering that immediately appealed to me and solved a bit of a design problem I was having. Now, many years later, I am trying to emulate my friend's planting by growing it on the south-west gable end of my own home. It is a self-clinging climber with large leathery leaves, often 15cm long. Once established, and come summer, it is covered in domed flowerheads.

GROW I have found that keeping the plant well watered and mulched, particularly when establishing, pays dividends. As a vigorous climber that flowers on previous-season and new-season wood, pruning to shape is the only maintenance required.

Type
Evergreen
climber
Flowering
Summer
**Height/
spread**
12m x 4m
Position
Full sun, part
shade, full
shade
Soil
Moist, well-
drained
Hardiness
USDA 8b/9a
/ RHS H4

Type
Shrub rose
Flowering
Summer
Height/spread
2m x 1.1m
(can be more)
Position
Full sun
Soil
Any
Hardiness
USDA 6b/7a /
RHS H6

Rosa **Jude the Obscure ('Ausjo')**
Rose [Jude the Obscure]

Having spent much of my early career sorting out other people's roses or pruning public rose gardens, I cannot say that I am the greatest rose fan. But living in a country cottage there is something quintessential about roses in the garden and I admit to having quite a few. So why this one in particular? For me, a rose must have a scent and Jude the Obscure does not disappoint on this front. It has a strong fragrance that lingers in the air. I grow this near my front door so it greets me and my visitors whenever we come and go; even the postman has commented on its merits.

I have trained this repeat- and free-flowering rose up a wall where it is now approaching 3m, but it can easily be pruned to the height you want. The flower is a large chalice of a soft yellow with an apricot or old parchment hue that gives a warmth and depth to it. The fragrance is strong and fruity, reminiscent of a sweet white wine but with a hint of something tropical going on.

GROW When establishing roses it is important to ensure adequate and regular watering, particularly in the first couple of years and during dry spells. Watering should be aimed at the soil – avoid getting water on the foliage as this may encourage fungal diseases. Once established, roses are deep rooted and watering is only important in longer dry spells. Twice yearly feeding, once in early spring and again in mid-summer, with a balanced rose feed or general fertiliser. A mulch of organic matter after irrigating and feeding newly planted roses is also recommended, but avoid taking the mulch too close to the stem as this can cause disease and plant failure.

Cistus ladanifer
Common gum cistus

The intoxicating smell of this Mediterranean shrub transports me to memories of special times: walking in the rugged terrain of Greece through insect-buzzing olive groves with the ever-present fragrance of cistus. On one occasion I passed through a small hillside village and two elderly gentlemen playing backgammon in a shaded taverna looked up as I approached. "You crazy Englishman", they said – walking in the midday sun made it obvious I was English. They invited me to join them and I spent a pleasant afternoon in the shade. Beside the veranda on which we sat, large plants of *C. ladanifer* grew, their resinous leaves glistening in the sun and their wonderful fragrance filling the air. To this day, the scent takes me back to that now distant memory.

GROW Little maintenance needed. The plant will not tolerate hard pruning but you can gently remove spent flowerheads. Plants become straggly in time and it is usually best to remove old plants and replace with new. Readily propagated by seed or softwood cuttings.

Type
Evergreen shrub
Flowering
Summer
Height/spread
2.5m x 1.5m
Position
Full sun, sheltered
Soil
Well-drained,
inclined to become
chlorotic on thin
chalky soil
Hardiness
USDA 8b/9a / RHS H4

JACKIE CURRIE
Garden designer,
Surrey, UK

Jackie Currie has been a garden designer for some two decades and co-runs Euphorbia Garden Design. For the last seven years she has held the National Collection of *Allium*, winning awards at RHS Chelsea and Hampton Court Flower Shows for her collection displays. *euphorbia-design.co.uk*

Allium ⭨
Ornamental onion

I love the colours, shapes and architectural look of allium flowers. Many bloom early in the spring border, giving colour before the main event, but there are so many that if you pick the right ones you can have alliums flowering from spring until autumn. As a garden designer, I had always used the common, readily available and reliable varieties *Allium hollandicum* 'Purple Sensation', *A. cristophii* and *A. sphaerocephalon*. But I became bored and decided to trial some new varieties up at the allotment I share with my husband to see if I could extend the season and get them to flower reliably for several more years. After one season testing 50 varieties that were new to me, I was hooked. I am now the National Collection holder. Asking me to choose a single favourite is impossible as there are so many good ones. My top picks are as follows. For colour, *A. hollandicum* 'Purple Sensation'. For early colour, *A. jesdianum* 'Early Emperor'. For late colour, *A. wallichii*. For reliability and beauty, *A.* 'Violet Beauty'. For bees, *A. siculum* (though bees love all alliums). And finally, for people who don't like alliums, *A.* 'Eros'. These particular recommendations range in height from 60cm–1m.

GROW I split alliums into three groups for the gardener: the 'leave in', the 'leave in, lift and split every two to three years', and the 'lift and bake'. That doesn't mean you put the last group in the oven! Instead lift, clean, dry and keep them somewhere like a shed or greenhouse at about 20°C before replanting in autumn. This mimics the dry and hot summer weather of the bulbs' native habitat. All the favourites I've mentioned sit in the 'leave in, lift and split every two to three years' group to keep them flowering.

Plant alliums at a depth that is twice the height of the bulb. The leaves will appear first, some of them as early as November (don't panic, the frost won't bother them). The flowerhead then appears from the centre of the plant and, depending on the allium, the leaves may start to die off. You can tidy these off as they die (but it doesn't matter if you don't). After flowering, leave the seedheads on or cut off. If left on, they will spread seed all over.

Type
Bulbous perennial
Flowering
Spring, summer, autumn
Height/spread
15cm–2m x 50cm
Position
Full sun, part shade, open unless a woodland species
Soil
There is an allium for all soil types
Hardiness
USDA 9a–6b / RHS H4–H6

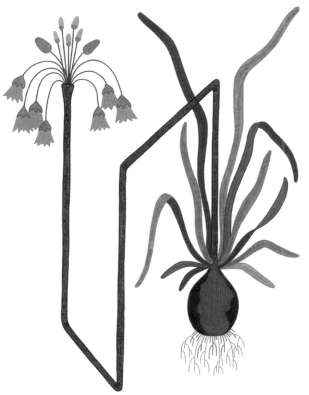

LEIF BJARTE KROGSTAD
Garden designer and
landscaper, Haugesund,
Norway

Leif Bjarte Krogstad started a landscape business in his early twenties.
Over the years he and his wife Anne developed their interest in garden
design and today they run a company combining design and builds.
komplettutemiljo.no

Acer shirasawanum 'Aureum' →
Golden full moon maple

It is very hard to choose between plants, but I consider this one of my overall
favourites. Its shape and size make it a great choice in many gardens,
especially in smaller spaces. The way the leaves are set up, in a true Japanese
cloud-like geometry, gives the plant a soft and eye-catching form. Most of all
I am very fond of the leaf colour. It goes from lime-green in early spring to dark
yellow later in summer, ending with orange in autumn. This plant really both
stands out and blends in in any planting. In our own garden it is planted in
well-drained soil under a huge pine tree that gives it half shade. As a backdrop
there is a beech hedge that gives it a soft and tender contrast. In Norway the
common name, *måneskinnslønn*, means 'moonshine maple', and alludes to
its almost glowing leaves in the evening. In our garden we also light it with a
spotlight from underneath, which makes it glow even more during the long
Norwegian summer nights.

GROW It thrives best in part shade and often gets a bit sunburned if planted in direct
sun. Plant in compost-enriched, well-drained soil. In my part of Norway, this plant rarely
grows more than about 3m high. In Norway we do not give awards to plants as in the UK
– we probably still have a bit too much Viking blood left in our veins, so our vocabulary
and ways of communicating are very minimalistic, so to speak – but if you are looking for
a great plant for half shade in your own garden, this is a really good choice.

Type
Deciduous
tree
Flowering
Spring
**Height/
spread**
8m x 8m
Position
Part shade,
sheltered
Soil
Moist, well-
drained
Hardiness
USDA 6b/7a
/ RHS H6

KAREN LEYS
Garden designer and
grower, Plants, Shoots and
Leaves, Jedburgh, Scotland

Karen Leys is a horticulturist who founded the nursery Plants, Shoots
and Leaves in 2010. She is a specialist grower of epimediums and hardy
geraniums and a cut-flower farmer. *plantsshootsandleaves.co.uk*

Type
Herbaceous perennial
Flowering
Spring, summer, autumn
Height/spread
45cm x 90cm
Position
Part shade, full shade
Soil
Moist, well-drained
Hardiness
USDA 6b/7a / RHS H6

Epimedium 'Domino'
Barrenwort 'Domino'

I chose this epimedium because it is one of the most reliable I
grow and possibly the most floriferous – it never fails to flower and
has a definite 'wow' factor. I always sell out of it at flower shows.
   I bought my first 'Domino' after seeing it in flower at Koen Van
Pouke's nursery in Belgium when on holiday there one September.
It has quite an impact as ground cover in shady areas or as part
of a woodland garden. It produces masses of arching spikes of
large, pinkish-white spurred flowers with maroon tips and buds
over long spiny leaves, which are speckled bronze in spring. It
flowers from spring to summer and can repeat flower in autumn.

GROW Likes leaf mould added at planting. Deadheading can extend
flowering and repeat flowering. Shelter from cold winds. Remove old
tatty foliage in late winter. Epimediums are also resistant to rabbits and
deer and tolerant of drought if the soil is humus-rich.

SARAH PAJWANI
Gardener, Berkshire, UK

Sarah Pajwani is a gardener who has created a much-celebrated two-acre garden at St Timothee. The private garden is open regularly through the National Garden Scheme. *instagram.com/sarahpajwani*

Type
Evergreen grass
Flowering
Summer, autumn
Height/spread
2.5m x 1m
Position
Full sun
Soil
Moist, well-drained
Hardiness
USDA 8b/9a / RHS H4

Stipa gigantea →
Golden oats

I love grasses for the soft and relaxed feel they bring to a border. They are a great foil for flowers. *S. gigantea* was the first grass I bought. I chose it specifically to add height, structure and year-round interest to a new border and as a lighter alternative to evergreen shrubs. I bought eight of them to run along the length of the border (large and backed by a hornbeam hedge) to give rhythm and cohesion, as well as height to link it with some tall, upright poplars behind. It's a tall grass, but one that is easy to accommodate even in smaller spaces, which I've done elsewhere in the garden. Even after the feather plumes are cut back at the end of winter, the green ball of grass acts as a great foil to the swathe of daffodils running through the border. The feather plumes then start up again in spring, giving a softness to summer perennials and then bringing golden tones and catching the light beautifully throughout autumn.

GROW This is a super-easy grass to grow. It is hugely drought tolerant, hardly self-seeds and the only maintenance required is a cut back of the spent feather plumes at the end of winter. I do this carefully by hand and with secateurs. It's more time consuming, but it's not a busy moment of the year and it means the plants continue to look good throughout spring. I like to trim the plumes as far back as possible to avoid ragged ends showing. I then go around the base of the plant, cutting out the dead, straw-coloured leaves. The last job is to do a quick and easy trim of the ends – pulling the whole clump together with one hand and cutting off the tatty straw tips. My soil is slightly alkaline clay. It gets baked in the summer and is claggy and wet in the winter, but the stipa is happy. I never feed or water it.

Melica uniflora f. *albida*
White-flowered wood melic

Type
Deciduous grass
Flowering
Summer
Height/spread
50cm x 1m
Position
Part shade, full shade
Soil
Moist, well-drained,
Hardiness
USDA 6a–1 / RHS H7

This is a delicate and beautiful small grass that brings light and movement to borders in partial and full shade. After being cut back fully at the end of winter, it quickly grows to a clump of fresh lime-green grass before throwing up delicate wands of flowerheads topped with what looks like grains of rice that catch the light perfectly and look so delicate and pretty. Photos never do this grass justice, but visitors to the garden always ask about it. Eventually the lime-green fades to straw, which lasts and provides interest throughout winter.

GROW Just needs a complete cut back at the end of winter. It self-seeds a fair bit in my garden, but it's easy to weed out or pot up to form new plants.

Type
Deciduous grass
Flowering
Summer, autumn
Height/spread
1.5m x 1m
Position
Full sun, copes with
some shade
Soil
Moist, well-drained
Hardiness
USDA 6b/7a / RHS H6

Calamagrostis × acutiflora 'Karl Foerster'
Feather reed grass 'Karl Foerster'

I love the softness and textural interest that grasses give to the garden, as well as how they catch the light and bring a sense of movement, swaying in the wind. Above all, I like the fact they are genuine year-round performers. 'Karl Foerster' is tall and strongly upright. I use it in two different ways: first, as a transparent screen where something evergreen would feel too heavy, and second, to give strong vertical accents in a mixed border. It's an early grass to get going, bouncing back quickly after its winter cut back to form a mound of lush green by the end of spring, with flower stems pushing up from early summer. By late summer, these have turned to straw, giving another colour to set against the summer flowers. It then goes on strongly through autumn and winter, where it has proved itself to be highly resilient to batterings by storms and snow.

GROW No maintenance needed other than simply cutting to the ground at the end of winter. Unlike some grasses, I've not found this self-seeds at all.

Type
Evergreen subshrub
Flowering
Spring, summer
Height/spread
1.5m x 1.5m
Position
Full sun
Soil
Well-drained
Hardiness
USDA 8b/9a /
RHS H4

Euphorbia characias subsp. *wulfenii*
Mediterranean spurge

This is a large evergreen shrub with huge structural interest. It looks wonderful right across the year, but I value it particularly for its branched open shape and interesting foliage in winter and throughout spring, when it throws up huge heads of zingy green flowers. It brings excitement and energy into the garden and the green is a great backdrop for spring bulbs and early perennials. In summer, it becomes a gentler and smaller presence in the border, acting as a soft green foil to all the flowers.

GROW I grow these in open, sunny and well-drained borders. I've found them hugely drought tolerant and they cope with harsh, cold winters equally well. The only maintenance needed is an annual cut back of the flowers. I tend to do this towards the end of spring, cutting the stems right back. They often still look good at this stage, but the summer flowers are growing and I like to give them space. As soon as the lime-green heads are removed, the euphorbia almost halves in size. So it is big and exciting when not much else is, then quieter and smaller when the main flower show gets going. It self-seeds a bit, but not much, and has given me the joy of many free plants.

Cornus sanguinea 'Midwinter Fire'
Dogwood 'Midwinter Fire'

This shrub is the absolute star of my garden for a full five months of the year – precisely the five months when it can be difficult to keep excitement, energy and warmth in the garden. I love all the dogwoods for their autumn foliage and winter stem colour, but 'Midwinter Fire' is exceptional because of the variety of tones of its stems, ranging from yellow to orange to red. It is perfectly named, really looking as if it is on fire, and so alive – it's the beating heart of my winter garden. A bonus was discovering how good its autumn foliage is, turning butter yellow before the leaves fall and the stems become the star. If cut back at the end of winter, it becomes a gentle lime-green foil for border flowers throughout the summer. The biggest downside of the plant is that it

Type
Deciduous shrub
Flowering
Summer
Height/spread
2.5m x 2.5m
Position
Full sun, part shade
Soil
Moist, well-drained
Hardiness
USDA 6b/7a / RHS H6

suckers, particularly after really wet spells. But I put up with this for the beauty it brings. I grow it in several spots in the garden – as a long hedge behind one of the borders where the colour intensity of the stems is multiplied, and also as a lone statement shrub in another border.

GROW I have found it slower to establish than other dogwoods and also more fiddly to prune. But given that the only maintenance it needs is a once-a-year cut back at the end of winter, maintenance is pretty easy. For the first couple of years, I tended to cut back stems by only a third and then, as the plant became more established, began to cut back one in every three stems to the ground and the remaining stems by roughly half. The plant may need occasional watering in its first year to establish. Requires full sun for optimum stem colour but copes with some shade.

Erigeron karvinskianus
Mexican fleabane

This has to be the easiest and longest flowering of all my plants. It's also desperately pretty. It's a small white and pink daisy that's perfect for edging paths and at the front of borders. From spring to autumn it is constantly in flower with no need for any deadheading. Soft and pretty, it's loved by bees and butterflies, so it also brings life and movement into the garden. I love its habit of self-seeding into paving cracks, giving the garden a sense of time and making things feel relaxed. It's even done this into north-facing walls in full shade – places where little else grows.

GROW I use this as a simple way to edge a path. It's easiest to establish in sunny, well-drained soils, but it has adapted to growing in very heavy clay here. It self-seeds readily but is easily kept in check. Give it a light cut-back at the end of winter.

Type
Perennial
Flowering
Spring, summer, autumn
Height/spread
50cm x 1m
Position
Full sun, part shade
Soil
Well-drained
Hardiness
USDA 7b/8a / RHS H5

Type
Herbaceous perennial
Flowering
Spring, summer
Height/spread
35cm x 30cm
Position
Full sun, part shade
Soil
Well-drained
Hardiness
USDA 8b/9a / RHS H4

Heuchera '**Black Taffeta**'
Coral bells 'Black Taffeta'

I use heuchera a lot in my garden as an easy front-of-border plant that offers so many different colours to contrast with other foliage and flowers. 'Black Taffeta' is one of my favourites as it is particularly vigorous and tough, and also easy to propagate. It has some of the darkest leaf colour, getting ever blacker as the sun and heat intensify, and looks great with strong bright colours. Its flower spires are a pale pink – so pale as to be almost white. It's in my 'red bed' along with reds, oranges, yellows and blues and sat next to some lime-green hakonechloa. It makes for a strong, vibrant and exciting mix of colours.

GROW Keep it in check by cutting off any chunks outgrowing their space. I tend to do this in autumn and I've found that stems plunged into a pot of compost will root over the winter and form strong new plants by spring, ready for any new areas or to give away to friends. Leaf colour is best in full sun.

CLAIRE HATTERSLEY
Biodynamic gardener,
Weleda, Derbyshire, UK

Claire Hattersley has worked in Weleda's biodynamic garden for over 20 years, growing and processing Demeter-quality botanical ingredients for the company's natural medicines and skincare products. *weleda.co.uk*

Matricaria recutita
Scented mayweed

There's nothing more uplifting than seeing (and smelling) an aromatic field full of scented mayweed (better known as German chamomile) with its billowing clouds of fragrant yellow-centred flowers. This is such a safe and easy-to-use herbal: use it to make a salve for inflamed and irritated skin, a tea to calm and aid digestion, or even a hair rinse to lighten the colour of your locks. At Weleda we harvest and dry the roots in early spring to make a remedy that helps with teething in babies. We also harvest the flowering herbs (everything above ground) in early summer to create products for problem skin prone to spots and acne. Chamomile in general is nicknamed the 'physician's plant' as it can revive sick plants if grown nearby. It can also help prevent your seedlings damping off – just spray them with cooled chamomile tea. It makes a useful companion plant for many vegetables, including brassicas, onions, beans and cucumbers, as well as apple trees and basil.

It's a plant that quickly reveals its calming personality, quieting the garden team's excited chatter within minutes of them starting the harvest! I love how it is an expression of air and light – from its finely divided, feathery leaves to each flower's 'sacred space' inside the yellow cone-shaped centre (cut one in half to see – this is the best method of correctly identifying this important medicinal herb). It flowers prolifically in early summer and readily self-sows, which can be good or bad depending where you're growing it.

GROW This is usually classified as an annual, but you get the biggest and most floriferous plants if you grow it as a biennial over two seasons. Sow thinly in late summer on to firm ground. Firm seeds in after sowing. There's no need to cover them as they need the light to germinate, but it's best not to sow on windy days as they can easily blow away.

It's pretty robust once established, and will keep growing into a leafy rosette throughout winter/early spring, then send up its flowering stems in mid- to late spring. Once the plants reach full size the following year, they may need some support, especially if grown on an exposed site.

Type
Annual
Flowering
Summer
Height/ spread
20cm x 90cm
Position
Full sun
Soil
Well-drained but firm
Hardiness
USDA 6a–1 / RHS H7

HARRIET RYCROFT
Gardener and speaker,
Cotswolds, UK

Harriet Rycroft is a container gardening expert. Formerly the head gardener at Whichford Pottery for nearly 14 years, she now gives talks and demonstrations and writes about container gardening. She gardens for private clients in the Cotswolds and maintains some 300 planted pots at her home. She is the author of *Pots*. *harrietrycroft.com*

Cobaea scandens →
Cup and saucer vine

When I was at Whichford I used to spend very little money on plants for the pots, growing a huge number from seed and cuttings. I have never been keen on limiting myself to well-behaved dumpy little 'patio plants' in pots – I like to include rangy annuals, trees, tall perennials and climbers in the bigger containers. *C. scandens* quickly became a favourite and I have grown it regularly ever since. I love the way it grows fast! It has gusto and ambition and doesn't care whether you plant it in a pot or in the ground: if it has sufficient warmth and moisture it will grow up the canes you give it, then its exploratory tendrils tipped with tiny grappling hooks reach across and grab anything they can – wires, branches, ivy, rough stonework, passing gardeners – and carry on upwards like Jack's beanstalk. On the way to the clouds it produces big, ding-dong bells followed by fat oval pods full of neatly packed papery seeds. The muted purple or cream flowers mean that wayward behaviour is tolerable as it never distracts too much, no matter what colour scheme it is photo-bombing.

   C. scandens is a perennial plant from Mexico but here in the UK it is most commonly grown as a tender annual. Sometimes it will survive winter in a sheltered position, but for container purposes I compost the plants once the frost has killed the top growth and sow fresh seed in the spring.

GROW It's easy to grow from seed (I use a propagator heated to about 15°C but a warm windowsill will probably do). I sow it on edge (to reduce the chance of the seed rotting) in general-purpose compost mixed with perlite, lightly covering it with compost. After an initial pause it grows fast and if you aren't careful you will end up with a tangled forest of seedlings so it's important to prick out/pot on promptly (I put one or two seedlings into a 1–1.5 litre pot), giving them a stick to climb up.

   After hardening off I like to plant it at the back of mixed summer plantings in large pots placed near a wall so that it can climb up existing wall plants such as ivy or (vigorous) roses. You can keep it on a large obelisk but it really isn't a plant for gardeners who like to remain in total control.

   If growing in a container it's easier to keep it in a position where hot midday or evening sun won't fry it, so that it remains happy and lush.

Type
Perennial climber, grown as an annual
Flowering
Summer, autumn
Height/ spread
5m x 2m
Position
Full sun, sheltered
Soil
Moist, well-drained
Hardiness
USDA 10b / RHS H2

REBECCA MCMACKIN
Director of horticulture,
Brooklyn Bridge Park, New
York, USA

Rebecca McMackin is an ecologically obsessed horticulturist. At Brooklyn Bridge Park she oversees 85 acres of diverse parkland managed with the dual purposes of cultivating beauty and encouraging biodiversity. She lectures, writes and designs the occasional garden. *rebeccamcmackin.com*

Type
Herbaceous
perennial
Flowering
Spring,
summer
**Height/
spread**
50cm x 50cm
Position
Full shade,
part shade
Soil
Adaptable,
but prefers
slightly
acidic loam
Hardiness
USDA 7b/8a
/ RHS H5

Tiarella cordifolia ↘
Foam flower

Plants in public parks require beauty and brawn. In our park, they must also have ecological functionality. *T. cordifolia* is somehow a darling spring flower, painting a cloud of white and beloved by bees, while also doing the hard work of thriving in a low-maintenance, high-pressure environment. Tiarellas and many related saxifrages have the smart strategy of keeping their fall foliage on for the winter in northeast USA. They're not exactly evergreen, but an 'ever-purple' ring of persistent foliage gives fall colour, winter interest, and holds the ground layer for the plant, inhibiting all interlopers from germination. New foliage and pretty flowers emerge in spring, and flowers are immediately sought out by bees who often lack floral resources. The plant also supports a specialist bee, who relies on its pollen for reproduction. A solver of many problems, we plant this by the thousands. Cultivars are available with all sorts of garish foliar mutations, from purple shapes to orange leaves, but I prefer a straight species plant with a diverse genetic array.

GROW This is a rugged plant. Ideal conditions are mesic (moist), dappled shade but it will thrive in sun with moisture and dry shade as well. Needs literally nothing after establishment. *T. cordifolia* is best planted en masse, as the drifts of flowers create a stunning spring show. They can be combined with spring phlox for a white and blue effect that is now arguably a modern classic. Due to their persistent and stubborn foliage, tiarellas also makes a marvellous green mulch.

Type
Herbaceous
perennial
Flowering
Spring,
summer
**Height/
spread**
1m x 50cm
Position
Part shade,
full shade,
can take
full sun with
reliable
moisture
Soil
Ideally the
side of a
moist, rocky
ledge
Hardiness
USDA 7b/8a
/ RHS H5

Aquilegia canadensis
Canadian columbine

Every spring, when the columbine blooms, we know that the ruby-throated hummingbird is not far behind. The red and yellow flowers, like nearly all red and yellow flowers of the Americas, are bird-pollinated and welcome hummingbirds back from their winter migration to Mexico. Columbine is part of a wave of red blooms that start around the Gulf of Mexico and announce the birds as they travel to and up the east coast. The aquilegia flowers are charming little bells, facing down to protect their nectar from spring rains, seeding in and popping up all over the garden. They are lovely, but it is the dynamic between flower and pollinator that makes the plant so special. Birds, like bees, have four photoreceptor cones in their eyes, but while bees are shifted to the UV spectrum, birds are shifted to the red. Birds see reds in ways we can only imagine, but bees, we think, see reds and greens alike, barely able to differentiate between them, which effectively hides red flowers from bees. Hummingbirds, then, have them all to themselves.

GROW It likes to be on lean, moist soils, growing out of rocks, hanging off a cliff and will make do in between paving stones. Thrives in most garden conditions and will go from dry shade to full sun if given moisture. Prefers a bit of shelter but I am always amazed at the places I see it happy – on rooftops, in sidewalk cracks – it's adaptable. Needs literally nothing after establishment. It will self-sow, so seedheads should be removed outside of its native range. Greens up early in spring and makes a good companion for bulbs.

KIRSTY WILSON
Herbaceous supervisor,
Royal Botanic Garden
Edinburgh, Scotland

Kirsty Wilson is an award-winning garden designer, BBC TV presenter
and herbaceous supervisor at the Royal Botanic Garden Edinburgh.
getplanting.co.uk

Meconopsis (Infertile Blue Group) 'Slieve Donard'
Himalayan blue poppy 'Slieve Donard'

As a student at the Royal Botanic Garden Edinburgh, I was captivated by its fragile beauty and iridescent blue blooms, a colour rarely seen in nature. I also saw this blue spectacle while working in America at Longwood Gardens, which forces the blue poppies to flower every year in spring and displays them in its world-class conservatory. People travel from all over just to see them – they call it 'blue poppy mania'. I always make a pilgrimage to see them in full bloom each year at Scotland's Branklyn Garden, which is home to the National Collection of *Meconopsis*. The plant originates from the Sino-Himalayan region, where it grows at high altitudes that experience heavy rainfall in summer, then monsoon conditions and heavy snowfall in winter. For this reason it thrives in our Scottish climate where the heavy rainfall and cool summers ensure it won't dry out.

GROW Meconopsis are hungry plants and dislike full scorching sun. In the wild, they grow in nutrient-rich soil frequented by passing yaks, so the plants benefit from a yearly mulch such as leaf mould or composted bark. You can apply this in spring or autumn but ensure the crown of the plant is not over-mulched and that the mulch around the plants is roughly 5cm deep.

This blue poppy can be propagated vegetatively through division, which is sometimes quicker than growing plants by seed. It's also an effective way of rejuvenating an old congested clump and, once divided, should result in more flowers. Do this in autumn to reduce stress on the plant and when conditions for the divided plant clump to root and grow are optimal. It's best to lift the plants out for dividing with a border fork, gently raising each clump at the edges. Once they're out, divide them with your hands as they are delicate plants and can be killed if brutally separated with a spade. The divided plants may take two to three years to bulk up and grow to a flowering size, so patience is key, just like with all gardening. You can divide a three- to four-year-old good-sized flowering clump and produce 10–20 new pieces for replanting. This process can be repeated each year.

If growing from seed, it is important to liquid feed the seedlings. To ensure they don't become pot bound, prick them out early and pot them on so they have room to establish good root growth. When the young plants are big enough you can plant them out in your garden, where you will be richly rewarded.

Type
Short-lived
perennial
Flowering
Summer
**Height/
spread**
1.5m x 50cm
Position
Part shade,
sheltered
to prevent
wind
damage
to flowers,
likes cold
and wet
summers
Soil
Moist, well-
drained,
acid, neutral
Hardiness
USDA 6b/7a
/ RHS H6

SARA VENN
Gardener and founder of
Incredible Edible Bristol,
Bristol, UK

Sara Venn founded Incredible Edible Bristol in 2014 after a career
working in nurseries and growing plants for urban regeneration
projects, flower shows and private clients. The organisation supports
communities to use lost, unloved spaces by creating food gardens.
thecommunitygarden.co.uk

Type
Perennial
Flowering
Summer,
autumn
**Height/
spread**
2.5m x 1.5m
Position
Full sun,
sheltered
Soil
Well-drained
Hardiness
USDA 7b/8a
/ RHS H5

Cynara cardunculus Scolymus Group ↘
Globe artichoke

Much of the planting we support at
Edible Bristol has to be able to withstand
the ravages of city life, and globe
artichokes do this magnificently. They
are architectural, productive and often
the last thing you expect to see growing in
a park or by the side of a road. They are
easily propagated by splitting them each
year. The silvery foliage is beautiful and
the huge flowers are edible while in bud
and great for pollinators once they open.

GROW They are really not fussy plants at all.
Their silver foliage means they can cope in
crazy hot conditions. They are challenging to
grow from seed, so are best propagated by
splitting the roots early in spring. Then they will
need a good watering and a mulch to settle
them in. After three years or so, they will be
super productive. People are always amazed
that they are growing in the city centre and
available for free!

Type
Tuberous
perennial
Flowering
Summer,
autumn
**Height/
spread**
Depends on
variety
Position
Full sun,
sheltered
Soil
Well-drained,
moisture-
retentive,
fertile
Hardiness
USDA 9b/10a
/ RHS H3

Dahlia
Dahlia (SEE ILLUSTRATION PAGE 89)

One of the most difficult things to do in a tiny space,
especially if it's rented and you are growing in pots,
is to have things that flower for a long time. Dahlias,
however, begin flowering in summer and go on to
the first frosts. They are very happy in a container, so
make the ideal plant for a tiny space. There is such
a range of colours and different forms, and they are
great as cut flowers.

GROW The only thing they need to be successful is a
mulch of good, peat-free compost twice a year and
to be kept frost free in winter, which is fairly easy with
some fleece. Feed weekly once they come into leaf and
deadhead to keep the blooms coming.

JINNY BLOM
Founder, Jinny Blom Studio,
London, UK

Jinny Blom has created over 500 landscape gardens based around her core ethos of sustainability to place. These include RHS Chelsea Flower Show gardens for the former Prince of Wales and Laurent-Perrier (a gold-medal winner). She is an artist in residence for Chelsea & Westminster Hospital, a board member of the Therapeutic Landscapes Network in the USA, and sits on the Gardens Committee for Waddesdon on behalf of the Rothschild Foundation. *jinnyblom.com*

Genista aetnensis
Mount Etna broom

Many years ago I visited Maurice Catlin, the renowned grower and owner of Manor Farm Nurseries, a trade nursery in Northamptonshire. Maurice was a lovely man – a solid, traditional plant grower of repute – and we had a great day looking at all his work. I noticed a single, small, stringy and unprepossessing plant in a pot that piqued my curiosity. "That's *G. aetnensis* and it's my gift to you," he said. Maurice had grown it from seed. Since that day, it has lived in increasingly larger containers at my home in London, ending up in a galvanised dustbin before I planted it in my garden. I called it Maurice. Never have I loved a plant more. It grew like crazy once it was planted out and before long I had the most beautiful small tree tapping on my bedroom window.

I adore plants that survive in the most improbable conditions. That is why *G. aetnensis* is such a favourite. Ascending Mount Etna is a visceral experience. Squeaking and skidding over the clinker-like ash that shrouds its slopes, it is astonishing to see the proliferation of these delicate trees emerging from the pumice, prone at any moment to being engulfed in volcanic emanations of mist and smoke. That such a sweet scent could counterbalance this pungent atmosphere, transporting one's nostrils to somewhere so transcendentally beautiful, is nothing short of miraculous.

Maurice's billowing clouds of exquisite perfume filled my house every summer from its heavy tresses of yellow pea flowers. I might have been imagining it, but I could sense the sulphurous emanations of its Etna home lurking within the reedy perfume. It is a broom, yet also a stunning small tree of unusual form. Tidy people won't like it as it sheds needle-like leaves and drifts of seed pods. It also has a tendency to have weak roots, hates heavy soil and blows over when you least want it to, namely when it has reached exactly the right size and shape and coiled itself round your heart. Maurice eventually succumbed to an elderly London rat gnawing through his roots. However, his offspring live on. I grew two more from seed and they are waiting patiently for me to plant them out in my new garden.

GROW Born to abuse, *G. aetnensis* needs little to thrive. It likes free-draining soil and some atmospheric moisture – after all it is from a seaside volcano. Prune with care to ensure you end up with a beautiful form rather than ugly stubs where branches were. Not much controls its shape – it has a unique character that is best enjoyed as it is.

Type
Semi-evergreen
small tree or shrub
Flowering
Summer
Height/spread
8m x 5m
Position
Full sun, warm, dry
Soil
Light, well-drained
Hardiness
USDA 7b/8a / RHS H5

SID HILL
Designer and gardener,
Sid Hill Ecological Gardens,
Cornwall, UK

Sid Hill is an award-winning designer, gardener and ecological artisan who trained at the Eden Project in ethnobotany and landscape design. He creates landscapes and plantings that echo wild plant communities and is passionate about working with plants to solve contemporary issues. *sidhillecogardens.com*

Type
Rhizomatous perennial
Flowering
Summer, autumn
Height/ spread
1m x 1m
Position
Full sun, part shade
Soil
Moist, well-drained, poorly drained
Hardiness
USDA 6a–1 / RHS H7

Persicaria bistorta →
Common bistort

Imagine a beautiful wildflower meadow with diverse flowers, scents and buzzing with bees. These wild plantings have captured people's imaginations for generations. Now imagine walking through this planting, foraging edible flowers for salads, leaves for a stir-fry and roots for roasting. Over the years I have been experimenting with creating edible wildflower meadows. These are plantings designed in line with plant ecology, by applying aesthetic design theory and combining edible plants found in meadow habitats around the world. They're biodiverse, beautiful and provide a truly varied diet. This sets the stage for how I select my favourite plants for my compositions: I select them for their ability to survive, their ecological sociability, beauty and ethnobotanical uses.

Bistort is one of my favourite plants because the functional and aesthetic benefits it provides are incredible. It is adaptable and tough, coping well in a variety of climates and growing conditions. Its natural habitat is wet meadows. These are lush and competitive environments where it has adapted to compete with its neighbours, so consider this when growing it in the garden. I remember the bistort in a garden I worked in as a teenager: there was an herbaceous border, cram-packed with plants and every year or two the bistort had to be divided because it outgrew its space. Some might call it invasive – I like to say 'successful'.

It also has a long history of use as a food plant in the UK. It has edible roots, leaves and seeds. It is important to harvest the leaves when they are young because they become tough as they age. The leaves have a mild flavour, which makes them great for bulking up salads or using as a pot herb. In the north of England, bistort is also known as dock and, each year, in a small town called Mytholmroyd, there is a World Dock Pudding Championship. People come together from neighbouring towns to cook dock pudding – bistort is mixed with wild leaves and vegetables, oatmeal and butter. The pudding is then fried as a patty and served with bacon and eggs as a breakfast.

GROW Prefers wet and fertile conditions, but it can grow well in a variety of soils. I have seen it growing well in dry alpine meadows in the Alps, boggy ground and woodland edges. When it becomes too big for its boots, divide it and give it to friends.

Malva moschata
Musk mallow

Musk mallow is a special plant to me. It is a reliable wildflower to grow from seed and a staple of the cottage garden for good reason. I blend it into my edible meadow seed mixes. Unusually for perennials, it flowers in its first year from sowing, making it a very useful plant to fill spaces. The leaves and flowers are edible and a great addition to salads and you can also eat them as a beautiful garnish. I use them regularly throughout spring and summer.

GROW It can be a long-lived perennial in the right conditions. I find it prefers an open position on a semi-dry, free-draining soil. Reliable grown from seed in situ and works well as a filler plant. I regularly see this plant growing on road verges in Cornwall among grasses, but it can be pushed out of plantings if the growth of other plants is vigorous. You can always rely on it to self-sow and germinate when the soil is disturbed.

Type
Perennial
Flowering
Summer, autumn
Height/ spread
1m x 50cm
Position
Full sun
Soil
Moist, well-drained
Hardiness
USDA 7b/8a / RHS H5

CHARLES DOWDING
Gardener, writer and
teacher, Somerset, UK

Charles Dowding has brought the virtues of no-dig gardening to a
worldwide audience and huge numbers of gardeners rejoice in the
simplicity of his methods and the time saved. He has written many
books and offers courses in no-dig gardening and growing vegetables.
charlesdowding.co.uk

Allium cepa ↘
Onion

Type
Annual,
biennial
Flowering
Summer
**Height/
spread**
45cm x 5cm
Position
Full sun, part
shade
Soil
Any
Hardiness
USDA 8b/9a
/ RHS H4

I love all the different variations of onion, and there are many. One plant, so many
possibilities. Onion bulbs and leaves are tasty, sweet and refreshing, edible raw
or cooked, and available for most of the year. They look beautiful in the garden,
especially in late spring to early summer when the upright leaves grow tall and
lush. When I see that amount of leaf on a bed of bulb onions, it gives me a warm
feeling that food will be available for much of the year. Leaf growth is healthiest
through late spring and they have an alluring presence at this stage. A rule of
thumb is that the more growth onions can make before summer solstice, the
larger your harvest of bulbs will be.

Homegrown organic onions pack a lot of punch compared to commercial
onions, which are mostly grown with synthetic fertilisers, making them mild and
easy to prepare, but they have less aroma and pungency. Onions grown in dug
soil and with the recommended wide spacings involve a lot of weeding and
work for the amount of harvest. But with no dig, closer spacing and compost
rather than fertilisers, they are easy to grow and harvests are so good. Their
tidy leaves also make them ideal for pots. They can grow against a wall and
especially like the extra warmth in spring.

I have type 1 diabetes and eat a lot of onions. They are my staple vegetable,
ahead of potatoes. My favourite time of year for eating them is late winter
through to spring as green salad onions. I'm convinced they are a fantastic boost
to the immune system, especially when they're homegrown and thus have added
microbes from healthy soil.

Salad onions are bred to grow long, whiter stems, while bulb onions are
bred to swell at the base. There is a fine line between these categories, a
quality difference. Shallots are another tasty variation. Best results come from
respecting the varietal descriptions, but it's possible to grow salad onions for
bulbs, bulb onions for eating green, and shallots grow lovely shoots in spring
from bulbs for salad onions. For salad onions, try 'White Lisbon' and 'Lilia'
(which has long red stems and is most attractive); for bulb onions, try
'Sturon' for its high yield of round bulbs and 'Red Baron' for dark red bulbs.

GROW When I started gardening in 1981, most people were growing onions from sets rather
than seeds. I heard of one grower who had volunteers helping him who planted 10,000 sets
the wrong way up! I also knew growers who were using multi-sown module plants. I don't
know how long multi-sowing had been around before that, but it's not a new practice. I
bought some multi-sown transplants in 1983 and appreciated the benefit of using them,
then adopted and developed the method. The more I do it, the more it intrigues me –
plants growing alongside their mates!

Cooperation, not competition. For food we grow them for their first-year stage, of
stems and then bulbs. They overwinter as bulbs, then grow again and flower in the second
summer. You can also overwinter them as seedlings, for bulbs the following summer (for
storing until mid-winter). As seedlings or bulbs, onions are hardy to –10°C or even lower.

Close spacing works well with no-dig beds. Onion leaves can grow 45cm in a sheltered
spot and need just 5cm space if grown singly. If you till, dig or rotovate, a wider spacing is
needed to control weeds. Mildew is a factor. If your climate is damp, space a little wider.
In wet summers, mildew is difficult to avoid. If you spot grey mould on leaves, it's best to
pull the onions straight away and use them, because they won't store. Any soil can grow a
decent onion, but best results come from adding sufficient organic matter on the surface.

MARK SPENCER
Consultant botanist,
Isle of Wight, UK

Dr Mark Spencer is an internationally respected botanist, a writer, public speaker and TV presenter. As a forensic botanist, he has worked on missing person enquiries, murders and serious crimes. *markspencerbotanist.com*

Eupatorium cannabinum
Hemp agrimony

Type
Herbaceous perennial
Flowering
Summer, autumn
Height/ spread
2m x 1m
Position
Full sun, part shade
Soil
Any, except very acidic
Hardiness
USDA 6a–1 / RHS H7

As a child, I was entranced by a large hemp agrimony plant growing in the lane by my grandparents' house. Every summer, the plant was a beacon for a vast array of insects: hoverflies, beetles, bees, wasps and butterflies. Thousands of tiny flowers made fluffy, dusky pink clouds at the top of the six-foot giant that towered over my head. The humid air was made marzipan-sweet by the blooms, and below in the light shade the jagged, lobed leaves cast crazy patterns in the sunlight. Decades later, the plant has gone, the lane has been tidied and although the air still hums with insects, they are fewer and more subdued.

Hemp agrimony is one of many native plants that are beautiful and important for wildlife. It is generally common across much of the cooler parts of Europe, although much less than it once was. It is adaptable and enhances modern herbaceous schemes as well as wetland plantings.

GROW This herbaceous plant is easy to grow, thrives in most reasonably moist soils and tolerates light shade. The best locations for it are the back of the border or by a large pond. Leave the shaggy, spent seedheads until spring (to attract birds and provide shelter for insects). Cut the plant to the ground in early spring once growth restarts. Staking is generally not needed, except in very windy locations.

Type
Herbaceous perennial
Flowering
Spring, summer
Height/ spread
1.2m x 50cm
Position
Full sun
Soil
Any, except very acidic
Hardiness
USDA 6b/7a / RHS H6

Centaurea nigra and *C. scabiosa*
Common and greater knapweed

As environmental change increases in intensity, we all need to do our bit. Many of us are concerned about bees, but there are many other insects – such as hoverflies, butterflies, moths and beetles – that are important plant pollinators. Knapweeds are some of our most valuable plants as pollen and nectar sources for insects. They are also emblematic of our meadows and grasslands in high summer, their vibrant plum-purple, thistle-like flowers contrasting wonderfully with the straw-yellow fading heads of grasses. Shamefully, over 97 per cent of our meadows have been destroyed since the mid-twentieth century, and these plants are now far less common than they once were.

Common knapweed is the more widespread and is also the more variable – some forms have tight button-like flowerheads (each head is a 'composite' of dozens of individual flowers), others are more shaggy-topped, akin to an exploding firework. Greater knapweed is taller and has heavily dissected leaves, and is largely restricted to areas where limestone or chalk rock underlies the soil. The larger, starburst flowers are beautifully framed by silver-trimmed bracts clasping the flowerhead. The main colour for both is purple-pink, but pale pink and white forms do occur. As a teenager, I grew a white-flowered form of common knapweed and it was one of the most reliable plants in the garden. The spent, silvery flowerheads of greater knapweed are especially attractive.

GROW These plants are easy to grow. Plant and watch! Common knapweed thrives in most soils and, once established, will even thrive in drier soils. Greater knapweed prefers chalky soils but will grow in neutral soil. Both can tolerate light shade, but flowering will be greatly reduced. The best locations are mid-border, wildflower meadows or in prairie-style plantings. Leave the seedheads until spring (they will attract birds such as goldfinches and provide shelter for insects). Cut the plant to the ground in early spring once growth restarts.

CHRIS BEARDSHAW
Horticulturist, garden
designer, broadcaster,
Cotswolds, UK

Chris Beardshaw is best known for his work with *Gardeners' World*, *The Flying Gardener* and *Gardeners' Question Time*. He is also the founder and creative director of Chris Beardshaw Design, which has collected over 35 awards, including 13 RHS gold medals. His books include *100 Plants that Almost Changed the World*. *chrisbeardshaw.com*

Rosa 'Souvenir de la Malmaison'
Rose 'Souvenir de la Malmaison'

Type
Climbing rose
Flowering
Summer, autumn
Height/spread
5m x 90cm
Position
Full sun, sheltered
Soil
Moist, well-drained
Hardiness
USDA 6b/7a / RHS H6

The rose of the perfect cottage garden, this plant is a unique combination of delightful sensory appeal, delicate artistic poise and infectious joyfulness. Individual blooms become modestly bowed by the thronged massing of multitudinous petals, each sumptuously curled, coiled and curved to offer a mesmerisingly complex face of unrivalled perfection. Spicy, sweet fragrance permeates from the generously numerous blooms, which are large, quartered and flat. Shades of raspberry lemonade in the heart of the flower evolve to blushed cream on the outer wave, all complemented by lead-tinted emerald foliage, which is unusually healthy and vigorous if the roses in our Cotswold garden are anything to judge by.

But perhaps as delightful as the physical plant itself is the story of how it emerged. A member of the sought-after and select bourbon group, it is thought its origins lie in a chance cross between roses planted as hedges on a tiny Indian ocean island. The volatile volcanic landscape was variously named Theemai Theevu, Santa Apolónia and Île Bourbon before eventually becoming Réunion Island. In the early 1800s China roses and damasks were used as hedge planting, and the seeds of the bourbons are thought to originate from these parents.

The 'Souvenir de la Malmaison' cultivar also tells of the passion of Empress Joséphine of France, Napoleon Bonaparte's first wife, for roses and the extravagant rose garden she created at her Château de Malmaison home. Josephine bought the then near-derelict château while Napoleon was warring in Egypt, convincing him to invest in revitalising its structure and grounds. One fundamental element of this was a *jardin à l'anglaise*, an English rose garden – the world's finest. Such was Josephine's enthusiasm and persuasiveness that while sourcing the garden's more than 250 rose varieties, she apparently even convinced the warring parties of England and France to allow her flower consignments through the blockades.

It is from such convoluted and implausible lineage that this horticultural delight emerges, a plant with the breeding to grace the grandest of schemes but a modesty that allows it to be a player in even the humblest of plots.

GROW Originally grown as an unassuming bush less than 1m high, the climbing form of this variety is well worth seeking out as it offers an ideal blend of plant and flower proportions. Those nodded heads whisper of intense summer evenings from lofty heights when the plant is draped through pergolas or over arches and arbours.

SARAH MEAD
Head gardener, Yeo Valley
Organic Garden, Bristol, UK

Sarah Mead works alongside her husband, farmer Tim Mead. She opened Holt Farm Gardens under the National Garden Scheme before taking the plunge and founding the Yeo Valley Organic Garden some 20 years ago. Sarah now leads the garden team. *yeovalley.co.uk*

Malus transitoria
Cut-leaf crab apple

M. transitoria is what we at Yeo Organic Garden call a 'diva plant'. For the 10 days it is in flower in spring, you cannot see any branches for the blush-pink blossom that opens to white. It's a stunner! In autumn, the leaves turn yellow and the tree bears small yellow fruits.

GROW Plant this low-maintenance tree somewhere where you can get up close to it. It's not fussy at all and is a perfect small ornamental tree for more modest spaces. Despite its looks it is remarkably tough.

Type
Deciduous tree
Flowering
Spring
Height/spread
8m x 8m
Position
Full sun, part shade
Soil
Moist, well-drained
Hardiness
USDA 6b/7a / RHS H6

Type
Annual
Flowering
Summer, autumn
Height/spread
1m x 50cm
Position
Full sun
Soil
Well-drained
Hardiness
USDA 8b/9a / RHS H4

Phacelia tanacetifolia ↘
Fiddleneck

Phacelia has got everything a gardener could want and more. It is normally sold as a green manure, but it is so much more than that. Standing at over 1m high, it has the most extraordinary and dynamic electric-blue flowers that curve back on themselves. Hoverflies, lacewings, ladybirds and bees go mad for it. What's more, you can grow it cheaply from seed pretty much any time of year. It flowers roughly eight weeks after sowing, is fully hardy and tolerates almost all soil types. It also makes a great cut flower and once it has finished flowering, you can dig it in to improve the soil structure.

GROW A great plant for successional sowing. Direct sow every eight weeks and you should get a six-week flowering period.

PETER MILNE
Co-founder, Nunhead
Gardener, London, UK

Peter Milne's passion for gardening – engendered while growing up on his family's farm in New Zealand – led him and his Colombian partner Alejandro Beltran to give up their corporate jobs to open a group of community-based garden shops in London. *thenunheadgardener.com*

Dicksonia antarctica →
Soft tree fern

Type
Evergreen tree fern
Height/spread
4m x 4m
Position
Full shade, part shade, sheltered
Soil
Moist, well-drained, acid, neutral
Hardiness
USDA 9b/10a
/ RHS H3

Although a native of Australia, *D. antarctica* reminds me of my New Zealand homeland. To enjoy it here in our garden in London is a real luxury. Seeing it move in the wind and watching it unfurl its new fronds from the top of its trunk evokes so many memories for me – of travels through the beautiful rainforests near where I grew up and of seeing it when visiting gardens with my parents. The unfurling frond is a strong emblem in New Zealand and that in itself provides me with a connection to home.

We have a lovely grouping of three at staggered heights on the shadier side of our garden as you look out through the window. I also planted one in a large pot in our front garden. They create a truly exotic feel, adding height and drama without blocking out too much light. They are easy to grow and, as evergreens, look great all year round. I have underplanted them with ferns and hostas, a combination that also transports me to the tranquil, native bush of New Zealand.

The 'trunk' is basically the decaying remains of earlier growth that forms a medium through which the roots grow. They have the presence of a tree, but without some of the downsides. For example, they don't need pruning (other than to clear away faded or damaged fronds once a year), and they provide beautiful filtered light without creating heavy shade for neighbouring plants. They also don't suck moisture and nutrients out of the surrounding soil or drop leaves or bark. They make you feel calm just by looking at them.

GROW Water, water and water some more – they will reward you year after year with their prehistoric furry claws that unfurl into long exotic fronds. For best results, concentrate your watering on the crown and 'trunk'. Water daily when first planted and regularly thereafter. Boost their growth during the growing season by applying a diluted seaweed-based fertiliser to the crown.

Trim away old fronds, which generally die back in a very short period of time at the beginning of spring. Do this just before they send out a host of fresh fronds for the coming season. Old fronds should be cut back to 10–15cm from the trunk – it is best not to cut them too close to it. The old frond stalks help form the trunk as it increases in height. They only grow 3.5–5cm per year, and as the price is generally based on size, I suggest planting in a pot to gain yourself some instant height.

They grow best in a sheltered position out of prevailing winds. The crown and trunk should be protected during prolonged cold spells in winter. Their Achilles heel is the crown at the top – this should be covered with straw and the trunk wrapped in frost fleece during the coldest months of winter. Best grown in partial to full shade. However, mine all receive a fair amount of direct sunlight and I find that as long as you keep watering, they thrive in a sunny position.

SUSYN ANDREWS
Consultant horticultural taxonomist, Devon, UK

Susyn Andrews is a world-renowned horticultural taxonomist. Her chief expertise is in the identification and naming of woody plant collections. She worked at the Herbarium at the Royal Botanic Gardens, Kew, for several decades, was the senior editor of *Taxonomy of Cultivated Plants* and co-author of *The Genus Lavandula*. She now serves on several scientific and horticultural committees.

Lavandula angustifolia Melissa Lilac ('Dow4')
English lavender [Melissa Lilac]

This is a stunning and reliable lavender with dense, striking flower spikes of violet-blue with a white centre held on long-flowering stems. It also has a strong fragrance. It was selected by Peter Carter in New Zealand and was launched in the UK by Downderry Nursery, Kent in 2003. It has potential as a cut flower.

GROW Let it breathe, grow in an open position and do not crowd it. Do not overfeed or over water. Cut back after flowering to foliage.

Type
Evergreen shrub
Flowering
Summer, autumn
Height/spread
1m x 50cm
Position
Full sun
Soil
Well-drained, hot, dry sites
Hardiness
USDA 7b/8a / RHS H5

Type
Evergreen tree or shrub
Flowering
Spring, summer
Height/spread
8m x 4m
Position
Full sun, part shade
Soil
Any, but not soggy or wet
Hardiness
USDA 6b/7a /RHS H6

Ilex aquifolium 'Handsworth New Silver' ↘
Holly 'Handsworth New Silver'

This is such a reliable holly that always looks good. It was introduced into cultivation before 1850 and was one of the more successful hollies introduced by the well-known nursery firm of the period, Fisher, Son & Sibray of Handsworth in the West Midlands.

'Handsworth New Silver' can be grown as an evergreen shrub or tree. The young leaves are shrimp-pink, becoming dark glossy green and paler grey-green with a broad cream or white margin. Dark purple stems set off the foliage. This is a female cultivar, carrying bright red berries that are freely produced. It looks good planted against a dark background or grown with other dark foliaged plants.

GROW Full sun is better, but the plant will cope with dappled shade.

Indigofera howellii 'Reginald Cory'
Howell's indigo 'Reginald Cory'

This spectacular shrub deserves to be more widely known. The original collection of this plant was from Yunnan, China by George Forrest in 1917. The species is named after Edward Butts Howell (1879–1952), who worked for the Chinese Maritime Customs Service and was a good friend of Forrest. The cultivar name commemorates Reginald Cory (1871–1934) of the Duffryn estate near Cardiff, who was one of the main sponsors of Forrest's 1917 expedition. The plant has small pinnate leaves and produces long, tapering spikes of good deep pink, pea-like flowers. It has an exceptionally long flowering period, lasting from the end of spring until the first frosts. The fruits are narrow, chestnut brown pods.

GROW Water well when planting and in dry periods for the first year. Stake on a windy site. The plant is a legume and does not need feeding. No pruning required, either.

Type
Deciduous shrub
Flowering
Summer, autumn
Height/spread
3m x 3m
Position
Full sun, open or against a wall
Soil
All, especially good on hot, dry sites
Hardiness
USDA 7b/8a / RHS H5

JOHN ANDERSON
Keeper of the gardens, Windsor Great Park, Berkshire, UK

John Anderson trained at the National Botanic Gardens Glasnevin in Dublin and the Royal Botanic Gardens, Kew. He was previously head gardener at Inverewe Gardens in Scotland and Exbury Gardens in Hampshire. In 2020 he received the Veitch Memorial Medal, the RHS's highest award for horticulturists born or living outside Britain. *windsorgreatpark.co.uk*

Tecophilaea cyanocrocus
Chilean crocus

When I became head gardener at Mount Usher Gardens in County Wicklow, Ireland, this was one of the gems it had successfully been growing outdoors since it received material from Kew in the 1950s. The then-head gardener, Miley Manning, carefully showed me how to look after these wonderful corms and get them to flower outdoors each year in spring. We lifted them every autumn, removing the small corms, potting them in a free-draining soil and placing them in the glasshouse to grow on. The mature corms – about the size of a ten-pence piece – were replanted in the sandy loam with a coarse stone on top to prevent the slugs from nibbling them in the early spring. We placed a layer of small-gauge chicken wire over the top of the soil, hidden by the gravel, to prevent mice from getting to the corms over the winter. The *pièce de résistance* was collecting sheep droppings in a bucket in winter (the nearby Wicklow Mountains are famous for their sheep), then letting them dry into a powder and applying this before flowering in spring to get the deepest gentian blue blooms. It worked! When I came to Mount Usher it had 20 corms and when I left 20 years later there were 200. The cultivar *T. cyanocrocus* 'Leichtlinii', which I also grew at Mount Usher, has larger flowers and white centres, while *T. c.* 'Violacea' has purple flowers.

GROW Grow in sunny but cool areas to prevent the corms from drying out in hot summers. Best alongside a wall or in a raised alpine bed, ideally with some summer shade. May need protecting from wet winters. Note that Irish summers are not as hot as many parts of the UK and its annual rainfall is around 90cm.

Type
Cormous perennial
Flowering
Spring
Height/spread
10cm x 10cm
Position
Full sun
Soil
Well-drained, pH 6–7
Hardiness
USDA 10b– 9b / RHS H2–H3

CAMILA ROMAIN AND MARIANNE MOGENDORFF
Founders, Wolves Lane Flower Company, London, UK

After working in the fashion and theatre industries respectively, friends Camila Romain and Marianne Mogendorff took a rare chance to lease a 40m urban glasshouse with a small outdoor plot and began learning on the job, growing scented, seasonal and sustainable blooms for floristry. *wolveslaneflowercompany.com*

Dahlia 'Cornel Brons'
Dahlia 'Cornel Brons'

Dahlias come in every shade and hue imaginable but if pushed to choose 'a real doer', I [Camila] would choose the stalwart variety 'Cornel Brons'. It flowers prolifically on long, strong stems, has a good vase life of about four or five days and is a pretty ball dahlia. In our first full season of growing flowers Marianne was on maternity leave and I was overwhelmed and exhausted by the never-ending to-do list of weeds, seeds and staking. To top it all off we suffered an extreme bout of drought and incessant heat in London that summer, which made trying to grow anything in that inhospitable glasshouse a grim endurance test. Fortunately, I was prevented from throwing in the trowel altogether by the dahlia patch outside that, despite my lack of any specialist knowledge at the time, pumped out the blooms through the heat and gave me something to cut for customers. I'm loath to limit myself to one variety ('Jowey Winnie', 'Senior's Hope' and 'Darkarin' are also real favourites), but 'Cornel Brons' is a deliciously warm but not garish orange shade that seems to go with practically everything and responds valiantly to us cutting it really hard. Dahlias are real workhorses and keep us in bloom until the first frosts. Without them I might have packed it all in after that summer!

GROW The new growth on all dahlias can be delectable to slugs and snails. Start your tubers or cuttings in pots and keep them somewhere protected from garden pests and any rogue cold snaps that could wipe out their new growth. We treat the ground with nematodes, a natural biological control, before planting out our dahlias.

We feed our dahlias with an organic seaweed feed or homemade comfrey feed every two weeks to keep these workhorses happy. Pinch out the leading stem to around two leaves at the beginning of the season to encourage a branching, bushy plant. Water deeply once or twice a week during a hot summer.

At the end of the season cut down the dead foliage after a first frost or, if no frost is forthcoming, when it seems to have run out of steam to produce more flowers. We leave our dahlias in the ground for approximately two seasons before digging them up in anticipation of the third season, then divide the tubers to make more plants. If your plot is very exposed, cold and wet, consider digging your tubers up at the end of each season and storing them in a crate of spent compost in a greenhouse or shed.

Type
Tuberous perennial
Flowering
Summer, autumn
Height/spread
1m x 1m
Position
Full sun
Soil
Moist, rich, well-drained
Hardiness
USDA 9b/10a / RHS H3

Type
Herbaceous perennial
Flowering
Winter, spring
Height/spread
10cm x 20cm
Position
Full sun, part shade
Soil
Moist, well-drained, humus-rich
Hardiness
USDA 6a–1 / RHS H7

Primula vulgaris
Primrose (SEE ILLUSTRATION PAGE 222)

When I [Marianne] was a child, Mother's Day was a serious yearly ritual between my dad and me. We'd get up at the crack of dawn (probably 7am, in reality), put wellies on over pyjamas and creep out of the back door and into the garden. What was so exciting about these early morning ventures was that literally anything was fair game for the picking. Armed with the kitchen scissors, I would scan the beds and anything that caught my eye would be snipped for the vase. No matter whether Mother's Day fell early or late in the year, the primroses were an unfailing, delicate presence – pale lemony yellow, also the rare rhubarb pink varieties, were treasured finds in the grass. Although short stemmed, they looked exquisite in a bud vase to accompany mum's breakfast in bed, and they'd still make it upstairs with droplets of dew clustered on their tiny faces.

Primroses aren't showstoppers in the cutting garden, but in bygone days they were bought and treasured by Londoners on Primrose Day (the annual holiday that marked the death of Prime Minister Benjamin Disraeli). With Mother's Day being the UK's second most commercially important day for cut flowers (Valentine's Day being the other, when virtually nothing is blooming in the UK!), it is wonderful to celebrate mothers and mother figures with a truly seasonal little flower that heralds the garden returning to life. Growing and treasuring the primrose makes us all appreciate the subtle turnings of the season and helps us remember that even such a diminutive and humble flower can lift our spirits at such a cold and unflowery point of the year.

GROW Once established in the garden, primroses are brilliantly self-sufficient, naturalising and spreading gradually through the grass over the years. Most gardeners would be happy to divide some plants to start a collection in a new garden, meaning it can be a thrifty addition to your garden and one which will reward you over time. They seem relatively unbothered by slugs and snails and need no staking or feeding, perhaps just a deadhead after the flowers are spent to help them build up strength for the next year. They perform best under trees or shrubs.

BEX PARTRIDGE
Floral artist, Devon, UK

Bex Partridge specialises in using dried flowers – which she grows and dries herself using sustainable and ecological practices – to create long-lasting designs and displays for events, retail spaces and homes. *botanicaltales.com*

Type
Annual
Flowering
Summer, autumn
Height/spread
50cm x 50cm
Position
Full sun, may require some staking if exposed
Soil
Well-drained, loam, sand
Hardiness
USDA 10b / RHS H2

Xeranthemum annuum
Annual everlasting

I grow many flowers to dry in my garden and this is the one that has won my heart. I first discovered it a few years ago and it quickly became my favourite for the ease with which it grows and its evolution while growing. Most images online and on seed packets show upright, bright purple blooms on silvery-leaved stalks. But the reality is that the flowers start out a vibrant purple and then evolve into alluring shades of metallic silver with gold patinas. Best sown directly as an annual in early spring, it is fuss free and a real time-saver in comparison to other everlasting annuals such as strawflowers, which need to be sown under cover and involve pricking out and growing on. It requires little care once it gets going and can be left to go over to achieve those patina hues, allowing the bees and butterflies to get their fill before cutting to use. It works well as a fresh flower and makes a brilliant dried flower, retaining its shape and colour beautifully to bring an extra something special to displays.

GROW Sow directly into soil in early spring, thinning out and replanting any thinned seedlings, as they transplant well. Succession sow for endless flowers throughout the summer. Don't over water; do feed regularly and cut back the entire plant to hang out to dry.

MONA ABBOUD
Gardener and National
Collection holder,
London, UK

Mona Abboud has spent 20 years creating an award-winning garden that is home to the National Collection of *Corokia*, as well as other unusual New Zealand plants. She is the author of *Corokia – My Adventure*, and she regularly gives talks to horticultural societies. *monasgarden.co.uk*

Pseudopanax
Lancewood

Pseudopanax: you either love it or hate it! I, however, am a great fan. It looks so prehistoric, like something out of a dinosaur movie, particularly the most aggressively spiky ones, such as *P. crassifolius* and *P. ferox*. They have so much attitude. Young plants have serrated, downward-facing, leathery leaves, while mature plants produce smaller, smoother, upward-rising leaves. This strange transformation of leaf shape is believed to be because the plant evolved alongside tall predators such as the moa, a now-extinct flightless bird. Once the shrub had grown high enough to avoid the attention of this lofty, leaf-eating creature, it would sprout adult leaves – and it continues to do so, despite the disappearance of the moa around 600 years ago. Other species such as *P. arboreus*, have a gentler appearance, with larger, soft fleshy leaves.

GROW Best positioned in an area where it will have maximum impact. Grow in a fairly sheltered location in rich, well-drained soil. Can be pruned in early autumn or spring.

Type
Evergreen
shrub or tree
Flowering
Summer,
autumn
**Height/
spread**
12m x 2.5m,
but varies
depending
on species
Position
Full sun, part
shade
Soil
Well-drained,
neutral, acid
Hardiness
USDA 8b/9a
/ RHS H4

Type
Evergreen shrub
or small tree
Flowering
Summer
Height/spread
60cm–4m x 1.5m,
depending on
species and variety
Position
Full sun, part shade,
sheltered
Soil
Rich, well-drained
Hardiness
USDA 9b/10a
/ RHS H3

Lophomyrtus
New Zealand myrtle

I became interested in this genus when I realised that New Zealand plants could be the next step after Mediterranean plants – and in this particular case, also because lophomyrtus resembled corokia in its growing habit and leaf form. My first acquisition was *Lophomyrtus × ralphii* 'Kathryn', which became a showstopper in my garden when it reached 2.5m tall. It wows visitors with its vibrant burgundy-chocolate colour, particularly when covered with small, round, white flowers in summer, glowing against the dark, rich background of its leaves. People feel compelled to touch the leathery puckered leaves, as they say they feel like plastic. I later visited Gary Firth's garden in Haywards Heath, which is home to the National Collection of *Lophomyrtus*, where I discovered *L. bullata* and *L. obcordata* as well as numerous cultivars of *L. × ralphii*, a cross between the two. As a result, I had a strong desire to plant more in my garden and found some lovely cultivars – notably the dwarf, bronze-tinged *L. × r.* 'Pixie' and the velvety chocolate 'Black Pearl'. This genus fits in perfectly with my favourite palette of colours: the contrasting yet complementary purple bronze set against blue-grey.

GROW Plant in a sheltered position protected from drying winds. Planting in full sun encourages stronger leaf colour. Prune either in spring or after flowering. Water during droughts. Frost hardy to –5°C, but can be even hardier in a sheltered position.

Corokia cotoneaster
Wire-netting bush

Type
Evergreen shrub
Flowering
Spring
Height/spread
3m x 2.5m
Position
Full sun, part shade, sheltered
Soil
Well-drained
Hardiness
USDA 8b/9a / RHS H4

Corokia plants are incredibly versatile, can be topiarised and fit into any style of garden. They make an excellent alternative to box, which has been decimated throughout Europe. Unlike box, they produce flowers in the spring. Some of the cultivars change from green to bronze in winter as well. As natives of New Zealand, they are drought, salt and wind tolerant and most of them are hardy to $-10°C$. Being of Mediterranean origin, I fell in love with *Corokia × virgata* 'Yellow Wonder' because it resembled an olive tree. Truly a plant for all seasons, it has tiny, star-shaped flowers in spring and colourful berries in autumn.

GROW An easy plant to grow – all it requires is good drainage. It benefits from an occasional seaweed liquid feed. Can be pruned during the growing season.

Type
Evergreen shrub
Flowering
Summer
Height/spread
2.5m x 1.5m
Position
Full sun, sheltered
Soil
Well-drained
Hardiness
USDA 8b/9a / RHS H4

Ozothamnus rosmarinifolius 'Silver Jubilee' →
Ozothamnus 'Silver Jubilee'

Ozothamnus is a small genus of evergreen shrubs. I am particularly attracted to delicate blue-grey foliage, which is my favourite leaf colour, and the silver, rosemary-like foliage of *O. rosmarinifolius* glows throughout the year. Its lightly scented, white-pink achillea-like flowers are a bonus, particularly as they attract pollinators. I grow it along with its grey-leaved close relation helichrysum.

GROW Prune in spring or lightly after flowering if you want to restrict height and to shape. Avoid winter wet by planting in very well-drained soil.

Type
Evergreen sedge
Flowering
Summer
Height/spread
50cm x 50cm
Position
Full sun, part shade, sheltered
Soil
Moist, well-drained, humus-rich
Hardiness
USDA 9b/10a / RHS H3

Uncinia rubra
Red hook sedge

I can't remember when this plant appeared on my radar. It was certainly way before I decided to focus on my favourite leaf-colour combination – purple-bronze contrasting with blue-grey. But it fits right in with my main palette. It's a wonderful plant for the front of borders: in my garden I have a row in front of a border of restios and also grow them under a corokia hedge, where they fit in with the bronze sheen of *C. buddleioides* 'Coco' or contrast with the blue-grey tinge of *C. × virgata* 'Geenty's Ghost'. These plants pop up through the garden, lighting it up like little flames. They are native to the southern hemisphere, and they are called hook sedge because their seeds hook on to passing animals. They gradually form tussocks of reddish-bronze foliage followed by flowering stems, and there are now new interesting cultivars such as 'Everflame' and 'Firedance'.

GROW Plant in moist but well-drained soil. A sunny position promotes leaf colour, but the plant is equally happy in part shade. Cut back every year to promote vigorous growth and divide every few years in late spring. Comb out any dead leaves and flowers in spring.

HANNAH AKEHURST
Horticulturist and farmer,
East Sussex, UK

Hannah Akehurst has worked with urban farms, school gardens and private gardens. She designed the Grown in Dagenham traineeship at Growing Communities Dagenham Farm, teaching unemployed parents how to grow and harvest produce. *instagram.com/hannah_grows*

Type
Biennial
vegetable
**Height/
spread**
60cm x 45cm
Position
Full sun
Soil
Moist, well-
drained,
fertile
Hardiness
USDA 9b/10a
/ RHS H3

Beta vulgaris cicla var. *flavescens* **rainbow chard**
Chard 'Rainbow Chard'

I didn't know about chard until I started working at Growing Communities. The head grower, Alice Holden, would show me how to harvest armfuls of verdant leaves in a matter of minutes. I was astonished at how bountiful a crop it was and how rapidly it grew back. It could be described as somewhere between spinach and beetroot, but is grown for its leaf and tasty midrib.

In the kitchen I find chard far superior to spinach, holding its form when cooked. It's beautiful wilted then dragged around the pan with olive oil and garlic. I grow both Swiss chard, which has deliciously chunky white midribs, and rainbow chard, whose centres range from hot pink to canary yellow. Chard is packed full of vitamins so a brilliant addition to any kitchen garden, but I've also seen it boldly claiming its place in adventurous herbaceous borders, adding colour and lushness.

GROW Chard is not a heavy feeder, but it will be in the ground for a substantial amount of time, so it's good to add organic matter to the soil before planting out. Start out with nutritious soil, and you are unlikely to need any additional feed. Chard can also be grown in pots, just allow sufficient space between plants to prevent downy mildew. Grow from seed in spring to early autumn. By starting them in module trays you give them the best chance against slugs, which can be known to enjoy a nibble. Once the seedlings have a few leaves, plant them out, spacing them roughly 25cm apart. They are a low-maintenance crop and just require watering during dry periods. I like to harvest my chard by cutting straight across the plant, near to the base but just above the smallest growing leaves. This encourages tender new growth and helps air circulate between the plants. If it starts to bolt, cut back the flowering stem to encourage further leaf growth.

CLAIRE DAVIES
Gardener, London, UK

Claire Davies joined Monastic institution Charterhouse in 2009 to restore the gardens, a project that took nearly ten years. Charterhouse was founded in 1611 and is still home to a community of 'brothers'. A former illustrator and photographer, Claire has written and photographed a book about the gardens called *Behind Walls. thecharterhouse.org*

Paeonia lactiflora **'Bowl of Beauty'**
Peony 'Bowl of Beauty'

I planted peony 'Bowl of Beauty' in the old cloister garden at the Charterhouse in semi-shade. It flowered the first year and has never let me down, forming a mass of 80cm-high blooms every year. There is always a sense of anticipation when the shoots and buds appear in spring after a long cold winter. The buds themselves are beautiful – tight, bright pink spheres that open up into cupped bowls with a centre of cream petaloids. They look exotic but are remarkably easy to grow. They are also excellent cut flowers.

GROW Do not plant them too deep as this will dissuade them from flowering. It is wise to support them before they reach full height so they don't become top heavy. Add a general-purpose feed in spring. Cut back dead stems in autumn. Divide in autumn.

Type
Herbaceous
perennial
Flowering
Spring, summer
Height/spread
80cm x 80cm
Position
Full sun, part shade,
sheltered from
strong winds
Soil
Moist, well-drained,
humus rich
Hardiness
USDA 6b/7a / RHS H6

ASHLEY EDWARDS
Head gardener, Horatio's
Garden London & South
East, London, UK

Ashley Edwards looks after the garden at the Royal National Orthopaedic
Hospital in Stanmore, a sanctuary for patients with spinal injuries run
by the Horatio's Garden charity. He was previously the gardener at
Strawberry Hill House, Twickenham. *instagram.com/plantsforwellbeing*

Sorbus aucuparia ↘
Rowan

My name in Old English translates as 'ash tree meadow',
so I feel an affinity to these plants, which are also known
as mountain ash trees. Rowans are found growing wild in
the UK and across most of the northern hemisphere and
for centuries have been used for their timber, fruits and
ornamental value. They also have a rich history of folklore
that includes being used to ward off evil spirits and being
crafted into dowsing rods. I love to learn about traditional
uses of plants, so this has drawn me even closer to this
magical tree. It is a great tree to have in the garden and
there are many attractive cultivars available to suit any
space. The thing I love most about it is the year-round
interest it provides. Gorgeous creamy white flowers in
spring, delicate pinnate leaves in the summer, followed
by vibrant berries and stunning autumn colour.
The silver bark becomes craggy with age and
can be fully appreciated in winter. It is also a
fantastic tree for wildlife, used as a pitstop for
pollinators in spring and providing a buffet
for birds in the autumn. Could you ask for
any more from a single plant?

GROW If buying from a nursery, make
sure you choose a healthy tree that is not
obviously rootbound. I've found planting
in autumn is always best, as it gives the
tree a chance to establish roots and settle
in during the cooler part of the year. It's a
tough specimen that doesn't require any
special treatment. It's tolerant of most
sites and is great for towns and cities as it
copes well with pollution.

    If your site is windy, you may want to
stake your tree for the first year or two.
Water it well in the first five years of its life
and it should establish good, deep roots to
provide for itself. Mulching will keep down
competition from weeds and grass and
provide nutrients. You shouldn't need to
prune, but do cut out any branches that
begin to rub or become damaged to keep
the tree looking its best. Try collecting and
sowing seed from a local tree (taking care
not to over harvest) as it will be better
matched to your climatic conditions.

Type
Deciduous tree
Flowering ·
Spring
Height/spread
10m x 8m
Position
Full sun, part shade,
it copes well with exposed
sites and cold
Soil
Well-drained, acid,
neutral loam, sand
Hardiness
USDA 6b/7a / RHS H6

163

ELEANOR BURTON
Records officer, Ōtari
Native Botanic Garden,
Wellington, New Zealand

Eleanor Burton worked at Victoria University in Wellington in gardens that were mostly made up of New Zealand native plants. She trained as a tree surgeon before working at Ōtari Wilton's Bush, a garden dedicated to native plants. She has been there for over 20 years. *wellingtongardens.nz*

Celmisia semicordata
Large mountain daisy

I like the *Asteraceae* (daisy) family. Some years ago in winter I was looking for something to draw and I reasoned that celmisia are all-white daisies with very similar flowers, but the foliage varies considerably. This has led to a slightly obsessive interest in *C. semicordata*, which is the largest species, and also happens to be one of the easiest to grow. A perennial herb, it has spear-like, stiff leaves up to about 30cm long. They are covered in a silvery pellicle, and have a white midrib and a white tomentum on the underside. The flowers are single large daisies, up to about 10cm across, held well above the leaves. The seedheads are also attractive.

Type
Perennial
Flowering
Summer
Height/ spread
50cm x 50cm
Position
Full sun, part shade
Soil
Moist, well-drained
Hardiness
USDA 7b/8a / RHS H5

GROW I can't grow *C. semicordata* in the ground as it is very susceptible to phytophthora, a soil-borne fungal disease. Fortunately it is quite happy in a big pot with a lot of root room. Although pretty hardy, it doesn't like to dry out completely or get too wet. It needs regular watering in summer and repotting every second year. This is an alpine plant so will not like too much humidity.

Aciphylla squarrosa
Bayonet plant

Why have I chosen this plant? Sheer cussedness. These are very attractive structural plants in a garden, but as the common name implies (taramea or speargrass in New Zealand) they are very spiny and can be a bit trying to look after. When I first started gardening in the rock garden at Ōtari there were a number of these, and I eventually developed a sort of sixth sense as to where they were, so they stopped sneaking up behind me!

Type
Perennial
Flowering
Spring
Height/ spread
2.5m x 1.5m
Position
Full sun, but not fussy,
Soil
Well-drained, deep enough for the formation of a tap root
Hardiness
USDA 6b/7a / RHS H6

GROW These are very hardy and not too picky about growing conditions. The main challenge is how to extricate the weeds from around them without being used as a pin-cushion. The best method is to use a large fork, push it under all the leaves on one side of the plant, then stand it up and dig it in firmly. This gives access to the weeds that have established under that side of the plant. They should not be planted too close together or the above process becomes impossible. Flowers should not be cut off the plant as the hollow stems can fill with water and cause the base of the plant to rot. They can eventually be pulled off.

Clematis paniculata
Puawānanga

Unlike most New Zealand native plants (which are notorious for having small, inconspicuous and usually green flowers), this is very showy. Easily missed for most of the year, in spring it covers its host tree in large white flowers. My plant at home grows up a tree next to the path, and in spring the flowers hang low, ensuring they are seen by everyone who goes by.

GROW An evergreen climber with glossy leaves and large white flowers, this plant likes a cool, moist root run and sun to flower. Otherwise it is not too picky. In the wild it climbs into the forest canopy, so it's a good idea to give it something fairly tall to climb. It is dioecious (male and female on separate plants), so you will only get the fluffy seedheads in summer if your plant is female. Most commercially grown plants are male, as the male flowers are generally larger. Mulching around the roots can help stop it drying out.

Type
Evergreen climber
Flowering
Spring, summer
Height/spread
8m x 6m
Position
Roots in shade, flowers in sun– it can climb quite a long way to achieve this
Soil
Moist, well-drained
Hardiness
USDA 7b/8a / RHS H5

JOEL ASHTON
Director, Hazelwood
Landscapes and Wild Your
Garden, UK

Joel Ashton designs and implements wildlife havens in gardens. His work has featured on shows such as *Springwatch* and he is an ambassador for the Butterfly Conservation and the British Dragonfly Society. He is the author of *Wild Your Garden*. hazelwoodlandscapes.com

Lotus corniculatus
Bird's foot trefoil

This is a perennial herbaceous plant, gaining its common name from the shape of the seed pods on the stalks. Its alternative common name of 'eggs and bacon' relates to its colouration when first emerging. It is a vital food source for the common blue, dingy skipper and green hairstreak butterflies, as well as the six spot burnet moth. It is easily grown and looks great as underplanting or in pots/baskets, where it also trails.

GROW An easy-to-grow plant, it establishes well and self-seeds. It's also great in a lawn – it survives fairly close mowing and is often found in ancient meadows. It has a long flowering period. Cut back in autumn to promote fresh growth in spring.

Type
Herbaceous
perennial
Flowering
Summer
Height/spread
20cm x 20cm
Position
Full sun
Soil
Well-drained
Hardiness
USDA 6a–1 / RHS H7

Type
Herbaceous
perennial
Flowering
Summer, autumn
Height/spread
2.5m x 50cm
Position
Full sun
Soil
Moist, well-drained
Hardiness
USDA 8b/9a / RHS H4

Verbena bonariensis
Purple top

Another favourite of many butterflies and bees. It looks fantastic (with good architectural value) anywhere in a border thanks to its fine stems with flowers (neat and compact) at the very top. The sturdy stems allow it to support other plants, as well as allow them to find light and be seen from all angles. It's long-flowering, with blooms from summer to autumn.

GROW It needs staking on occasion as in semi-shade it can reach for the light. Cut back in spring rather than autumn as it can suffer die-back if cut back in damp and cold conditions. A fine layer of mulch protects the plant during winter.

Lythrum salicaria
Purple loosestrife

A fantastic plant for damp areas and great for pollinating insects – many butterflies and bees are drawn to its rich nectar. A colourful plant often seen on the banks of rivers, it is fast growing and reaches a good height.

GROW Prefer soils that stay relatively damp. It is clump-forming and hardy. Seeds can be collected for sowing in spring or autumn.

Type
Herbaceous perennial
Flowering
Summer
Height/spread
1.5m x 50cm
Position
Full sun, dappled shade
Soil
Moist, poorly drained, fertile
Hardiness
USDA 6a–1 / RHS H7

Type
Short-lived
perennial
Flowering
Spring, summer
Height/spread
60cm x 45cm
Position
Part shade
Soil
Moist, well-drained
Hardiness
USDA 6b/7a / RHS H6

Silene dioica
Red campion

An absolutely stunning spring plant that flowers for a long period and attracts a vast number of pollinating insects. A delicate wildflower, it flowers in late spring and summer, and is perfect for areas in part shade. It's often seen on the edge of woodlands and meadows.

GROW If sowing from seed it will not be happy in very fertile soil, as it prefers low-nutrient meadow areas. Perfect as a naturalising plant, it provides a vital early nectar source for pollinating insects. Seeds can be collected and sown in spring or autumn. Deadhead regularly to promote more flowers.

TAYSHAN HAYDEN-SMITH
Landscape designer,
London, UK

Tayshan Hayden-Smith is a landscape designer, CEO of Grow2Know CiC and a semi-professional footballer. As the Grenfell Guerrilla Gardener he initiated the 'Grenfell Garden of Peace'. He is of mixed heritage and is passionate about diversifying horticulture and keen to empower young people through gardening. *grow2know.org.uk*

Musa →
Banana

At a primary school fair in Notting Hill, I was given £5 to spend on anything I wanted. While other children went home with sweets and toys, I came home with a small banana tree. I always used to have a banana with my Weetabix cereal in the morning and in my 10-year-old mind, I thought this might be the beginnings of my London banana farm. Of course, the banana tree has never borne any edible fruit, but still stands strong in my mum's garden in west London. It is a tree that not only reminds me of my childhood and a moment I cherish with my mum, but also of my Caribbean roots.

GROW My plant has been through it all. It has always been outside and never been brought indoors, yet it still stands and is going strong. I wouldn't advise everyone to leave bananas without protection in winter, though. Fortunately, our small garden is extremely enclosed and we live in a built-up area. I believe the surrounding conditions have allowed this tree to thrive.

Type
Perennial
Height/ spread
4m x 2.5m
Position
Full sun
Soil
Well-drained
Hardiness
USDA 10b / RHS H2

ÅSA GREGERS-WARG
Head gardener, Beth Chatto's Plants & Gardens, Essex, UK

Åsa Gregers-Warg is responsible for the day-to-day upkeep and development of the world-famous, seven-acre Beth Chatto's Plants & Gardens, where she has worked since 2001. *bethchatto.co.uk*

Ferula communis
Giant fennel (SEE ILLUSTRATION PAGE 108)

Not to be confused with the edible fennel *Foeniculum vulgare*, this spectacular giant umbel never fails to impress with its dramatic presence, towering above everything else. An attractive mound of finely cut foliage makes a perfect foil for spring-flowering bulbs and the lime-green heads of *Euphorbia characias* subsp. *wulfenii*. In early summer a stout stem erupts through the feathery foliage, bolting towards the sky revealing large, acid-yellow umbel flowers. It looks wonderful against a blue sky. Equally impressive, but perhaps more graceful and elegant is *Ferula communis* subsp. *glauca*, with its greyish-green foliage and purple-tinted stems topped with slightly ochre-tinged yellow flowers. Not everyone has room to grow these giants, so *F. tingitana* 'Cedric Morris', the Tangier fennel, might better suit smaller gardens. This distinctive fennel has glossier, stiffer foliage and only reaches a height of 1.5m.

GROW Seedlings should be pricked out into deep pots to allow the tap root to develop. Place the young plants directly in their final position as they resent transplanting. Choose a position that mimics its native habitats where it is found on rocky slopes and scrubby grassland. It usually takes two to three years to gather enough strength to flower, but it's well worth the wait. As it's dormant in summer, it leaves a large empty gap in the border as the foliage withers. This is not an issue if you plant it behind a lavender or cistus, combined with perennials that continue to add interest through late summer and autumn such as *Gaura lindheimeri*, salvias, hylotelephiums and agapanthus. Sometimes short lived, particularly if grown on heavier soil, it will self-seed if there's open ground. It has proved to be reliable in our Gravel Garden, which was planted in the early 1990s.

Type
Herbaceous perennial
Flowering
Early summer
Height/ spread
3.5m x 1m
Position
Full sun, open
Soil
Well-drained
Hardiness
USDA 9b/10a / RHS H3

ANDREW & HELEN WARD
Owners, Norwell Nurseries,
Nottinghamshire, UK

Andrew and Helen Ward set up Norwell Nurseries in the early 1990s and now grow over 2,500 different species and cultivars, and hold the National Plant Collection of *Astrantia* and hardy chrysanthemums. The nursery is known for its innovative sandbeds where tricky-to-grow plants thrive. Andrew is trained in plant genetics and plant breeding. *norwellnurseries.co.uk*

Chaerophyllum azoricum
Hairy chervil

This is a rarely seen member of the cow parsley family (*Apiaceae*) that I [Andrew] have chosen primarily for its scent. Its grey-green, slightly soft and hairy foliage appears early and is attractive in its own right, but is different from that of other umbellifers in that it isn't finely divided and is more like that of the excellent foliage plant *Melianthus major*. As the season progresses it forms an impressive mound of self-supporting foliage and stems that become covered in countless umbels of white, lacy flowers that last for six weeks. These have a strong and delicious scent of old-fashioned soap with a hint of bubblegum. The smell can be carried on the air up to ten metres away and customers have been known to snap them up as soon as they catch a whiff of their nostalgia-inducing perfume of freshly washed grandmother. Planted around it are *Phlox paniculata* cultivars, which carry the scent after it has finished, and symphyotrichums, which provide autumn colour.

GROW While its close, pink relation *Chaerophyllum hirsutum* 'Roseum' is more commonly grown and great for shady areas, *C. azoricum* is easy to grow in sunny or lightly shaded spots. Although it comes from the Azores, we have found it very hardy, going down to −12°C without injury and remaining undamaged by late frosts. Unlike many in the family, it is not short-lived and very perennial. It requires no special cultivation and grows well in a mixed herbaceous border that doesn't get waterlogged in winter.

Type
Perennial
Flowering
Spring, summer
Height/ spread
1.2m x 1m
Position
Full sun, part shade
Soil
Well-drained
Hardiness
USDA 7b/8a / RHS H5

Erythronium 'Joanna'
Fawn lily 'Joanna'

My [Helen] first favourite is the spring bulb 'Joanna'. The strong shoots push through in late winter before the fresh green leaves become overlaid with a patina of brown marbling and the freely produced flowers open a delicious creamy-lemon, gently aging to soft pink later in spring. This provides a beautiful combination of colours and in a typical cool spring gives a five-week show. Many years ago at a Leeds Hardy Plant Society meeting, we were asked for this plant but didn't have it or even know it. The gardener was effusive in her praise of it and so we kept a look out and bought it when we saw one for sale. Although it was expensive, unusually for us we bought not one but three bulbs, trusting the wonderful description. It was a great investment. It has never failed to delight us each spring and is a firm favourite with customers. We always sell out every year – often prior to flowering when people remember it from previous years.

GROW This grows in woodland conditions and enjoys being under later tree cover, as once flowered it quickly dies back down again. We have had it in our woodland now for about 20 years, so it has seen some very low temperatures, but it reliably reappears in slowly greater numbers each spring. It is important that the dormant bulbs do not get too desiccated in very dry summers. A bucket of water in a dry summer would stop this happening. We propagate in early autumn by digging up the clumps and taking off bulbils. It is sterile and does not set seed.

Type
Bulbous perennial
Flowering
Spring
Height/ spread
30cm x 60cm
Position
Part shade, sheltered
Soil
Rich, moist
Hardiness
USDA 7b/8a / RHS H5

Astrantia major 'Can Candy'
Astrantia 'Can Candy'

We house the National Plant Collection *Astrantia* and this is my [Andrew] favourite of a wonderful group. As the year wears on it gets increasingly harder to provide flower colour in a shady garden, but astrantias in their silvers, limes, pinks, reds and burgundies flower in summer and then again in autumn, and are great for shady places, especially if it isn't too dry. 'Can Candy' also has personal connections for me. A good friend of mine, Trevor Edwards, bred it. In 2019 an RHS assessment committee came to look at our astrantia collection and, after much discussion, 'Can Candy' was awarded an RHS Award of Garden Merit.

    Astrantias are in the *Apiaceae* family, but look very different from typical cow parsleys, with small flowers backed by a large ruff of bracts, which provide the majority of the colour. In a group where many different named varieties look similar, this is a distinct, vigorous variety that flowers heavily but is not very tall and after a few years makes a clump that is easily divided in spring. The flowers are soft pink, the bracts are large, and the very centre is bright pink, but the main colour is silver, netted with veins of pink and green. The backs of the bracts are highly visible and add to the impression of the inflorescence looking like a striped fairground tent.

GROW In a dry summer the foliage may look tatty, but it can all be removed along with the old flower shoots. If it looks fine, just remove the old flowers and then add a handful of fertiliser and, if dry, a bucket of water to maximise the autumn show. Although they thrive in shade, we also grow ours in mixed herbaceous borders in full sun, just don't let them bake dry. They are good for heavy clay soils and can survive being waterlogged. In the shade, we combine with flowers such as pulmonarias, erythroniums and *Tulipa sprengeri*; in the sunnier borders it works well with border phlox and *Erigeron annuus*.

Type
Herbaceous perennial
Flowering
Summer, autumn
Height/ spread
60cm x 60cm
Position
Full sun, part shade, shade
Soil
Moist, well-drained
Hardiness
USDA 6a–1 / RHS H7

Chrysanthemum 'Mrs Jessie Cooper'
Chrysanthemum 'Mrs Jessie Cooper'

We were delighted to be awarded a Plant Heritage-dispersed National Plant Collection of hardy chrysanthemums along with Judy Barker and Hill Close Gardens, Warwickshire. Most people think of chrysanths as large, tender exhibition types or short-lived 'pot mums' bought from garage forecourts. They don't realise there are over 150 completely hardy varieties that flower when everything else has finished in the garden, typically from mid-autumn to the end of the year. These tend to be spray types with single flowers that are excellent for cutting, but there are also pompoms, semi-doubles and full doubles, many of them honey scented and providing much-needed nectar and pollen to support late-flying insects, especially bees. 'Mrs Jessie Cooper' is one of the latest to flower, producing large (7.5cm across) single, bright cerise flowers with a green-yellow eye. They light up the garden and provide joy when all around is looking sad. The foliage is distinct, dark green, healthy and more lobed than the lacy. My [Helen] mum, a keen plantswoman, introduced us to this group in the early 1990s when she bought us *C.* 'Innocence' after we moved to Norwell, and she has always produced lots of 'Mrs Jessie Cooper' cuttings for us. When our eldest son was christened, we cut armfuls to decorate the church and our house, so it remains not only a favourite because of its fabulous colours, but also because of the lovely memories.

GROW We divide and take cuttings in spring. 'Mrs Jessie Cooper' is strong and survives −21°C with us. Try to provide a well-drained neutral to alkaline soil, although it isn't fussy – ours is heavy clay that gets very wet in winter. Hardy chrysanthemums are happy in mixed herbaceous beds – we have tall *Allium* 'Forelock' and earlier-flowering *Papaver orientale* cultivars with some of ours to provide mid-summer colour before the chrysanthemums start to shine. We have also trialled chrysanths in our sandbeds, where they are thriving.

Type
Perennial
Flowering
Autumn
Height/ spread
90cm x 70cm
Position
Full sun, sheltered
Soil
Well-drained, neutral to alkaline
Hardiness
USDA 6a–1 / RHS H7

BECKY CROWLEY
Cut-flower gardener
and garden designer,
Sheffield, UK

Becky Crowley established the organic cutting garden at Chatsworth
House in Derbyshire, home of the Duke and Duchess of Devonshire,
and has also worked at the celebrated Floret flower farm in the US.
beckycrowley.com

Digitalis
Foxglove

Foxgloves have something of the wild about them. I enjoy seeing the native
Digitalis purpurea decorating the edges of woodlands around Britain as well
as in forest openings in the Pacific Northwest, USA. In late spring I always want
to have some of their magic in the garden, though I tend to select white and
apricot varieties to bring light to a shady spot. I've planted many in the partial
shade of young hedgerows, though I find they also flower well in sun, provided
they have moist soil to grow in. Being fully hardy, the plants over-winter in their
first year before going on to produce their tall spires of nectar-rich blooms the
following spring and summer.

When using for floristry I cut them before most of the blooms have been
pollinated, as these soon drop. The tall leading spires look magnificent in large
arrangements and bring the spirit of a woodland to lavish evening events. For
smaller arrangements, the shorter side shoots are ideal. You can couple them with
peonies, another flower that, like the foxglove, marks the transition of spring into
summer. The first of the roses make great companions too.

Digitalis purpurea varieties tend to be biennial and should be sown in late
spring so they have a full year to grow before sending up their spires. It can
be a bit of a stretch to make time to sow next year's biennials when you're so
busy taking care of the current season's plants, but it is absolutely worth it. The
biennials are such a useful group of plants for helping knit spring into summer
with flowers, avoiding a disappointing gap between the end of the spring bulbs
and the start of the annuals and perennials. Other biennials I like to have in the
garden include honesty (*Lunaria annua*), sweet rocket (*Hesperis matronalis*) and
forget-me-not (*Myosotis sylvatica*). Sweet William (*Dianthus barbatus*) is another
helpful addition as it lasts such a long time in bouquets and farm-shop bunches.

Not all foxgloves are biennials. *D. × mertonensis*, also known as the strawberry
foxglove, is a short-lived perennial. It is lower growing with a chunkier form
than the *D. purpurea* varieties, but the dusky pink, slightly hairy flowers make
it a beautiful addition to both the garden and floral arrangements. At Floret,
we combined *D. × mertonensis* with the later-flowering *D. ferruginea* 'Gigantea'
in plantings designed to attract pollinators. 'Gigantea', often called the rusty
foxglove, is a tall and very upright perennial with smaller blooms that are tight
on space for big bumblebees (though they do their best), and better suited to
daintier honey bees. I like to sow strawberry and rusty foxgloves along with other
short-lived perennials such as aquilegias and lupins at the same time as the
biennials in spring, as they also appreciate a full year to grow before flowering.

Other foxgloves well worth a place in a cutting or ornamental garden include
D. lanata 'Café Crème' (woolly foxglove) and *D. lutea* (straw foxglove), both of
which are lower growing than the others. I love to include them all if I can!

GROW Most *D. purpurea* forms are biennial and I sow these in late spring for flowers the
following year. But if you miss the boat, plant the newer F1 varieties, which flower in their
first year from an early sowing. I tend to sow these in module trays under glass in early
spring, choosing varieties from the Dalmatian Series or Camelot Series and treat them as
annuals. The seed is so fine I barely cover it when sowing. Foxgloves can tolerate a range
of soils but like moist (though not wet) roots; this is especially important if grown in sunnier
situations. I think of foxgloves as a woodland edge plant and I like planting them in this
way within a garden, but I've also known them to grow well in brighter, more exposed spots.

Type
Biennial,
short-lived
perennial
Flowering
Spring, early
summer
**Height/
spread**
1.5m x 50cm
Position
Part shade,
full sun (if
soil is moist)
Soil
Unfussy
Hardiness
USDA 6a–1
/ RHS H7

JOY LARKCOM
Vegetable grower and author, West Cork, Ireland

Joy Larkcom is often described as the 'doyenne of the kitchen garden' and is a respected vegetable gardener and writer. Her accolades include a lifetime achievement award from the Garden Media Guild and the RHS Veitch Memorial Medal. She is the author of several ground-breaking books, including *Grow Your Own Vegetables*, *The Organic Salad Garden*, *Creative Vegetable Gardening*, *Oriental Vegetables* and the semi-autobiographical *Just Vegetating*.

Allium sativum ↘
Garlic

Some of my most vivid memories from a 1985 trip to China to research oriental vegetables are of garlic. To most Westerners, garlic conjures up mature, dried bulbs with white cloves, but in China garlic is seen as being more diverse and all parts are used at different stages. Young green leaves are eaten fresh or blanched, a whole young plant with an immature bulb can be used, and some of the 'hardneck' types are grown for their flowering stems and flowers.

An abiding memory is of an old lady with a garlic stall in a Chengdu market. Besides her stock of large pink and white garlic bulbs she had a range of cloves graded by size. These included 'rounds', mainly for planting, and peeled cloves, which I imagined fondly were for the busy housewife. As for the garlic flower stems, I was completely baffled when I first saw these long, slightly twisted stems with flowerheads still attached in a Beijing market. I was lucky enough to get a taste of them as a side dish later, dressed in oil and soy sauce. Absolutely delicious.

Unlike onions, bolted garlic goes on to produce sound bulbs. True garlic is not found in the wild, but the ancestral garlic is thought to have come from central Asia. The Chinese are known to have cultivated it since at least 3000 BC. Pink and red-skinned garlic is generally considered better flavoured than white, and flavour is probably influenced by climate and how it is grown... and cooked. The longer it is cooked, the milder it becomes.

GROW Garlic is technically biennial, though if left in the ground it will behave like a perennial. It is hardy and needs a cold period in its early stages, followed by warm temperatures while growing. Planting in autumn is usually preferable to spring, but in poor conditions it can be started in modules in autumn and then planted out in spring. Good drainage is essential, especially in the winter months, but moisture is needed in spring when leafy growth is at its height. Garlic is susceptible to the pests and diseases that attack onions, so never plant where onions have recently been grown. Plant large cloves where available (gently split from mature bulbs) about 18cm apart each way (smaller cloves can be closer). Plant upright – it's not always obvious! – and with at least 2.5cm of soil above them. Harvest them in mid-summer when the leaves are starting to fade. Dry them off thoroughly over two weeks, either outside in wind and moderate sun, or in racks indoors. Garlic bruises easily, which shortens its storage life, so always handle it carefully.

Type
Bulbous perennial
Flowering
Summer
Height/spread
50cm x 30cm
Position
Full sun, open
Soil
Deep, well-drained, sandy loam; avoid very acid and freshly manured soils; moderate fertility
Hardiness
USDA 8b/9a / RHS H4

ANNABEL WATTS
Head gardener, Munstead
Wood, Surrey, UK

Annabel Watts worked at Munstead Wood for 11 years prior to becoming head gardener there in 2013. In that time she has become at one with the cycle of the garden and finds being well-organised (a skill she picked up in her previous career as a PA) as necessary in an office as it is in running a sizeable garden. *munsteadwood.org.uk*

Azalea and *Rhododendron* ↘
Azalea and rhododendron

Through my work I have come to admire the azaleas (now officially listed under rhododendrons by taxonomists) and the rhododendrons at Munstead Wood. They are the original specimens planted by Miss Gertrude Jekyll, so they are well over 100 years old. They are situated in her 'decorative woodland' away from the formal garden. They had been neglected for many years, but following professional advice, they have now been exposed to more light and air, and any dead wood has been removed. One forgets that the original owner would not have seen them at the height they are now and I feel quite a responsibility towards these precious plants. Over the years they have survived all sorts of weather conditions, unsympathetic owners and two world wars, and every year their spectacular blooms never cease to amaze me.

The varieties I particularly look forward to are the strong colours, such as: 'Fama', best described as Victoria plum-red with an orange throat; 'Gloria Mundi', a dazzling orange with a blotch of egg-yolk yellow; 'Coccinea Speciosa', a red-orange; and 'Pallas', which has coral-red blooms. On closer inspection, the buds are as beautiful as the flower itself. To add to this explosion of joyful colours is a swathe of *Azalea luteum*, which provides a heavenly scent that accompanies the visitor as they meander through the paths. The sight and fragrance last a few weeks, if we are lucky weather-wise, for it just takes one downpour and the blooms will spoil and then the display is over for another year.

It has been difficult to identify many of the rhododendrons, nevertheless they make a magnificent sight at the end of spring, especially since we cleared away a plant Jekyll introduced to the woodland, *Gaultheria shallon*. It had rampaged through the area and is difficult to eradicate, however, since removing it from the base of the rhododendrons, the hard work has paid off and has made a huge difference to their glorious annual display.

GROW Soon after flowering, we prune the azaleas to retain a goblet shape and to keep each specimen separate from its neighbour, as well as to allow plenty of light and air to circulate among them. Jekyll wrote of making a clearing in her woodland to plant her collection of azaleas in the only peaty area, which is close to ideal conditions for them. When they are not in leaf it is interesting to see the grid-like way she planted them. If only she knew what a spectacle they would go on to make all these years later.

Type
Evergreen and deciduous trees and shrubs
Flowering
Spring, summer
Height/spread
Varies
Position
Dappled shade
Soil
Acid
Hardiness
USDA 6a–1 / RHS H7

JESS EVANS
Head gardener,
Knightshayes Court,
Devon, UK

Jess Evans is head gardener at the National Trust's Knightshayes Court in Tiverton. Trained at Royal Botanic Gardens, Kew, she has also worked as senior gardener at Tintinhull Gardens and for Monty Don at Longmeadow. *nationaltrust.org.uk/knightshayes*

Schefflera taiwaniana
Taiwanese schefflera

I love this plant. If it is growing in a garden where it is happy, it can become a very tall tree with beautiful leathery palmate leaves. The leaves have a faintly tropical appearance and are generally evergreen when sheltered. It is in the same family as ivy (*Araliaceae*), and so has similar inflorescences and seeds. I have seen it grown beautifully in Cornwall and have grown it myself – we have a couple planted at Knightshayes. I have also visited the National Collection of *Araliaceae* a couple of times, and there are some beautiful plants in this family. I do think a lot of plants that don't have large colourful inflorescences can get missed out – the leaves of many plants are also beautiful and are often the best things about them.

GROW Scheffleras are fairly hardy but struggle if exposed to freezing cold winds or frost, so a sheltered spot in good soil and full sun is best. If happy, they can put on the best part of a foot a year, so give them space if possible. That won't happen everywhere, though, so don't worry about it taking over the whole garden immediately. It requires little cultivation care once planted and growing well. It may need watering and feeding to settle it in but should look after itself after then. The dead leaves may occasionally need removing and clearing away.

Type
Evergreen shrub or tree
Flowering
Summer
Height/ spread
4m x 2.5m
Position
Full sun, part shade, sheltered
Soil
Moist, well-drained
Hardiness
USDA 8b/9a / RHS H4

Magnolia grandiflora
Bull bay

If I absolutely had to select one plant that is my favourite, it is this magnolia at the point just when the flowers are opening. It's a large tree with beautiful dark, shiny, evergreen leaves that are velvety brown underneath. The flower buds are held tightly early in the year and surrounded by golden velvety tepals. The large flowers themselves are slightly citrus scented and when they first open are perfectly white.

GROW These are often seen growing near buildings and walls because it was thought they would not be hardy in the UK, so would benefit from the protection. They can become large trees if given the space but grow well near walls too – though you need to prune them occasionally to keep them away from windows and doors. This is best done after flowering. You can prune back to two to four buds of the main structure if training and to keep them in shape and size. If grown in the open, they require little pruning but it is always worth keeping an eye on crossing branches and dead wood, and to make sure the crown is raised where needed. Tidy up dead leaves around their base as these can comprise a significant amount of organic matter that can cause an issue for other plants if left on the ground. This may not be a problem in open situations but can be a challenge against buildings.

Type
Evergreen shrub or tree
Flowering
Summer, autumn
Height/ spread
12m x 8m
Position
Full sun, part shade, sheltered
Soil
Moist, well-drained
Hardiness
USDA 7b/8a / RHS H5

TOM KNUDSEN
Head gardener, Tivoli,
Copenhagen, Demark

Tom Knudsen grew up at his parents' plant nursery; he graduated in
landscape engineering in 1991. He has been head gardener at the historic
Tivoli amusement park in Copenhagen since 2004. He often contributes to
TV programmes and articles as a horticultural expert. *tivoli.dk*

Geranium **Rozanne ('Gerwat')**
Geranium [Rozanne]

This is the perfect spreading plant for ground cover as it has a long
flowering period and the most beautiful blue flowers. Strong and fast-
growing, it will bloom through the summertime and until the first frosts.
It's very good in combination with trees, bushes and other perennials.

GROW Easy to grow. Make sure to water when very dry in summer. Remove any
remaining foliage from the previous year in early spring. If used in pots, plant it
at the edges.

Type
Herbaceous
perennial
Flowering
Summer, autumn
Height/spread
1m x 1m
Position
Full sun, part shade
Soil
Moist, well-drained
Hardiness
USDA 6a–1 / RHS H7

Cephalaria gigantea →
Giant scabious

An amazing plant that produces the most wonderful
flowers at the end of long stems. It gives rich variation
to the flower bed; it is both light and graceful at the
same time, providing some 'power' and fullness to the
planting. Very good for insects.

GROW Easy to grow, self-seeding, frugal and does not require
that much attention. Can be planted in beds as well as pots.

Type
Herbaceous
perennial
Flowering
Summer
Height/spread
2.5m x 1m
Position
Full sun, part shade
Soil
Moist, well-drained
Hardiness
USDA 6a–1 / RHS H7

Type
Deciduous tree
Flowering
Spring, summer
Height/spread
25m x 10m
Position
Full sun, sheltered
Soil
Moist, well-drained
Hardiness
USDA 6b/7a / RHS H6

Robinia pseudoacacia **'Nyirségi'**
False acacia 'Nyirségi'

If you have a large garden this tree is almost perfect. A big tree with an
open habit, it has an irregular growth form, green leaves and thorny, light
brown shoots and white flowers in hanging clusters that attract bees.
Sculptural as a stand-alone tree.

GROW Prefers a warm and sunny place. This variety is stronger and more
windproof than others of the same species.

Thalictrum **'Splendide'**
Meadow rue 'Splendide'

An adorable and beautifully graceful plant with delicate foliage
and the most stunning small flowers. Very good as a 'pop-up'
plant in between other groups of plants.

GROW Self-sowing. It can be planted in beds as well as pots. Protect
against strong winds so the stems don't break.

Type
Perennial
Flowering
Summer, autumn
Height/spread
1.5m x 50cm
Position
Part shade, sheltered
Soil
Moist, well-drained
Hardiness
USDA 6b/7a / RHS H6

Type
Rhizomatous
perennial
Flowering
Summer, autumn
Height/spread
1m x 50cm
Position
Full sun, part shade
Soil
Light, well-drained
Hardiness
USDA 6a–1 / RHS H7

Echinacea purpurea 'Magnus'
Purple coneflower 'Magnus'

Compact plants with large, long-lasting flowers. The seedlings are super decorative as well, right up until the first frosts. Very good for butterflies.

GROW Easy to grow and self-sowing. Let the stems and leaves stay for the winter and avoid cutting back until next spring – this is to avoid water accumulation in the cavity of the stem, which can cause freezing during winter.

Molinia caerulea subsp. *arundinacea* 'Transparent'
Purple moor-grass 'Transparent'

A light and graceful grass whose stems sway in an amazing way. Perfect in combination with *Verbena bonariensis* and large-flowering dahlias.

GROW This can be planted in beds as well as pots, and it can be used in between other perennials as well in between bushes and under trees.

Type
Deciduous grass
Flowering
Summer
Height/spread
2.5m x 1.5cm
Position
Full sun, part shade
Soil
Moist, well-drained
Hardiness
USDA 6a–1 / RHS H7

Type
Deciduous tree
Flowering
Spring
Height/spread
10m x 6m
Position
Full sun, part shade
Soil
Moist, well-drained
Hardiness
USDA 6b/7a / RHS H6

Sorbus commixta 'Dodong'
Japanese rowan 'Dodong'

If you want a smaller tree in your garden this could be a fine choice, with its white flowers, orange fruits and lovely autumn foliage in shades of orange and red. A strong tree that allows plantation underneath. The flowers attract bees and insects.

GROW Grow as a solitary tree or use in groups.

Amelanchier laevis
Smooth serviceberry

A light, medium-sized shrub with white flowers in clusters. Later in the summertime it will have small red-black fruits that attract birds. It also has autumn foliage with stunning colours of yellow, orange and red.

GROW Can advantageously be stemmed up so that there is room for vegetation underneath.

Type
Deciduous shrub
or tree
Flowering
Spring
Height/spread
8m x 8m
Position
Full sun, part shade
Soil
Moist, well-drained
Hardiness
USDA 6a–1 / RHS H7

Type
Deciduous tree
Flowering
Spring
Height/spread
5m x 2m
Position
Full sun, part shade
Soil
Moist, well-drained
Hardiness
USDA 6a–1 / RHS H7

Malus 'Makamik'
Crab apple 'Makamik'

A small tree with an open habit, perfect for the smaller garden or as a solitary tree in a smaller bed with ground-cover plants underneath. Dark red flowers in spring, beautiful red foliage and red fruits in autumn. The flowers attract bees and insects.

GROW Very good if you want to add some height to a smaller bed.

GERALD LUCKHURST
Landscape architect,
Portugal

Gerald Luckhurst is a landscape architect and garden historian with an extensive knowledge of subtropical and Mediterranean garden flora. His work involves both historic restoration and contemporary garden design. He lives between Sintra, Monsaraz and Funchal in Portugal.

Dichorisandra thyrsiflora →
Blue ginger

The botanic garden where I work in Funchal lists the common name as dicorisandra, but not surprisingly my garden staff prefer the English common name, blue ginger. It is not, however, related to the true gingers. It belongs to the same family as tradescantia and callisia, which is *Commelinaceae* (the spiderwort family).

Some plants have an elegance that infuses their whole assembly. This is one such. It has an architecture that is composed of repeating modular parts, rather like that of bamboo: statuesque but slender. Its colour scheme is discreet yet striking, as though composed for haute couture. The general impression is of dark green highlighted by the blue flowers. Yet there is so much more going on in the details. The leaves have a strong pale midrib on long, dark leaf blades, which is the characteristic that makes this plant so reminiscent of members of the ginger family, such as alpinias and hedychiums. They taper to a graceful drip point and the jointed stems are freckled with maroon dots, the joints marked with stains of the same colour. The flowers are bunched at the top of the canes like a flowering wand. They are rather more purple than blue and have yellow stamens and a white eye.

The upright bearing and snazzy dress sense make this plant a gift to the garden designer. The subtle variations in tone mean it can be mixed with accessory plants that highlight its virtues. In one of my garden designs, it is paired with the equally elegant *Zantedeschia aethiopica*, grasses and, in the background, dark blue hydrangeas and garnet-coloured philodendrons. This is a garden composition that has grown to maturity over a period of twenty years without substantial intervention or replanting, a characteristic I value highly in any planting scheme.

GROW This has a 12-month flowering season, at least in Madeira. Maintenance is reduced to removing spent canes after flowering. It is dead easy to propagate, so much so that this plant is never found in nurseries on the island: people just help themselves to a snip. After writing this, that 20-year-old planting described above will probably suffer from severe finger blight!

Like most subtropical garden plants, blue ginger needs plenty of water and appreciates well-nourished soils. It is reported as naturalised in the Sydney region of Australia, probably due to discarded garden waste. I have not seen garden escapees in Madeira.

Type
Perennial
Flowering
Spring, summer
Height/spread
2m x 1m
Position
Part shade, but will take full sun with adequate moisture
Soil
Grows well in Madeira's heavy volcanic clay
Hardiness
USDA 12 / RHS H1b

ANDREW BEALE
Managing director, Beale Arboretum and Beales Hotels, Hertfordshire, UK

Andrew Beale is the eighth generation of Beale to run his family's hotel and is also responsible for the 35-acre Beale Arboretum. Founded by his grandfather, the arboretum now comprises more than 4,000 trees and three Plant Heritage National Collections. *westlodgepark.co.uk/arboretum*

Type
Deciduous tree
Flowering
Spring, summer
Height/spread
3.5m x 3m
Position
Full sun, dappled shade, exposed, sheltered
Soil
Thrives in the clay found in the Thames basin, which is either sodden or bone dry, which hints at its adaptability
Hardiness
USDA 6b/7a / RHS H6

Cornus kousa
Kousa

Trees, particularly from the US, are generally too big for the typical suburban garden, but the Japanese do everything at a smaller scale. The dwarf acers are the most famous of the Japanese trees, but here is a compact dogwood that manages two remarkable seasons each year. Late spring brings a profusion of small white bracts, making the tree look like it is covered in a blizzard of snow. And the bracts last much longer than a petal would, up to eight weeks or so depending on conditions. In the autumn, the teardrop-shaped leaves turn purple, with reds, golds and green also featuring. A lovely tree.

GROW The tree thrives in UK conditions, which are not dissimilar to those in Japan – both are maritime nations. Plant it in a square hole so the roots have to force themselves out at the corners, add mulch or swell gel to the soil mix, water well for the first two seasons, then leave alone unless there are drought conditions.

Taxodium ascendens 'Nutans'
Nodding pond cypress

It is rare to find a truly four-season plant. Most have at best two good seasons, while many are only at their peak for a few weeks. The pond cypress, however, provides interest in almost every week of the year. In spring the miniature 'leaflets' grow vertically to a final height of about 10cm and look absolutely stunning (and a bit otherworldly). In summer the same leaflets bush out and start curling over. In autumn, the tree turns the deepest rust colour. And in winter, as this is a deciduous conifer, it loses its foliage and shows off a very attractive fastigiate skeletal habit (like a rocket ice lolly). A monoecious tree, it produces male pollen cones and female cones that look like miniature footballs. It's narrow enough to plant in a medium-sized garden and will give years of pleasure.

GROW The pond cypress lives in standing water in the south-eastern North America, but adapts remarkably well to UK conditions. Follow the same planting advice as listed for the first tree in this selection.

Type
Deciduous conifer
Flowering
Spring
Height/spread
7.5m x 3m
Position
Full sun, dappled shade
Soil
Clay, loam
Hardiness
USDA 6a–1 / RHS H7

Type
Evergreen conifer
Flowering
Spring
Height/spread
4.5m x 3m
Position
Full sun, dappled sun, exposed, sheltered
Soil
Adaptable
Hardiness
USDA 6a–1 / RHS H7

Picea abies 'Acrocona'
Norway spruce 'Acrocona'

A remarkable tree, best in spring when a profusion of pink female cones, coupled with thousands of male pollen cones and the previous season's opened female cones, adorn it. Unusually, most of the cones grow at the tips of the branches and, as the tree expands the next year, it cannibalises and absorbs these cones into its branch structure as it pushes outwards. The tree does not have a strong leader, so grows outwards in a rather haphazard habit. In autumn its teardrop-shaped leaves turn a beautiful red.

GROW Follow the same planting advice as listed for the first tree in this selection.

Type
Deciduous tree
Flowering
Spring
Height/spread
4m x 4m
Position
Full sun, dappled sun, shade (although the fruits will ripen better in sun)
Soil
Adaptable
Hardiness
USDA 6b/7a / RHS H6

Malus 'Evereste' →
Crab apple 'Evereste'

Malus trees are ideal for a typical British garden. Not only are they compact in size, but they benefit from two great seasons, with creamy white blossom in spring and fruit in autumn – and there's the added bonus that you can make crab apple jelly from the fruits. Malus apples come in all sizes and colours, and we have over 40 varieties in the Beale Arboretum, but for me this variety is the best of the lot, because of its beautiful miniature cox's orange pippin-style apples, with their dolls-house-like yellow, orange and red patterning. Astringent until late mid-autumn, these become much sweeter after that.

GROW Follow the same planting advice as listed for the first tree in this selection.

Crataegus tanacetifolia
Syrian haw

The totemic hawthorn indicates the kind of spring we're experiencing each year, given that it is due to burst into flower on or around May 1 (May Day). In the past 30 years I have observed a wide variation in flowering dates in the Beale Arboretum, ranging from early April in a hot season to as late as early summer if the winter has been prolonged. Global warming? Maybe, although as a geographer I am loath to mix up weather with climate.

In general crataegus are very decorative when allowed to grow to tree height, but are most commonly seen in hedgerows, where their nasty thorns keep livestock in and unwanted intruders out of farmers' fields. But the Syrian haw has no thorns, grows no higher than 3.5m, and has the most delightful tansy velvet leaves, plus lots of creamy spring flowers and yellow autumn fruit or haws.

GROW Follow the same planting advice as listed for the first tree in this selection.

Type
Deciduous tree
Flowering
Spring, summer
Height/spread
3.5m x 3m
Position
Full sun or dappled shade
Soil
Adaptable
Hardiness
USDA 6b/7a / RHS H6

Type
Deciduous tree
Flowering
Spring
Height/spread
9m x 4.5m
Position
Full sun; hornbeams are a woodland species, so can grow closely in shady conditions
Soil
Adaptable
Hardiness
USDA 6a–1 / RHS H7

Carpinus betulus 'Quercifolia'
Oak-leaved hornbeam

I could have chosen much more beautiful hornbeams from our National Collection, such as *Carpinus betulus* 'Fastigiata' or *C. b.* 'Pendula', but I have instead gone for this biological oddity. We have various mixed-species trees here, and I don't really like any of them, although they are endlessly fascinating. Why anyone would mix *Laburnum* and *Cytisus* to produce the graft chimaera that is + *Laburnocytisus* 'Adamii' is beyond me. But the oak-leaved hornbeam is an old cultured form that isn't really in a balanced state: the oak-shaped leaves, with their deep lobes, are steadily replaced by pure hornbeam leaves as the tree reverts to full-blooded hornbeam. So it is a tree that is constantly undergoing reversion to its native form, and I think that's why I like it – because it refuses to accept the meddling that we humans have done to it.

GROW Follow the same planting advice as listed for the first tree in this selection.

JEREMY FRANCIS
Owner, Cloudehill Gardens,
Victoria, Australia

From the late 1960s to 1990, Jeremy Francis farmed a 5,000-acre wheat and sheep property in Western Australia. In 1990, he sold the farm and moved to the Dandenong Ranges into a historic nursery/flower farm that featured plants going back to the 1920s – and also lots of weeds. Cloudehill is now one of Australia's finest gardens and nurseries. *cloudehill.com.au*

Type
Shrub
Flowering
Spring,
summer
**Height/
spread**
2m x 1m
Position
Part shade
Soil
Well-
drained
Hardiness
USDA 8b/9a
/ RHS H4

← *Darwinia carnea*
Mogumber bell

This incredibly rare and rather lovely plant was actually described and collected from our farm. There were only about 15 or so plants in the original population and by the time my family owned the property these had long vanished, leaving *D. carnea* extinct. It was also growing in Perth, in the famous Kings Park and Botanic Garden – annoyingly, however, they were all grown from cuttings from the one original plant in the wild, and self-infertile. The Kings Park Mogumber bells never produced seed, so the darn thing was thought thoroughly extinct. However, in very recent years, another tiny population has been found on a hilltop just east of Mogumber, and the Mogumber bell is back with us again. *Darwinia* is an intriguing genus, growing mainly on mountaintops on the south coast of Western Australia. There are no mountains around Mogumber, need I add, and ours is a bit of an outlier. I understand that darwinias were named for Erasmus Darwin, the grandfather of Charles.

GROW Ensure excellent drainage.

Miscanthus
Eulalia

I've been collecting and working with perennials and ornamental grasses since the mid-1970s. Christopher Lloyd very kindly helped me source a number of grasses when I visited Great Dixter in 1988. (My wife, Valerie, happened to have a family member who was a neighbour.) I had the chance to spend half a day with the great man tracking down people such as Beth Chatto and Ernst Pagels. Pagels supplied several *Miscanthus sinensis* selections, also *Calamagrostis × acutiflora* 'Karl Foerster' and 'Overdam' – they all came through the highly convoluted Australian plant quarantines between 1990 and 2005.

I still class grasses as some of my favourite plants and I created a new grass garden recently using *Stipa gigantea*, *M. sinensis* var. *condensatus* 'Cosmopolitan', *M*. 'Graziella', *M*. 'Flamingo', *M*. 'Sarabande', and also a seedling that has cropped up in Cloudehill that's behaving like a hybrid between *M. nepalensis* (which I've loved and lost) and another of my introductions to Australia, *M*. 'Gracillimus'. My seedling looks very exciting, with narrow leaves and all the grace of 'Gracillimus' as well as the pendulous tawny flowers of *M. nepalensis*. And the foliage seems to be evergreen! Very mysterious and also very useful.

Out of an interest in First Nations culture I also grow the glaucous form of kangaroo grass, *Themeda triandra*. Aboriginal cultivation of the landscape (using the firestick) often seemed to centre around promoting this grass, both for its flour and also because kangaroos love the fresh shoots. Kangaroo grass is an intriguing beast, growing all the way from South Africa to the eastern shores of the Middle East and to coastal India and Australia. Its range duplicates the migration route of Australia's First Nation peoples 65,000 years back. Is this coincidental?

GROW In among the grasses I use various salvias and agastaches in softer colours.

Type
Grass
Flowering
Autumn
**Height/
spread**
2.5m x 1.5m
Position
Full sun
Soil
Moist, well-
drained
Hardiness
USDA 6b/7a
/ RHS H6

PETER MOORE
Plant breeder,
Hampshire, UK

Peter Moore is a plant breeder with over 40 plants to his name. He started his career at Hillier's Nurseries in the early 1960s and raised the first choisya hybrid, C. 'Aztec Pearl'. He moved to Longstock Park Nursery in 1997 and became keeper of the National Collection of *Buddleja* in 2005. *bredbypetermoore.co.uk*

Choisya × dewitteana **White Dazzler ('Londaz')**
Mexican orange [White Dazzler]

After the success of raising *Choisya* 'Aztec Pearl', I used another Mexican species, *C. dumosa*, as the pollen parent and crossed it to create a compact hardy evergreen plant. It is suitable for a border or patio pot, flowering in the spring and autumn, and has been in the top ten plants sold at the nursery for many years now, a testament to its reliability.

GROW Give the plant a light prune after spring flowering. Apply an organic fertiliser or garden compost in late spring. For pot-grown plants, apply a liquid feed through the summer.

Type
Evergreen shrub
Flowering
Spring, autumn
Height/spread
1m x 1m
Position
Full sun, part shade
Soil
Well-drained
Hardiness
USDA 8b/9a / RHS H4

Buddleja **Berries and Cream ('Pmoore14')**
Butterfly bush [Berries and Cream]

I'm the keeper of the National Collection of *Buddleja* at Longstock Park Nursery. One day I found a single variegated flower on a spike of *B. davidii* 'Royal Red' – by carefully collecting its seed I raised several buddleja with less or more variegated flowers. By repeating the process over several years I raised a plant with bicoloured purple and white flowers and a few flowers on each raceme that were either wholly white or wholly purple.

GROW Apply organic compost in the autumn and organic fertiliser in early summer. I prefer to prune in early spring, reducing the bush by 50–75 per cent. In recent years in the UK, we have experienced very late spring frosts, especially in my garden (a frost pocket close to a river) and the low temperatures have done considerable damage to all buddleja cultivars. Buddleja is root hardy, so grows away from the base in early summer. To extend the flowering period into early autumn, remove all the dead flowers every two to three days and water if very dry. More nectar will give you more butterflies.

Type
Deciduous shrub
Flowering
Summer, autumn
Height/spread
4m x 1.5m
Position
Full sun, part shade
Soil
Moist, well-drained
Hardiness
USDA 6b/7a / RHS H6

Type
Evergreen shrub
Flowering
Winter
Height/spread
1m x 1m
Position
Full shade, part shade, sheltered
Soil
Moist, well-drained
Hardiness
USDA 7b/8a
/ RHS H5

Sarcococca hookeriana **Winter Gem ('Pmoore03')**
Sweet box [Winter Gem]

This hybrid form (*Sarcococca hookeriana* var. *digyna* 'Purple Stem' × *S. h.* var. *humilis*) has inherited the best qualities of both its parents. It has larger than average leaves, which are a glossy, rich green, as well as highly scented white flowers in winter, followed by spherical glossy red berries that ripen to black. Tough and tolerant of most conditions, it is especially valuable for shadier areas.

GROW Can easily be grown in a container – one of the original plants has been growing happily in a large pot for 10 years.

Escallonia Showstopper ('Pmoore20')

Escallonia [Showstopper]

An amazing new introduction that brings together characteristics from the larger, more outstanding escallonia flowers of some of the newer breedings with a bushy, compact and almost mound-forming cultivar that produces a great dome of summer colour.

GROW Apply an organic fertiliser in early summer. Lightly prune after flowering. Can be cut back very hard after 10 years and will shoot from the base. Loves full sun, but protection in very cold frost pockets (subject to late spring frosts) may be necessary.

Type
Evergreen shrub
Flowering
Summer
Height/spread
1.2m x 80cm
Position
Full sun
Soil
Well-drained
Hardiness
USDA 8b/9a / RHS H4

NICK BAILEY
Garden designer,
London, UK

Nick Bailey is a garden designer and plantsman, *Gardeners' World* presenter, author and speaker. He has designed and managed gardens on four continents over the last 30 years, including the Chelsea Physic Garden in London, and has written gardening books including *365 Days of Colour in Your Garden*. nickbailey365.com

Zaluzianskya capensis ⬊

Night phlox

South Africa has huge and diverse flora, including one of my favourite plants, *Z. capensis*. I first encountered it in my twenties when I was working in Johannesburg at the famed Brenthurst Garden. One evening as I wandered through the vast plantings, I was overwhelmed by a delicious scent, the likes of which I'd never experienced: I'd just met *Z. capensis*. By day this diminutive Capetonian plant can easily go unnoticed, but as dusk draws in, it owns the night. The petals, which are deep red on their backs, flex inwards during the day and look like little red berries. At dusk, they unfurl to reveal near-iridescent white faces and a sublime, unique scent. Sitting somewhere between Parma Violets and vanilla, the perfume of a single plant can fill a garden on a warm night. I've grown it every year since I first met it and have introduced it to, frankly, anyone who will listen. It's easy to grow and happily blooms for about 60 nights.

GROW Easily grown from seed – best surface sown and covered in vermiculite. Start it in mid-spring for blooms come mid-summer. I usually prick out several plants together as it has a straggly habit and several grown this way form a fuller plant. It is best grown and shown off in two-litre terracotta pots and its scent is most appreciated when grown in a slightly protected area that's still part of the garden.

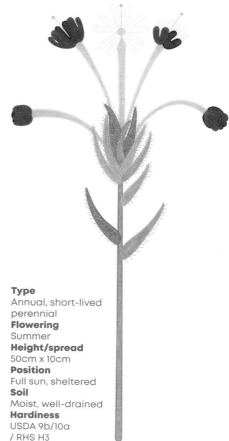

Type
Annual, short-lived
perennial
Flowering
Summer
Height/spread
50cm x 10cm
Position
Full sun, sheltered
Soil
Moist, well-drained
Hardiness
USDA 9b/10a
/ RHS H3

RAINER SCHMIDT
Landscape architect and
urban planner, Munich,
Germany

Professor Rainer Schmidt is a landscape architect and urban planner. In
1991 he opened offices for landscape architecture in Munich and Berlin,
and in 1997 another branch in Bernburg/Saale. He became a professor
for landscape architecture and design at the Beuth University of Applied
Sciences in 1991. He is also a guest professor at the Beijing University and
the University of California, Berkeley. *rainerschmidt.com*

Paulownia tomentosa →
Foxglove tree

P. tomentosa has long been one of the most common park trees. It creates a
special atmosphere during spring, as the fragrant, violet-blue blossoms come
out before the leaves emerge. The trees are undemanding when it comes to
the location and soil – they can even be planted in regions endangered by
frost, which is perfect for climate change. It can also reserve a huge amount of
water and that way easily survives dry periods. Known as *blauglockenbaum* in
Germany, this tree grows really fast, is strong and is resistant to various insects.
The heart-shaped leaves are spectacular because of their size, more than 30cm
long. It makes a good specimen tree.

GROW The first few years are quite critical and the trees have to be protected from cold
and wind. Since the roots are pretty strong, the location has to be chosen carefully so
they don't destroy any pipes or building structures. Easy to care for, they tolerate heat
and need some warmth, so are suited to the urban climate.

Type
Deciduous
tree
Flowering
Spring
**Height/
spread**
12m x 8m
Position
Full sun, part
shade
Soil
Well-
drained
Hardiness
USDA 7b/8a
/ RHS H5

CEL ROBERTSON
Flower farmer, Norfolk, UK

Cel Robertson started Forever Green Flower Company in 2013, supplying
sustainably grown flowers to local farm shops, florists and wedding clients.
Originally trained as a garden designe, she runs workshops alongside
flower farming and is the author of *Cut Flowers. forevergreenflowerco.co.uk*

Type
Herbaceous
perennial
Flowering
Spring,
summer
**Height/
spread**
80cm x
50cm
Position
Full sun, part
shade, open
Soil
Moist, well-
drained
Hardiness
USDA 6a–1
/ RHS H7

Astrantia major **Sparkling Stars Series**
Masterwort 'Sparkling Stars'

As a cut-flower grower, I'm always looking for varieties that perform well in
the vase. Astrantia is a popular cut flower, but the Sparkling Stars Series is
something special. It comprises separate pink, burgundy and white tones,
with larger-than-average flowers held in well-branched heads on straight
stems. It's definitely an upgrade on some of the species types. Sparkling Stars
is among the first astrantias to start flowering in spring. If deadheaded, the
plants continue to produce stems at a slower rate through summer. As a
bonus, the larger flowerheads are good to cut for drying for use through winter.
They are also beneficial plants for wildlife and can be found humming with
hoverflies and bees when in flower.

GROW The astrantia is easy to grow and I've found it to be tolerant of a range of
conditions. Moist soil is said to be preferable, but I grow mine on a sandy loam that dries
out quickly. We are located in one of the driest areas of the country (in Norfolk) and I have
added a lot of compost to my beds over the years, which has improved their moisture
retentiveness. While it does grow in shade, it is more floriferous in better light. If you want
to cut the flowers, wait until the pollen is visible on the central bloom – this must be fully
open as otherwise it will wilt in the vase. I feed with seaweed meal in the spring and always
mulch my beds with 5cm compost. The plants do not need any special support, but they
benefit from weekly irrigation if it is dry once the plants are growing in spring. Lack of water
at this stage negatively affects flowering. Cut down to ground level in autumn/winter once
the foliage has died back. Plants may be easily divided in the autumn.

MICHAEL PERRY
Hortpreneur, Suffolk, UK

Michael Perry, AKA Mr Plant Geek, is a gardener and broadcaster who aims to share his enthusiasm for plants and gardens with as wide a range of people as possible through his social media channels and regular TV appearances. *mrplantgeek.com*

× *Petchoa* BeautiCal
Petchoa (BeautiCal Series)

Type
Annual
Flowering
Summer, autumn
Height/ spread
30cm x 40cm
Position
Full sun, part shade
Soil
Moist, well-drained
Hardiness
USDA 9b/10a / RHS H3

I've always been interested in new breeding, and this comes from one of the best breeding stables in the world. The BeautiCal Series is the unique marriage of a petunia and a calibrachoa, giving you weatherproof blooms in a fantastic range of shades: cappuccino, milkshake and caramel. The growth is open and the flowers are produced on top of the plants in a well-balanced manner. They are perfect in basket mixes, with a little bit of careful colour coordination. Unlike many big floppy petunias, they bounce back after a storm, usually within minutes!

GROW Their billowing habit means that they suit baskets as well as pots. Don't underestimate how intense the colours can be during the height of summer. They flower for an exceptionally long period too – even up to the first frosts. Feed with potash for best results and extended flowering.

Type
Hardy, half-hardy shrubs, depending on variety
Height/ spread
Up to 50cm x 50cm
Position
Full sun
Soil
Well-drained, gritty
Hardiness
USDA 7b–10a / RHS H5–H3

× *Mangave*
Mangave

I love new trends, and this plant has got everybody talking. It's a unique hybrid between agave and manfreda, a perhaps little-known plant. They are basically outdoor succulents and look absolutely amazing, like nothing else in your border. They are also super easy to grow, drought proof and a heck of an architectural sight! I've got quite a few at home – they're quite collectable, like the toys you get in cereal boxes. They are also really flexible plants to grow – if you want them to, they will grow; if you don't water them, they just stay as is, not complaining a jot. The succulent rosette of growth is rather eye-catching, and look out for the range of varieties – they have stripes, spots and many different colourings.

GROW These are showpiece plants, so give them space to show off. Even though I'm a fan of mixed containers, you probably won't have much space for any other plants when you grow mangave in a pot. They look amazing in drought-tolerant planting schemes too, adding that touch of the exotic. They will need to be relatively dry over the winter, so make sure drainage is adequate.

Type
Perennial
Flowering
Summer
Height/ spread
50cm x 50cm
Position
Full sun
Soil
Well-drained, alkaline, neutral
Hardiness
USDA 6a–1 / RHS H7

Sedum takesimense Atlantis ('Nonsitnal') →
Takeshima stonecrop [Atlantis]

Now here's a plant that could be described as high resolution. It has variegated foliage, which offers a gold lining to the bright green leaves and golden flowers that appear during the summer. This is a real show-off plant, but one that's easy to grow. You can use it in dry borders, in pots... anywhere you want carefree gardening. It looks good all year round, because even when the flowers aren't on the plants, there's enough to catch your eye.

GROW I plant it where I want a real dose of colour. It's a great companion plant to other drought-lovers, such as cape daisies, in containers. It's also excellent ground cover and keeps moisture locked in. It will barely need watering, as it stores so much water in its flat succulent leaves.

186

JANE SCOTTER
Owner, Fern Verrow,
Herefordshire, UK

Jane Scotter is the owner and farmer of Fern Verrow, which has operated as a biodynamic farm for more than 25 years. It grows seasonal vegetables, fruit and flowers for restaurant Spring in London. *fernverrow.com*

Type
Annual, biennial
Height/spread
1m x 50cm
Position
Any, avoid
prolonged periods
of hard frost
Soil
Any, but not too wet
or it may rot and
attract slugs
Hardiness
USDA 7b/8a / RHS H5

Cichorium intybus var. *foliosum*
Radicchio

I love radicchio on so many levels, and always get carried away each year, growing tens of varieties. Taste is the most important thing, with beauty a close second. The different colours are always thrilling and original, like 'Castelfranco', with its green leaves spotted with what looks like blackcurrant juice. Other varieties come in all tones of pink and magenta, only to darken over the winter. When harvesting on a cold day and coming across a beautiful specimen glowing like the flesh of a blood orange, it is warming to the eyes and spirit.

GROW Though this is technically a biennial, it is eaten before it goes to seed, so treated as an annual. Start germination at the end of July (mid-summer) and have them in the ground by late August for a good supply of large heads in winter. It likes the warmth of autumn to get going, but needs the cold to really develop flavour and colour. Keep weeded and water well in late summer so plants grow to full size before the shorter days arrive.

CAROLYN DUNSTER
Gardening writer and
planting designer,
London, UK

Carolyn Dunster is the author of *Cut & Dry: The Modern Guide to Dried Flowers from Growing to Styling* and *Urban Flowers: Creating Abundance in a Small City Garden*. She has exhibited at RHS Hampton Court, winning the People's Choice Award. She writes about flowers, plants and gardens for gardening and lifestyle magazines. *instagram.com/carolynrdunster*

Nigella damascena
Love-in-a-mist (SEE ILLUSTRATION PAGE 74)

I love this plant as it was one of the first flowers I grew myself from seed and I have had it in my garden ever since for over 20 years. It is so easy to grow in any soil and under any conditions and requires no complicated pricking out or planting on. It gives a first-time gardener masses of confidence as it germinates quickly and the results are so satisfying.

Each flower is a little work of art that produces a stripy balloon-shaped seedhead that makes for a fantastic dried display. The flowers come in a range of jewel-like colours, from pinks and blues to deep maroon. They stand upright with a single flower on each stem that is supported by delicate, feathery bracts. They are perfect for a cottage-garden style of planting and can be picked by the handful for vase arrangements. Their flat heads also make them easy to press.

Type
Annual
Flowering
Spring,
summer
**Height/
spread**
50cm x 50cm
Position
Full sun, part
shade
Soil
Well-
drained,
alkaline,
neutral
Hardiness
USDA 9b/10a
/ RHS H3

GROW Sow seed in the autumn. The more thinly you sow the better, but you may need to remove the occasional seedling if they are growing too close together. This will produce a batch of early flowers from late spring the following year onwards. If you sow more seed again in spring, you will have a succession of flowers taking you right through summer and into autumn. You'll only have to buy one packet of seeds as it self-sows so prolifically that you will end up with loads of flowers for free. You can save your own seed for redistribution if you decide you want it to grow in another place. There is no need to feed, but watering occasionally when very dry will keep the flowers coming, as will regular picking.

MIDORI SHINTANI
Head gardener, Tokachi
Millennium Forest,
Hokkaido, Japan

Midori Shintani is head gardener at the Dan Pearson Studio-designed Tokachi Millennium Forest where she merges 'new Japanese horticulture' with wild nature. She trained at Minami Kyushu University and in 2002 moved to Sweden and trained at Millesgården sculpture garden and Rosendals Trädgård biodynamic gardens. She writes and lectures. *tmf.jp*

← *Sanguisorba hakusanensis*
Korean burnet

I have a serious sanguisorba obsession. Growing the *Sanguisorba* genus is my life's joy. Regardless of varieties, I have always loved their unique characters and comparing their differences. It is too tough to choose one favourite! But I introduce *S. hakusanensis* as my favourite here, because this extraordinary species is one of the longest relationships I have had in the garden. In Japan, the common name is karaitosou – named after *karaito*, the silk thread introduced from China – for the plant's beautiful thread-like stamens. The Latin name means 'from the Haku mountain'. Its grey-green scalloped leaves thrive here and form a decorative pinnate clump. Before the flowering stems come up in spring, its huge clump looks like a big bird resting its wings. After the dramatic appearance at the beginning of the growing season, upright stems gradually start arching with masses of pink flowers and their silk-thread stamens gracefully capture the sunlight.

GROW One plant spreads over 1.2m in my garden. It has a tendency to droop, which is more noticeable in older plants. I recommend allowing them to follow their natural habit rather than trying to make them stand up with supports. It's one of the plants I would like to grow in a garden with a steep slope. Splitting a mature plant is quite a moment – you will be overwhelmed by the strength of its root system grabbing at the earth to live!

Type
Herbaceous
perennial
Flowering
Summer,
autumn
**Height/
spread**
1.5m x 1.5m
Position
Full sun, part
shade
Soil
Moist, well-
drained
Hardiness
USDA 6b/7a
/ RHS H6

NOËL KINGSBURY
Garden designer, author
and teacher, Portugal

Noël Kingsbury is a writer, teacher, garden/planting designer and horticultural consultant. Best known for his ecological and naturalistic approach to planting design, he has written more than 25 books, several in collaboration with Dutch plantsman Piet Oudolf. He is co-founder of learning platform Garden Masterclass. *noelkingsbury.com*

Salvia
Sage

Salvias are useful in so many situations and always beautiful. For late-season colour, look to *Salvia uliginosa* or *S. guaranitica* 'Blue Enigma'; for variegated foliage, the subshrub *S. officinalis* 'Icterina' forms low clumps with visual texture. On dry soil, *S. nemorosa* hybrids look striking with yellow achilleas in early summer, and as the season progresses, *S. sclarea* var. *turkestanica* can take up the baton. For planting among rough grasses, try the tall and robust *S. glutinosa*. And for meadow planting, *S. pratensis*. For nutrient-poor limestone soils, repeat-flowering varieties of *S. nemorosa*, *S. × superba* and *S. × sylvestris* will flower profusely in early summer, become dormant later in the season as the soil dries out, then make a recovery later in the autumn as the rains return (and if cut back after the first flush). There are countless forms, scents and colours – simply choose those that thrive in the given conditions you can offer (rather than defying them) and garden in tune with nature, which will not only reward you (your back and your bank balance) but also the local wildlife.

GROW Many salvias look their best planted in small- to medium-sized clumps of three to five plants. They can be tender or hardy, so ensure you know what you are growing. Take cuttings in spring.

Type
Annual,
perennial
Flowering
Summer,
autumn
**Height/
spread**
1.5m x 60cm,
varies
depending
of form
Position
Full sun, part
shade
Soil
Well-
drained
Hardiness
USDA 10b–1
/ RHS H2–H7

**ANDRÉE DAVIES &
ADAM WHITE**
Directors, Davies White
Landscape Architects, UK

Andrée Davies and Adam White specialise in connecting communities, families and children with nature through imaginative and award-winning public space design. They deliver resilient schemes that are good for people and planet. *davieswhite.co.uk*

Type
Herbaceous
perennial
Flowering
Summer, autumn
Height/spread
50cm x 50cm
Position
Full sun,
part shade
Soil
Any
Hardiness
USDA 6a–1 / RHS H7

Alchemilla mollis →
Lady's mantle

This is one of those underdog plants, very common, often overlooked and considered a weed by some. But we always use it in our work with children because it has beautifully shaped wavy-edged leaves that capture droplets of water after it rains that seem to shine like diamonds. 'Let's go and see the fairy jewels' is something we often hear in our children's gardens after the rain. Its attractive foliage lasts all summer long and it also has acid-green flowers that smell of cherries.

GROW It's so easy to grow pretty much anywhere and it self-seeds when it gets established. It's tough too, so doesn't mind if you accidentally tread on it – as often happens in our playful public gardens – and it will rebound happily. Cut back dead foliage in spring ready for the new growth.

Eupatorium maculatum **Atropurpureum Group**
Eupatorium Atropurpureum Group

We want our planting schemes to reflect nature and not be too perfect, so we often choose plants that capture the qualities of their wild relatives. We also want to use plants that are beneficial for wildlife. This eupatorium fits the bill perfectly. It has a wild-looking habit, grows very tall with strong stems so it doesn't fall over or need staking. Best of all it is loved by butterflies. There are lots of different types, but this is the best in our view: tall and elegant with antique rose-coloured flowers later in the summer.

GROW Easy to grow, but does better in a dampish situation. Can be cut back to ground level in late winter ready for new growth.

Type
Herbaceous
perennial
Flowering
Late summer
Height/spread
2m x 1m
Position
Full sun, part shade
Soil
Not fussy
Hardiness
USDA 6a–1 / RHS H7

Type
Deciduous tree
Flowering
Spring (but the
flowers are not the
main event here)
Height/spread
12m x 8m
Position
Full sun, part shade,
pretty resilient
Soil
Any
Hardiness
USDA 6b/7a / RHS H6

Fagus sylvatica **'Pendula'**
Weeping beech

This is our favourite tree for den building. It has low, sweeping branches that touch the ground in a beautiful, elegant arc and make the perfect place to scramble under and create your own place to curl up and daydream. This tree features in our Back to Nature garden at RHS Wisley. If you are passing that way, call in and take a look at our much-loved and characterful tree. The grass underneath its branches has been worn away by all the children and families who have enjoyed sitting there. It also boasts an excellent autumn colour that shines like gold in low autumn light.

GROW You need a lot of space for this tree – it's best in large gardens or parks. It can be pruned into shape when young if necessary. Like all new trees, it needs plenty of water until it is established, then it is pretty easy to look after.

Fragaria vesca
Alpine strawberry

Foraging for edible plants adds another layer of fun to the planting schemes we design for children. We usually put all the edible plants in one bed together to help children understand which they can eat and which they can't. These tiny strawberries pack an amazing flavour punch and the hunt for a perfectly ripe, tiny, bright red fruit is well worth it. The fruits are also loved by blackbirds and it's often a race to see who can get to them first. Neat, clump-forming, semi-evergreen plants, they also have shiny leaves and white, star-shaped flowers. They seem to flower and fruit all summer and into autumn. Over time they spread by sending out runners that root and form a new plant.

GROW Easy to grow in most situations. They like a bit of shade, but because they're so small any surrounding plants give them some protection. They can be tidied up in spring if needed.

Type
Stoloniferous perennial
Flowering
Summer
Height/spread
30cm x 1m
Position
Full sun, part shade, some protection appreciated
Soil
Any
Hardiness
USDA 6b/7a / RHS H6

Pelargonium 'Cola Bottles'
Geranium 'Cola Bottles'

We are always trying to get children interested in plants and horticulture and to help them feel the benefits of a nature fix. This little pelargonium is great in a pot on a windowsill or balcony; you don't need a garden to grow it. The giveaway is in the name – it smells of cola! When we take it along to our workshops in primary schools the students are amazed and like to put a few of the leaves in their pocket to take home and surprise their friends with.

GROW Old plants can become quite woody, so this is often grown as an annual. It's easy to grow in a pot on a sunny windowsill or outside in summer. It's not frost hardy so needs to come indoors in winter. It has pink flowers that are most prolific in summer and the grey-green foliage persists all year round. Deadheading will prolong flowering. Like most pelargoniums the aromatic leaves smell strongest when grown in hot and sunny conditions. Don't over water.

Type
Perennial
Flowering
Spring, summer, autumn
Height/spread
30cm x 20cm
Position
Sunny spot in the house, or on a patio or balcony
Soil
Gritty soil with very good drainage
Hardiness
USDA 9b/10a / RHS H3

Prunus 'Tai-haku'
Great white cherry

Cherry trees are so common in our towns and cities that we often pass them without a second thought. But they have a fascinating history. Most of them originate from Japan and there is the lovely story of Collingwood 'Cherry' Ingram, who is said to have helped reintroduce varieties of cherries from his garden in England back to Japan following a decline there in the mid-twentieth century. Cherries seem to embody that Japanese aesthetic of simplicity and clarity, none more so than the great white. Its fleeting large, white, single flowers make it all the more of a treasure to look forward to each spring and this is one of the reasons we used it in the design for the London Blossom garden.

GROW This cherry tree is suitable for a small garden and has a wonderful wide-spreading canopy that is like a roof of blossom over your head in spring. Best to plant it in a place where it won't need controlling, as cherries don't respond well to pruning and tend to die back. It needs plenty of water until it is established, then it is pretty easy to look after.

Type
Deciduous tree
Flowering
Spring
Height/spread
6m x 8m
Position
Full sun, part shade
Soil
Any
Hardiness
USDA 6b/7a / RHS H6

SHARON COOKE
Curator and head gardener,
Andromeda Botanic
Gardens, Barbados

Sharon Cooke is curator and head gardener at Andromeda Botanic Gardens, and course director, tutor and business owner at Passiflora, the company responsible for the management of the Gardens. She trained as a garden designer in the UK. In 2008 she emigrated to Barbados, her parents' birthplace. *andromedabarbados.com*

Passiflora edulis f. *flavicarpa* →
Yellow passion fruit

I love plants that are native to the region and this is not only a vigorous tropical climber with a wonderfully beautiful flower, it also bears the delicious passion fruit. The purple and white flowers are beautiful, about 10cm in diameter, almost surreal with their showy corona and prominent anthers. The golden yellow fruit is sweet to tart and can be eaten by just scooping out the pulp-covered seeds. So, a rampant vine with attractive dark green, glossy, three-lobed leaves, beautiful bee-attracting flowers and delicious fruit. Perfect.

GROW Give the vine sun to maximise flower and fruit production. It is a major food source for the caterpillar of the gulf fritillary butterfly; cover the plants with netting when they are young as these spiky caterpillars can eat them. Very fertile soils will produce a vine with plenty of leaves, as will growing the vine in shade. Grow in moderately fertile to poor soils with good drainage.

Type
Evergreen
climber
Flowering
Spring
**Height/
spread**
15m x 4m
Position
Full sun
Soil
Well-
drained
Hardiness
USDA 11 /
RHS H1c

Plumeria obtusa
Frangipani

The *Plumeria* genus comprises many flowering trees. *P. rubra* is wonderful as it is strictly deciduous so its seasonal nature is appealing. By contrast, *P. obtusa* tends to keep most of its leaves, only shedding them in extremely dry conditions. But it is not the evergreen nature of this species that is appealing – its scent can be detected when you are far from the tree, particularly very early in the morning. But it doesn't matter if I'm not awake early enough as the tree drops its flowers daily and the discarded flowers are also divinely scented, large and beautifully white against a green lawn. Almost daily I pick them up and smell them. The scent is so intoxicating and it connects me to this garden in a wonderful way.

GROW At Andromeda we leave the flowers where they fall so visitors can smell them. Leaves may fall with extended periods of dry weather. Although not required, prune when young in late autumn to early winter for a bushier plant. Take care if pruning, as they have a milky sap that can irritate the skin.

Type
Evergreen
shrub or tree
Flowering
Spring
**Height/
spread**
7m x 7m
Position
Full sun, part
shade
Soil
Well-
drained
Hardiness
USDA 12 /
RHS H1b

Type
Herbaceous
perennial
Flowering
Summer, autumn
Height/spread
2.5m x 50cm
Position
Full sun, open
Soil
Moist, well-drained
Hardiness
USDA 8b/9a /
RHS H4

Verbena bonariensis
Purple top

This is a super plant, providing height without density and is perfect for hot, dry areas. Graceful and see through, they do not spoil the views beyond. The clusters of lilac flowers are like jewels hanging in the air. Wonderful! They work well in gravel gardens and are beloved by bees, birds and butterflies. Red admiral butterflies and hummingbird hawk moths feed from them all the time here in Barbados. The latter are especially fascinating to watch. It grows quickly: from seed to flower within months.

GROW Leave the spent flowerheads as birds will be extremely grateful. Cut down the dry stems when new basal growth starts in the spring. If you want a tall plant by a sunny window that will not spoil the view, *V. bonariensis* is ideal.

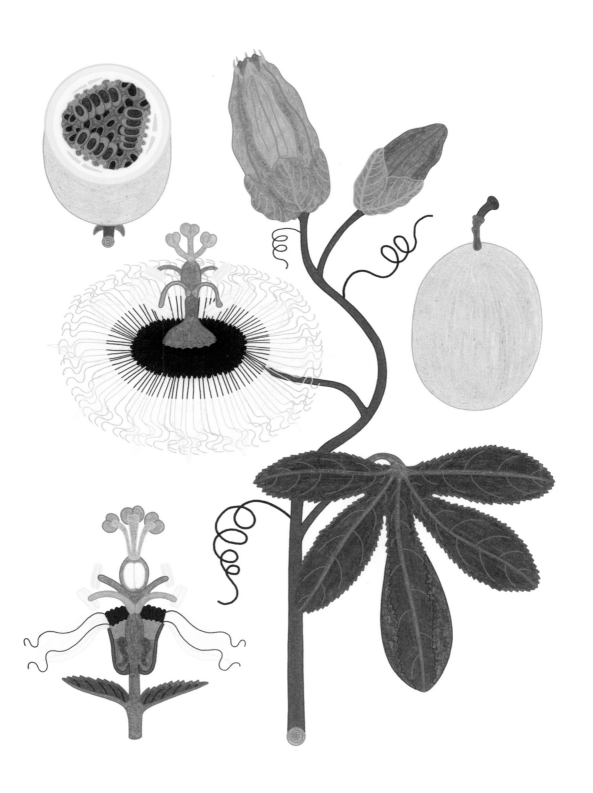

Hebe 'Green Globe'
Hebe 'Green Globe'

It was quite difficult to choose my favourite hebe because I like so many of them. They have a long flowering season (I've even seen them flowering throughout the winter), bees love them, they come in a range of sizes and they are evergreen. Why is 'Green Globe' my favourite? It is amazingly neat. The small, bright green leaves are almost like scales. It is dense and grows naturally into a sphere with little pruning required. These globes create perfect pauses in planting schemes and this variety makes a good substitute for box in certain situations. The white flower clusters add to the delightful nature of this shrub.

Type
Evergreen shrub
Flowering
Summer, autumn
Height/ spread
50cm x 50cm
Position
Full sun, part shade
Soil
Moist, well-drained
Hardiness
USDA 9b/10a / RHS H3

GROW The globes provide a strong structural shape and are great at unifying an eclectic garden space. The plants can be used as a ground cover if planted en masse. Hebes grow well in pots. If you want a small box plant, get 'Green Globe' instead! No special care needed – prune lightly to maintain shape.

Allium hollandicum 'Purple Sensation'
Dutch garlic 'Purple Sensation'

When I was 'gardenless' I bought some fake flowers – not something I normally do but these were simple yet interesting, like huge lollipops with tiny flowers in a large globe. Perfect for my flat and some tall narrow vases I had bought. I had thought that this 'plant' was simply some person's imagination. Later that year I was watching highlights from the RHS Chelsea Flower Show and there they were! I was amazed (and perhaps I felt a bit silly for assuming these didn't exist in real life). I fell in love with them. The tiny flowers are star-shaped and hundreds are packed into a 10cm-diameter sphere. So, when I started my own garden, I planted so many, as well as other varieties including *A. sphaerocephalon*, another lovely plant. But 'Purple Sensation' remains my favourite. An added benefit? Bees love them too.

Type
Bulbous perennial
Flowering
Summer, autumn
Height/ spread
1m x 50cm
Position
Full sun
Soil
Moist, well-drained
Hardiness
USDA 6b/7a / RHS H6

GROW Plant bulbs in autumn. Plant lots of them in a few groups in your garden. The globes provide a strong structural shape. Leave the spent flowerheads as these are also attractive.

Type
Annual climber
Flowering
Summer, autumn
Height/spread
2.5m x 2.5m
Position
Full sun
Soil
Well-drained
Hardiness
USDA 9b/10a / RHS H3

Tropaeolum majus
Nasturtium

Nasturtiums are easy to grow and they give back so much. The flowers come in a range of hot colours as well as near white, and they bloom well into the autumn. Bees love them, which is always a great reason to plant them. The climbing plants will scramble quickly up netting or a trellis, adding a wonderful wildness to the garden. The trailing varieties are perfect in pots or hanging baskets. The attractive leaves can get very large, especially in fertile soils. Although much is written about the edible flowers, I prefer the taste of the young leaves, which are absolutely delicious in salads or with eggs and soft cheeses.

GROW Nasturtiums can self-seed prolifically – fabulous for many gardeners – but remove the seeds to prevent this from happening, if you wish.

Zinnia elegans
Zinnia

If you enjoy seeing hummingbirds, bees and butterflies in your garden, plant zinnias. If you want a colourful display at 1m or 30cm in height, plant zinnias. If you want an easy plant that will grow and flower quickly, plant zinnias! Definitely one of my favourite plants. They flower quickly – six weeks after sowing the seeds – and the single pink and orange are my favourite cultivars. I plant them together for a dazzling display. Varieties come in a range of colours and heights. The flower is typically daisy-like with single and double ray florets.

Type
Annual
Flowering
Summer, autumn
Height/ spread
1m x 50cm
Position
Full sun, sheltered as they do topple over in strong winds
Soil
Moist, well-drained
Hardiness
USDA 10b / RHS H2

GROW I plant en masse for a long-lasting colourful display. For those gardeners in colder climates, collect the seed and sow the following year. In the tropics, zinnias will self-seed and germinate during the rainy season. Zinnias are annuals that love the heat.

Strongylodon macrobotrys
Jade vine

The jade vine really has to be seen to be believed. It has the most unique and incredible flower colour. If you walk underneath these flowers when the plant is in full bloom, you will be simply mesmerised by its colour and it feel as if you are truly walking through paradise. The colour is jade and when the light is just right, it has a luminous quality that is unforgettable. If you are lucky, to add to the magic, you might see a hummingbird sipping on its nectar-rich flowers. When they fall, the flowers change colour to purple. Once experienced, it is remembered forever. It really seems out of this world.

Type
Evergreen climber
Flowering
Spring
Height/ spread
20m x 4m
Position
Part shade, sheltered
Soil
Moist, well-drained
Hardiness
USDA 13 / RHS H1a

GROW This is a tropical plant that grows near rivers in the forests of the Philippines and is a rampant climber. It can grow through a tree but it is better appreciated if grown on a very tall, sturdy frame. The flowers can grow to 90cm, so you need lots of headroom. Prune after flowering. Water often.

Type
Evergreen shrub
Flowering
Spring, summer, autumn
Height/ spread
Varies
Position
Full sun, part shade
Soil
Well-drained
Hardiness
USDA 9b/10a / RHS H3

Ixora
West Indian jasmine

When I first started my role at Andromeda Botanic Gardens, there were extended periods of drought. It was stressful simply trying to keep plants alive, as there was no functioning irrigation system. However, what these extended dry periods enabled me to do was to watch and discover which plants were quite happy in that environment. Droughts do not seem to bother these plants at all. They continued to flower throughout. This is a huge bonus for those gardening in areas with extended dry periods. You will be told that ixoras need acid soil, but Barbados is a coral island with alkaline soils aplenty and ixoras are one of the most common plants. Yes, every once in a while a plant will show yellow foliage – proof of chlorosis – but generally they thrive and I've even seen them growing directly out of limestone boulders! I have chosen the genus and not the species because I love so many of them. These are wonderful shrubs – some are large with big leaves while others are dwarf. Some are scented. What do they have in common? They are always flowering; the flowers come in a range of colours – red, yellow, white, pink and orange – and hummingbirds love them.

GROW It's great having a plant that responds well to shaping. Plant as a hedge, or dwarf varieties provide excellent ground cover. Little care is needed – trim to keep the required shape and size. Wonderful clusters of flowers are super at providing both structure and colour.

PAUL MILLS
Curator of living collections,
Ganna Walska Lotusland,
California, USA

Paul Mills started his career in 1990 at Abbey Garden Cactus and Succulent Nursery in Carpinteria. He has worked in Mexico, setting up field monitoring sites for threatened cacti, and at conservation and ethnobotanical garden El Charco del Ingenio. In 1995 he started working at Ganna Walska Lotusland as a cactus and succulent specialist. *lotusland.org*

Aloe dorotheae
Sunset aloe

Gardening in hyper-arid California can be tricky, so I often gravitate toward succulents and drought-tolerant plants that can fend for themselves. The clump-forming *A. dorotheae* is a beautiful small aloe that is great either in a rockery or a pot. As its common name implies, it has fantastically coloured leaves (when in strong sun) that fade from red to orange to yellow, accentuated by white teeth along the margins and occasional white mottling. On top of that, it has orange-red flowers during winter. This species, although common in cultivation, is critically endangered in the wild, being known to be from one degraded site in Tanzania.

GROW This plant's one downfall is that it is a little tender, but it has survived down to –3°C with me. It likes strong, full sun and, like most succulents, infrequent water. It's not too picky about soil, but would enjoy a fast-draining, well-aerated soil if you're in wetter climes. A very carefree plant that should be kept dry and has low fertiliser needs.

Type
Succulent perennial
Flowering
Winter
Height/spread
30cm x 60cm
Position
Full sun, open
Soil
Well-drained
Hardiness
USDA 10b / RHS H2

Begonia gehrtii
Begonia gehrtii

Even though I garden in the land of perpetual sun, I do have some shade-loving plants in pots in a corner of the north side of our house. In my opinion, *B. gehrtii* has some of the most interesting and distinctive foliage of any plant, period. This is a rhizomatous begonia from Brazil with ovate, textured leaves that appear as if they've been crinkled up and then flattened back out. They are very brittle and crack very easily when being handled. Flowers are white and fairly unexciting compared to the leaves. At Lotusland, we had one under a South African fig tree, whose marble-like fruits would plummet down destroying the leaves.

GROW As I've found with some other begonias, when you find its happy place, never move it again. I grow this plant under an eave outside with some chamaedorea palms as companions, which help to keep the area more humid. Most begonias are heavy feeders so regular fertiliser is best.

Type
Rhizomatous perennial
Flowering
Spring, autumn
Height/spread
50cm x 1m
Position
Very sheltered, full shade
Soil
Rich, well drained
Hardiness
USDA 10b / RHS H2

Type
Perennial
Flowering
Summer, autumn
Height/spread
1m x 50cm
Position
Full sun, part shade, open but sheltered from drying winds
Soil
Loamy, moist, well-drained
Hardiness
USDA 10b / RHS H2

Salvia discolor
Andean silver-leaf sage

I tend to grow more drought-tolerant, California native salvias such as *Salvia apiana*, *S. brandegeei* and *S. leucophylla*, but I was really attracted to *S. discolor* when I first saw it. The flowers, which are so deep purple they appear black, are a dramatic contrast to the silvery calyxes and undersides of the leaves. Hailing from the Peruvian Andes, this species can take more water than its Californian counterparts. It is low maintenance and very politely seeds itself in cracks in bricks and between rocks. Like other salvias, it is a great addition to an insectary or habitat garden.

GROW This plant is in flower much of the year in my garden. It appreciates some midday shade. Like most salvias, it should be deadheaded when it has finished flowering and can be cut back for more compact growth.

Type
Succulent perennial
Flowering
Varies
Height/ spread
90cm x 1.2m
Position
Open, full sun
Soil
Dry, well-drained
Hardiness
USDA 8b/9a / RHS H4

Agave parryi var. *truncata* →
Parry's agave

Like most agaves, this plant is ferociously spined (which I kind of like until I have to get a weed out from under it), extremely sculptural and will make a statement no matter if it's in the garden or a pot. I like this form of *A. parryi* for its more silvery, stout and individual leaves, perfect symmetry and overall more compact growth than the others. This plant does great on a steep, sunny slope in my garden where other plants have shrivelled – there's no plant tougher when it comes to heat and dry conditions. On top of all that, it's extremely hardy to cold, surviving well below freezing temperatures and has been successful in gardens of higher latitudes. The majority of plants of *A. parryi* var. *truncata* in cultivation originated from plants collected by noted agave expert H. S. Gentry in Durango, Mexico in 1951. Although agaves are called 'century plants' – because it's said they flower once every 100 years, which I guess is more or less true – this and many other agaves typically flower within 25 years. It's known as artichoke agave in the US and maguey in Mexico.

GROW A great addition to any succulent or rock garden and looks great individually or as a mass planting. Once established it doesn't need a thing. Agaves are favourites of gophers and can be prone to mealybugs.

Eriogonum arborescens
Santa Cruz Island buckwheat

Anyone growing plants in California should be focused on using natives. I find it very interesting that one of the earliest proponents of using and popularising California natives was English horticulturist Theodore Payne, who is credited with the introduction of this species into cultivation. *E. arborescens* is a must-have native plant that is a local endemic found on our Channel Islands here in Santa Barbara County. The islands are home to many other endemic plants and, because of the rich marine environment, they are often referred to as the Galapagos of the north.

The name of this plant is a bit of a misnomer – it isn't very arborescent but more of a small shrub. It has an appealing branching structure with brown stems that contrast with the fine grey foliage, and flowers profusely spring through to autumn with attractive dry flowers and seedheads. Like the majority of plants in the *Eriogonum* genus, *E. arborescens* is a great plant for attracting beneficial insects and for habitat gardens. It seeds itself around the garden, popping up between rocks, but not enough to become weedy. Although summer watering can be the death knell for many natives, I have seen this plant looking fantastic in irrigated settings.

Type
Evergreen shrub
Flowering
Spring, summer, autumn
Height/spread
1m x 1.5m
Position
Full sun, open
Soil
Tolerant of clay
Hardiness
USDA 10b / RHS H2

GROW A monthly watering is adequate. No special needs. Keep drier through the summer and in wetter climates. Can be pruned to keep it compact and promote new growth.

197

BARRY GRAIN
Head gardener,
Cholmondeley Castle
Gardens, Cheshire, UK

Barry Grain worked in a wide variety of gardens before arriving at Cholmondeley Castle, where he is responsible for orchestrating the day-to-day management of the gardens, guiding their long-term evolution and expanding the plant collections. *cholmondeleycastle.com*

Rosa 'Queen of Denmark'
Rose 'Queen of Denmark'

Type
Shrub rose
Flowering
Summer
Height/spread
1.5m x 1.25m
Position
Full sun, part shade, shelter from the prevailing wind
Soil
Lightly acid, rich in organic matter, moisture-retentive
Hardiness
USDA 6a–1 / RHS H7

Roses have been a theme during my career and 'Queen of Denmark' is my favourite of all. For me, it has all the characteristics of what a good rose should be. Bred in 1826, it is one of the best of the old roses. Like some old roses, it does not repeat flower, which some would find disagreeable, but I feel summer flowerers give you a little something that repeaters do not. It is a vigorous plant with a good upright habit and strong constitution. I also find it perfectly healthy and unaffected by fungal diseases such as rust and rose black spot. The foliage is elegant with soft grey-green hues, but as with any good rose, it is the flowers that make it. They open soft pink from charming buds and have an intoxicating old rose fragrance that lingers in the air.

GROW My top tip is to spray roses every two weeks with liquid seaweed, which acts as a general tonic and also helps keep foliage healthy. 'Queen of Denmark' is at its best in mixed borders, especially in cottage-garden style planting schemes. Partner it with soft-textured perennials, such as *Geranium phaeum* 'Samobor', *Nepeta racemosa* 'Walker's Low' and *Gillenia trifoliata*.

As roses are gross feeders, adding a mulch of organic matter every spring will add nutrients to the soil and help moisture retention in summer. I recommend feeding every six weeks with rose feed from mid-spring until the end of summer. Keep roses well watered during dry weather. After flowering, prune extension growth back to within the framework of stems, which helps the wood ripen for the following summer. Formative pruning in the dormant season should be light.

Primula florindae
Tibetan cowslip

Type
Perennial
Flowering
Summer
Height/spread
1.2m x 90cm
Position
Full sun, part shade, open
Soil
Damp, neutral
Hardiness
USDA 6a–1 / RHS H7

I love primulas in all their forms and this is a hugely impressive variety that should be more widely grown. Its preference for damp conditions makes it a versatile plant for a problematic spot in the garden. In the wild you find it in marshes and along the banks of streams, which gives you a good idea of how it performs best in cultivation. It is vigorous and quickly produces a large rosette of leaves. In favourable conditions the flowers can reach up to 1.2m tall and hold 40 individuals per umbel – which is why it's sometimes known as the giant cowslip. As if that weren't enough, the scent of the flowers is richly sweet and can carry on a warm breeze for many metres. Like most primulas, it is also easy to propagate, either by dividing the rosettes or by seed sown fresh. A plant that just keeps on giving – and a real conversation starter.

GROW This is a really easy plant to grow provided it has the damp soil that it would have in the wild. It looks at its best in large drifts near water and partners well with iris, hosta and moisture-loving ferns. It must have a damp root zone if planted in full sun, but does equally well in dappled shade.

Daphne bholua 'Jacqueline Postill'
Daphne 'Jacqueline Postill'

Anyone who knows this plant would surely agree that every garden should have one. It takes up little room and is a highly useful addition to any border. Daphnes are prized by gardeners the world over but are tricky to grow well and not always hardy. However, 'Jacqueline Postill' is particularly robust and grows in a broad range of conditions in my experience. I have had great success with it in both damp and dry soils as well as very exposed sites. Only the coldest of winter winds seem to cause a bit of light leaf drop. The leaves are elegant and produced on fine upright stems, which make it a good accent shrub year-round. The magic happens in winter when it starts flowering and continues well into spring, taking the brunt of all the inclement weather thrown at it, and still it shouts for more. The flowers are born all along the stems, which gives a charming effect. Pink-purple on the outside and white within, they have a delicious scent that emanates across the entire garden.

GROW Really easy to grow, this plant needs to be placed where the flowers and fragrance can be enjoyed to the full – close to a garden path or entrance way. Flowering for so long takes its toll, so apply a good feed of liquid seaweed as a general tonic.

Type
Evergreen shrub
Flowering
Winter, spring
Height/spread
2m x 1.5m
Position
Full sun, part shade, sheltered
Soil
Well-drained
Hardiness
USDA 8b/9a / RHS H4

Type
Deciduous tree
Flowering
Spring
Height/spread
20m x 15m
Position
Full sun, part shade, sheltered
Soil
Moisture-retentive, well-drained
Hardiness
USDA 7b/8a / RHS H5

Cercidiphyllum japonicum →
Katsura tree

Surely this has to rank as one of the great delights of the whole botanical world. I love it! It is an amazing tree that changes dramatically through the seasons and although it can make a large specimen, there are now plenty of dwarf selections suitable for smaller gardens. The best forms have elegant branches that sweep down to the ground and look quite distinguished in winter. In early spring the flowers appear – try to get a female form as the effect is better. These are very small, but are produced in huge quantities and are a vivid cerise colour, making them highly conspicuous, especially in full sun. The new foliage is a lovely bronze and emerges as the flowers fade. This then changes to a fresh lime green once fully developed. But autumn is when this tree is really at its best. The leaves start to change to a rich butter-yellow and produce an amazing scent of caramel that emanates across the garden. I have had the privilege of enjoying this bonanza on the slopes of Mount Emei in China and it is an experience I treasure.

GROW Strategically place this in the garden so that the autumn scents can be best enjoyed. It always looks good near water. Add balanced fertiliser in spring and apply a mulch of leaf mould annually.

Acer palmatum 'Seiryū'
Japanese maple 'Seiryū'

I have always had a love for Japanese maples and for me 'Seiryū' has all the qualities that a great one should have. It has an upright form that makes it look almost tree-like and also allows you to enjoy its beautiful branching habit. The green leaves are fresh looking and graceful and very finely dissected. In autumn they transform to a mix of orange, red and purple with the colours lasting for many weeks before they finally fall.

It is generally a robust plant, it thrives in a range of conditions. It should be placed with plenty of room to become the focal point it wants to be, but also to ensure the best habit and branching. This is simply a terrific plant that will not disappoint.

GROW With acers it is all about developing a strong attractive form. Like others of its kind, 'Seiryū' continues to produce new growth well into autumn, which tends to be thin and ultimately dies when the frosts get hold of it. Prune this out when the plant is in full leaf in spring to tidy up the appearance. I look to carry out formative pruning on mine every few years as soon as they come into full leaf. Carefully selecting the thinnest lateral branches for removal accentuates the form to best effect. Mulch with leaf mould in autumn and keep young plants well watered during establishment.

Type
Deciduous shrub
Flowering
Spring
Height/spread
4m x 4m
Position
Full sun, part shade, shelter from late frosts and drying winds
Soil
Moist, well-drained
Hardiness
USDA 6b/7a / RHS H6

Paeonia × suffruticosa 'Yachiyo-tsubaki'
Japanese tree peony

Tree peonies are among my favourite plants, not just for their impressive flowers, but also for the architectural quality of their foliage, which seems to complement almost anything in the garden. This is my personal favourite, as frankly it's a perfect plant. It is vigorous and easy to grow, quickly becoming an upright plant with a form that makes it perfect for the border. Spring shoots are a warm red and followed by graceful bronze foliage. Even the buds have presence, and they open to reveal delicate, semi-double flowers with long petals that are charmingly frilled. The flowers are the perfect shade of soft pink to complement the bronze foliage.

GROW The flowers are large and heavy, which can be problematic, especially on young plants, so good staking is essential for both presentation and to avoid damage to the stems. I do this by using hazel or birch rods, which blend in well with the plant and make the process quite subtle. I tie them gently with string 10–15cm below the flowerheads to provide good support but also to allow light movement in the breeze. Deadhead after flowering to an outward-facing bud to promote a good bushy form. Apply a balanced fertiliser as buds swell in spring and a high potash feed in late summer to help with winter hardiness. Young buds and growth can be damaged by late frosts.

Type
Deciduous shrub
Flowering
Late spring, summer
Height/spread
1.25m x 1.25m
Position
Full sun, sheltered
Soil
Well-drained
Hardiness
USDA 7b/8a / RHS H5

ANNIE DELLBRIDGE
Head gardener, Fullers Mill
Garden, Suffolk, UK

Annie Dellbridge has managed Fullers Mill, a seven-acre waterside and woodland garden filled with rare and unusual plants, since 2010. The site is owned by Perennial, a charity that helps people in horticulture build and live better lives. *perennial.org.uk/garden/fullers-mill-garden*

Abelia mosanensis
Fragrant abelia

In summer, this plant's pink-blushed white flowers give off an amazing fragrance that fills the air, before leaving behind 'glowing' red calyxes. In autumn the leaves turn shades of fiery reds and oranges before they fall. A well behaved and extremely garden-worthy shrub.

GROW Plant by a seating area or not far from the front door to enjoy the scent. It's easy to look after – prune as required, although this is seldom necessary.

Type
Deciduous shrub
Flowering
Spring, summer
Height/spread
2m x 2m
Position
Full sun, part shade, sheltered
Soil
Well-drained, neutral to alkaline
Hardiness
USDA 6b/7a / RHS H6

Type
Tuberous perennial
Flowering
Late spring, early summer
Height/spread
50cm x 50cm
Position
Part shade, sheltered
Soil
Moisture-retentive, acid to neutral
Hardiness
USDA 8b/9a / RHS H4

Arisaema candidissimum
White-spathed jack in the pulpit

A. candidissimum adds an interesting touch to a semi-shaded area. Even when the flowers have faded the large, trifoliate leaves are bold and attractive. It is easy to grow and reliable with exotic-looking hooded spathes in pink and white stripes (reminiscent of stripy sweetshop paper bags). Visitors to Fullers Mill always ask about this plant as it is seldom seen in private gardens.

GROW Easy to take care of, but prefers semi-shade and a good, humus-rich soil.

Euonymus oxyphyllus
Korean spindle

This is one of the very best spindles, with wonderful red autumn leaf colour and stunning seed capsules with dangling orange seeds. A joy to see at every stage throughout the year. The delicate and tiny, pale pink-peach flowers are beautifully marked and worth looking out for in early summer.

GROW Easy to care for. Best grown in full sun to encourage autumn leaf colours. Prune if required to improve shape.

Type
Deciduous shrub
Flowering
Spring
Height/spread
2.5m x 2.5m
Position
Full sun, part shade
Soil
Well-drained
Hardiness
USDA 6a–1 / RHS H7

Type
Bulbous perennial
Flowering
Summer
Height/spread
1.5m x 50cm
Position
Full sun, sheltered
Soil
Moist, well-drained
Hardiness
USDA 6b/7a
/ RHS H6

Lilium regale
Regal lily

A wonderfully scented 'old fashioned' lily with a white, wide and open trumpet flower that has a purplish-pink back to it. It's easily recognisable by its scent and large flowers. It's also very easy to grow – lily bulbs die back in the winter and reappear in the early summer, with no special winter care required – and it can be easily fitted between other plants or grown in pots. Brings back memories of gardens long ago.

GROW Easy to look after. Best grown in full sun. Dig plenty of compost into the ground before planting to help retain moisture. Put a stake in to support the plant as it grows taller. Check for lily beetles each day.

ARNE MAYNARD
Garden designer,
Monmouthshire, Wales

Arne Maynard's garden designs draw out the essence of a place, responding to the landscape, history and buildings within and around it to create a quality of harmony and belonging. Bold lines and a strong architectural framework are characteristic of his work, while soft plantings provide a lush and expansive counterbalance. *arnemaynard.com*

Verbascum blattaria f. *albiflorum* →
White-flowered moth mullein

This wonderful blush-white verbascum is a fabulous anchor plant in the border, which we thread through as if it has self-sown. We tend to plant it annually, but given time to establish, it will naturally self-sow, creating a soft veil-like haze that connects other plants and brings the whole planting scheme together. It has crinkly, lobed, dark green leaves producing an evergreen basal rosette. A single, narrow flower spike stands at about 1.2m tall with widely spaced white flowers that have pink- and purple-flushed centres.

GROW Allow to self-sow and thread through the border.

Type
Biennial
Flowering
Summer, autumn
Height/ spread
1.5m x 50cm
Position
Full sun, exposed
Soil
Well-drained, alkaline
Hardiness
USDA 6b/7a / RHS H6

Iris germanica 'Immortality'
Bearded iris 'Immortality'

As a garden designer I seek out plants that give added value to a planting scheme. This iris flowers in spring and again in autumn, with gorgeous, ruffled, pure-white petals that fall away from a sun-yellow centre. It's an easy plant to maintain, is perfect for cut flowers and suits gardens of all sizes.

GROW Easy to grow and has the additional benefit of being fairly drought tolerant once established. Ensure good drainage to prevent rot issues. Full sun is best. Can be split in the autumn when the clump gets too large.

Type
Rhizomatous perennial
Flowering
Late spring, late autumn
Height/ spread
80cm x 60cm
Position
Full sun, part shade
Soil
Well-drained, humus-rich
Hardiness
USDA 7b/8a / RHS 5

Geranium × cantabrigiense 'St Ola'
Cranesbill 'St Ola'

Hardy geraniums are the stalwarts of herbaceous borders but it's rare to find a white one with such a vigorous habit. This one has the added bonus of white flowers that take on a pale pink tinge as they age, underpinned by lush and aromatic dark green leaves that turn red in autumn. It's the perfect ground cover for growing under shrubs or roses.

GROW This is an easy plant to establish and maintain. Can be divided easily in autumn.

Type
Herbaceous perennial
Flowering
Late spring, summer
Height/ spread
50cm x 50cm
Position
Full sun, part shade
Soil
Well-drained, moist
Hardiness
USDA 6b/7a / RHS H6

Lilium 'Honeymoon'
Tree lily 'Honeymoon'

This hybrid, ornamental trumpet lily can reach heights of up to 2.5m, making it a standout plant in a herbaceous border. Its stature and striking, exotic-looking, beautifully scented, pale yellow flowers help elevate planting schemes. I love its exuberance and its impact. It will improve and multiply year after year, while its blooms are perfect as cut flowers as they have a long-lasting perfume.

GROW Plant at the back of the border and leave undisturbed. Full height will be reached at the end of its third growing year. Ensure good drainage to avoid bulb rot.

Type
Bulbous perennial
Flowering
Late summer, autumn
Height/ spread
2.5m x 40cm
Position
Full sun, part shade
Soil
Well-drained, moist
Hardiness
USDA 6b/7a / RHS H6

Sanguisorba hakusanensis 'Lilac Squirrel'
Korean burnet 'Lilac Squirrel'

I love all sanguisorbas but this one is absolutely beautiful. Long, graceful, lilac-pink tassels appear above grey-green dissected foliage in summer. Ideal for romantic summer planting schemes and prairie-style borders and meadows. They work particularly well in combinations with *Dierama* (angel's fishing rod), *Thalictrum* (meadow rue) and dahlias, bringing a feathery lightness to the scheme with their soft movement and texture.

GROW Plant in semi-fertile, moist soil. Flowers best in full sun. Allow to become established in the border and self-seed to thread through more structural plants within the scheme.

Type
Rhizomatous herbaceous perennial
Flowering
Summer, early autumn
Height/ spread
1.5m x 1.5m
Position
Full sun, part shade
Soil
Moist, well-drained
Hardiness
USDA 6b/7a / RHS H6

Tulipa linifolia (Batalinii Group) 'Bronze Charm'
Tulip 'Bronze Charm'

Spring-flowering bulbs are a joy to combine in any garden design. They provide that lift we all look forward to as their colours and forms break through the hardened ground after the long winter. This delicate, low-flowering species tulip does best when allowed to naturalise. We like to plant it in drifts, in chippings together with *Pulsatilla* (pasqueflower) and other species bulbs. The pale yellow flowers have a dark orange tinge in early spring.

GROW This does well grown in chippings among other early spring-flowering bulbs and perennials. Prefers a sheltered position.

Type
Bulbous perennial
Flowering
Spring
Height/ spread
15cm x 10cm
Position
Full sun, sheltered
Soil
Well-drained, alkaline, neutral
Hardiness
USDA 7b/8a / RHS H5

Dahlia excelsa 'Penelope Sky'
Tree dahlia 'Penelope Sky'

A wonderful introduction from Crug Farm Plants, this Mexican dahlia gives height and strength to the border. It forms clumps of strong, dark, sturdy stems with several opposite branches emerging from cup-shaped nodes. In the upper part of the plant, these hold pinnate foliage and large, lilac-purple, star-shaped flowers that bloom from mid-summer to the first frosts.

GROW Prefers a sunny, warm spot in fertile soil. Best protected from severe frost either with a generous mulch or by lifting the tubers.

Type
Tuberous perennial
Flowering
Summer, autumn
Height/ spread
3m x 40cm
Position
Part shade, but tolerates full sun
Soil
Moist, well-drained, humus-rich
Hardiness
USDA 9b/10a / RHS H3

Aconitum 'Blue Opal'
Monk's hood 'Blue Opal'

This is a late-flowering, healthy cultivar with leathery, dark green leaves and strong, sturdy purple-brown stems that do not require staking. As its name suggests, it has light violet-blue hooded flowers that bring a welcome splash of colour at the end of the garden's flowering season. A brilliant plant to extend the border into autumn and bridge the gap between seasons.

GROW I love that this doesn't need to be staked. It's really very strong and can withstand some late-summer rain and wind.

Type
Herbaceous perennial
Flowering
Late summer, autumn
Height/ spread
1.5m x 50cm
Position
Part shade but tolerates full sun, sheltered
Soil
Any
Hardiness
USDA 8b/9a / RHS H4

Daphne × *transatlantica* Eternal Fragrance ('Blafra')
Daphne [Eternal Fragrance]

I have used this summer-flowering daphne a lot in recent years and it has not disappointed. It has unusual compact growth, a long flowering period and provides delicate wafts of perfume each time you pass. It works well planted by a well-used doorway in order to get the most out of its scent, but also as structural underplanting in a shrub border or as a low hedge.

GROW Grow in semi-fertile, moist soil, in sun (not dry) or part shade. Once planted avoid replanting – daphnes do not respond well to being transplanted. Requires minimum pruning. Be aware that all plant parts are toxic and sap may cause irritation to exposed skin.

Type
Semi-evergreen shrub
Flowering
Spring, summer, autumn
Height/spread
1m x 1m
Position
Full sun, part shade
Soil
Moist, well-drained
Hardiness
USDA 7b/8a / RHS H5

Rosa Jude the Obscure ('Ausjo')
Rose [Jude the Obscure]

If I had to choose only one rose, this would be it. Introduced by David Austin in 1995, it can be trained as a shrub rose within a border scheme (I favour hazel domes for structure) or as a climber. It has lovely creamy-yellow, chalice-like flowers and repeat flowers for most of the growing season, so you can cut it for the house.

GROW Prune in autumn for plenty of new growth and flowers the following spring. Like all shrub roses, this performs well with regular pruning and training. It is a truly versatile rose with large, incredibly perfumed flowers.

Type
Shrub rose
Flowering
Late spring, summer
Height/spread
1.2m x 1.2m
Position
Full sun, part shade
Soil
Well-drained, moist
Hardiness
USDA 6b/7a / RHS H6

ARABELLA LENNOX-BOYD
Principal, Lennox-Boyd Landscape Design, Lancaster, UK

Italian by birth, Arabella Lennox-Boyd has been designing for more than 45 years and has landscaped more than 400 gardens, including six RHS Chelsea Flower Show gold medal gardens. She is a trustee of the Chelsea Physic Garden and the Tree Register of the British Isles, and serves on the council and scientific panel of the International Dendrology Society. *arabellalennoxboyd.com*

Paeonia × *suffruticosa* 'Joseph Rock'
Tree peony 'Joseph Rock'

'Joseph Rock' has magnificent early summer flowers with a beautiful shape and scent, as well as a romantic history. There is also the added pleasure of seeing how varied each shrub can be both in flower and foliage colour. I have many of them in my garden near Rome. I bought a few from a good nursery that specialises in peonies near Viterbo called Centro Botanico Moutan and I have grown all the ones I have in the UK from their seed.

GROW Likes a sunny position that is not too wet and can grow well in the UK and Europe. Allow it plenty of space when planting. It is not particularly demanding, but it could do with a feed if the soil is poor. Although very hardy, it doesn't like a late frost.

Type
Deciduous shrub
Flowering
Summer
Height/spread
1.2m x 1.5m
Position
Full sun, part shade
Soil
Best in loamy soil but not too fussy
Hardiness
USDA 6b/7a / RHS H6

HILARY COLLINS
CEO, Hardy Eucalyptus,
Worcester, UK

Hilary Collins has over 40 years of nursery experience and 30 years of landscaping experience and is an acknowledged UK expert on eucalyptus trees. She is the author of several eucalyptus guides and with her husband Stephen runs an award-winning nursery, which is the largest eucalyptus nursery in the UK. *hardy-eucalyptus.com*

Eucalyptus parvula
Kybean gum

Type
Evergreen tree
Flowering
Summer
Height/ spread
10m x 8m
Position
Full sun
Soil
Moist, well-drained, boggy
Hardiness
USDA 7b/8a / RHS H5

There are approximately 1,000 eucalyptus species and subspecies. Out of those, around 100 or so can be grown in various locations across the UK. Each one has a different 'personality': differing height, leaf colour, leaf shape and habitat requirements. I love them all and to choose just one is an almost impossible task. However, I like plants that are useful as well as beautiful and *E. parvula* ticks so many boxes that it is possibly my number one species. Beautiful and well-behaved, it can be maintained as a small- to medium-sized, neat, evergreen tree, making it ideal for the smaller garden. It has lovely smooth, tactile bark in golden coffee with some violet-grey and russet tones, and a light, open canopy that allows for underplanting. Its delicate, chalky, French-blue leaves with the typical eucalyptol aroma make it a mainstay for armfuls of cut foliage, and with careful crop management it can be harvested at just about any time of year.

E. parvula usefully has a lignotuber (a woody doughnut-like structure situated where the trunk meets the root plate) and so responds very well to coppicing, pollarding and shearing, so it can be trained in many different ways. These include as a small multi-stemmed bushy tree ideal for privacy screening; as a large, bushy shrub, when it slightly resembles a hebe on steroids and can be deployed in borders; as a potted tree grown in large Air-Pot containers placed inside decorative pots; and trained as a standard and kept trimmed – think of a lollipop bay tree but with more attitude! With management you can keep it as short as 2.4m or up to its natural 10m and anywhere in between. Extremely hardy, it is an ideal candidate to grow as a windbreak or shelterbelt.

At a maturity of around 10-12 years, the trees can be coppiced to provide a crop of poles or firewood logs. They will then regenerate off the lignotuber to produce another stand of trees, with no replanting required. Furthermore, when planted on farmland *E. parvula* will keep honey bees fed with a good supply of nectar and pollen in what can sometimes be an agricultural bee desert.

GROW To keep your eucalyptus happy but also in good shape, prune in spring (in the UK, do this around March 18, which is National Eucalyptus Day) and again, on the new wood only at the end of spring or beginning of summer. Unless growing specifically for cut foliage, refrain from pruning at any other time of year. Keep free of grass and weeds around the base of your young tree because additional vegetation will seriously slow down establishment and could even kill the tree.

Ensure your tree has been Air-Pot grown, then it will have the correct form of root system and so will not fall over when mature. Avoid eucalypts grown in smooth-walled pots; they are a liability. Also, hardiness in eucalyptus is governed by seed provenance: younger eucalypts and those fed a high-nitrogen diet are more susceptible to frost damage. To encourage deep rooting and fast establishment, plant between spring and autumn. Water copiously, twice a week in the first growing season with you.

E. parvula can be successfully grown as a multi-stemmed shrub in a container provided you are prepared to pot on at the recommended intervals and to supply it with sufficient water and food during the growing season. If not watered enough, it becomes thin and spindly, dropping its lower leaves and looking sad and crispy.

Type
Evergreen tree
Flowering
Summer
Height/ spread
7m x 5m
Position
Full sun, part shade
Soil
Moist, well-drained, boggy
Hardiness
USDA 7b/8a / RHS H5

Eucalyptus neglecta 'Dargo Plains'
Omeo gum 'Dargo Plains'

This is a small eucalyptus with a big personality, determined to express it; big leaves, square juvenile stems and a powerful aroma. Once planted it grows very quickly, then after about seven years it slows right down. New growth in early summer is a striking pinky-purpley bronze with a white wax overlay, while juvenile leaves are huge, rounded and glossy peacock-green, which in a cool moist climate (most of the UK) take on a wonderful purple tinge. Juvenile leaves persist for between seven and 15 years before the adult leaves make an appearance. These are large, broad lanceolate and sage-olive green. Mature bark is variable, being smooth or rough, while colours are lime-custard through to pewter. Beloved by bees, the small white flowers appear in large groups of seven to 15 buds per umbel, followed by globular gumnuts.

In winter, our *E. neglecta* provides welcome night-time roosting for dozens of goldfinches. You can see them all snoozing away when you stand quietly underneath the tree and shine a torch up into the canopy. The name *neglecta* is not because you can plant it and forget it, but because the botanists (bless them!) neglected to initially classify it as a distinct species. In fact, *E. neglecta* stands alone in the eucalyptus classification series *Neglectae*, meaning it is botanically unique.

GROW See general care advice for *Eucalyptus parvula* given opposite.

Eucalyptus pauciflora subsp. *debeuzevillei*
Jounama snow gum

Named after botanist and ecologist Wilfred Alexander Watt de Beuzeville (1884–1954) of Bombala, New South Wales, the Jounama is the hardiest of all eucalypts and has even been introduced to Norway, which is impressive! It is a good specimen tree, growing slowly to form a small- to medium-sized mallee (multi-stemmed) tree with an attractive crown. A striking species for a winter interest or xerophytic garden, it is also a good choice for a pot when grown in an Air-Pot container inside a heavy decorative pot. Its tough foliage, resilient to salt-laden winds, makes it great for planting in coastal locations – once well established, it can be pruned to provide an excellent windbreak. Young shoots and emerging leaves are a striking translucent copper-crimson with a white bloom, beautiful when back lit by the sun. Its juvenile foliage consists of huge, 'boxy' angular blue leaves of an incredibly thick leathery texture. Adult foliage is blue-green maturing to glossy olive-green. It has a beautifully patterned bark of smooth pewter-grey to porcelain-white with an additional mosaic of russet, cream, olive and silvery-grey, which shreds in ribbons from the trunk and branches. White flowers in groups are followed by woody gumnuts.

Type
Evergreen tree
Flowering
Spring, summer
Height/ spread
12m x 4m
Position
Full sun, sheltered
Soil
Well-drained
Hardiness
USDA 7b/8a / RHS H5

GROW See general care advice for *Eucalyptus parvula*. Root rock for young eucalypts must be avoided at all costs. Prune as previously advised, as this management technique allows for this gum's finer, more fibrous root system to establish. In extreme conditions, it may also be necessary to stake the young tree. Once established for two to three years, it can then be allowed to grow tall.

This gum is very well adapted to survive harsh winter conditions. Mulching with a very thick layer of bark chips will act as a root duvet. However, should the tree be cut down by harsh weather conditions, it usefully has a lignotuber, which means that it can be coppiced and grown as a multi-stemmed specimen shrub or tree. In addition, like most eucalypts, it has a dense population of dormant epicormic buds lying just beneath the bark on the lower trunk, which will generate new shoots if the tree is pollarded. However, snow gums generally do not respond well to regular, aggressive coppicing.

MIGUEL OGANDO DOS SANTOS
Landscape designer,
Urquhart & Hunt, UK

Miguel dos Santos is a landscape designer at Urquhart & Hunt, a studio based in Somerset that specialises in contemporary restorations of gardens with a focus on ecology and nature. *urquharthunt.com*

Vitis vinifera ↘
Grape vine

This is a very special plant to me that I have held dear since my earliest memories of gardens and gardening. It's a very underrated plant that offers so much through its simplicity, versatility and year-round spectacle. Intricately cut leaves spring out from the dark, twisted bark on bright vigorous green stems and, as spring turns to summer, the (almost) invisible flowers swell up through to late autumn. This is when the vine will shift into darker tones of orange to dark red for stunning autumn foliage, and bunches of grapes ripen. It is adaptable to colder and wetter climates, it can tolerate pruning and it puts on an amazing display with very little effort.

GROW It needs as much sun and warmth as you can give it, though it will tolerate most soil types as long as it's well drained. Prefers to be planted sheltered from wind. You can get creative with pruning. Requires little care, though it may need staking in the first year.

Type
Perennial climber
Flowering
Summer, autumn
Height/spread
6m x 10m
Position
Full sun, sheltered
Soil
Moist, well-drained
Hardiness
USDA 8b/9a / RHS H4

MARK DUMBLETON
Head gardener, Oudolf
Field, Hauser & Wirth,
Somerset, UK

Mark Dumbleton is the head gardener at art gallery Hauser & Wirth in Somerset, working with the esteemed plantsman Piet Oudolf. A love and respect for plants was instilled in him from a young age and most of what he does today stems from the basic principles his family taught him as a child. *hauserwirth.com*

Amsonia hubrichtii
Arkansas bluestar

Type
Herbaceous
perennial
Flowering
Spring, summer
Height/spread
1m x 1m
Position
Full sun, part shade
Soil
Any
Hardiness
USDA 6a–1 / RHS H7

Personally, I don't have a favourite plant – I've grown too many to choose just one. Every plant makes me smile, be it one of the grasses which make up a lawn, the weeds I must remove or the most intricate of orchids. When you begin to understand how plants work as organisms, their aesthetics, ease of maintenance and so on are superseded. Every plant has its place and mode in nature and therefore is of equal value. With this in mind I have chosen what seems to be a favourite with visitors, *A. hubrichtii*. It is one of the most admired and asked about plants in the garden. As well as being popular it is also particularly resistant to drought, pests and disease and extremely easy to maintain once established, while providing virtually year-round interest.

Amsonias perform right from the start of spring, with their unusual asparagus-like new shoots topped with dark blue buds. Panicles of light blue, star-shaped flowers appear in spring and last for weeks on end. The plant continues to grow during flowering, reaching approximately a metre in height. It then takes a back seat, providing a great foil for later-flowering plants with its delicate green, willow-like leaves and gently arching shrub-like habit. When autumn arrives, the amsonia takes centre stage once more as its leaves flush a beautiful golden yellow, which provides punctuation throughout the borders here. During the winter the stems remain erect and fade to white, topped with attractive elongated seed pods.

GROW Best propagated from cuttings as it is slow to grow from seed and not the easiest plant to divide, which may account for its near absence in popular cultivation. It takes a few years depending on conditions to reach full size, but patience is rewarded with an extremely tough, long-lived plant. For this reason, I would recommend buying as large a pot size as possible or growing on smaller plants as they tend to get lost in an established border. After establishing I have found little if any need to feed, prune or water these plants. In spring I remove as much of the old stems as possible with secateurs without damaging the newly emerging buds.

I have only ever grown these plants in full sun and feel this is where they perform best. Amsonias grow well here, where the garden is fully exposed and aligned north to south with little to no shelter from the wind or cold. Don't plant it in a pond or a desert, but most soil types should be fine. The elusive, magically 'moist but well-drained', perfectly nutritionally balanced soil advice always makes me smile. To make my point, if I gave you this perfect soil and it never rained, the amsonia along with every other plant, would die regardless. How well a plant does is a culmination of endless variables specific to our locality that, as gardeners, we have to learn to mitigate or use to our advantage.

ISABEL AND JULIAN BANNERMAN
Garden designers and builders, Somerset, UK

Isabel and Julian Bannerman are award-winning gardeners, garden designers and builders by royal appointment to the former Prince of Wales. They have been designing gardens together since 1983. They strive to create places for living. They are also writers and photographers. *bannermandesign.com*

Philadelphus →
Mock orange

Julian and I both cherish childhood memories of this plant, especially of its sensational orangey and heart-warming smell in early summer. The first to flower in is usually *Philadelphus coronarius*, a native of southeast Europe with abundant, creamy, star-like flowers and a scent that can catch you by surprise metres away. Philadelphus used to be a staple of all British cottage and country gardens, but big round shrubs have become less popular since the fashion for grasses and perennial plantings came in. Nevertheless, we always include them in our designs because they give body, form and, in this case as in that of many others, scent to a garden. The leaves are not distinguished – except perhaps those of golden *P. coronarius* 'Aureas' – which makes for a small, intensely fresh green shrub that does well in part shade. Most varieties are hardy, except those from the deserts of Arizona and New Mexico, and there are also some evergreen ones, such as *P. karwinskyanus*, though we have never obtained or grown it.

GROW Height and spread will vary depending on species and cultivar. We don't prune our philadelphus plants much – we like them as big, wild-looking bushes. Occasionally we want a particular shape, such as a fountain in a flower bed, which means keeping varieties such as *P.* 'Starbright' tight at the stem to allow other border plants to grow, and encouraging them to spill out high up with lots of flowers. Some varieties such as *P.* 'Manteau d'Hermine' just naturally form small mounds – useful as froth at the front of a border. Others, such as the delicious bubblegum-scented *P. mexicanus*, need to be left alone as they resent pruning.

Type
Deciduous shrub
Flowering
Summer
Height/spread
2.5m x 1.5m
Position
Full sun
Soil
Any
Hardiness
USDA 6b/7a / RHS H6

BRENDA LEESE
Gardener, Windermere, UK

Dr Brenda Leese studied botany and biochemistry. After moving to Windermere in retirement she joined the Lakeland Horticultural Society, which manages Holehird Gardens. Here she helped develop a National Collection of *Daboecia*. She is the author of *There She Grows: Women in Plant Names*. *holehirdgardens.org.uk*

Erigeron karvinskianus
Mexican fleabane

I have chosen this plant for its delicacy and seeming simplicity, though the *Asteraceae* family is anything but simple in the structure of its flowers. Daisies are ubiquitous, but this plant is special. I particularly like the way the plants place themselves between stones and slabs in paths and flower so profusely. In the Lake District they grow less well than further south and I have to grow mine in pots, but the effort is definitely worth it. The common name, fleabane, gives the wrong impression of such a lovely plant.

GROW Happy on most types of soil and will grow anywhere but prefers a sunny location. It is also drought tolerant. It requires very little maintenance.

Type
Perennial
Flowering
Spring, summer, autumn
Height/spread
50cm x 1m
Position
Full sun
Soil
Well-drained
Hardiness
USDA 7b/8a / RHS H5

Daboecia cantabrica 'Bicolor'
Irish heath 'Bicolor'

Heathers are not the most popular plants these days, but I like to think that the plants in the genus *Daboecia* are different. They are characterised by large, very attractive flowers in the form of bells and should really be cultivated more widely in gardens. At Holehird Gardens I manage the National Collection of *Daboecia*. 'Bicolor' is my favourite cultivar because, unusually, it has pink and white flowers on the same stem, hence its name. The oval leaves are glossy green on the upper surface with silvery hairs on the lower side, providing an attractive whitish sheen. The flowers are much larger than other heathers (*Erica* and *Calluna*) and are shaped like bells. In 'Bicolor' they can be purple or white, often on the same stem. Other flowers can be individually variegated in purple, white and mauve. These heathers are natives in Ireland, western France and north-western Iberia, where they grow in exposed locations on moorland and in mountainous areas. This means they are very tolerant of exposed growing conditions and thrive in sheltered as well as open areas. They grow rapidly and look good when they merge to produce a range of colours across a bed.

GROW In general, all daboecia, not just the 'Bicolor', are evergreen. However, it is noticeable that many do not retain any leaves during the winter and can have the appearance of dead-looking sticks! This can be dispiriting and unnerving and prompts regular checks on progress, but I have learned not to despair. They will eventually recover and develop their leaves in the usual way. To complicate matters further, this does not happen every winter and sometimes they remain green throughout. Like all heathers, daboecias prefer a lime-free, slightly acidic soil, which mimics their moorland habitat. They are easy to grow, being very hardy. However, they do not tolerate drying out. They take 5–10 years to reach their maximum height and spread.

Plants may be trimmed either immediately after flowering or after winter. If seedheads are left in place over winter, they may protect the rest of the plant from frosts. When trimming, it's best not to cut back to bare, leafless stems but to trim only those stems bearing leaves. Trimming back to the base of the flower spike or harder will help reduce the extent to which the plants become leggy. Eventually the plants will become excessively woody and may need to be trimmed more extensively, and eventually replaced.

An application of general fertiliser in the spring is beneficial for all heathers. And all heathers are best planted with conifers, as happened in the 1970s and 1980s when heathers were popular. There is a good reason for this – removing fallen deciduous leaves from among heather plants is not to be wished on any gardener, as they become entangled with the heather stems!

Type
Evergreen shrub
Flowering
Summer, autumn
Height/ spread
50cm x 50cm
Position
Full sun, part shade
Soil
Moist, well-drained, acid
Hardiness
USDA 7b/8a / RHS H5

Omphalodes luciliae
Rock forget-me-not

I have chosen this plant because it features in my second book *There She Grows Again*, being named after the wife of well-known Swiss botanist Edmond Boissier (1810–1885). The story of his wife Lucile is a poignant one and deserves retelling. In 1840 Lucile Butini married her cousin, Edmond, twelve years older than her, and often accompanied him on trips in search of plants. He had inherited a fortune from his family and could have had a life of idleness, but decided instead to take up botany and went on to become one of the most prolific plant collectors of the nineteenth century. Unfortunately, on one of his trips to Spain and Algeria in 1849, Lucile died of an infection aged only 27. Her husband named *O. luciliae* in memory of his wife because its flower colour was the same blue as her eyes. Edmond found it difficult to recover from the loss and in 1877 he named another plant with blue

Type
Perennial
Flowering
Summer
Height/spread
15cm x 15cm
Position
Full sun, part shade
Soil
Moist, well-drained
Hardiness
USDA 8b/9a / RHS H4

flowers after her, *Chionodoxa luciliae* (also known as Lucile's glory of the snow). After such a story and Edmond's obvious affection for his wife, how is it possible not to love these plants?

GROW The plant is a native of Turkey and of the family *Boraginaceae*. It is useful as ground cover in beds and under shrubs in borders, and is frequently grown in rock gardens. Feed in spring and water regularly. Do not allow to dry out. Cut back after flowering. Tolerant of mild frosts.

Type
Annual climber
Flowering
Summer
Height/spread
2.5m x 50cm
Position
Full sun, part shade, sheltered
Soil
Moist, well-drained, rich
Hardiness
USDA 9b/10a / RHS H3

Lathyrus odoratus
Sweet pea (SEE ILLUSTRATION PAGE 49)

The sweet pea is my favourite of all plants. It is a member of the *Fabaceae* family. The unusually shaped flowers are beautiful, strongly perfumed, have an attractive range of colours and last for most of the summer. My father grew them when I was a child. Later, at my wedding, I wanted to have them in my bouquet but the florist said they would not last and allowed them just for the bridesmaids! This is their downside – they do not survive well once picked but they do need to be gathered to allow more flowers to be produced.

GROW They can be grown easily from seed but are susceptible to frost damage. Sweet peas like to have their roots growing in deep soil, so sow in a tall pot. After germination, prick out around supporting stakes or trellis once all chance of frost has gone. Pinch out the tips of the plants to encourage bushing and greater production of flowering stems. Do not allow to dry out. Water well and feed occasionally. Once flowering, pick the stems to encourage more flowers to be produced. They should flower for most of the summer in the UK.

Scabiosa 'Butterfly Blue'
Scabious 'Butterfly Blue'

This belongs to the *Caprifoliaceae* (honeysuckle) family. I have chosen it because of its versatility in the garden and the attractive colour of the flowers. I particularly like to grow it in a pot on its own, though it also mixes well with other plants. I was unaware of one of its common names – pincushion – but this describes its appearance so well. As its name suggests, it is attractive to butterflies and from observation bees like it too! It produces its attractive large blue flowers during the summer and autumn, and cutting off the dead flowerheads after flowering encourages more to be produced. It is so easy to grow in almost any environment and needs hardly any attention. It looks especially attractive in mixed herbaceous borders or pots, and provides colour in wildflower meadows. This cultivar is a sterile hybrid that produces nectar, but does not set seed.

Type
Perennial
Flowering
Summer, autumn
Height/spread
40cm x 40cm
Position
Full sun
Soil
Well-drained
Hardiness
USDA 8b/9a / RHS H4

GROW Seeds can be sown in autumn and kept inside over winter ready for planting out in spring. They do not set seed themselves but can be propagated by division of the clumps that form over a number of years. The plants should be kept well watered, particularly if grown in pots.

DAVID FORD
Vice chair, RHS Tender
Ornamental Plant
Committee, Surrey, UK

David Ford is vice chair of the RHS Tender Ornamental Plant Committee, overseeing plant trials and round table assessments, He is chair of the Surrey Group of Plant Heritage and also the holder of the National Plant Collection of *Chaenomeles*.

Chaenomeles speciosa 'Kinshiden'
Japanese quince 'Kinshiden'

It is hard to pick a single cultivar of *Chaenomeles* since it is a reliable genus of plants, but I think *C. speciosa* 'Kinshiden' stands above many of the others because of its colour and form. It is one of the last to open its buds in spring but, when it does, it produces a wonderful display of lime-coloured double flowers. These fade towards white as they age for a truly beautiful display. This is always a plant that is much photographed and commented upon when the collection is open to the public, partly, I think, because the genus evokes images of single red or orange flowers and this cultivar's large (about 3cm across), subtle blooms challenge these preconceptions. Although not the most generous fruiter, it does produce small, green-yellow edible fruit in autumn. But it's easy to forgive such a shortcoming given its memorable spring display.

Type
Deciduous shrub
Flowering
Spring
Height/spread
2.5m x 2.5m
Position
Full sun, dappled shade for good blooming
Soil
Well-drained, acid, neutral
Hardiness
USDA 6a–1 / RHS H7

GROW Chaenomeles happily grow in the open or trained against a wall. They are not fantastic competitors with other plants, particularly when young, so make sure your plant isn't crowded by neighbours. They also make good container plants, but hate having their roots sitting in water when planted in a pot that's too large, so start small and work up to your desired size of container. Pot on every one or two years. In Japan, chaenomeles are regularly used for bonsai and will adapt to any size of container you want – 20 litres is fine, but they go even bigger!

Chaenomeles can grow with or without direct sunlight, but none bloom well in deep shade. Although they grow in alkaline soils, they perform best in neutral to acid. Very alkaline soil makes them prone to chlorosis, particularly in dry summers, which can prove fatal over time. Not an ideal plant if you have chalky soil!

Take cuttings of material that is one or two years old immediately after the plant has finished blooming. Always ensure that the growing tip of the stem is still intact. In open soil, a mulch once a year keeps your plant happy. In a container, a monthly feed of a half-strength proprietary plant food, ericaceous if possible, during the growing season keeps it growing well. A couple of good high-potash feeds as the buds are forming in late winter helps ensure a good bloom.

Chaenomeles occasionally bloom on material that is a year old, but more normally on material that's older. Undertake formative pruning after it has flowered in spring to encourage the plant to branch strongly, but any resulting new shoots are unlikely to bloom the following year – more likely the year after that. A light prune of the year's growth during the brief dormant period in early winter encourages the formation of flower buds further down the stem on older growth.

Type
Rhizomatous perennial
Flowering
Summer, autumn
Height/spread
1.5m x 1m
Position
Full sun, part shade
Soil
Well-drained, especially if over-wintered outside
Hardiness
USDA 10b / RHS H2

Canna 'Phasion'
Canna 'Phasion'

I have grown this plant for over 30 years and every year it reaffirms its right to a place in my garden. It has large, paddle-shaped purple-bronzy leaves intricately striped with pinks, oranges and greens, and produces an explosion of bright orange flowers held high above the foliage. It shouldn't work, but somehow it manages to pull it off to create a majestic and architectural masterpiece. It is sold under a plethora of synonyms, from 'Tropicanna' to 'Volcano', 'Inferno' and 'Mexicana'. But while the name changes, the importance of this plant does not. Gardens require structure as well as beauty and 'Phasion' provides truly monumental summer impact. It happily grows in both containers and open soil. Grown en masse to fill a large border, it can provide a powerful summer punch in open ground, and it also works exceptionally well as a 'dot plant' providing a focal point in a bedding scheme. It is also an elegant sculpture grown on its own in a container.

GROW Choose a bright and sunny position, but requires some protection from hot direct sunlight in summer. It can suffer wind damage if too exposed. Watering requirements change as they grow. During winter and when they first come into growth in spring, be careful not to over water and keep them on the dry side. As they begin to grow more strongly, increase watering. In open soil, protect them over winter with a good depth of mulch.

Containerised canna can be successfully overwintered dry. Simply cut down the foliage once it has been attacked by frost and move to a frost-free shed. Some are hardier than others and this one has not suffered in an unheated shed, even when temperatures have fallen to –15°C. As temperatures rise in spring, the plant lets you know when it is ready to grow by sending new shoots up. Water sparingly until the risk of frost has passed. Frost-affected new shoots will not bloom, so do not be tempted to keep them. They are liable to rot over winter and the decay can travel down into the rhizome and kill the plant, or at least a part of it. A word of warning: if grown for too long in a container it tends to wedge itself in so tightly that destroying the pot becomes the only way to get it out. You can divide it when it starts growing again in spring, but be sure that each rhizome you divide has a strongly growing new shoot. In containers, feed weekly with a balanced plant food over the growing period.

There is some disagreement over whether cannas require deadheading. You can do this as soon as a flower is over: snap off the developing seed pod. The plant will then produce new buds on that flowering spike and new flowering spikes at the leaf nodes along it. However, many argue this is fiddly, that the additional flowering spikes detract from the plant's architectural value, and that the rounded and spiked seed pods are too attractive to remove. The choice is yours.

Dianthus **'Doris Allwood'**
Perpetual flowering carnation 'Doris Allwood'

Every greenhouse in the country deserves to have a space set aside for these magical flowers. The blooms are simply amazing but the intoxicating scent is unparalleled. Many visitors to my greenhouse often comment that they remind them of their childhoods and the plants their grandparents grew. Perpetual flowering carnations have fallen out of favour in the last couple of decades, but you will never truly understand why we persist with the Edwardian custom of putting a carnation in our buttonholes at weddings until you have grown them and savoured their sweet clove aroma. I have chosen 'Doris Allwood' because she is an outstanding mixture of beauty, colour and scent. It has stripes of the most incredible metallic-looking lilac/silver in its soft salmon flowers and is technically classified as a 'fancy' – a magical bloom that looks more like an illustrator's fancy than a real, growing flower. You may know *Dianthus* 'Doris', the hardy garden pink, and this plant is named after the same Doris, who was the wife of Montagu Allwood, one of the three brothers who founded Allwoods, which in its time became the world's largest dianthus nursery.

GROW Despite the delicacy of their blooms these plants can become quite large. Mine regularly end up in 15-litre containers. But they become woody after a couple of years, so it's best to take cuttings and start again. I find spring cuttings the most successful. A little bottom heat helps them to get away faster. Cuttings can be 'stopped' by taking out the central shoot once they have started growing to encourage the plants to bush out. Feed with a weak high-potash feed every couple of weeks from spring. You can increase the strength as the plants start to produce buds. Deadhead to encourage further blooms. The flowering stems require support – either tie in each one individually or use loops of wire on a central cane.

Type
Perennial
Flowering
Spring, summer, autumn
Height/spread
1.5m x 35cm
Position
Full sun, a cool greenhouse plant that can be taken outside during summer in a sheltered position
Soil
Well-drained compost
Hardiness
USDA 10b / RHS H2

BRIGIT STRAWBRIDGE HOWARD
Bee advocate, wildlife gardener and amateur naturalist, Cornwall, UK

Brigit Strawbridge Howard writes, speaks and campaigns to raise awareness of the importance of biodiversity, with a focus on native wild bees. Her debut book, *Dancing with Bees*, was shortlisted for the Wainwright Prize. She is patron of the charity Caring for God's Acre. *beestrawbridge.blogspot.com*

Echium vulgare →
Viper's bugloss

If someone were to wake me in the middle of the night and tell me I had space to grow just one flowering plant, the first to pop into my head would be *E. vulgare*. I absolutely love this plant, not only for its vibrant blue flowers, but also for its immense value to bees and other pollinating insects. Unlike most plants, which only produce nectar for short periods of time, its flowers make nectar all day, every day across its long flowering season. It is resilient in drought conditions and, not only is it able to protect the nectar inside the flower in extremely hot conditions, but it can also prevent it from being flushed away in heavy rain. This is a truly magnificent plant that I can't recommend highly enough.

GROW Like other native wild plants, viper's bugloss grows well in impoverished soil – the first time I came across it was on a shingle beach in Dungeness in Kent. But bring it into your garden, plant in a rich perennial border, and it will almost quadruple in size. I allow it to self-sow, then lift the plants and pot on.

Type
Biennial
Flowering
Summer
Height/spread
1m x 50cm
Position
Full sun, open
Soil
Tolerant of a range of well-drained soils
Hardiness
USDA 6a–1 / RHS H7

Onobrychis viciifolia
Cock's head

Cock's head, also commonly known as sainfoin, is right up there with viper's bugloss and wild mignonette as a magnet for pollinators. Having seen this plant flowering en masse as a cover crop and been impressed by how popular it was with insect visitors, I couldn't wait to try it on the allotment. It is now thriving there: the pea-like flowers are a beautiful shade of pink, and I now have some growing at the front of the perennial borders too.

GROW Easy to grow from seed and, if you cut back after its first flush, it usually flowers again.

Type
Perennial
Flowering
Summer
Height/spread
70cm x 60cm
Position
Full sun, part sun
Soil
Dry, limestone
Hardiness
USDA 8b/9a / RHS H4

Reseda lutea
Wild mignonette

Chosen for similar reasons to *Echium vulgare*, this is a brilliant plant for pollinators, especially some of the shorter-tongued solitary bees. Honey bees love it too. I've been growing wild mignonette in our garden for a few years now, and at least two of the species of solitary mining bee that visit it for pollen have begun to nest in the soil beneath it – the soil conditions that wild mignonette enjoys are also perfect for these insects. Unassuming and easy going, it produces tall spires of pale greenish-yellow flowers in early summer and would make a delightful addition to any garden.

GROW Easy to grow from seed. Plant it alongside various nepetas of similar height – the purple and yellow flowers look spectacular together. Both make good cut flowers.

Type
Biennial, short-lived perennial
Flowering
Spring, summer
Height/spread
60cm x 60cm
Position
Full sun, open
Soil
Well-drained
Hardiness
USDA 8b/9a / RHS H4

BENJAMIN POPE
Head gardener, West
Sussex, UK

Benjamin Pope leads a team that maintains and develops a private garden in West Sussex. He is a lecturer at the Chelsea Physic Garden for the English Gardening School and West Dean College of Art and Conservation. He has a RHS Master of Horticulture and is a member of the RHS Herbaceous Committee. He is the author of *What to Sow, Grow and Do: A Seasonal Garden Guide. theworkinggarden.com*

Geum 'Mai Tai'
Avens 'Mai Tai'

I find geums such good garden plants for late spring and summer, shining bright when in flower and then happily sitting back among their neighbours. Recent breeding has produced some amazing colours and 'Mai Tai' is a great example. Its gorgeous flowers hold a semi-double ruff of attractive soft peach petals tinged with dark pink, held nodding above small, neat mounds of fresh green foliage on thin, elegant, burgundy stems – a winning colour combination for the garden or vase.

GROW Easy to grow in any reasonable soil, which is what makes them so handy to use in the garden. In thin soils and in sunnier spots they benefit from a mulch of well-rotted compost or manure. They're perfect for planting around the base of roses or other shrubs, where they'll enjoy a little shade for a part of the day. Deadheading stems once flowers have faded encourages a little repeat flowering, while cutting back in the dormant period (winter to spring) and mulching keeps the plant looking smart and happy. Dividing plants in early spring every three to four years maintains vigour and promotes flowering.

Type
Herbaceous perennial
Flowering
Spring, summer
Height/spread
30cm x 40cm
Position
Full sun, light shade, sheltered
Soil
Any, with added organic matter
Hardiness
USDA 6a–1 / RHS H7

Type
Rhizomatous perennial
Flowering
Spring
Height/spread
2.5m x 50cm
Position
Part shade, light shade, sheltered
Soil
Moist, well-drained, with added organic matter
Hardiness
USDA 6b/7a / RHS H6

Disporum longistylum 'Night Heron'
Long-styled disporum 'Night Heron'

I love a choice woodlander and this is a great example. It's a classy form of *Disporum cantoniense* selected by one of the great plant hunters of our time, Dan Hinkley. For me it captures that feeling of the rare and exotic, while remaining relatively easy to grow and hardy in southern parts of the UK. Whether in a container or border, it always makes a sophisticated statement in the garden. Its slender stems hold small, shiny, dark leaves that provide both an exotic contrast to other foliage and the perfect setting for its loose, terminal clusters of elegant, lime-green, bell-shaped flowers, which fade to a softer cream.

GROW This isn't the quickest to bulk up, so grow to a decent size in a container before planting out to help with establishment. Alternatively, keep it happy in a border by ensuring it has space for the first few years and an annual mulch of leaf mould or compost. Other woodland plants such as hostas and ferns make good companions. It may need protection from late frosts, which will damage the new stems as they begin to emerge. Leaving the old foliage up until late spring offers some protection. Remove old stems annually so as not to detract from the current season's growth.

Arisaema ringens
Cobra lily

I have a soft spot for arisaemas and have found this one to be super reliable. It's pest and disease free and makes a great addition to my container display from the moment it wakes up in early spring right through to when it dies back in autumn. It has two, sometimes three large, glossy, emerald-green trilobed leaves that sit horizontally above the unusually shaped flowers. It overwinters in the soil as a round corm, with both leaves and flowers emerging at the same time.

GROW I grow them in large containers underplanted with low ferns or London pride (*Saxifraga × urbium*) and numerous early spring bulbs. Plant in a free-draining compost with added organic matter to ensure they don't dry out in summer or sit wet in winter. Liquid feed with a weak organic fertiliser during the growing season and/or top dress with organic compost/mulch in spring.

Type
Bulbous perennial
Flowering
Spring, summer, autumn
Height/spread
50cm x 50cm
Position
Light sun, part shade, sheltered is best to recreate a woodland-edge environment
Soil
Rich, moist, well-drained
Hardiness
USDA 8b/9a / RHS H4

Type
Deciduous tree
Flowering
Spring
Height/spread
5m x 5m
Position
Full sun, part shade, sheltered, open, but avoid highly exposed locations on coasts
Soil
Any, apart from those that sit wet through winter
Hardiness
USDA 6b/7a / RHS H6

Malus transitoria
Cut-leaf crabapple

My first encounter with this tree was in a garden in Lancashire. It was in full bloom and almost sparkling as the morning light touched the hundreds of small, pure-white flowers. I later discovered that its yellow autumn fruitlets were equally as demure, yet can put on a spectacular show in high numbers. The leaves turn a golden yellow before falling. All three – flowers, fruits and leaves – enhance the tree's delicate appearance. Although it has much ornamental interest, it is natural-looking enough to comfortably sit in most garden spaces.

GROW Although a small tree, it has a large, broad canopy and so should be planted where it has enough space to grow into a beautiful specimen. In the early years, formatively prune by removing any awkward crossing branches in winter and lightly tip dominant stems in mid-summer to encourage a well-branched habit. As with all trees, mulch after planting to feed and reduce competition from other plants and weeds while it establishes. Temporarily stake if required and be sure to water during dry periods. It requires minimal pruning – just remove dead, diseased and dying branches during winter.

Type
Bulbous perennial
Flowering
Spring
Height/spread
40cm x 10cm
Position
Full sun, light shade
Soil
Rich, moist, well-drained
Hardiness
USDA 6b/7a / RHS H6

Narcissus 'Pipit'
Jonquil 'Pipit'

There is nothing quite like a daffodil returning after winter to inspire spring optimism and one of my favourites has to be the charming and reliable 'Pipit'. It produces narrow green leaves early in the season, which are soon followed by stylish flowers that reference the classic daffodil, but with a little more sophistication. Being a jonquil type, it has multiple flowers on one stem that open a soft lemon-yellow and turn to a creamy-white as they age, creating a most pleasing display.

GROW Plant in rich, free-draining soil in full sun for the best repeat flowering. I use them in the cut-flower beds and borders, growing alongside perennials and hardy annuals, which hide the foliage in late spring as it dies down. As with all narcissi, remember to deadhead after flowering to ensure the bulb has more energy for the following year's display. Plant bulbs in autumn and mulch soil surface with well-rotted organic matter to feed and reduce competition from weeds.

Type
Deciduous conifer
Height/spread
5m x 6m
Position
Full sun, open but
protected from the
harshest weather
Soil
Appreciates moist
and heavy soils but
grows reasonably
well in all but the
direst of conditions
Hardiness
USDA 6a–1 / RHS H7

Metasequoia glyptostroboides
Dawn redwood

This was one of the first trees I was introduced to at the start of my
horticultural education and it has remained a firm favourite. As well as
having a fantastic Latin name to pronounce and much horticultural
merit, it also has a romantic history – once thought lost from modern
flora, it was discovered growing in central China.

It's a beautifully shaped tree with a conical habit and straight central
trunk, which gives it a smart appearance throughout the year. The
peeling bark is a warm orange and the delicate foliage is the brightest
green when emerging in spring, before turning orange in autumn and
leaving bare stems for winter. Older specimens often develop interesting
twisted roots that sit exposed above the ground.

GROW Planting close to a water source promotes vigorous growth, while
reflecting the glowing autumn foliage. No pruning required, but remember to
water well if conditions become dry while establishing.

Persicaria orientalis
Gentleman's cane

This plant is a great annual that will liven up the garden from late summer
into autumn with its glowing magenta flowers. I use it in the borders and
pumpkin patch where its height guarantees it sits above other plants and
creates a seasonal focal point. Full of vigour, it produces a thick central
stem and lush, relatively large leaves from spring to summer. As summer
continues, sprays of hot pink flowers begin to appear, softly arching to
create vibrant tassels that get better as autumn approaches.

GROW Shaking the flowers from late summer onwards usually dislodges any
ripe seed, which can be collected and sown in autumn for the following year.
The seed needs a period of cold to germinate, so place in a cold frame or
outside during winter to ensure good germination in spring. Grown as a hardy
annual it will happily self-sow in mild parts of the country; seedlings can be
moved or potted on and then planted in a desired location. Alternatively,
sowing in autumn produces a spring germination and plants can be grown on
in pots before planting out, avoiding slug damage that can be fatal for young
plants. Watering after planting and during dry conditions ensures healthy
growth, while an occasional liquid feed is beneficial if grown on light soil.

Type
Annual
Flowering
Summer, autumn
Height/spread
1.5m x 60cm
Position
Full sun, part shade,
avoid strong winds
Soil
Any, but grows
shorter in drier,
well-drained ones
Hardiness
USDA 8b/9a / RHS H4

KATE MCEVOY
Founder member, Real
Seeds, Pembrokeshire, UK

Kate McEvoy has been growing and selling vegetable seed since 1998. She also spends time writing, campaigning and teaching about seed saving; she aims to encourage all gardeners and growers to produce at least some of their own seed. Real Seeds sells open-pollinated seeds suited to organic/low-input methods. *realseeds.co.uk*

Chenopodium berlandieri

Huauzontle

Huauzontle (also known as Aztec broccoli) is such an easy plant to grow. It looks striking and is so good to eat. As a chenopod it isn't affected by flea beetles, cabbage white caterpillars or leaf miners, making it the perfect summer green vegetable. Sow as the weather warms up in late spring and, once established, it will grow to over 1m tall, with delicious edible leaves.

The best bits are the masses of flower shoots, which you gather just before they show their tiny yellow petals. Pinch out the top 7.5cm of each flower stem (which will have both leaves and flowers) and boil or steam them. These 'huauzontles' have a great texture when cooked, with a very slight crunch. They're not in any way chewy but don't go completely soft like spinach does. They are great to mix in with rice, potato cakes, couscous or stir-fries, providing an easy way to make simple dishes special. If you're a particularly keen cook, search online for 'huauzontles' to find lots of Mexican recipes for fritters and more. Half a dozen plants will supply you with shoots from mid-summer right through to autumn.

GROW The main tip is to sow in modules – the seedlings look like the wild English plant fat hen, so it's easiest to start them in a tray then plant out at around 45cm spacing once they're established. Like all leaf greens, they need watering in dry weather for best establishment, but once they're growing well they are very robust. They benefit from a reasonably fertile soil with some compost or manure added.

Type
Annual
Flowering
Summer, autumn
Height/ spread
1.5m x 80cm
Position
Full sun, open
Soil
Moist, well-drained, reasonably fertile
Hardiness
USDA 6b/7a / RHS H6

Capsicum pubescens 'Alberto's Locoto'

Apple chilli 'Alberto's Locoto'

I've been growing this unusual chilli for more than 25 years, since we were first given the seeds by a Bolivian friend living in Cambridge. Since then I've grown a few other *C. pubescens* varieties, but I've yet to find another that performs as well in UK conditions or is as exceptionally tasty. The plants have softly furred leaves, pretty purple flowers and black seeds. They're big, handsome plants, especially later in summer when covered in masses of bright red fruit. The chillies have thick flesh, which is medium to hot but with a particularly fruity flavour. They freeze really well and they also make a good hot chilli sauce.

GROW Like all chillies, these are best started in late winter with a little heat – if you have the option, an electric propagator is ideal. They'll grow large, so if you're planning to keep them in a container, they either need a good-sized pot or one plant to an up-ended grow bag, which works well. They're more tolerant of cool weather than many chillies, so can do well outdoors in a sunny sheltered pot on a patio in warmer areas.

They are most commonly grown as annuals but are in fact short-lived tender perennials. In milder years they overwinter in our polytunnel here in Pembrokeshire with just a cover of fleece to keep the frost off. They survive well in a conservatory or other warmer, under-cover spot. If you do plan to overwinter them, don't cut back. They'll look untidy, but leave them be until they are well into growth in the spring. Provide good fertile soil with plenty of manure or compost and feed container-grown plants once the first fruits have set.

Type
Perennial
Flowering
Summer
Height/ spread
1m x 1m
Position
Full sun
Soil
Fertile, such as a grow bag
Hardiness
USDA 10b / RHS H2

CHRIS BAINES
Campaigner, writer
and broadcaster, West
Midlands, UK

Chris Baines is a pioneering champion of wildlife gardening and works as
an environmental adviser to industry and government. He first appeared
on *Gardeners' World* in 1979 and was one of the original presenters of
Countryfile. His most recent film, *The Living Thames*, has won awards
across four continents. His book *How to Make a Wildlife Garden* is
regarded by the RHS as a classic.

← *Primula vulgaris*
Primrose

I love the pure simplicity of our native primrose. This is a wildflower that
can hold its own in any garden. The pale creamy-yellow of the flowers
glows in the low light and dappled shade of broadleaved woodland,
and that same luminous quality lights the path to my front door as a
first real harbinger of spring. In detail, the primrose is exquisite. One of
my very first natural history lessons came when my dad showed me
the two contrasting forms of primrose flower – the pin form, where the
female stigma projects to catch the pollen, and the thrum form, with
its projecting anthers cleverly designed to powder the earliest bees.
Pick a posy of primroses and their perfume will delight you, and when
the seed pods ripen, look out for the garden ants that carry the seeds
away to plant in some new corner of the garden.

Primrose plants form a flattened rosette of crinkled green leaves, with
the individual flowers growing from the centre on thin 10cm single stems.
A single clump may produce more than a hundred flowers in a season,
beginning with the last of the winter snow and frost, and providing a
perpetual display for a month or more. As the rest of the garden bursts
into leaf and begins to dominate, the modest primrose simply fades
into the shadows. It is the ideal foil for spring bulbs such as snowdrops,
crocuses and grape hyacinths, and I particularly like to see primroses
mixed in among a carpet of pale-blue forget-me-nots. The primrose is
one of the few native wildflowers with an RHS Award of Garden Merit.

Primroses are wildflowers of the sheltered hedgerow, stream bank
and sunlit woodland glade. These are habitats that have been lost from
much of our wider countryside, but a mature garden can make the
perfect substitute. My own small wildlife garden serves as a sheltered
woodland glade in Wolverhampton's urban forest, and the primroses
seem to love it. When I made the very first wildlife garden at the RHS
Chelsea Flower Show back in 1985, I combined primroses with sweet
woodruff, sweet violet and wood anemones, and the public seemed to
be astonished and enchanted by the romantic pastel-coloured carpet
this produced.

GROW Primroses spread readily from seed, but as long-lived herbaceous
perennials they also lend themselves to division and replanting every two or
three years. They perform best in sheltered sunlight and dappled shade, so the
base of a hedge or the front of a flower border are ideal, but in my own garden
they have seeded into the edge of paths within my veg patch, where they
produce a constant crop of seedlings for passing on to friends. The pure native
primrose readily cross-pollinates with polyanthus and cultivated primrose
cultivars, but I much prefer the pure simplicity of the original. I have gardened
on sand and on clay, and primroses have always thrived.

Type
Herbaceous
perennial
Flowering
Spring
Height/spread
10cm x 10cm
Position
Full sun, part shade,
sheltered
Soil
Moist, well-drained
Hardiness
USDA 6a–1 / RHS H7

JAMES GRAINGER
Senior gardener, Coleton Fishacre, Devon, UK

James Grainger studied at RHS Rosemoor and since then has developed a passion for gardening in harmony with nature and promoting gardens not just as beautiful spaces, but as flourishing wildlife habitats. *nationaltrust.org.uk/coleton-fishacre*

Aloysia citriodora
Lemon verbena

When my partner and I were on a cycling tour of New Zealand, we heard a cyclone was forecast to hit and sought refuge with a wonderful couple on the Coromandel Peninsula. After a hearty dinner, we sat in front of the log burner playing cards, laughing and sipping mugs of steaming lemon verbena tea. I am not a huge fan of herbal teas but found it refreshing and relaxing. As soon as we returned home and I discovered that I was able to grow lemon verbena here in Devon, I planted some in a sunny border. Whenever I smell the delicious sherbet lemon scent, I am transported back to that 'hyggelicious' moment.

Native to South America, *A. citriodora* is a deciduous, bushy shrub, with whorled, lance-shaped, heavily scented, lime-green leaves. Panicles of tiny lilac-white flowers appear in late summer. I like to grow it with *Eryngium planum* as the two have similar growing requirements and the combination is aesthetically pleasing. The electric blue flowerheads of the sea holly harmonise with the green foliage of the lemon verbena, I also find that the woody framework of the lemon verbena helps to support the flower spikes of the sea holly, which tend to flop after heavy summer rain. Another bonus is that the strong scent of the lemon verbena masks the decidedly less pleasant scent of the eryngium. At Coleton Fishacre, we also grow the less widely available 'Spilsbury Mint' cultivar, which, as the name suggests, has a dominant spearmint scent and flavour.

GROW Prune to within one or two buds of a permanent woody framework in spring after the threat of frost has passed. Pick and dry leaves before the shrub comes into flower to ensure you have a supply over winter (drying the leaves enhances the scent and flavour). Propagates easily from softwood cuttings. A dry mulch in autumn helps to insulate roots.

Type
Deciduous subshrub
Flowering
Summer
Height/ spread
2.5m x 1m
Position
Open, sunny, in frost prone areas in the UK grow against a south-facing wall or in a container, which can be moved under glass during cold spells
Soil
Poor, dry, well-drained
Hardiness
USDA 9b/10a / RHS H3

Type
Rhizomatous herbaceous perennial
Flowering
Summer, autumn
Height/ spread
1m x 1m
Position
Full sun
Soil
Well-drained, moderately fertile
Hardiness
USDA 6b/7a / RHS H6

Artemisia ludoviciana 'Valerie Finnis'
Western mugwort 'Valerie Finnis'

Silver is such a versatile colour in a garden designer's palette. It harmonises with any other colour without clashing (although I fully endorse breaking the conventional colour rules from time to time). This is one of the purest silver-foliaged plants available and can be used to great effect in a border. It is a rhizomatous, clump-forming perennial with silvery-grey leaves with cut margins. In mid-summer it produces panicles of yellow-brown flowers (but you're not growing this plant for its flowers).

At Coleton Fishacre we use it with *Pittosporum* 'Tom Thumb', *Heuchera* 'Binoche' and *Hylotelephium* 'José Aubergine', all of which have a deep purple colour. Next to brown soil, these dark colours can appear underwhelming and muted, but placing them alongside a contrasting (lighter) colour boosts their visual energy. 'Valerie Finnis' achieves this perfectly.

GROW If left to flower, 'Valerie Finnis' will flop and lose its impact. I would recommend giving it a 'Chelsea chop' to encourage younger, bushy growth. It propagates well from semi-ripe cuttings, although annual division in spring is just as successful at increasing stock. It dies back over winter, but rather than removing the dead foliage, I prefer to leave it looking 'untidy' until spring. This has the double benefit of creating useful spaces for hibernating insects and providing a degree of insulation and protection during cold weather.

Rosa glauca
Red-leaved rose

This changed my perception of roses, with which I have always had a love-hate relationship. While their scent and beauty are undeniable, here in the often wet West Country, black spot is a common problem. In my experience *R. glauca* displays greater resistance. Native to the mountainous regions of central and southern Europe, this vigorous shrub rose has an arching habit with reddish, thorny stems. Many roses behave like divas, clamouring for attention while in flower, before receding into the background once the flowers fade, but *R. glauca* is more demure. The simple, pink flowers contrast gracefully with the greyish-purple foliage. Later in the year, red hips continue to provide seasonal interest.

When deciding how to incorporate plants into a scheme, it is important to consider what it brings to a border, especially when not in flower. From the moment that this rose comes into leaf until the last hip falls from the naked stems, it provides great design value. It also seems to be a bit more tolerant to extended periods of hot, dry weather than many other roses.

GROW I use this rose in a mixed herbaceous border, emerging through a carpet of forget-me-nots. Many of the hardy geraniums, alliums or catmints make good bedfellows. The foliage is great for use in floral displays. Avoid deadheading if you want rosehips. Mulch with well-rotted manure in spring and keep pruning to a minimum to avoid spoiling the naturally arching habit – a light prune in spring should be sufficient.

Type
Shrub rose
Flowering
Summer, autumn
Height/ spread
2m x 1.5m
Position
Full sun
Soil
Well-drained, moderately fertile, moist
Hardiness
USDA 6a–1 / RHS H7

JEAN-MARIE AVISARD
Head gardener, Claude Monet's House and Gardens, Giverny, France

Jean-Marie Avisard began working at the Giverny gardens in 1988, having started out at the Château de Tournebut in Aubevoye. *giverny.org*

Tricyrtis hirta →
Japanese toad lily

I have chosen *T. hirta* because it is relatively unknown. I feel it deserves a place in the spotlight, having noticed here in Giverny how much people appreciate discovering its dark green, slightly downy, lanceolate leaves and speckled flowers, which range from yellow to white and mauve. Visitors find it magnificent, regularly comparing it to an orchid. It is easy to grow, bringing pleasure to even beginner gardeners as long as they have taken care to plant it in a suitable soil and position. It does particularly well alongside hostas, heucheras, rhododendrons and ferns.

GROW Ideally, plant it in autumn. You can multiply the clump by division in autumn, too. It requires soil rich in organic material so do not hesitate to incorporate well-rotted manure as well as compost. Always keep the soil cool, avoiding exposure to burning sunshine. Remove the wilted stems and add a little well-rotted manure in autumn when digging over the beds. While it's resistant to disease, pay attention to slugs and snails as vegetation revives in spring.

Type
Rhizomatous perennial
Flowering
Summer, autumn
Height/ spread
1m x 50cm
Position
Full shade, part shade
Soil
Moist, well-drained
Hardiness
USDA 6a–1 / RHS H7

225

ED BOLLOM
Head gardener, Gordon
Castle Walled Garden,
Morayshire, Scotland

Ed Bollom has worked at Gordon Castle since 2015. He was previously
senior gardener in charge of production for the former Prince of Wales at
Highgrove and also worked at Allington Castle for Sir Robert Worcester.
gordoncastle.co.uk

Cucurbita pepo, C. maxima, C. moschata →
Pumpkins and squash

I love the exuberance of squash and pumpkin plants. With their
weird and wonderful fruit and vigorous trailing foliage snaking
across the veg patch, they just seem so bountiful by the end
of the summer. Any plant that looks good and tastes great is
a winner for me. Many varieties of squash have surprisingly
beautiful trumpet-shaped flowers, such as the ornamental
gourd 'Cobra', which has lovely delicate white flowers. They can
be grown over arches and obelisks to add height to your plot
and the fruit comes in many shapes and sizes, from tiny little
patty pans to vast carriage-sized whoppers, such as *C. maxima*
'Mammoth' and 'Atlantic Giant'. They also range in colour from
blues and purples through to bright red and burnt orange.

My favourites are the small and perfectly formed *C. pepo*
'Jack be Little' and the majestic *C. maxima* 'Turk's Turban', with
its fantastically striped and knobbly fruit. I like to grow several
varieties together alongside nasturtiums, which add a splash of
colour and provide edible flowers earlier in the summer.

Squash are dead easy to cook – just cut them into chunks and
roast in the oven with a little olive oil, sea salt and a few sprigs
of rosemary. For smaller varieties, cut off the top, add a knob of
butter and pop them in the microwave for a couple of minutes.
You can scoop the creamy nutty flesh straight from the shell of
the squash, thus avoiding any washing up!

GROW If you're serious about growing pumpkins or squash, you need
to give them lots of room to spread and sprawl over the ground through
the summer, so you may want to put them in a dedicated bed or even
plant them in your compost heap. Given room to roam free, they are
fabulously rewarding plants.

As with courgettes, sow two seeds per pot in mid-spring onwards,
keeping them warm. Carefully harden them off before planting into
warm soil from early summer. Give them at least a square metre per
plant. However careful you are, young pumpkins and squash always
seem to sulk for a couple of weeks after planting, but if you feed them
every couple of weeks with tomato fertiliser and keep them well watered
and sheltered from cold nights and strong winds with a sheet of garden
fleece, they should soon start snaking across your plot. You can guide
the long shoots into spirals to save space but in the walled garden we
just let them grow where they like, often out of the veg beds and across
the paths.

Pumpkins are ready for harvesting in autumn before the first frosts
and should store until at least Christmas. Squash are divided into
summer and winter types. Summer squash are harvested through
the summer when they are small with soft skins and tender tasty
flesh. Winter squash are allowed to mature into the autumn and are
harvested before the first frost.

Type
Annual
Flowering
Summer, autumn
Height/spread
50cm x 3m or more
Position
Full sun, preferably
sheltered from strong winds
Soil
Moist, well-drained
Hardiness
USDA 10b / RHS H2

BRIE LANGLEY
Botanical horticulturist,
Royal Botanic Gardens,
Kew, UK

Brie Langley works in Kew's Palm House as a horticulturist. She trained with the RHS and Cambridge University Botanical Garden. She lives in a small flat with pots on every windowsill and annoys her housemates by stealing all of the small plates to go under them. *kew.org*

Tillandsia usneoides

Spanish moss

Air plants were first becoming popular when I was getting into horticulture, with every garden show having at least one stand dedicated to them. I was entranced. The soft elegance of *T. usneoides* struck me from afar and I knew I had to take the plunge. I draped the flowing locks over a dried *Dahlia imperialis* stem (as you do!) on my bedroom windowsill. The light softened through the grey trichome hairs covering every surface (which allow the plant to take in water and nutrients) and the pale green chaos hung in graceful swathes, floated in the breeze and brought a calm rhythm to the room. Every so often a flower would appear, but only if I took the time to look. If just looking at plants is good for our mental health, caring for them must be an act of mindfulness. *T. usneoides* is that plant that makes you stop for a moment and smile.

GROW Bathrooms are brilliant for air plants because of the high humidity – you could even make a natural shower curtain out of this plant! Part sun indoors is best; a very hot spot with direct sun will lead to it looking like barbed wire. You can put it outdoors in a warm, sheltered area in summer (just keep an eye on night temperatures, above 15°C is best). Allow this plant to hang and move with the wind, if possible; it gives a marvellous effect.

    T. usneoides is easily propagated vegetatively – simply tear or cut the required chunk from the mother plant. In its native habitat in the Americas, this helps it cope with damage caused by wind or animals, and helps it to spread. At home, it means you can rest easy if children or pets get a little too hands-on, though it does take a while for each piece to grow to a decent size.

    If you can, mist over or water every day until the plant changes colour from grey to green, but don't worry if not. You can also water by leaving it in a bucket of water (or a sink) overnight once a week, more often if extremely dry and hot. Once a month or so, add a little orchid feed to the bucket. You can tell if your plant needs more water just by looking at it: when well watered, the leaves are plump and a little greener; when dry, they are thinner and greyer. In hard-water areas, try to use filtered or mineral water, at least some of the time, as the limescale may block up the trichomes and stop the plant taking in water. Another method is to use water from a kettle, as much of the limescale will have been removed. Just allow it to cool first!

Type
Epiphytic perennial
Flowering
Spring, autumn
Height/spread
2m x 1m
Position
Part sun, can be put outdoors in a warm, sheltered spot in summer
Soil
None
Hardiness
USDA 11 / RHS H1C

Type
Epiphytic perennial
Flowering
Spring, summer
Height/spread
50cm x 50cm
Position
Full sun, part sun, can be put outdoors in a warm, sheltered spot in summer
Soil
None
Hardiness
USDA 11 / RHS H1C

Tillandsia juncea

Rush-like air plant

I have only just learned the name of this plant. When I first bought one, I hadn't a clue, so I called him Geoffrey. In the humid air of the UK's west coast this plant got to a colossal size – I could barely squeeze him into the bucket to water him and by the time it came to moving house he had outgrown the plastic carrier bag I'd lined up to transport him in. He did not enjoy Cambridge so much: my room was too dark and the hard water was a shock. So, I have now bought Geoffrey #2, or *T. juncea* as he is properly known. So far, this plant is enjoying sitting in the bathroom, getting doused in water each day from the shower. He hasn't grown nearly as quickly in London, but he is still green. There is hope.

    T. juncea has long, dusty green blades held stiffly upright in a whorl, all growing from a grey-brown rounded base. With high humidity and low light, the blades will spread and fall outward, forming a wide bowl in the shape of two cupped hands. With more light, the leaves will be held upright, almost like a grass or sedge. Flowers are a vivid purple tube crowned with bright yellow protruding stamen. They are held high in clusters on a long, thick, scaled stem in the centre of the plant.

GROW If outdoors over summer, keep an eye on night temperatures, above 15°C is best. Even indoors, temperatures next to a window can be cold in winter, so move to the heart of the room overnight. A bright and humid bathroom is perfect. Be careful with how you display this plant, the ends of the leaves are brittle and prone to snapping. Although this is purely aesthetic and will not harm the plant, it is very annoying! In the right conditions it can easily reach 20cm across in two years, so make sure the holder is either big enough, or that you can easily remove your plant if it starts getting too big. If there's no space in the bathroom, a bright windowsill is perfect.

For watering and feeding tips, see the advice for *Tillandsia usneoides* opposite. After watering, allow it to dry upside-down to stop the water sitting in the base of the plant and causing rot. If you find that leaves become rotten, remove the affected areas but be careful to avoid the growing tip at the base. It is best just to cut off the affected leaf rather than tear off a leaf if it is not ready to come away.

Propagate by seed or simply separate the pups (small plants that grow from the mother plant) when they are roughly a third the size of the parent.

Type
Bulbous perennial
Flowering
Autumn
Height/spread
10cm x 50cm
Position
Full sun, part sun
Soil
Well-drained
Hardiness
USDA 9b/10a
/ RHS H3

Oxalis melanosticta
Black-spotted wood sorrel

I first came across this plant while working in the alpine section at Cambridge University Botanic Garden and I just love how tactile it is. For years I kept a large pot of it outside that flowered every year like clockwork and never complained. Keeping *O. melanosticta* indoors all year round is a little more challenging, but hopefully my tips will go some way towards ensuring a healthy plant you'll want to show off.

Foliage lasts all the way from autumn to spring, when the plant will die down and lie dormant over summer. Its fluffy green shamrock leaves stand 7–10cm above the soil surface, forming a graceful dome. Bright yellow vase-shaped flowers blast through the foliage in early autumn like trumpets – the flowers only open in daylight hours, so take the time to enjoy them when you can.

These days there is a lot of experimentation (yielding fantastic results) with growing alpines in pure sand or gravel with no soil whatsoever. It is generally the winter wet that gets them and this method allows maximum drainage. If in doubt, go for a mix of loam with a high proportion of sand and gravel for a raised bed or alpine trough. If using a pot, consider exchanging gravel for pumice as this will help keep the pot light for moving around (you may wish to store it in a corner while dormant and reintroduce it to your display when the foliage returns).

GROW Keep this little one where you can easily spot it from a window in the morning – catching sight of the bright flowers gives a little lift to the day. Even better, consider planting in a raised bed or wall you often pass. Stroking the foliage brings an almost childlike joy. If planted outside, cultivation is a doddle. Leave the rain to do the watering and just keep an eye on any weeds that might swamp it. Remove any dead leaves when the plant starts to die down and watch for snails and slugs. Alpines are often grown with a layer of fine gravel covering the soil surface, which not only looks good but also lifts the leaves from the wet earth and keeps our slimy friends at bay.

If growing in a pot, check the watering each week by either feeling the top layer of soil with your finger or by picking up the pot by the rim with both hands, and rocking it slightly forward and back to feel the balance. If well watered, the pot will feel heavy, with the weight even throughout the pot. If you feel the weight is only in the top half of the pot, water! Water well until the water comes out the hole at the bottom of the pot and the soil is wet all the way through.

Always use terracotta pots for alpines. Not only do these look good, but they are also slightly porous, allowing excess water to escape and protecting the plant's roots from rotting. If grown in a very wet area where drainage is an issue, consider keeping pots in a covered porch or a naturally drier part of the garden, such as at the base of a wall or very close to the house. If you have no access to outside space, keep on a cool, bright windowsill away from a radiator and check the watering every week. Pots can be placed to one side when not in growth, but don't forget to water a little every three weeks or so. Pots should be refreshed every two to three years, during the dormant months. Gently remove the bulbs from the pot along with any dead or rotten material. Discard the old soil and replace with new, planting to a depth of three times the size of the bulb. Keep the bulbs quite close together, 2cm or so, to maintain a full and lush appearance. Give *O. melanosticta* an extra kick by feeding once every two to four weeks when in growth with a general plant feed.

Type
Perennial shrub
Flowering
Summer
Height/spread
1.5m x 2m
Position
Full sun, sheltered
Soil
Well-drained, sandy
Hardiness
USDA 9b/10a /
RHS H3

Teucrium fruticans
Tree germander

When I first moved to London, I lodged in a townhouse and maintained the garden as part of the rent. A mature walled plot filled with beautiful shrubs in a tangle of romance and thorns, it felt like the secret garden of Frances Hodgson Burnett's novel. I even found a large *Hibiscus syriacus* under the billows of wisteria from next door. Halfway down the path was a grey giant, toppling the rose arch and threatening to take over the path. This *T. fruticans* must have been 2m wide and a good 2m tall, incredibly happy in its sheltered position and sandy loam bed. The evergreen shrub has green leaves with dusty grey undersides, which are held in opposite pairs along tall, furry, grey stems topped with a blue/purple flower reminiscent of salvia or rosemary. And this one flowered constantly, all year round. It proved an excellent backbone to my regeneration and replanting of the garden.

GROW *T. fruticans* is a large shrub that grows quickly in one season – be sure to give it space. It is perfect for a dry garden – in fact, it seems to thrive on neglect! Give it a well-drained soil and sunny position and it will ask for nothing in return. Though I do advise you water every week, more if dry, for the first few weeks until it is established. Try to leave all the watering to the rain after that, unless very dry.

Tip back young plants and shape mature specimens with shears in winter. You can also prune hard to encourage bushy growth – these plants come back strongly from regenerative pruning. *T. fruticans* can be shaped into relaxed forms or hedges but does not have the compact growth required for formal topiary. Potted specimens need adequate drainage and regular pruning.

Propagate tree germanders from semi-ripe cuttings. Mature specimens can sucker; these can then be removed to form a separate plant. Cut a sucker so that the removed part has a good number of roots, then keep in a pot for six months to bulk up the root system before planting out.

230

EDWINA VON GAL
Landscape designer and
founder of Perfect Earth
Project, New York, USA

In 2008, while designing the park for the Biomuseo in Panama, Edwina von Gal founded the Azuero Earth Project to promote native species reforestation on the Azuero Peninsula. In 2013 she created the Perfect Earth Project, a non-profit supporting toxin-free landscapes. In 2021 she launched Two Thirds for the Birds – a call to action to landscape professionals to make all their projects habitat friendly. *perfectearthproject.org*

Coreopsis tripteris '**Gold Standard**' ↘
Tickseed 'Gold Standard'

I am focusing on native plants these days as part of my new initiative Two Thirds for the Birds. I choose plants that are great performers and need little care, so as well as selecting this beautiful, yellow-flowered coreopsis, I would also like to mention the plants: *Aster* 'October Skies', *Zizia aptera*, *Tiarella* 'Brandywine' and *Baptisia tinctoria*.

The thing I most prize in a plant is how well it interacts with adjacent plants. Does it mingle nicely, loose but not floppy, spreading but not aggressive? Do its blooms last a long time or develop interesting seedheads? And, of course, I look for lots of ecosystem value.

Many of the new native plant selections (or 'nativars') are bred for compactness, which I guess looks tidy, but they tend to stay separate and solid. I am going for airy plants like these so that things grow through each other, hold each other up, and maybe even cover for each other's seasonal low moments.

GROW I am now, finally, trying to follow the old edict: right plant, right place. It solves most cultural problems if a plant is growing in a place most similar to where it evolved. I am no longer interested in growing something difficult. Why? I have enough that depends on me.

Type
Perennial
Flowering
Summer,
autumn
**Height/
spread**
2m x 2m
Position
Full sun, part
shade
Soil
Moist, well-
drained
Hardiness
USDA 7b/8a
/ RHS H5

DEBS GOODENOUGH
Organic gardener, Isle of Wight, UK

Before stepping down in 2020, Kew-trained Canadian Debs Goodenough was head gardener to the then Prince of Wales and Duchess of Cornwall at Highgrove for 12 years, developing the garden to organic principles and advising teams at other royal properties.

Philadelphus coronarius 'Aureus'
Mock orange 'Aureus'

I've long grown varieties of philadelphus for their intoxicating scent in early summer, but had never grown the golden form until I worked for the then Prince of Wales. He uses the plant to lighten areas of semi-shade and for its aroma, which is all the more surprising given that its flowers are so buried among the gleaming golden foliage. The bright yellow leaves (best in spring) are a wonderful feature useful in woodland situations and in areas that you need to highlight or draw the eye. When I first started in horticulture I wasn't fond of golden-foliaged plants, but my opinion changed when I saw them used in the right position. They make a wonderful backdrop to dark-foliaged plants such as *Lunaria annua* 'Chedglow'.

Type
Deciduous shrub
Flowering
Summer
Height/ spread
2.5m x 1.5m
Position
Full sun, part shade, sheltered
Soil
Well-drained
Hardiness
USDA 6b/7a / RHS H6

GROW Best grown in good light but with shading from the fiercest of sun (which can scorch the leaves). Early foliage can be damaged in exposed windy positions. Tolerates dry conditions, but grows best in free-draining soil with adequate moisture to maintain good growth.

This is generally an 'easy care' shrub. Water to establish the planting and add an annual mulch to maintain vigour. Prune to help shape the plant – hard to rejuvenate or regularly (every other year) to maintain new growth from the base.

Propagation is from semi-ripe wood cuttings in early summer or hardwood cuttings in winter.

Iris × hollandica
Dutch iris

I enjoy having cut flowers in the house and taking bouquets to friends when I visit, cut from the garden if possible. As the daffodil and tulip season wanes, Dutch irises are already starting to offer stems for cutting. These are strong and last a good week in a vase, often having first one, then another flower to enjoy.

This form of iris is so easy to care for and reliable, and offers a particularly good range of flower colours from pale purple or blue to yellow, white or bronze tones, sometimes bicoloured or with a yellow throat. All the tones mix well together in bouquets, while single forms accentuate cut tulips in a vase.

A row or two for cutting is a real delight in spring, especially as they will deliver good cutting material year after year.

Type
Bulbous perennial
Flowering
Winter, spring
Height/ spread
1m x 50cm
Position
Full sun, part shade, sheltered or staked in exposed positions
Soil
Moist, well-drained
Hardiness
USDA 7b/8a / RHS H5

GROW The foliage takes until mid-summer to die down completely, naturally feeding and increasing the bulbs for the following year. This is the only unattractive element about the plant and not necessarily helpful in a border. But you can always lift them and allow them to die down in a tray, replanting the bulbs in late summer. Every three years lift the bulbs and gift them to friends to keep the rows from expanding, then add new colour form to the group.

Dutch irises are inexpensive to buy and you could consider them 'throw-away' items, but I find this hard since they perform so well in following years. I've tried them in meadow situations, but they are not long lasting. They grow well in most soil conditions, enjoying an annual mulch of compost.

Oxalis triangularis subsp. *papilionacea*
Purpleleaf false shamrock

It's great when you find an easy-care, versatile plant that can be used in imaginative ways that surprise even well-seasoned gardeners – and this is a plant that does that. Often viewed as a pretty greenhouse or indoor plant, purpleleaf false shamrock is not so notably used outdoors for pot work or planters. But its deep purple foliage and pale pink flowers throughout the growing season are just as charming and effective on their own as they are in combination with contrasting or complementary foliage or flowering plants. When I lift the plants in autumn, I have the difficult decision of whether to keep them going on my windowsill through the winter (as they look so attractive) or to dry them off and keep them as dormant rhizomes for the following year. It always depends on how full the windowsills are already...

GROW Grow in pots or use to 'bed out' small areas or planters. A container combination that I recommend with this plant is *Solenostemon scutellarioides* 'Campfire' (which has burnt orange foliage with purple hints) and *Begonia* 'Benitochiba' (silvery purple foliage, which is almost, but not quite, frost hardy and lasts long into autumn). Hanging baskets are another good use for it, but there are many more innovative situations to try.

Grow outdoors late spring to mid-autumn, indoors year-round, or with frost protection in a greenhouse. Don't be dismayed after you first put the plants outside for the summer – they tend to mope for a week or two until they adjust to their new climatic conditions.

If growing outside, bring them indoors for winter and allow them to go dormant by withdrawing water but don't allow the rhizome/bulb to desiccate. Repot and initiate growth in early spring with an occasional liquid feed during the growing season. Propagate by division or seed.

Type
Bulbous perennial
Flowering
Summer, autumn
Height/spread
15cm x 50cm
Position
Full sun, part shade, sheltered
Soil
Moist, well-drained
Hardiness
USDA 9b/10a / RHS H3

Ipomoea alba
Belle de nuit

There are always those plants that are fun to grow but a tiny bit challenging depending on the year – some years they perform well, others not so well if you live in the UK. This is one of those. Technically a perennial from tropical and subtropical regions of North and South America, it is either grown in a greenhouse in the UK or treated as an annual and grown outside. It loves the heat and shorter day lengths, so flowers best in late summer or early autumn. Its alternative name of 'moonflower' comes from its white, round-shaped blooms (like full moons) that flower in the evening giving off a most fragrant scent. It looks like flowering bindweed on steroids, so is wonderful for provoking a multitude of raised eyebrows.

GROW Nick the hard seed coat, soak the seeds for a couple of hours, then sow. Germination is quite quick, but if you are growing them outside, do not put them outside until you put out your runner beans. Give them a sunny position near to where you will visit them in the evening when they are in flower. Fertilise when first establishing. Keep the soil moist, but not saturated.

Type
Climbing perennial
Flowering
Summer, autumn
Height/spread
1.5m x 4m
Position
Full sun, sheltered
Soil
Well-drained
Hardiness
USDA 10b / RHS H2

Anemone apennina
Blue anemone

I came across this plant in the garden of a house in which I lived for years; it took a long time to realise that it wasn't a superior blue form of *Anemone nemorosa* (which is wonderful yet painstakingly slow to establish) but in fact a robust Mediterranean species ready to charm anyone with its graceful foliage (which emerges as the snowdrops disappear) and carpet of beautiful blue-rayed flowers. I say robust, as the area I first found it growing in was a ground elder nightmare, and it seemed very happy, flowering well before the ground elder had properly woken. It spreads easily, accentuates naturalised bulb plantings and disappears as spring wanes.

GROW Blue anemone is a beautiful ground cover below hydrangeas before they take over all the space around them. They also accentuate emerging peonies in conjunction with hellebores, and look good with any bulb display growing higher than 40cm. It's also particularly useful under deciduous trees and shrubs and it just glows when struck by the occasional ray of sunshine. Most importantly, blue anemone isn't competitive and can be removed readily with a gentle tug.

Although it is supposed to come readily from seed – and I'm sure it spreads around my garden that way – I find it is easiest to propagate 'in the green' by lifting clumps, cutting large rhizomes into pieces the size of a large pea, and potting up three to four to a pot. Allow the foliage to die down and plant the pot any time that suits – you can even wait until it reappears the following season. Grows in dry ground but spreads more readily where there's some ground moisture, at least in winter. A pot of blue anemone makes a most desirable gift to a fellow gardener.

Type
Rhizomatous perennial
Flowering
Spring
Height/spread
15cm x 50cm
Position
Performs best in dappled shade
Soil
Any, apart from saturated ground
Hardiness
USDA 6b/7a / RHS H6

Corylus avellana 'Rotblättrige Zellernuss'
Hazel 'Rotblättrige Zellernuss'

I love hazel as it supplies the garden with pea sticks, poles and bindings for making structural pieces, and any remaining bits can be used as kindling for winter fires. They are beautiful structural plants that are always good to have growing innocuously in a shrubbery, so to come across one as ornamental as this is an absolute delight! This form of red hazel doesn't need to be a shy wallflower but can take pride of place in a border or in a backdrop for more ornamental plantings. It produces long pink catkins in late winter and early spring followed by deep red-purple foliage in spring and nuts that are red on mature specimens. I have begun replacing some of my ordinary hazel with this variety. I will leave a few specimens to get to flowering- and nut-producing size to see if the local red squirrels enjoy them as much as I do!

GROW To take advantage of the wonderful colouring of the leaves and catkins, grow where you can see the light coming through the foliage. Planting with an artistic eye for light and colour is an important element that the Prince of Wales used a lot at Highgrove, particularly with the Japanese maples.

Full sun gives best red colour to leaves but this can grow in semi-shade. It can be grown in a shelterbelt or hedging but also looks lovely against contrasting shrubs. If space allows, groupings are best, but individual specimens can make dramatic focal points and are tough enough to withstand exposed situations.

Coppicing allows changes to borders or shrubberies on a cyclical basis, giving constant renewal. You can coppice as an ordinary hazel, making it useful for producing pea sticks and poles. Doing so also helps maintain foliage cover and promotes new shoot growth, but compromises catkin and nut production. Take hardwood cuttings in winter.

Type
Deciduous shrub or small tree
Flowering
Spring, summer
Height/spread
5m x 3m
Position
Full sun, part shade
Soil
Moist, well-drained, alkaline, neutral
Hardiness
USDA 6b/7a / RHS H6

ISSY CROSSMAN
Grower and florist, Flower
Appreciation Society,
London, UK

Issy Crossman is part of Hackney-based floral studio Flower Appreciation
Society, which transformed a disused backyard into a cutting
garden in order to grow flowers for its arrangements and workshops.
theflowerappreciationsociety.co.uk

Cosmos bipinnatus
Cosmea

A very easy cut flower! It is simple to grow from seed, easy to germinate
and produces a multitude of blooms throughout late summer until the first
frosts. The more you cut them, the more they flower. And though they look
delicate, they have good vase life. They come in shades from white to pink
and pale yellow. We particularly love 'Cupcake' and 'Fizzy Rose Picotee'.

GROW Pinch out stems when they are about 20cm tall to encourage bushy growth.
Stake your plants and keep on top of deadheading to prolong the season.

Type
Annual
Flowering
Summer, autumn
Height/spread
2m x 40cm
Position
Full sun
Soil
Moist, well-drained
Hardiness
USDA 9b/10a / RHS H3

Rosa **Margaret Merril ('Harkuly')**
Rose [Margaret Merril]

One of our all time favourite roses for cutting. Scent is very important
when arranging flowers, and Margaret Merril really does have the most
beautiful fragrance. It looks stunning, with delicate, open-faced petals
in creamy white with a blush-pink sheen. It is also repeat flowering.

GROW Water weekly in the flowering season with a comfrey fertiliser to keep
your rose happy and producing lots of blooms. We plant geraniums, nepeta
and calendula underneath our roses, as they are great companion plants for
deterring pests. Prune in early spring.

Type
Shrub rose
Flowering
Summer
Height/spread
80cm x 60cm
Position
Full sun, sheltered
Soil
Moist, well-drained
Hardiness
USDA 6b/7a / RHS H6

Type
Annual
Flowering
Summer
Height/spread
50cm x 50cm
Position
Full sun, good for
coastal areas
Soil
Well-drained,
loam, sand
Hardiness
USDA 9b/10a
/ RHS H3

Eschscholzia californica
California poppy

Very easy to grow in pots, drought tolerant and will grow in poor soil as
long as it has lots of sun. The blooms look delicate and dainty with their
frilly, silky petals and wispy leaves. But despite their fragile appearance,
they have a good vase life and last well in arrangements. We love the
range of colours they come in, with pops of bright orange, soft peach
and pearlescent pale yellows and pinks. Excellent, bushy border filler.

GROW Keep cutting the blooms to prolong flowering. Very easy to sow – we just
sprinkle the seeds directly on to the soil in spring for flowering that year or in
autumn for flowering the following year.

Type
Perennial
Flowering
Summer
Height/spread
1m x 1m
Position
Full sun, sheltered
Soil
Well-drained
Hardiness
USDA 11 / RHS H1c

Pelargonium capitatum
Rose-scented geranium

Pelargoniums produce some of our favourite scents of all time – they
smell like summer and come in an amazing array of aromas from citrus
and peppermint to rose. Their bushy, feathered leaves in vibrant greens
look beautiful in seasonal flower arrangements. They are sturdy when cut
and have a good vase life.

GROW Not frost tolerant. Very easy to take cuttings from, so a good beginner
plant if you want to try propagation.

JO CAMPBELL
Head grower, Restaurant
Andrew Fairlie, Perthshire,
Scotland

Jo Campbell has been growing vegetables, edible flowers, microgreens and herbs for Michelin-starred chefs throughout her gardening career. She worked in the kitchen gardens at Raymond Blanc's Le Manoir aux Quat'Saisons before working at the Secret Garden for Restaurant Andrew Fairlie. *andrewfairlie.co.uk*

← *Mertensia maritima*
Oysterplant

This is an unusual plant to grow in the garden, but its increasing popularity in fine dining has made the seeds and plants more widely available. Its fleshy, succulent, blue-grey leaves have an oyster-like flavour reminiscent of its natural seashore habitat, and their spoon-like shape make them perfect for serving as canapés or as an accompaniment to fish. They also add an element of seafood flavour to vegetarian and vegan dishes. A member of the borage family, it is a low-growing plant that produces trailing stems with clusters of bright blue edible flowers at the end, hence its alternative name of 'sea bluebell'.

GROW Oysterplants can be challenging to grow as productive crops, rather than for ornamental rockery gardens. I grow two areas of oysterplants: one to harvest and another that I allow to flower in order to collect the seeds for sowing. The seeds need the cold to germinate, so stratification is required. Sow the seeds from autumn in a cold frame to overwinter, or store the seeds in sand in a refrigerator, sowing in late winter.

Grow in pots in cold frames, in raised beds in a soil-based substrate or in open ground and rockeries. They prefer dry to moderate moisture. Feed regularly with a seaweed feed. They dislike root disturbance so don't move them once they're established. Susceptible to slugs and snails.

After harvesting the leaves, place them in a bowl of cold water before you use them to retain their freshness.

Type
Perennial
Flowering
Summer
Height/spread
10cm x 50cm
Position
Suits a bright location but grows in part shade
Soil
Mimic its natural growing environment along the coasts of northern Scotland and Greenland by supplying good drainage and a sandy or medium loamy soil
Hardiness
USDA 7b/8a / RHS H5

Coriandrum sativum 'Confetti'
Coriander 'Confetti'

I have chosen coriander for its sheer culinary versatility. It can be grown as a microgreen for its leaf and the seeds can be harvested green and then pickled. Roots can be ground into a paste for cooking. You can complement any vegetable garden by growing edible flowers throughout, and the dainty, lacy, pinkish-white flowers of herb coriander stand tall above other crops, attracting beneficial insects, hoverflies, bees and pollinators. When there is a glut of flowers, use them sparingly in dishes – fresh with seafood they add the same signature lemony, citrus flavour as the leaf; dried in a food dehydrator they can be turned into an aromatic powder and used as a seasoning. Coriander 'Confetti' has feathery foliage similar to carrot tops, but is still edible and has the same flavour profile.

GROW I grow a patch of coriander specifically to produce flowers and seed, sacrificing the leaf. That way, there are no frustrations with the plant prematurely bolting under stress and the flowers are produced quicker. My preferred variety for flower production is 'Confetti', which is sturdy and stocky, making it easier to stake and support. Planting in blocks as opposed to traditional rows enables you to stretch layers of pea/bean netting over the top to support the stems as they grow. The hard seeds can be soaked overnight to aid germination. I multi-sow modules in spring indoors to germinate in the warm, which can take up to 14 days, and then plant outside. Water in dry weather.

Type
Annual
Flowering
Summer, early autumn
Height/spread
1m x 25cm
Position
Full sun for flowers and seed production
Soil
Fertile, well-drained
Hardiness
USDA 7b/8a / RHS H5

Stachys affinis
Chinese artichoke

Chinese artichokes, commonly known by chefs as crosnes, are a crop worth growing on the basis that they are rarely seen in shops. The plant is a prolific producer of small, pearly white tubers that have a juicy, crunchy, crisp texture. Thin-skinned, these can be eaten whole to appreciate their sweet, nutty fresh flavour, while blanching them in boiling salted water with lemon juice preserves their white colour. Finished in a brown butter, they're lovely paired with wild mushrooms, or dress them with olive oil in an autumnal salad of earthy beets, bitter chicory, walnuts and sorrel. They're the perfect autumnal and winter crop.

Chinese artichokes are a member of the mint family and they have the same spreading growth habit. Their green, slightly furry leaves have a similar shape to mint and mauve flowering stems.

GROW Having battled with most pests and diseases with many other crops in the kitchen garden, I find this relatively pest free. A native to Asia, it can easily be grown in the UK climate with little maintenance. You can purchase and plant seed tubers in spring. I prefer to start them in seed or plug trays then plant them out once the shoots appear. Tubers can be planted directly outside but are susceptible to mice damage. Stretching a pea/bean net across the top of the foliage to support it as it grows prevents the growth from falling over. Water during dry weather – applying a mulch helps to retain moisture. Cut the flowering stems off to allow the plant to divert its energy into developing the tubers below.

Harvest the tubers when the foliage dies back in mid-autumn onwards – dig as and when required. Seed tubers can be expensive to buy so I reserve some tubers as seed stock for the following year and store them in damp compost over winter in a cool, light place. Cleaning the soil from the tubers can be challenging: try putting the tuber in a garden sieve and shaking under a hosepipe. Alternatively leave some in the ground to regrow the following year. It's shallow growing and if a piece of root is left in the soil after digging and harvesting, it will sprout up the following year – grow it in a separate area to keep it under control.

Type
Tuberous perennial
Flowering
Summer
Height/spread
50cm x 50cm
Position
Full sun, open
Soil
Well-drained, not too manure-rich, otherwise there will be lush green plant growth and few tubers
Hardiness
USDA 6a–1 / RHS H7

RACHEL DE THAME
Horticulturist, broadcaster and garden writer, Gloucestershire, UK

Rachel de Thame is a regular presenter on *Gardeners' World*, the author of several books and a columnist for *The Sunday Times*. She is also vice president of conservation charity Plantlife, an ambassador for the National Gardens Scheme and patron of the British Iris Society. *racheldethame.com*

Cephalaria gigantea
Giant scabious (SEE ILLUSTRATION PAGE 174)

My first encounter with this tall, rangy perennial many years ago prompted a eureka moment. I'd previously given disproportionate priority to perennials of middling and short heights in mixed and herbaceous planting schemes. *C. gigantea* encouraged me to look up. I realised the importance of scale and that tall plants can encompass delicacy and transparency. I like to use it towards the front or corner of a border, where the pale lemon, scabious-like flowers – beloved by pollinators – dance atop slender stems, offering veiled glimpses of other plants beyond.

GROW Cut back after flowering to encourage further intermittent flowers. Can be allowed to self=seed to achieve an informal effect.

Type
Herbaceous perennial
Flowering
Summer
Height/spread
2.5m x 1.5m
Position
Full sun, part shade
Soil
Well-drained, moist, humus-rich
Hardiness
USDA 6a–1 / RHS H7

JONATHAN SHEPPARD
National Plant·Collection
holder, Lincolnshire, UK

Jonathan Sheppard left London for Lincolnshire more than ten years ago and transformed a two-acre plot into a home for cottage-garden favourites and wildlife. He now holds the National Plant Collections for *Alcea* and *Cosmos bipinnatus*. britishhollyhocks.wordpress.com

Cosmos bipinnatus 'Lemonade' and 'Xsenia'
Cosmea 'Lemonade' and 'Xsenia'

Type
Annual
Flowering
Summer,
autumn
**Height/
spread**
1m x 50cm
Position
Full sun,
sheltered
Soil
Moist, well-
drained
Hardiness
USDA 9b/10a
/ RHS H3

Many people assume most *Cosmos bipinnatus* are just the pinks and whites, but if you are looking for a lovely yellow, then 'Lemonade' has to be on your list. Not one of the taller cosmos that can become thuggish, 'Lemonade' is quite compact and produces lemon-yellow flowers with a white-ringed centre.

For me, cosmos is a must-have for anyone who loves the informality of the cottage-garden planting, with fantastic flowers from summer until the first frosts. While many could be described as a bit showy, striving to be the star of the garden, sometimes a plant wows by being more classy and understated. That's why I also love *C. b.* 'Xsenia'. It has subtle pink petals flushed with an apricot colour, which deepens as the flowers age to a lovely terracotta that glows in the sunshine. Not the biggest, brightest or boldest, but a beauty.

GROW To get the best out of your cosmos you have to be prepared to deadhead... and then deadhead some more. That way you ensure you have a continuous flourish of flowers until the time comes when you want the plant to produce seed, which you can allow to self-sow in situ. Provide a feed once a week during flowering.

Type
Biennial or
short-lived
perennial
Flowering
Summer,
autumn
**Height/
spread**
1.5m x 30cm
Position
Full sun
Soil
Well-
drained
Hardiness
USDA 7b/8a
/ RHS H5

Alcea 'Halo Cream' →
Hollyhock 'Halo Cream'

I have always enjoyed growing lots of different hollyhocks. 'Halo Cream' is a lovely variety that looks spectacular when the sun shines behind it on a summer's evening. It is a single variety, so is a great plant to grow to benefit pollinators. It has big green foliage leading to tall spires with multiple flowers.

Prior to establishing the National Plant Collection of *Alcea* I never really grew 'doubles'. I always thought they weren't for me, yet I have had to change my views. William Chater is perhaps the name most associated with hollyhocks, and many doubles bear his name. 'Chater's Salmon' is a beauty, with flowers that easily compete with those of a peony in my view – lush, voluptuous and just a superb salmon-pink that is a joy to behold in any garden.

GROW The biggest threat to hollyhocks is rust and it's one of the reasons why the plants fell out of favour. In spite of that, hollyhocks are well worth growing for their blooms. Using an anti-fungal spray can help combat rust. If it does appear, remove infected foliage. They are generally known as biennials, or more recently short-lived perennials, because of the view that rust can weaken plants on an ongoing basis. So, even though many hollyhocks can come back each year, some may need replacing after a time. They may require staking in really exposed locations. Provide a seaweed feed once a week during the growing season. Once flowering has taken place, collect the seed and then cut back to the ground.

DAN PEARSON
Landscape designer,
horticulturist and writer,
Bath, UK

Dan Pearson is an award-winning landscape designer, horticulturist,
gardener and writer with an internationally recognised design practice.
He is an expert in ecological naturalistic plantings that support wildlife
biodiversity. *danpearsonstudio.com*

Paeonia delavayi →
Delavay peony

Type
Deciduous shrub
Flowering
Spring
Height/spread
2.5m x 1.5m
Position
Full sun, part shade,
sheltered
Soil
Moist, well-drained
Hardiness
USDA 6b/7a / RHS H6

I have grown this plant since I was 19 and working at Edinburgh
Royal Botanic Garden in the early 1980s. I collected seedlings
from beneath the parent plants there and grew them on in my
parents' garden in Hampshire. In 1997 I took one of those plants
for my garden in Peckham and then, in 2010, I potted up a number
of seedlings from that plant when I relocated to Somerset. I
have six of these third-generation plants at the entrance to the
garden at Hillside, where I live today. As they are seed-raised,
the flowers can vary in both shape and colour, ranging from
almost mahogany brown to blood red. A ruff of stiff, waxy petals
surrounds a large boss of golden stamens. The flowers have an
exotic, spicy scent and are very attractive to honeybees.

As small shrubs they provide good, mid-height structure
and volume in the planting through all seasons. I love it for its
coppery young foliage, which is early and remarkably frost
hardy. The foliage colours well in autumn and is held through
the winter, when it blackens and resembles ornate wrought iron,
particularly when overlaid by a crust of sparkling frost. In late
autumn, bladder-shaped seed pods break open to reveal almost
spherical seeds of shiny black, which fall to the ground and
germinate freely to produce seedlings that I now pot on and give
to friends and clients.

GROW Peony seeds can take up to two years to germinate. Sow them
in moist compost in a 9cm pot and leave in a sheltered place such as
a cold frame or cool greenhouse. Ensure the pots are kept damp in
summer. Once they've germinated, grow the seedlings on for another
year before transplanting to their final position.

In the garden I have these underplanted with richly coloured early
tulips as spring companions and scarlet schizostylis for autumn colour.
I have also allowed the short-growing brick-red *Lathyrus rotundifolius*
to scramble over them, which gives them an extended season of
flowering interest.

Mulch with well-rotted manure in spring. Prune out the eldest stems
as plants mature in winter to make way for new wood.

ANTON ROSENFELD
Knowledge officer, Garden Organic, Coventry, UK

Dr Anton Rosenfeld has worked for Garden Organic, the UK's leading organic-growing charity, since 2003, running projects that encourage people to grow more organic fruit and vegetables. He also writes regularly for horticultural and gardening magazines. *gardenorganic.org.uk*

Brassica juncea
Chinese mustard

We were shown this plant by an old Vietnamese couple who had a plot on a large allotment in Birmingham. It was beautifully tended with flowers dotted between the vegetables. There was a whole array of plants, including wonders such as edible chrysanthemums and shark-fin melon (*Cucurbita ficifolia*), but this plant stuck in my memory. I was handed a small piece of leaf to try and I was instantly taken. It was a delicious blend of mildly hot and spicy mustard with a hint of sweetness. I really wanted to secure a supply of those leaves! They kindly gave me a pinch of home-saved seeds to take away. With their agreement, we added it to Garden Organic's Heritage Seed Library, so others would have access to it too.

The plant turned out to be easy to grow, and also easy to save seeds from (although you need to keep it away from other flowering brassicas to avoid it crossing). The slightly serrated leaves have a white midrib and can be used in salads or briefly cooked in stir-fries. The bonus I found was that just before it flowers, it produces lots of small florets that are like lime-green, mini-broccoli spears. They add a crunchy mustard zing to a salad!

GROW This plant can be grown most of the year, but can be knocked back a bit by a really cold winter day and does better in a slightly sheltered spot. It runs to seed a lot more quickly from spring sowings, but if you sow in mid- to late-summer, it keeps going all the way through till the next spring. As a brassica, it is vulnerable to the whole list of woes that brassicas suffer, including flea beetles, cabbage white butterflies and pigeons. Sow into trays first and then plant out at 50cm spacing once they have developed three or four true leaves. Then it is just a case of regularly harvesting the outer leaves until the plant starts to flower and stops producing good quality ones.

Type
Annual, biennial
Flowering
Summer, autumn
Height/ spread
1m x 50cm
Position
Full sun, part shade
Soil
Silt loam, rich in nutrients and organic matter, neutral to slightly alkaline
Hardiness
USDA 8b/9a / RHS H4

Momordica charantia
Balsam pear

I love the alien-like look of the fruits produced by this plant, but my first encounter with them was not a positive one. I just bought a load from a market stall and added them to a stir-fry. It was so bitter that it was completely inedible. However, once an Indian friend cooked a dish with it, I was hooked. When prepared properly, balsam pear, also known as karella or bitter gourd, still has a slightly bitter flavour, but it's paired with a slight nuttiness that is quite addictive.

A sprawling climber, with deeply lobed leaves and yellow monoecious flowers, it is a challenge to grow in the UK, but if you find the right varieties and grow them under glass, they can be very productive.

GROW I have found the Chinese varieties with smooth skin are not only more productive than the heavily wrinkled Indian types, but also taste less bitter. Balsam pear has a hard seed case so it is best to pre-germinate the seeds on a damp paper towel in a plastic box in a warm place. As soon as roots start to emerge, carefully place them root down in seed compost in an 8cm pot in a 1cm-deep hole. Allow to grow in a warm place, and transplant to their final position when they have three to four true leaves. Plant 50cm apart and provide a trellis for them to climb. Once the plants reach the top of the trellis, pinch out the growing point to keep them a manageable size (they will grow to at least 2m unchecked). Also remove any side branches that don't have female flowers (these have a swelling of the fruit forming underneath). Harvest the fruits while they are still green.

Type
Annual climber
Flowering
Summer
Height/ spread
2m x 2m
Position
Full sun, in a glasshouse with plenty of warmth
Soil
Rich, well-drained, loam
Hardiness
USDA 12 / RHS H1b

Brassica oleracea covo
African kale

If you visit a reasonable-sized urban allotment, chances are you will find somebody from Zimbabwe with a plot. I can almost guarantee they will be growing African kale, known as covo. This plant grows into a moderate-size perennial kale bush, providing you with a supply of greens all year round without having to worry about sowing seeds or messing around with planting out seedlings. It really does offer low-maintenance brassica growing. The greens are often cooked in a spicy peanut sauce that nicely complements their flavour. It is almost impossible to find the seeds of this plant in the UK, so the only way you can grow it is from a cutting. The best strategy is to find a Zimbabwean grower on an allotment, take an interest in what they are growing, and ask nicely for a few cuttings. It has worked for me so far!

GROW Cuttings are best taken between mid-spring and late summer. Break off a shoot and trim it to around 10cm long. Remove most of the leaves except the upper few and place them gently in some gritty compost, making sure you have at least two or three nodes under the ground. They might look a bit sorry for themselves for a few weeks, but once they take, they will start producing new leaves and perk up. Plant them out 90cm apart to give them enough space to grow into a bush.

You need to protect these plants from pigeons and caterpillars when they are small, but once they get larger, they are big enough to withstand a touch of herbivorous grazing. One fact I have learned is that pigeons cannot fly and eat at the same time, so they are only able to devour the lower leaves. Harvest leaves regularly, starting with the lower leaves. The plants grow happily in the same spot for three years and benefit from a top dressing of compost in spring.

Type
Annual, perennial
Flowering
Summer, autumn
Height/spread
1m x 1m
Position
Full sun, part shade, grows under a range of conditions
Soil
Heavier types such as silt or clay loam, rich in nutrients and organic matter, neutral, alkaline
Hardiness
USDA 6b/7a / RHS H6

Trifolium incarnatum
Crimson clover

This has to be one of the most spectacular green manure plants I've come across. I still have a vivid memory of gazing over a crimson sea of its cone-shaped flowers as far as the eye could see in the otherwise bleak landscape of the fens in Cambridgeshire. Green manures are underused by gardeners, but when you have versions that improve your soil and look as stunning as this, it may encourage a few more people to grow them.

Green manures don't always have to take up valuable space in your veg plots. You can grow them elsewhere and then, when you're ready, just chop up the foliage and spread it on your plots mixed with compost.

GROW Many books tell you to scatter the seed over the soil but I find this makes the plot a nightmare to weed as you can't distinguish the plants from the weeds. If you sow it in close rows (about 5cm apart), you can see where your plants are coming up and weed them easily. It takes longer to sow but you definitely save time on the weeding later on. Wait until the soil has warmed up in spring and rake over to remove clods. Make shallow grooves 5cm apart and drop in seeds. Aim for about 2g of seed per square metre. Cover the seed over lightly and firm down the soil to ensure that there is good contact between the seed and the soil. Clover seed does not germinate well if it is sown too deeply. Water well and keep moist until it germinates.

Allow the plants to grow. Chop down the foliage straight after flowering, before the plants go to seed and become tough, and use this mixed with compost to boost the fertility of your soil.

Type
Annual, short-lived perennial
Flowering
Summer
Height/spread
50cm x 40cm
Position
Full sun, part shade
Soil
Free-draining, loam, grows on poor fertility soils, tolerates slightly acidic pH but prefers neutral
Hardiness
USDA 10b / RHS H2

Colocasia esculenta

Taro

I love this plant because it is both multicultural and multifunctional. The African and Caribbean communities grow it for its tubers, which taste like a very creamy potato – nothing quite has the texture of a taro. The Indian community uses the large, spade-shaped leaves rolled up and carefully prepared with spices and gram flour in a most delicious snack that I can only describe as 'curried leafy swiss roll'. If neither of those appeals, it also makes an attractive houseplant with dark, glossy green foliage that brings a bit of jungle into your living room or conservatory. All that from a tuber that costs less than 10p from a West Indian market stall. (Note: only eat the leaves cooked and with the long midrib removed, as they can cause an allergic reaction in some people. Make sure you know what you're doing!)

GROW These plants are best grown from taro tubers that you can get from West Indian or Asian supermarkets or market stalls. I have found late summer a great time to buy them, as the ones in the shops always seem to have small sprouts at that time of year. Plant a tuber in a large pot of moist, rich potting compost. Allow it to sprout and keep moist. During the growing months from spring to autumn, it benefits from a nitrogen-rich plant food such as nettle feed.

Type
Perennial
Flowering
Summer
Height/spread
1m x 1m in a pot, but can grow into a larger plant unconstrained
Position
Full sun, part shade, best grown in a glasshouse, only grows outside in the UK in very sheltered spots in summer
Soil
Poor-draining loam or clay, they are grown in swamps in their country of origin
Hardiness
USDA 12 / RHS H1b

Smallanthus sonchifolius

Earth apple

Type
Rhizomatous perennial, grown as an annual
Flowering
Summer, autumn
Height/spread
1m x 1m
Position
Full sun, part shade
Soil
Well-drained, tolerates slightly acid soil but grows best at neutral pH
Hardiness
USDA 10b / RHS H2

I received a small earth apple – also known as a yacon – plant after doing a whirlwind tour of a community garden in London where I was overwhelmed by a host of plants I had never seen before. By the time it had endured a train and bike journey on a warm day, it was looking very much worse for wear, but I dutifully planted it out to see what would happen. It quickly perked up, and grew into a lush, tall plant with blue-grey, slightly hairy, heart-shaped leaves. By autumn it had produced a generous bucketful of large tubers. The tubers can be eaten raw and have a fresh nutty flavour when first harvested, but as advised I left a few of them to 'mature' until they were soft and juicy. They had the taste of a fleshy, nutty pear. I was bowled over by this plant. What a strange concept – a plant that produces an underground sweet, fruity-tasting tuber!

GROW The plant is quite late to produce tubers, so wait until the leaves have been killed off by frost to maximise your harvest. And wait until after the last frost of the year before carefully digging up – you need to get your fork down deeper than you would digging potatoes to avoid spearing the tubers.

To make new plants, ensure you save some of the crowns at the base of the stems. It is obvious where they are when you look at the plant. Divide them into small pieces and store in dry compost for the next season. From each plant you can get up to 10 new plants, so you quickly build up a collection. In spring, take your pieces of stored crown and put them in 12cm pots, buried about 2cm deep in potting compost, and place in a frost-free place indoors. Don't water them until they start to sprout or they will be in danger of rotting off. The plants should increase in size rapidly after about four weeks, and can be planted out after the last frost. They are reasonably large plants, so I place them around 60cm apart.

Lagenaria siceraria
Calabash cucumber

Ever since I first visited Asian shops, I have been fascinated by these vegetables – also known as dudis or bottle gourd – that look like a short, green baseball bat, so it was a bonus to find that lots of people were growing them in the UK. If you have a sheltered spot, they will quickly fill the space with a rampant vine of lobed leaves. They produce large, white monoecious flowers that come out at night and are pollinated by moths. A vine bearing lots of gourds is pretty heavy, so make sure you have a sturdy support. But the sight of a load of gourds hanging from the vine is pretty impressive. The gourds are like a courgette with a firmer texture, so are good for cooking in curries, but my favourite dish is a spiced Indian halva, where the gourd is grated and cooked with coconut milk, nutmeg, cardamom and almonds.

GROW The seeds are slow to germinate and often attacked by sciarid fly, so I recommend pre-germinating them on some damp paper towel in a warm place in late spring. As soon as the roots start to emerge, place them root downwards in a 1cm-deep hole in seed compost in an 8cm pot. When they have two to three true leaves, plant in their final position allowing 1m between plants. Make sure they have a very sturdy frame to climb up. They grow rampantly, so cut out the terminal shoot once they reach the height of the frame and shorten branches to three or four fruits to allow them to develop properly. You can harvest fruits at any size from 20cm to 60cm long. Make sure they are kept off the ground or they will quickly rot.

Type
Annual climber
Flowering
Summer
Height/spread
Needs continual taming or will easily fill an 18m polytunnel
Position
Full sun in a glasshouse, polytunnel, outdoors in a sheltered spot
Soil
Fertile, well-drained, loam
Hardiness
USDA 12–11 / RHS H1b–H1c

Symphytum × uplandicum 'Bocking 14'
Comfrey 'Bocking 14'

I love the history behind this plant. It is rumoured that botanist Henry Doubleday discovered the beneficial properties of the comfrey plant as a liquid fertiliser by accident when he was looking for a new material to provide the glue for stamps. This happy fortuity led to Lawrence D. Hills later continuing his important work, and naming the Henry Doubleday Research Association in his honour.

No garden should be without a comfrey plant – they provide valuable food sources for bumblebees and the leaves can be used to make an excellent feed for many plants. 'Bocking 14' has pale-green, spear-shaped, hairy leaves and produces bell-shaped flowers that range from blue through purple to pink.

GROW Make sure you use only the 'Bocking 14' variety, which doesn't produce viable seeds – common comfrey will set seed and rapidly take over your garden. It is best propagated through root cuttings. Take a small piece of root at least 2.5cm long and of a finger's thickness and bury 3cm deep in the soil in mid-spring when the ground isn't frozen. It will start to sprout and rapidly grow into a medium-size bushy plant. You can usually take around three harvests of cutting down to the ground – it depends on how moist and fertile the ground is. The leaves can be steeped in water to make a rich plant feed that is ideal for feeding tomatoes and other pot plants. Water the plants in very dry weather, and provide an annual top dressing of compost once a year in early spring.

Type
Perennial
Flowering
Spring, summer
Height/spread
1.5m x 1.5m
Position
Full sun, part shade
Soil
Unfussy
Hardiness
USDA 6a–1 / RHS H7

JUDITH QUÉRÉE
Owner and head gardener,
Judith Quérée, Jersey, UK

When Judith Quérée married a Jerseyman, they bought a derelict cottage in a beautiful valley on Jersey island. There they created an organic, naturalistic garden containing more than 2,000 mainly herbaceous perennials from all over the world. The garden also contains many sculptures and its three surrounding meadows are managed for wildlife. *judithqueree.com*

Corydalis elata
Fumewort

The intense blue of this corydalis – the name comes from the Latin for 'crested lark' – is so beautiful and so valuable for areas of part shade, where it mixes well with other shade-loving plants. As a true blue, this one shines out.

Originally from Sichuan province in China, it's a hardy perennial that doesn't die back completely, so you can see where it is even in winter. Ferny new foliage is a lovely acid-green colour with red veining. When happy, it spreads and grows into a large clump and, if you are really lucky, it will seed around.

GROW Not always the easiest plant to grow, it is quite particular, requiring perfect drainage with loose, friable soil. We add compost every year to ensure good, rich, moisture-retentive soil. Only grow in full sun when soil is sufficiently moist; it flowers better in partial shade.

Type
Perennial
Flowering
Spring, summer
Height/ spread
30cm x 30cm
Position
Part shade in a woodland mix
Soil
Moist, well-drained, acid
Hardiness
USDA 7b/8a / RHS H5

Salvia guaranitica 'Blue Enigma'
Anise-scented sage 'Blue Enigma'

This salvia gives height and colour to a border. The blue – a colour difficult to find in flowers – is really eye-catching. I grow it next to *S. g.* 'Argentine Skies', which is a lighter blue, and the two combine very well. 'Blue Enigma' flowers for weeks in late summer. It has tall, square stems with attractive green leaves.

GROW It likes our warmer climate in Jersey. Cut right down in winter and mulch with compost. You need to divide every four or five years and put 'sides to the middle', to avoid a gap developing at the centre of the clump.

Type
Herbaceous perennial
Flowering
Summer, autumn
Height/ spread
1.5m x 1m
Position
Full sun, sheltered, open
Soil
Fertile, well-drained
Hardiness
USDA 9b/10a / RHS H3

**BLEDDYN &
SUE WYNN-JONES**
Owners, Crûg Farm Plants,
Caernarfon, Wales

Based on the edge of Snowdonia, Bleddyn and Sue Wynn-Jones's Crûg Farm Plants nursery specialises in unusual plants propagated from over 19,000 collections gathered on over 90 expeditions. In 2011 they became the first exhibitors to win the president's award at the RHS Chelsea Flower Show with their debut display. *crug-farm.co.uk*

Holboellia brachyandra ⬊
Short-anthered sausage vine

For those not familiar with the genus *Holboellia*, what a shame, because you've been missing out. It is a really useful group of evergreen twining plants that some authorities are attempting to incorporate into the larger but fairly similar *Stauntonia* genus. They range in size from enormous to just a few metres and have scented flowers. *H. brachyandra* sits apart from the rest by producing an abundance of larger white flowers with a pleasant melon-like fragrance that almost hides the foliage from spring into summer. For us, this plant also evokes wonderful memories of a day spent with our dear friend and fellow collector Dan Hinkley in the lower forests of Vietnam's highest mountain in autumn 2003, which was before that particular area was cut back and cleared to the primary forest, wiping out all the small treasures we found that day, including this small climber that only bore a single fruit.

GROW Best grown in a relatively sheltered position in fertile, moisture-retentive but free-draining soil. Go for a sunny to partially shaded site that isn't excessively hot or dry with room for it to climb 5m to full height. It has withstood –15°C for short periods for us without ill effects. Feed annually.

Type
Evergreen climber
Flowering
Spring
Height/ spread
5m x 3m
Position
Full sun, part shade, shelter from freezing winds
Soil
Fertile, moisture-retentive, well-drained
Hardiness
USDA 7b/8a / RHS H5

Type
Evergreen shrub or small tree
Flowering
Autumn, winter
Height/spread
4m x 2.5m
Position
Full sun, part shade, sheltered
Soil
Moist, well-drained
Hardiness
USDA 7b/8a / RHS H5

Polyspora longicarpa
Long-fruited polyspora

Polyspora is an Asian genus only recently segregated from *Gordonia*, which is now confined to the Americas. It's a close relative of camellia and their flowers are unmistakably affiliated. Although technically trees – that's how you see the undisturbed plants in the wilds of northern Vietnam – they inevitably only form large shrubs in gardens. Their striking, deepest dark green and glossiest glossy leaves up to 21cm long make a wonderful foil for the large white (12–15cm across) camellia-like flowers that emerge in autumn in the wild, but appear all the way through winter in cultivation.

GROW Best grown in a well-drained fertile soil with good moisture retention. Go for a spot in full sun to light shade and sheltered from freezing winds. Hardy to –15°C for us as young plants.

JONATHAN WEBSTER
Curator, RHS Rosemoor,
Devon, UK

Jonathan Webster trained at Ventnor Botanic Garden on the Isle of Wight and at Cambridge University Botanic Garden. After several years working in private gardens, he joined RHS Wisley and in 2005 relocated to RHS Rosemoor. *rhs.org.uk/gardens/rosemoor*

Acer griseum
Paperbark maple

A tree I have loved since seeing the single specimen planted at RHS Wisley near the wild garden, Oakwood. It's a must-have in any garden with its amazing cinnamon peeling bark, compact habit and vibrant scarlet autumnal colour. I have several great examples here at RHS Rosemoor, especially a group of three in our winter garden, which provide impact all year round.

GROW If you have the space, a group of three is very impressive.

Type
Deciduous tree
Flowering
Spring
Height/ spread
12m x 8m
Position
Full sun, part shade, sheltered
Soil
Moist, well-drained
Hardiness
USDA 7b/8a / RHS H5

Cornus 'Norman Hadden'
Dogwood 'Norman Hadden'

This is one of the summer highlights at Rosemoor – a magnificent dogwood around 25 years old planted at the back of our lake. In summer it is covered in white flowers, making picturesque reflections in the water; in autumn the leaves turn yellow creating another spectacle.

GROW This is slow-growing and requires little attention.

Type
Deciduous shrub
Flowering
Spring
Height/ spread
6m x 6m
Position
Full sun, part shade
Soil
Moist, well-drained
Hardiness
USDA 7b/8a / RHS H5

Cotinus obovatus
Chittamwood

When I was an apprentice at Ventnor Botanic Garden there was a mature cotinus in the American beds – a small tree arching over the pathway, beautiful with its soft, smoke-like flowers in summer and warming red autumn colour. It's a great plant, which I have added to our arboretum here at Rosemoor.

GROW For some reason it is not widely available, but if you can source it, it is outstanding.

Type
Deciduous shrub
Flowering
Summer
Height/ spread
8m x 8m
Position
Full sun, part shade
Soil
Moist, well-drained
Hardiness
USDA 6b/7a / RHS H6

Prunus 'Tai haku'
Great white cherry

This Japanese flowering cherry has a real link with the history of Rosemoor. Noted plantsman Collingwood 'Cherry' Ingram – who was an authority on Japanese cherries – inspired former Rosemoor owner Lady Anne Palmer to become a keen gardener during a chance meeting that led to a lifelong friendship and fostered the estate's gardening heritage.

The oldest great white cherry we have was planted by Ingram himself, and blossoms beautifully by Lady Anne's old house.

GROW Plant in a sunny spot.

Type
Deciduous tree
Flowering
Spring
Height/ spread
8m x 8m
Position
Full sun
Soil
Moist, well-drained
Hardiness
USDA 6b/7a / RHS H6

CHRIS FLYNN
Head gardener, Dyffryn Gardens, Vale of Glamorgan, Wales

A Royal Botanic Gardens, Kew-trained horticulturist, Chris Flynn joined the National Trust in 2009 as assistant head gardener at Cliveden in Buckinghamshire before moving to Dyffryn as head gardener in 2015. *nationaltrust.org.uk/dyffryn-gardens*

Adenophora bulleyana
Lady bells

If ever I was to do the Ellen Willmott trick with a plant and sow seed secretly wherever I go, then this would be my plant of choice. I've used it previously paired with *Salvia microphylla* 'Bordeaux', *Ammi majus* and *Euphorbia* 'Golden Foam' as part of a bedding display where it added a perfect contrast through its lavender-blue flowers, flower form and presence of structural spikes, which really helped bring the display together. More recently I've been pairing it with the deep plum tones of *Rosa* Munstead Wood, *Persicaria amplexicaulis* 'Orange Field' and *Achillea* 'Salmon Beauty' as part of some new underplanting for a weeping malus, which is proving very satisfying. Maybe not the most obvious combination on paper, but there's just something about that colour and the longevity of the flowers that really lifts the border, providing enough contrast to stop it disappearing into an ethereal pink mass.

GROW I think this plant is so versatile and easy to grow, it will always be a favourite of mine. Quick to propagate, easy to grow and very floriferous.

Type
Herbaceous perennial
Flowering
Summer
Height/ spread
1m x 50cm
Position
Full sun, part shade
Soil
Moist, well-drained
Hardiness
USDA 7b/8a / RHS H5

Stewartia pseudocamellia **Koreana Group**
Deciduous camellia Koreana Group

Without doubt my favourite tree for a small garden, or any garden to be fair. Stewartias are renowned for their excellent autumn colouration, and the bright orange of this tree makes it one of the finest. It's not just about the autumn colour though; this beautiful small tree thrives in sun or part shade on a range of soils, even our very wet Welsh clay! The spring brings on its fresh apple-green leaves, which are followed by delicate, open white flowers in summer. Even in winter this garden hero doesn't disappoint, exhibiting the most stunning flaked cinnamon-coloured bark.

GROW Although not a large tree, this is certainly one that wants to be given space to take on its broadly ovate form. It has a light branching structure, so lends itself well to a lift in later life to accommodate underplanting.

Type
Deciduous tree
Flowering
Summer
Height/ spread
12m x 8m
Position
Full sun, part shade
Soil
Moist, well-drained
Hardiness
USDA 7b/8a / RHS H5

Type
Bulbous perennial
Flowering
Late winter, spring
Height/spread
10cm x 10cm
Position
Full sun, any aspect
Soil
Moist, well-drained
Hardiness
USDA 6a–1 / RHS H7

Iris **'J.S. Dijt'**
Iris 'J.S. Dijt'

I've always had a soft spot for miniature irises, perfect Lilliputian replicas of their blousy summer cousins. Although only a diminutive 10cm tall, this particular cultivar is a real standout. It flowers early so is a very welcome sight on a grim winter's day. The deep purple petals contrasting with a vivid orange patch really make it pop in a border amongst other early garden arrivals. There's something deeply satisfying about seeing them emerge each year as the clumps mature, and that bright orange spot can't fail to draw the eye of the intrepid garden visitor in winter.

GROW These survive from season to season in relatively well-drained soils with the benefit of full sun, forming robust clumps after just a few years.

Rhinanthus minor
Yellow rattle

This interesting little hemi-parasite has been a key plant for all of the meadow restoration that I've been involved in. Being a fairly prolific annual it will create large colonies quite quickly, latching on to the roots of rank grasses and reducing their vigour, allowing more delicate grasses and herbs to establish within the sward over time. As well as being incredibly useful they are very pretty close up, if a little unusual. The small, beak-like yellow flower protrudes from what will become the swollen spherical seed case which, when dried, gives the yellow or hay rattle its name. This is a very understated, grown-up plant with purpose, but your inner child can't help pulling a dry stem and giving it a good shake just to see if it lives up to its name.

GROW If you're willing to play the long game with meadow restoration/ creation, getting your cutting regime right and introducing yellow rattle will be two key components to success. To get the best results, sow the seed as fresh as possible at the end of the season, ideally having lightly scarified the area requiring inoculation, just to help get better contact between the rattle and the grass roots.

Type
Annual
Flowering
Summer
Height/spread
50cm x 10cm
Position
Full sun
Soil
Well-drained
Hardiness
USDA 7b/8a
/ RHS H5

Echinacea pallida 'Hula dancer' →
Coneflower 'Hula dancer'

This is another plant I will always take with me from garden to garden. The straight varieties will often produce flowers with lax outer petals, but 'Hula Dancer' will do it reliably and is just such a different form to other components within a border.

Though the structure of the plant is quite stately and leaves behind the typical, dark, cone-shaped seedheads synonymous with echinaceas, the lax habit and light pink shades of the outer petals add a real softness to a border without being the sort of plant to flop around and sit on your other prized blooms. The flowering stems rise high above surrounding planting, which also helps them with not being too heavy an element within a border. Another plus is that they seem to be fairly slug resistant, although I may have just jinxed that by saying so! The coarse hairs on the foliage seem to offer some protection as they emerge in late spring, meaning they form decent clumps in the border in just a couple of years.

GROW This plant is definitely made for large-scale, billowing, prairie-style schemes, or seems quite at home within a gravel garden amongst other light plants like molinias and perovskia.

Type
Rhizomatous
perennial
Flowering
Summer,
autumn
Height/spread
1m x 50cm
Position
Full sun, part
shade
Soil
Well-drained
Hardiness
USDA 7b/8a
/ RHS H5

JACQUIE FELIX-MITCHELL
Garden designer, Devon, UK

Jacquie Felix-Mitchell is founder of Oasis Garden Design creating gardens in Devon and beyond. She is also a writer and event speaker. She is a contributor to BBC's *Gardeners' Question Time*, and her work has been featured in newspapers and magazines. *oasisgardendesign.co.uk*

Betula utilis subsp. *jacquemontii*
West Himalayan birch

Type
Deciduous tree
Flowering
Spring
Height/ spread
8m x 4m
Position
Any
Soil
Well-drained
Hardiness
USDA 6a–1 / RHS H7

This is a medium-sized deciduous tree that grows extremely well in the UK, and it makes for a beautiful and gentle screen from the neighbours. It has lovely yellow-brown catkins in spring and the leaves turn gold in autumn. But for me it's all about the ghost-like peeling bark, which almost appears to shimmer, particularly in winter, as well as the grace of the branches as they move in the breeze. How happy was I to be able to plant three of these delightful trees in my garden. I call them the 'Three Spirits' – they symbolise the lives of my little family. The thing about trees is that we plant them for the future. They are a marker of hope and joy.

GROW I particularly like the fastigiate (upward growing) variety of this plant, and love to grow them in groups. Doing so stops them getting too big. You can wash the bark to make it gleam even more, but they look fabulous just as they are.

Type
Evergreen palm
Flowering
Summer
Height/spread
12m x 2.5m
Position
Full sun, part shade, sheltered
Soil
Well-drained
Hardiness
USDA 7b/8a / RHS H5

Trachycarpus fortunei
Chusan palm

Part of the *Arecaceae* family, this gorgeous architectural beauty has palmate leaves on stout stems and bears pretty panicles of small, cream-coloured flowers. I love the tropical feel of this plant, and the fact that it can cope with cold as well as drought conditions.

GROW Plant in well-drained soil in sheltered conditions, such as in a walled garden. It is generally pest- and disease-free, and no pruning is needed.

Phormium tenax
New Zealand flax

Type
Evergreen shrub
Flowering
Summer
Height/spread
4m x 2m
Position
Full sun, part shade
Soil
Moist, well-drained
Hardiness
USDA 7b/8a / RHS H5

I love how this plant says 'look at me!' – it is pure drama. The way the leaves flap in the wind also makes it great for distracting from traffic in urban areas. It's a plant that really anchors a space – it is architectural and clump-forming with long, strap-like leaves, and it has a tall flowering shoot with yellow or red flowers.

GROW Generally disease-free. Remove dead or damaged leaves in spring.

Type
Evergreen shrub
Flowering
Autumn
Height/spread
3m x 4m
Position
Full sun, shade
Soil
Well-drained
Hardiness
USDA 7b/8a / RHS H5

Fatsia japonica
Japanese aralia

This fatsia's leaves are very striking – they look like they should need a sultry heat to thrive, yet they cope with the worst of our UK winters. Want to screen out the neighbours, but be subtle about it? Grow some fatsias near your boundary. Job done. It also has small black fruits that birds love.

GROW Perfect for low-maintenance and informal gardens.

DAVE GOULSON
Professor of biology and
author, East Sussex, UK

Dave Goulson is professor of biology at the University of Sussex,
specialising in bee ecology. He has published more than 300 scientific
articles on bumblebees and other insects. He is the author of books
including *A Sting in the Tale*, *Gardening for Bumblebees* and *Silent
Earth*. He founded the Bumblebee Conservation Trust in 2006 and is an
ambassador for the UK Wildlife Trusts. *sussex.ac.uk/lifesci/goulsonlab*

Senecio jacobaea →
Common ragwort

Ragwort is a pretty, native flower that provides home and food to 77 different
insect species, 30 of which are entirely dependent on it. Ten of these insects
are endangered. Another 117 species of insect have been recorded visiting
the flowers for nectar or pollen – in my garden, it is especially popular with
small copper and small skipper butterflies, but it is also visited by hoverflies,
bumblebees, solitary bees, soldier beetles and more. In short, ragwort is
a wonderful plant for insect life. It is thus a shame that it is sometimes
demonised as a poisonous, invasive weed.

GROW Ragwort looks perfectly at home in the midst of an herbaceous border or in a
meadow area.

Type
Biennial
Flowering
Summer,
autumn
**Height/
spread**
1.5m x 1m
Position
Full sun
Soil
Well-
drained
Hardiness
USDA 6a–1
/ RHS H7

Type
Annual
Flowering
Summer
Height/spread
1m x 50cm
Position
Full sun
Soil
Well-drained
Hardiness
USDA 8b/9a
/ RHS H4

Phacelia tanacetifolia
Fiddleneck (SEE ILLUSTRATION PAGE 153)

Also known as blue tansy, this pretty annual plant is from North America
and is sometimes sold as a green manure. It is spectacularly attractive
to all sorts of short-tongued bees and hoverflies. The clusters of purple
flowers produce abundant nectar and plentiful purple pollen on very
long anthers that give the flowers a spiky appearance.

GROW It is very easy to grow from seed, germinating well and growing fast. In
warm weather it flowers within about eight weeks of sowing and continues to
flower for another eight weeks or so. Sow seeds in autumn for early flowering the
following spring, or any time through spring to early summer. If it is in a sunny spot
with a little soil disturbance to provide space for germination, it will self-seed.

Type
Perennial
Flowering
Summer, autumn
Height/spread
80cm x 80cm
Position
Full sun
Soil
Well-drained
Hardiness
USDA 6b/7a
/ RHS H6

Origanum vulgare
Oregano

Also well known as English marjoram, this is a great all-rounder: very
easy to grow, attractive to heaps of different pollinators and good for
cooking, too. It seems to be particularly attractive to butterflies, perhaps
even more so than buddleia – in my garden it often attracts gatekeeper
and common blue butterflies. It is a tough perennial native and it is
fine in a flower border, naturalised among grasses or in a pot near
the kitchen door for handy picking for cooking. Avoid the golden and
variegated garden varieties, which in my experience are not quite as
good for insects.

GROW It takes easily from softwood cuttings made in early summer, or you can
sow seeds in early spring.

Echium vulgare
Viper's bugloss (SEE ILLUSTRATION PAGE 217)

A gorgeous biennial wildflower that flowers in summer and is absolutely loved by bees of all types for its copious nectar. In the wild in the UK it thrives on the shingle in Dungeness on the Kent coast and along the sides of tank tracks on the chalky soils of Salisbury Plain in Wiltshire, helping to make these two places among the best sites for bumblebees.

GROW Likes a sunny, well-drained site. It does suffer from mildew in damp weather, and during winter it is prone to rotting on heavy clay soils. It is very easily grown from seed and it will self-seed given half a chance.

Type
Biennial
Flowering
Summer
Height/spread
1.5m x 40cm
Position
Full sun
Soil
Well-drained
Hardiness
USDA 6a–1 / RHS H7

Agastache foeniculum
Anise hyssop

Also known as blue giant hyssop, this is one of the very best plants for bees. When thriving on well-drained soil, it forms very attractive clumps of blue flower spikes up to 1m tall in late summer.

GROW I have found it very hard to get seeds to germinate, and plants have a habit of dying over the winter on my heavy clay soil, so generally this is not a plant for the beginner to grow from seed, but it takes well from cuttings.

Type
Herbaceous perennial
Flowering
Summer
Height/spread
1m x 50cm
Position
Full sun
Soil
Well-drained
Hardiness
USDA 9b/10a / RHS H3

Type
Perennial
Flowering
Spring, summer
Height/spread
1m x 50cm
Position
Full sun
Soil
Moist, well-drained
Hardiness
USDA 6a–1 / RHS H7

Nepeta racemosa
Dwarf catmint

Catmint is a fantastic cottage-garden classic, one of the best all-round garden plants for bees of a wide range of species. Somehow its gently sprawling, soft blue flowers manage to attract both long- and short-tongued bumblebees. It is very easy to grow almost anywhere, with a long flowering period from late spring through to the end of summer. No garden should be without some.

GROW Catmints root very rapidly from softwood cuttings or they can be grown from seed.

Symphytum × uplandicum 'Bocking 14'
Comfrey 'Bocking 14'

Comfrey is a great plant for bumblebees, visited by both long- and short-tongued species, the latter often robbing from holes bitten in the tops of the flowers. It has a long flowering period that peaks in late spring and early summer and is followed by smaller numbers of flowers right through to autumn, especially if it is cut back.

GROW Comfrey can be chopped down regularly and used to make excellent potassium-rich compost, or steeped in water to produce a foul-smelling but highly nutritive liquid compost for tomatoes. Very easy to propagate from root fragments.

Type
Perennial
Flowering
Spring, summer
Height/spread
1.5m x 1.5m
Position
Full sun, part shade
Soil
Moist, well-drained
Hardiness
USDA 6a–1 / RHS H7

SARAH RAVEN
Gardener, author and
teacher, East Sussex, UK

Sarah Raven runs growing, gardening, cooking and flower arranging courses at her farm Perch Hill. She founded her business from the kitchen table in 1999 as a seed catalogue. All the plants are trialled and tested, and she favours those that look or taste fantastic but are also highly productive. *sarahraven.com*

Dahlia 'Rip City' ↘
Dahlia 'Rip City'

I love dahlias – they are like bread and butter to a colour-loving gardener like me – and I particularly like the ones that fall into the rich palette of stained glass reds, oranges and purples. 'Rip City' is a brilliant colour, deep chocolate-crimson, and has a plush texture and flowerheads the size of small plates. But the main reason I love it is that it was the first dahlia I grew.

I saw them in Monet's garden in Giverny in 1999; dahlias were out of fashion then, but the sight of 'Rip City' converted me and I bought three plants from the nursery on the spot. When I got back to Perch Hill, I planted them with the similarly textured *Tithonia rotundifolia* and some chocolate cosmos. The dahlias romped, growing to nearly my height, and each week I cut bunch after bunch. There is no more generous flowering plant than the dahlia. I've been a huge fan ever since.

GROW 'Rip City' is quick-growing and vigorous with a good vase life. If you live in an area with mild winters, dahlias can be treated much like hardy perennials and can be left in the garden. After a hard frost, cut the dahlias back to within 10cm of the ground and mulch each crown deeply.

Type
Tuberous perennial
Flowering
Summer, autumn
Height/ spread
1.5m x 60cm
Position
Full sun
Soil
Moist, well-drained
Hardiness
USDA 9b/10a / RHS H3

Salvia involucrata 'Hadspen'
Rosy-leaf sage 'Hadspen'

Salvias are such fantastic garden plants. They flower for months, are drought-tolerant, are excellent in pots, loved by pollinators and can even be planted as companions to roses – plant the compact, shrubby types with pungent, aromatic leaves as a skirt beneath your roses and they will work as a natural fungicide.

It's almost impossible to pick just one, but I absolutely love the deep pink, velvety flowers of *S. involucrata* 'Hadspen'. It's a big, bold, showy salvia, flowering later than many of the others and with balloon-like calyxes that remind me of lotus flowers.

GROW With lots of grit added to its planting position and mulched deeply with 15cm over the crown, this salvia can survive winter outside. Take some cuttings as insurance.

Type
Herbaceous perennial
Flowering
Summer, autumn
Height/ spread
1m x 60cm
Position
Full sun
Hardiness
USDA 6a–1 / RHS H7

CHERRY CARMEN
Garden designer
and horticulturist,
West Sussex, UK

Cherry Carmen founded garden design, consultation and maintenance business Cherry Carmen Garden Design in 2013 and creates medal-winning gardens for the Association of Professional Landscapers and charity Perennial at shows such as RHS Hampton Court Flower Show and Gardeners' World Live. *cherrycarmen.co.uk*

Francoa sonchifolia
Wedding flower

The plant that ticks so many boxes! *F. sonchifolia* produces masses of delightful sprays of swaying flowers throughout summer and early autumn, after which the foliage gives autumnal colours and stays evergreen in winter. It suits any planting scheme – I have used it in contemporary projects as well as cottage gardens, woodland settings and in containers. An elegant, delicate and graceful plant. Why isn't it in everybody's garden?

Type
Perennial
Flowering
Summer
Height/ spread
1m x 50cm
Position
Full sun, part shade
Soil
Any, apart from waterlogged
Hardiness
USDA 8b/9a / RHS H4

GROW Best grown in full sun with moist soil. Give it a multipurpose feed in late spring to keep the plants healthy. The blooms last a long time as cut flowers. Protect from winter wet. Manual division in early spring.

Roscoea purpurea
Purple roscoea

Having grown up around southeast Asia I have a soft spot for tropical plants. This is an exotic cousin to ginger and it's easy to think that it isn't hardy – the flowers look like orchids! In fact roscoea is the easiest way to introduce an exotic look into your garden. It can be used in subtle but splendid ways – tuck it into a woodland planting scheme to add colour and texture or use it to amplify an Eastern-themed garden. *R. purpurea* flowers are usually lilac or mauve, but it also come in pinks, whites and red.

Type
Perennial
Flowering
Summer
Height/ spread
50cm x 50cm
Position
Part shade, full shade
Soil
Clay, loam, humus-rich
Hardiness
USDA 7b/8a / RHS H5

GROW Plant the tubers at least 15cm deep in fertile, humus-rich but well-drained soil. Choose a cool damp spot in the garden to prolong flowering time and put different varieties together for a more colourful display. Mulching may be necessary in particularly cold winters. Does not appear until late spring. Keep the flowers out of scorching sunlight.

Lagurus ovatus
Hare's tail grass

This is the most delightful ornamental grass. The soft, bunny tail-like seedheads are irresistibly cute. Yes, it's an annual, but sowing the seeds is worth the very little effort. I love seeing these readily growing along the south coast of England as it's a reminder of how easy to grow and hardy they are – they tolerate both drought and poor soils. Because they are so small they can be used at the front of borders or in gravel beds and Mediterranean settings. The seedheads are often cut and dried to use in flower arrangements.

Type
Annual grass
Flowering
Summer, autumn
Height/ spread
50cm x 50cm
Position
Full sun
Soil
Chalk, loam, sand
Hardiness
USDA 8b/9a / RHS H4

GROW Adding more nitrogen makes the grass greener and spread further but flowering suffers. It does best in almost poor, sandy soils in full sun and once it has formed a healthy clump is best left alone. I have found no problems sowing in spring directly where I want it and leaving it well into winter with the seedheads intact.

Athyrium niponicum
Painted fern

I love all ferns but this is one of the most rewarding and striking. There aren't many plants that give you silvery-grey, blueish-greens and a burgundy-purple all within one leaf. I love how I can use it in a woodland planting scheme to brighten up a dark corner but it can look just as at home in a modern garden surrounded by clean lines and architectural planting. As long as it doesn't dry out for long spells and stays out of full sun, it needs no attention and will come back bigger and better each year from spring to autumn. It is also rabbit and deer proof!

GROW Instead of throwing away the fronds you cut in autumn, place them over the crown of the plant to provide extra protection in case of a cold winter.

Type
Deciduous fern
Height/ spread
50cm x 50cm
Position
Part shade, full shade, sheltered
Soil
Moist, neutral, acid
Hardiness
USDA 7b/8a / RHS H5

Euphorbia ceratocarpa
Horned spurge

This is my favourite euphorbia. It grows light and airy compared to other types, which can feel heavy and brutish in a flower bed. It has dainty attributes, small glaucous leaves, pinky-orange wiry stems and possibly the longest-lasting blooms I know of. In a mild winter it can be in flower for 12 months. The wide yellow sprays of flowers are willowy, lacy and beautiful. This plant looks great in most situations – I love using it in gravel beds in particular.

GROW Don't be afraid to give this plant a haircut – you can be as harsh as you like. Cut the flowers to use inside and you will find it only encourages the plant to bush out and throw out more.

Type
Evergreen subshrub
Flowering
Spring, summer, autumn, winter
Height/ spread
2.5m x 2.5m
Position
Full sun, sheltered
Soil
Chalk, loam, sand, well-drained
Hardiness
USDA 8b/9a / RHS H4

Euonymus europaeus
Spindle

I remember seeing this tree for the first time walking through the countryside when I was younger. I was so captivated by the bright fruits hanging like jewellery in a hedgerow and couldn't understand why a plant that displayed such vibrancy at a pretty bleak time of year wasn't used more readily in private gardens. To this day I still don't see it being used enough. It only really comes into its own in autumn and winter, but it has so much more to offer. It attracts such a wide variety of wildlife, from birds to bees, insects, caterpillars and moths. The growth habit means it can easily be a hedge, shrub or tree. My favourite is when it has been grown as a specimen multi-stemmed tree, with a canopy kept low enough so that you can appreciate its unique fruits and seeds up close!

GROW When the plant is still young, prune in mid-spring to encourage a bushy habit. After pruning, give it a mulch of manure for healthy growth. Does particularly well on chalky soil or any well-drained site in full sun or part shade.

Type
Deciduous shrub or tree
Flowering
Spring
Height/ spread
4m x 4m
Position
Full sun, part shade
Soil
Any
Hardiness
USDA 6b/7a / RHS H6

RON FINLEY
Gangsta Gardener,
Los Angeles, California, USA

Known as the Gangsta Gardener, Ron Finley inadvertently started a horticultural revolution when he transformed the barren parkway in front of his South Central LA home into an edible oasis. The Ron Finley Project now teaches communities how to transform food deserts into food sanctuaries. *ronfinley.com*

Helianthus annuus →
Common sunflower

Sunflowers are such a special plant. No one can look at a sunflower without smiling. They are beautiful and come in a ton of different sizes, colours and varieties. They can be 12cm tall to several metres tall, and each flower can be 3cm to 60cm in diameter. Hundreds of thousands are planted in Fukushima, Japan to pull radiation out of the ground. They feed you and they feed pollinators (bees, butterflies and so on). I plant them in my parkway garden year round to make people smile. They drive by, they walk by, and they can see them from the Metro train. When they drive by they slow down like they are in Disneyland. It's my social experiment.

GROW What I do is start the seeds in a 7cm-deep tray or dresser drawer. I put cardboard or newspaper at the bottom, mix soil and compost, add the seeds very close together, and cover with more soil and water. Once they start to sprout, I use a spoon to take them out and plant them where they will live. This is because sunflowers do not like to be moved once they get to a certain height.

They are typically a spring/summer flower but in some places you can grow them year round. They do well in an open space. Sunflowers like full sun and will follow it, but can also grow in part shade. It's best to keep them in moist soil, as they are not a deep-rooted plant. You might want to stake them early for support.

Type
Annual
Flowering
Summer
Height/spread
Varies
Position
Full sun, part shade
Soil
Moist, well-drained
Hardiness
USDA 8b/9a / RHS H4

MALCOLM PHAROAH
Former head gardener,
Marwood Hill Gardens,
Devon, UK

Malcolm Pharoah started working at Marwood Hill Gardens in 1972. Marwood is a private 20-acre garden open to the public with four National Collections. Its *Astilbe* collection has been built up over 30 years and is one of the biggest in the world. *marwoodhillgarden.co.uk*

Astilbe 'Opal'
False goat's beard

I first became aware of astilbes while studying at RHS Wisley in 1972. As a student I got to go to the RHS Chelsea Flower Show and I still remember the garden created by the Bees of Chester nursery, which featured banks of astilbes. When I came to Marwood Hill Gardens there were already 10 or 12 different astilbes. As we started collecting more, I became aware of Georg Arends, a nurseryman in Ronsdorf in Germany who raised many of his own seedlings from the early 1900s until his death in 1959. His nursery was bombed by the Allies during World War II and he lost many of his cultivars forever. On a visit there I went to see a trials ground in Munich and was given several astilbes they didn't want any more. One of them was 'Opal'. We are now the only nursery to sell it in Europe, probably the world. Why is it so good? Well, it has a beautiful silvery pink flower with masses of flowerheads in summer offset by lustrous green foliage. This is what the National Plant Collections are all about – finding and conserving cultivars that could otherwise be lost.

GROW Astilbes prefer moist soil but there are many shorter varieties that tolerate dry conditions. Divide the plants regularly – not only does this give them more vigour, but it also gives you more plants. We divide ours every five or six years, from autumn to winter (though not in frosty conditions). Add some fertiliser when planting and they will reward you with plenty of flowers. They look good by a pond. Clear spent foliage after the winter.

Type
Herbaceous perennial
Flowering
Summer, autumn, winter
Height/spread
1m x 1m
Position
Full sun, part shade, open
Soil
Moist, well-drained, boggy loam
Hardiness
USDA 6a–1 / RHS H7

MARTIN DUNCAN
Head gardener and
landscape designer,
Arundel Castle, West
Sussex, UK

Martin Duncan was born and brought up in Zimbabwe. He has worked as head gardener to King Hussein and Queen Noor of Jordan, at Audley End House and Gardens, and in Bermuda as the senior superintendent for the Department of Parks. In 2018 he was awarded the Kew Guild Medal for distinguished services to horticulture. *arundelcastle.org*

Scaevola aemula
Fan flower

I am often looking for really pretty plants that will flower right through from early summer to autumn, and giving our visitors something different is often the challenge. I was delighted when I came across this plant at my local nursery – I was instantly drawn to its unusual fan-like petals and variety of subtle colours of blues, pinks and white. We have very large terracotta pots by our water rill, so we plant agapanthus as our centrepiece and then the fast-growing scaevola (which is native to Australia) surrounds it and cascades down over the pots, giving a really stunning display.

GROW Can be used as bedding, edging, in pots, in sunny window containers and even as part of rockeries. Good in warm, sunny conditions, also tolerates shade. Pots require regular watering.

Type
Perennial
Flowering
Spring,
summer
**Height/
spread**
15cm x 1.5m
Position
Full sun, part
shade
Soil
Well-
drained
Hardiness
USDA 9b/10a
/ RHS H3

Dierama pulcherrimum
Angel's fishing rod

Having been born and brought up in Zimbabwe by parents who were keen gardeners in their spare time, I was encouraged from an early age to appreciate plants. *D. pulcherrimum* is one of my favourites. Seeing the pink, nodding, bell-shaped flowers swaying in the wind on the hillsides of the Eastern Highlands in Zimbabwe was totally unforgettable. My mother took us on a special expedition to collect the seed and to this day I continue to harvest the seed and propagate these plants, all of which originate from that expedition over 55 years ago!

GROW This plant is especially effective growing among ancient tree stumps within the Stumpery Garden here at Arundel Castle. But it can look attractive in so many locations – its grass-like stems can sway above lower plants or look graceful and serene in a wildflower area, and it looks wonderful planted by water. Plant corms in mid-autumn or mid-spring. Remove old flower stems and faded foliage.

Type
Perennial
Flowering
Spring,
summer
**Height/
spread**
1.5m x 30cm
Position
Full sun
Soil
Well-drained,
rich
Hardiness
USDA 8b/9a
/ RHS H4

Allium christophii
Star of Persia

A. christophii is one of those plants that gives instant impact in any garden. Its enormous spherical flowerheads dominate the medium-sized plant. These are up to 20cm across and are made up of 50 or more star-shaped silvery-lilac flowers. From a landscape design point of view, it is incredibly versatile. It's my favourite plant to place in amongst English lavender 'Hidcote' within our Cut Flower Garden parterre beds – it's quite magical! Growing in amongst the lavender hides the unsightly leaves, too. Alliums are also excellent at attracting bees to any garden.

GROW Plant bulbs in autumn, 15cm deep and 20cm apart to avoid the flowers being too crowded. Avoid excessive soil moisture. Split and divide large clumps in autumn or spring.

Type
Bulbous
perennial
Flowering
Summer
**Height/
spread**
50cm x 50cm
Position
Full sun,
sheltered
Soil
Moist, well-
drained
Hardiness
USDA 7b/8a
/ RHS H5

Tulipa 'Angélique' ↘
Tulip 'Angélique'

This double-late, peony-flowered tulip is my absolute favourite as it's so incredibly versatile. Its petals are a soft blush-pink that deepens with age, with a rich apple-blossom pink developing at the edges and green markings on the outside. I include it in many of my spring designs and they always look stunning.

Arundel Castle has one of Britain's largest tulip festivals, with over 180 named tulips, and on average we plant 70,000 tulips each autumn. I plant 'Angélique' in our Peony Garden, which often fools our visitors who ask why our peonies are so early! We also plant it en masse in our Rose Garden, as they look beautiful, giving the illusion of a rose garden in flower. For a very pretty combination of blue and blush-pink we plant these tulips with blue forget-me-nots in both pots and our flower beds.

GROW The best time to plant your tulip bulbs is just before the first frosts. Plant at least 10cm deep. Ensure you check your tulip bulbs before buying or planting them, avoiding soft or rotten bulbs, as damaged bulbs are prone to disease. Plant bulbs densley in pots to give high impact and make sure you water them well in spring. Use other combinations with tulips such as forget-me-nots, primulas, wallflowers and pansies. To extend flowering time in pots, place in a shady, protected area once in full bloom.

Type
Bulbous perennial
Flowering
Spring
Height/spread
40cm x 15cm
Position
Full sun, part shade
Soil
Well-drained
Hardiness
USDA 6b/7a / RHS H6

261

JENNY BARNES
Head gardener,
Cottesbrooke Hall & Gardens,
Northamptonshire, UK

Jenny Barnes comes from a farming background, but studied forensic science and worked for the National Grid before retraining in horticulture. She then spent eight years in the Cotswolds working on three private estate gardens, and is now head gardener at Cottesbrooke Hall. *cottesbrooke.co.uk*

Wisteria brachybotrys f. *albiflora* '**Shiro Kapitan**' →
Silky wisteria

This has the fattest buds I have ever seen on a plant! We have it growing on a south-facing wall at Cottesbrooke Hall, and I was completely blown away the first time I saw it. In spring, the fist-sized buds open to strong, chunky racemes as thick as my arm, and although they may be shorter than some other varieties, they pack a serious visual punch. The flowers are borne before the leaves appear, so the effect is much more impactful, and the smell is enough to make you giddy. The wonderful gnarly, twisted stems also add great interest to a winter garden.

GROW This vigorous climber requires regular maintenance to keep it in check. Pruning in early spring and again in summer ensures the best flowering performance. People perceive wisteria pruning to be tricky, but in the UK an easy way to remember the basics is to prune to six buds in the sixth month and two buds in the second month. In June prune back the long whippy growth to six buds from the main stem and in February, further shorten these shoots to just two buds. I feed it in spring with a general all-round fertiliser.

Type
Deciduous climber
Flowering
Summer
Height/ spread
12m x 8m
Position
Full sun
Soil
Most types
Hardiness
USDA 6b/7a / RHS H6

Type
Rambler rose
Flowering
Summer
Height/ spread
8m x 4m
Position
Full sun, part shade, sheltered
Soil
Tolerant of poorer soils, moist, well-drained
Hardiness
USDA 7b/8a / RHS H5

Rosa '**Ethel**'
Rose 'Ethel'

I moved to the Cotswolds when I accepted my first gardening job and lived in the most quintessentially English, quaint, chocolate-box village, which seemed to be entirely made up of cow parsley, honeysuckle and slightly wonky stone cottages with roses around the doors. My neighbour (now a great friend) had a vigorous rambling rose that ran the full length of the front garden. Clouds of soft pink, beautifully scented flowers atop a thicket of sturdy yet flexible stems formed an impenetrable barrier that served to keep chickens in and dogs out. Vast limbs would occasionally be lopped off by the local farmer when it dared to sprawl a little too far into the lane and started snagging at passing tractors. Blooms would be cut for church flowers and hips would be saved for Christmas decorations. The rose was always affectionately referred to as 'Ethel'. When I eventually moved out of the village, I wanted to recreate this little snapshot of rural idyll, so I bought an 'Ethel' and patiently watched her grow. It was only when she flowered that I realised that the rose that had played such a big part in my happy Cotswold memories wasn't an 'Ethel' at all! To this day I have no idea what it was, but in the meantime the actual *Rosa* 'Ethel' has won my heart. A mass of pale pink, frothy flowers fill the garden with scent from early summer to the first frosts, and she is happy in all situations, including a north-facing wall. 'Ethel' is a star!

GROW 'Ethel' is a particularly vigorous rambler, so plant accordingly. The style of pruning that I love makes use of the huge quantities of flexible new growth that it throws out all summer. I like to loosely tie this new growth in as it is produced to ensure it isn't damaged by the wind; I then deal with it properly in the autumn when I prune following flowering. I like to feed after pruning with blood, fish and bone or a good general rose feed. I also like to give all roses a generous shovel of farmyard manure.

Kniphofia thomsonii var. *thomsonii* 'Stern's Trip'
Thomson's red-hot poker 'Stern's Trip'

I first saw this kniphofia at Pettifers gardens in Oxfordshire: its towering spikes of neon orange pokers were planted side-by-side with a hot-pink rose. It was love at first sight; I had to have one! Weeks later, with all obvious avenues exhausted, I resorted to Instagram for help in sourcing one. After following a few leads, all dead ends, I gave up. Fast forward 18 months and I received a message out of the blue asking for my address. Three days later, a tiny offshoot of 'Stern's Trip' arrived! I'm so grateful for the kindness of gardeners and their willingness to share.

Unlike most other kniphofias, 'Stern's Trip' more closely resembles an aloe, with the tubular, downward-facing flowers widely spaced along tall stems and strappy low-growing foliage. It's completely contradictory, but this is a very, very elegant plant that also shouts in your face!

GROW This gently spreads rather than forming clumps – something I love because it creates a more natural look as it gently settles into a border. Be sure to allow it enough room when positioning. It tolerates partial shade, but flowering is improved when placed in full sun. Dislikes sitting wet and cold. Propagate by division or offshoots.

Type
Perennial
Flowering
Summer, autumn
Height/ spread
1.5m x 1m
Position
Full sun, part shade
Soil
Moist, well-drained, sand, humus-enriched
Hardiness
USDA 8b/9a / RHS H4

Cynara cardunculus
Cardoon

Another impressive architectural plant that is basically a weed, offering statement grey foliage with strong purple flowers in autumn that can fill a large hole in a border. Striking evergreen, silvery-grey foliage provides year-round interest, and looks especially great in frosty winter months. In summer, chunky flower stems are topped with globe artichoke-like flowers that split open to reveal a crazy tuft of bright purple, like a giant common thistle. The bees love them. I find silver foliage useful in a border and the colour and size of these leaves offer a great contrast to more typical herbaceous planting. Cardoons are happy in most situations and hold themselves up well throughout a growing season. Any plant that performs reliably year after year with minimal mollycoddling gets a thumbs up from me.

GROW The lower leaves occasionally become yellow over time and can split off from the stem with the sheer weight of the plant. Make sure to cut these off and clear away debris to avoid an unhealthy and unsightly mass of rotting foliage that could become a haven for pests and disease.

Type
Herbaceous perennial
Flowering
Summer, autumn
Height/ spread
2m x 1.5m
Position
Full sun
Soil
Well-drained
Hardiness
USDA 7b/8a / RHS H5

Rosa 'Raubritter' ('Macrantha' hybrid)
Rose 'Raubritter'

When I first started gardening, one of the areas I was responsible for was a formal rose garden designed by Mary Keen. Surrounded by wavy yew hedges and with a large wooden pergola along its axis, it was split in half, each half divided into six beds edged with box. This rose was planted on the corner of a central bed where it sprawled untidily over the hedge and into the path. At the time, I didn't fully appreciate its lax habit (which I now value highly for certain training techniques), but I fell instantly in love with the huge, unique, cup-shaped, hot-pink blooms, which swamp the plant all summer. They look like pink golf balls!

GROW 'Raubritter' is sold as a ground-cover rose, but there are many other ways to use it. Using strong hazel poles to create a framework around the shrub can provide enough support for the rose to scramble skyward. Alternatively, plant on top of a retaining wall and allow it to tumble downwards. It can be susceptible to mildew, so prune to allow airflow.

Type
Shrub rose
Flowering
Summer
Height/ spread
1m x 2m
Position
Full sun
Soil
Moist, well-drained
Hardiness
USDA 6b/7a / RHS H6

Angelica archangelica
Angelica

Since I made the decision to change careers and become a professional gardener, I have worked exclusively in privately owned estate gardens. Thus the style I know best is that of the traditional English country garden, but it is always fun to add a twist. The houses, gardens and landscapes are usually of a fairly considerable size, so plants need to be large enough or showy enough to hold their own. *A. archangelica* certainly ticks these boxes, offering bold structure from spring right through until autumn. The limey-green foliage and flowers contrast well with absolutely everything, and bring a freshness to the borders. I'm a huge fan of biennials, and seeds sown in late summer mean one less thing to do in spring when time for a gardener is so sparse. Not that you'll ever need to sow the seeds again – angelica (or St Michael's flower as it's also known) is a rampant self-seeder and once you have one, you'll never be without it.

GROW Leave the seedheads standing at your peril. The easiest way to avoid an angelica forest is to cut the seedheads off before they start to drop. Sow seed in a tray to avoid waste, and plant back exactly where you want them.

Type
Biennial
Flowering
Spring, summer
Height/ spread
2.5m x 1.5m
Position
Full sun, part shade
Soil
Moist, well-drained
Hardiness
USDA 6b/7a / RHS H6

Pelargonium triste
Night-scented pelargonium

I have always gardened on estates, typically large houses with a combination of formal and informal gardens, a kitchen garden and a greenhouse full of tender plants. Every garden I've worked in has had a collection of pelargoniums kept in the affectionately named 'pellie house', and every collection has included a *P. triste*. Unlike the majority of pellies, it dies back to nothing and spends the summer dormant. I'm always so pleased to see the new leaves pushing through in early winter, reassured that I haven't killed it while it slept. It has attractive, feathery foliage with green-brown flowers from late summer to late winter. It is highly scented with cinnamon at dusk.

GROW Be careful not to over water while the plant is dormant in summer. Soil should be kept as dry as possible without drying out completely. Keep in a frost-free greenhouse. Plants can be propagated from cuttings, seed or division. Pelargoniums make fantastic houseplants: they're low maintenance and flower pretty much non-stop if looked after.

Type
Tuberous perennial
Flowering
Autumn, winter
Height/ spread
40cm x 35cm
Position
Full sun
Soil
Sandy
Hardiness
USDA 11 / RHS H1C

Philadelphus 'Belle Étoile'
Mock orange 'Belle Étoile'

This is 100 per cent my favourite scent in the garden! As a rule, I don't particularly like shrubs – I find the old twiggy growth a bit messy in the leafless winter months. But philadelphus flowers on new wood and so it's pruned after flowering to remove the old scruffy growth. This leaves just the elegant, clean new stems to stand through the winter, satisfying my tidy nature. I find *Philadelphus* a hugely versatile genus and have used it in a wide range of situations: formal borders, natural mixed hedges (left to their own devices) and even trained as a climber on a wall. 'Belle Étoile' has both the better fragrance and the longer-flowering period of the philadelphus varieties.

GROW Prune immediately after flowering in early summer. I like to put the prunings to use in place of pea sticks for staking small herbaceous plants such as geraniums. The stems are strong and branched, making them really effective. Leaving them until the following year should mean there's no chance of the stems rooting.

Type
Deciduous shrub
Flowering
Spring, summer
Height/ spread
1.5m x 2.5m
Position
Full sun, part shade
Soil
Moist, well-drained
Hardiness
USDA 6b/7a / RHS H6

KIM WALKER
Medical herbalist,
Handmade Apothecary,
Hertfordshire, UK

Alongside her work at Handmade Apothecary, Kim Walker is a foraging teacher and also researches the historic development of plant-based drugs at the Economic Botany Collection, Royal Botanic Gardens, Kew. She is the co-author of *The Handmade Apothecary* and *The Herbal Remedy Handbook*. kimwalkerresearch.co.uk

Crataegus
Hawthorn

On hearing I work at Kew, people often ask: 'Oh, how do I grow such and such...?' and I have to disappoint them. Many do not realise there is a whole batch of scientists and researchers behind the scenes working on all things plant based. It is an open secret that I am not a gardener, which is my colleague Vicky Chown's role within Handmade Apothecary. I am, however, an ardent forager. I consider the 'outdoors', whether that be urban waste ground or lush countryside, an extended garden of sorts. And just like a gardener, I harvest, prune and spread seeds, planting here and there to make sure that what I forage is replaced each year.

    Of all the plants I forage, hawthorn has my heart and, when I see it, I know summer is on its way. I love how the flowers grow close to the branches and wave like arms against a blue spring sky. Even though they are around for such a brief time, there's nothing quite like it for me. The beautiful spring and autumn displays are excellent for wildlife: pollinators love the flowers and birds love the berries. They are also said to attract fairies, so you can't really go wrong.

    You can buy many varieties for the garden and for looks, *Crataegus laevigata* 'Paul's Scarlet' is a gorgeous choice. However, I prefer its 'wilder' cousins, *C. monogyna* and *C. laevigata*, because they have more scent and flavour. Not only do the flowers provide a lovely spring show but the young blooms also have a tasty marzipan 'pop' to them. The tender young leaves and flowers, known as 'bread and cheese', are ideal lightly sprinkled in salads. As summer comes to a close, the small crimson fruits provide yet another seasonal spectacle. These are high in pectin, so are a jam-maker's friend. But my ultimate favourite use for them is to make a tasty hedgerow tipple, hawthorn brandy. Herbalists traditionally use this to treat heartache and anxiety, but it is also a luscious almond-infused liqueur and makes a lovely gift. To make it, fill half a 1-litre mason jar with ripe berries. Add a couple of tablespoons of sugar and fill to the top with brandy. Leave to macerate for a month, shaking occasionally, before straining and bottling.

GROW Like mini-apples, to which they are closely related, haw berries can vary wildly in taste, so nibble around the hedgerows to find a favourite for turning into recipes and remedies.

    Hawthorn can withstand exposure, and in the countryside you can see beautiful shapes growing alone in fields, sculpted wonderfully by the wind. Plants in full sun provide the most abundant flowers and fruits, but they are also happy in partial shade. I like seeing them left to become small trees, but they are ideal in hedgerows too. You need to leave them to get a little 'shaggy' as the flowers and fruit grow on two-year-old branches. Close, regular trimming produces only foliage. Like all wild things, they can be left to get on with it, but light pruning can keep them under control.

Type
Deciduous tree
Flowering
Spring
Height/spread
8m x 8m
Position
Full sun, part shade
Soil
Moist, well-drained
Hardiness
USDA 6a–1 / RHS H7

MARK DIACONO
Writer, grower and cook,
East Devon, UK

Mark Diacono is lucky enough to spend most of his time eating, growing, writing and talking about food. He has written ten books, including *Herb: A Cook's Companion*. He is passionate about encouraging people to grow even a little of what they eat. He was formerly an environmental consultant at River Cottage. *otterfarm.co.uk*

Type
Deciduous
tree
Flowering
Spring,
summer
**Height/
spread**
8m x 8m
Position
Full sun,
part shade,
sheltered
Soil
Moist, well-
drained
Hardiness
USDA 6b/7a
/ RHS H6

Morus nigra ↘
Black mulberry

There is no fruit more delicious than the mulberry. So succulent and juicy are these large, usually dark purple-black fruits when ripe – similar to big blackberries in appearance – that it is all but impossible to get them to point of sale before they dissolve under the weight of their ripeness. You have to grow them (or know someone who does) to eat them. Mulberries are also beautiful in form, tending to droop a little, creating a room under the branches that is wallpapered with ripe fruit. As they are self-fertile, just one tree gets you fruit, so they're perfect for anything from a small garden upwards. The tree is medium-sized with a lazy, irregular habit. It is late into leaf and its large, somewhat heart-shaped leaves can be used for stuffing (similar to how vine leaves are used in dolmades).

GROW Choose a plant that is a few years old or go for a hybrid such as 'Illinois Everbearing' – you won't be waiting so long for fruit. Prefers shelter and to be out of frost pockets. Not wildly fussy about soil as long as extremes of pH, waterlogging and very sandy soils are avoided. Prune for shape, size and to remove any areas affected by dieback. Slow growing.

Zanthoxylum schinifolium
Sichuan pepper

If this plant only provided its beautifully fragrant leaves, it would still be my number one, but in the second half of the year it also produces the most astonishing peppercorns. Becoming plump and green in early summer, these redden to a vivid crimson during the hottest weeks: they can be picked at any stage, often right until the end of the year. Bright, citrusy and full of peppery heat, they impart a delightful tingle – a gentle anaesthetising – to the tongue. Of the numerous zanthoxylum considered under the Sichuan pepper umbrella, this is my favourite for flavour and scent. The aromatic leaves are wonderful added to salads when young and succulent, the peppercorns are intensely flavoured, the branches often bear large spikes, and it's an important bee plant in early spring.

Type
Deciduous shrub
Flowering
Spring
Height/spread
4m x 4m
Position
Full sun, part shade,
sheltered
Soil
Moist, well-drained
Hardiness
USDA 6b/7a / RHS H6

GROW A perennial deciduous shrub that can grow to several metres high and wide, it is also happy to be kept smaller with the use of secateurs. Prefers shelter but tolerant of considerable imperfection in this regard – my pepper orchard grew well in a windy field. Not wildly fussy about soil as long as extremes of pH, waterlogging and very sandy soils are avoided. Prune for shape and size only.

267

CATHERINE MACDONALD
Principal landscape
designer, Landform
Consultants, UK

Catherine MacDonald leads the design team at Landform Consultants,
creating award-winning gardens at flower shows as well as gardens and
landscapes for private and commercial clients. She previously worked
for landscape designers Luciano Giubbilei, Christopher Bradley-Hole and
Anthony Paul. *landformconsultants.co.uk*

Pisum sativum
Garden pea

This plant has significance for me as, along with its many pea family
relatives, it was the key plant used in my gold-medal-winning RHS Chelsea
Flower Show display for the Seedlip Garden in 2018. We used unusual
snap and snow pea cultivars bred by Dr Calvin Lamborn in the twentieth
century. They not only looked good, but the pods tasted great too!

GROW Great grown on pea sticks.

Type
Annual climber
Flowering
Summer
Height/spread
2.5m x 1m
Position
Full sun
Soil
Any
Hardiness
USDA 10b / RHS H2

Type
Evergreen tree
Flowering
Spring
Height/spread
12m x 8m
Position
Full sun, part shade, shade
Soil
Most, except very wet
Hardiness
USDA 6a–1 / RHS H7

Taxus baccata
Common yew

This plant can be clipped into shapes extremely well to give
form and structure to a garden, whether it's topiary in a dome
or beehive form, as flat cushions or even as a hedge. It is a dark
green evergreen native that can provide a wonderful contrast or
backdrop to a soft perennial planting scheme.

GROW Don't over water – it does not like wet feet.

Nepeta govaniana
Catmint

This yellow-flowering nepeta has more versatility than the lilac species,
as it is happy in full sun or partial shade. The foliage has a lovely smell,
and it has an upright habit. The flowers last long through the summer.
I first used this in the Squires 80th Anniversary Garden at the RHS
Hampton Court Flower Show in 2016 and have loved it ever since.
It's a tricky plant to get hold of though!

GROW It prefers a cool soil and can be cut back after flowering for a potential
second flush.

Type
Perennial
Flowering
Summer
Height/spread
90cm x 60cm
Position
Full sun, part shade
Soil
Any
Hardiness
USDA 6b/7a / RHS H6

Type
Deciduous grass
Flowering
Summer
Height/spread
50cm x 50cm
Position
Full sun, part shade,
full shade
Soil
Most, humus-rich
Hardiness
USDA 6a–1 / RHS H7

Hakonechloa macra
Japanese forest grass

A plant regularly used in my planting schemes. Although it's
deciduous, the leaves develop reddish-brown tones in the
autumn that persist into winter – it's a great grass for structure
and texture. It looks very effective planted in bold swathes or
monotypic blocks.

GROW Easy to grow. Cut back the fronds in late winter before new growth
shows through. Divide in spring.

Blechnum spicant
Hard fern

I like using a range of ferns in shade but this one is a star performer and personal favourite: it is evergreen and native. I particularly love the feathery frond shape and compact habit.

GROW Easy to grow in most cool, moist, shaded sites.

Type
Perennial
Flowering
Spring
Height/spread
50cm x 50cm
Position
Part shade
Soil
Moist, well-drained
Hardiness
USDA 6b/7a / RHS H6

Type
Evergreen fern
Height/spread
50cm x 50cm
Position
Part shade, full shade
Soil
Moist, well drained, poorly drained
Hardiness
USDA 6b/7a / RHS H6

Epimedium pubigerum
Hairy barrenwort

There are a vast range of deciduous and evergreen epimediums to choose from: this one has evergreen foliage that is great for ground cover and small white flowers. I love their heart-shaped leaves and I like that the flowers on the deciduous forms appear before the new leaves. Of the deciduous forms, *E. × rubrum* is a great choice as its leaves are tinted red in autumn. Epimediums are probably my most used plant in planting schemes.

GROW Propagate by division in autumn or after flowering. Every few years, cut back the leaves in early spring before the flowers appear to refresh the look of these plants.

Salvia nemorosa 'Caradonna'
Balkan clary 'Caradonna'

This is a wonderful salvia. It has upright purple flower spikes on dark stems and is a star performer in sun-loving schemes. A favourite of bees, it can often repeat flower after a mid-summer trim.

GROW Deadhead the flower spikes for more flowers. It is drought tolerant once it's established.

Type
Insectivorous perennial
Flowering
Spring
Height/spread
30cm x 30cm
Position
Full sun, part shade, sheltered
Soil
Acid
Hardiness
USDA 6b/7a / RHS H6

Type
Perennial
Flowering
Summer
Height/spread
50cm x 50cm
Position
Full sun, part shade
Soil
Moist, well-drained
Hardiness
USDA 6a–1 / RHS H7

Sarracenia purpurea
Common pitcher plant

This is my 'wild card' nominee. I have a large collection of *Sarracenia*, a genus of carnivorous plants. They are great in bog gardens, wet areas and in pots, if well watered. *S. purpurea* is the species I started with. It has low-growing, purple-toned pitchers, but other species can have bright green, tall, architectural pitchers that look very elegant.

GROW Use acid potting medium and ensure it is kept moist. It's a lime-hating plant, so use distilled or rainwater to water.

MATT COLLINS
Head gardener, Garden
Museum, London, UK

Matt Collins is an author, journalist and head gardener at the Garden Museum. He trained in horticulture at the Botanic Gardens of Wales and writes a monthly column for *The Telegraph* in which he brings to life the native landscapes of familiar garden plants. His most recent book, *Forest: Walking Among Trees*, was shortlisted for an Edward Stanford Travel Writing Award. *gardenmuseum.org.uk*

Type
Rhizomatous
herbaceous
perennial
Flowering
Spring
**Height/
spread**
80cm x
50cm
Position
Full shade,
part shade,
can be
planted
facing all
directions
but south
Soil
Moist
Hardiness
USDA 6a–1 /
RHS H7

Uvularia grandiflora →
Bellwort

Gardeners tend to keep a mental list of tried-and-tested 'doers', robust plants that can be relied upon. Sunny spot go-tos for me include cistus, catmint and acid-green euphorbias; for shade, however, I would reach for *U. grandiflora*, also known as merry bells. This intriguing yet trustworthy woodlander does something spectacular in conditions unfavourable to many perennials, lighting up in a mound of luminous yellow pendant flowers just at the peak of spring. It belongs to the damp-loving, gloom-brightening North American troop that I love – trilliums, dicentras, erythroniums, tiarellas; plants that stand proud beside a forest fern and, like true performers, vanish altogether once the show is over.

As with most new plants at the Garden Museum, I trialled merry bells first in pots, placed beneath our large mulberry tree on a shady ledge that I consider 'experiment corner'. After a winning first year, however, they were quickly elevated to the permanent planting, sharing ground with a gentle mist of maidenhair ferns and wild strawberries. Here, they're able to grab visitor attention from close to the brick footpath that encircles the museum's courtyard: something seasonal, vivid and effortlessly cheerful. Gardeners inclined towards a softer colour palette have the option of *U. grandiflora* var. *pallida*, with its pale cream flowers.

Much like a disporum, polygonatum or arisaema, even, this plant possesses a shade-plant physique ever more popular in gardens today: slim, stylish and leafy, albeit with accentuated colour. There is a mysteriousness to its flowers – particularly in the handkerchief-like drop and twist of the petals – that invites a closer look. The foliage, meanwhile, bears the freshness of new-season beech leaves, almost glaucous in their clarity. Attractive seed pods follow in summer, before the plant dies back fully to the ground. A spectacular perennial woodlander!

GROW It enjoys a rich, fertile soil with plenty of moisture – it lives for leaf mould. When growing them in pots, therefore, I mix a generous handful of bark chippings into the potting compost to improve water retention. Although the stems of *U. grandiflora* are relatively slender and can sometimes climb to almost a metre high, never be tempted to stake them, as this is a sure way to ruin the magnificent, natural architecture. If placed in the shadow of a tree or sizeable shrub, wind is unlikely to cause damage. Watch for slugs and snails in early spring, although shoots are usually well-developed by the time molluscs are at their most destructive. Best grown in repeated, scattered clumps.

Fritillaria acmopetala
Pointed-petal fritillary

Type
Bulbous
perennial
Flowering
Spring
**Height/
spread**
60cm x 10cm
Position
Full sun
Soil
Well-drained
Hardiness
USDA 8b/9a
/ RHS H4

For a time, I worked in Suffolk in the former garden of painter and highly influential plantsman Sir Cedric Morris (1889–1982), discovering many of his unusual plants still flourishing in the overgrown grass. Among the most enchanting were the spirited spring fritillaries, and among these the pointed-petal fritillary truly captured my heart. I read somewhere that this graceful, bold-headed flower was Morris's favourite, too; he described it as possessing an 'aristocratic elegance and aloofness'. Perhaps aloofness is what kept it thriving all these years after Morris died, but its elegance is what made me take notice. Thrilled to have found this fritillary, I introduced it into the Garden

Museum's little courtyard garden, growing it in simple terracotta pots each spring. Unlike many exquisite fritillaries, it is a reliable perennial and can be trusted to return and even naturalise into drifts when let loose in garden soil. In the wilds of Turkey and Syria they contend with stony scrub and airy woodland, so the herbaceous roots and woody stems of a mixed border or rock garden do little to deter its vigour. I prefer to use pots only because I like to champion intriguing plants, particularly those whose entire physique – linear leaves, architectural stems and pendulous, bobbing flowers – deserves centre stage.

F. acmopetala is a tall yet sturdy perennial fritillary, capable of stopping one in one's tracks with its richness of tone and unique form. On the outside, the petals run from deepest maroon to lemon-yellow – this colouration mixed via subtle streaks. As the name suggests, the petal tips are reflexed and pointed at the ends, revealing an inside of astounding gold that glows in the afternoon sunlight. Its scent has been described as 'foxy', but it is fairly nondescript.

GROW Whether planted as bulbs in the autumn or 'in the green' in spring, these fritillaries like good drainage – waterlogged soil can rot the bulbs, particularly in pots. Plant directly into soil or compost that's had plenty of grit mixed in, and for best effect, grow in multiples of six upwards. After flowering, allow the foliage to die back before cutting down. Keep a watchful eye for scarlet-red lily beetles, which devour fritillaries – pick them off when spotted. Best placed somewhere slightly sheltered, given the taller-than-usual stems.

Type
Herbaceous perennial
Flowering
Spring, summer
Height/ spread
1m x 50cm
Position
Full sun, part shade
Soil
Moist, well-drained
Hardiness
USDA 7b/8a / RHS H5

Aquilegia canadensis
Canadian columbine

Aquilegias are known for their overtly intricate flowerheads – an array of decorative folds, spurred sepals and protruding stamens held aloft on graceful, slender stems. And although their variety is wide – from the bicoloured mountain columbines to the violet, burgundy and spiky white cultivars of the European *Aquilegia vulgaris* – if I had to pick just one, it would undoubtedly be the bright crimson species *A. canadensis* (also known as red columbine).

I began growing this perennial only a few years ago but fell completely head over heels on first sight. Its blazing red, showy flowers open from late spring through to early summer and are of course the main draw, but these are complemented perfectly by the airy foil of a delicate, fern-like foliage. It is a plant of the North American woodland glade, spanning the east coast from Canada down to Florida, and they are as magnetic for me as they seem to be for copious pollinators – bumblebees in Britain, hummingbirds in their American homelands.

As red columbine is among the plant species first introduced to Britain by the Garden Museum's patron saints, the Tradescants – the father and son were celebrity gardeners of the seventeenth century – it feels doubly fitting to be cultivating them in the museum grounds. I'm more often attracted to muted colours, but there's something so electrifying about this particular red; surely every gardener should have at least one bold indulgence in their planting palette.

GROW Like all columbines, *A. canadensis* is best treated as a biennial or short-lived perennial, putting out foliage in the first year and flowers by the second. Attractive papery seedheads follow in summer, which can be collected for future sowings. Although red columbine will happily occupy a mixed herbaceous border, I have enjoyed growing it in individual terracotta pots (about 25–30cm), as this enables me to bring them under cover if necessary to protect against protracted cold spells. Adding plenty of sharp drainage to the potting mix also ensures they won't sit in damp, clumpy soil. Best placed somewhere a little sheltered on account of the delicate stems, although exposure is rarely an issue. No feeding necessary. Water well during the growing season and cut away any fungal-infected foliage at the base, making way for fresh, unfurling leaves.

JOSEPH ATKIN
Former head gardener,
Aberglasney, Wales

Joseph Atkin was the head gardener at Aberglasney for more than ten years. Aberglasney covers some 10 acres and features 20 different garden styles. *aberglasney.org*

Camassia leichtlinii
Camassia

This is a wonderful addition to meadows, herbaceous borders, woodland gardens and bog gardens. The tall blue spires in the spring work brilliantly with other bulbs such as tulips. It will come back every year and, as long as there is some rain, it flowers for nearly two months.

GROW One of the most useful bulbs for heavy soil.

Type
Bulbous perennial
Flowering
Spring
Height/spread
1.5m x 50cm
Position
Full sun, part shade, sheltered
Soil
Moist, well-drained
Hardiness
USDA 8b/9a / RHS H4

Type
Perennial
Flowering
Summer, autumn
Height/spread
1m x 50cm
Position
Full sun, part shade
Soil
Moist, well-drained
Hardiness
USDA 7b/8a / RHS H5

Salvia 'Day Glow'
Sage 'Day Glow'

There are a few other salvias that are just as good, but this one just seems to flower all summer. Neon pink is not for everyone, but with the right companions it's amazing.

GROW Here in Wales, I've found this to be bone hardy.

Lathyrus odoratus 'Matucana'
Sweet pea 'Matucana'

The old ones are still the best, and that is certainly the case for me with this sweet pea. The colour seems to go with almost anything and it has an excellent scent.

GROW Water well and deadhead or pick regularly.

Type
Annual climber
Flowering
Summer, autumn
Height/spread
2m x 40cm
Position
Full sun, part shade
Soil
Moist, well-drained
Hardiness
USDA 9b/10a / RHS H3

Type
Deciduous shrub
Flowering
Summer
Height/spread
6m x 6m
Position
Full sun, part shade
Soil
Moist, well-drained
Hardiness
USDA 6b/7a / RHS H6

Cornus kousa 'Miss Satomi'
Kousa 'Miss Satomi'

All of the new bracted cornus are excellent plants, but this was the visitors' favourite at Aberglasney with its wonderful pink-tinged bracts. It has good autumn colour, interesting fruit and a wonderful, long-lasting floral display. It pretty much does everything.

GROW As a small tree, 'Miss Satomi' is neat and has a steady growth rate.

Type
Bulbous perennial
Flowering
Late winter, spring
Height/spread
25cm x 25cm
Position
Full sun, part shade
Soil
Moist, well-drained
Hardiness
USDA 6b/7a / RHS H6

Narcissus 'Cedric Morris'
Daffodil 'Cedric Morris'

This wonderful little daffodil comes into flower before Christmas and keeps going well into spring. It has classic lemon-yellow trumpet flowers.

GROW Perfect for a small garden where a long season of interest is required.

CLAIRE GREENSLADE
Head gardener,
Hestercombe House &
Gardens, Somerset, UK

For more than a decade Claire Greenslade has dedicated herself
to preserving the historical integrity of Hestercombe's gardens,
which encompass Georgian, Victorian and Edwardian designs.
hestercombe.com

Berkheya purpurea →
Purple berkheya

This plant grows on silvery thorny stems and produces great mauve daisies from
a rosette of grey spiny leaves. The reason I love it so much is that it has been
one of my greatest achievements at Hestercombe. Gertrude Jekyll's 1904 plan
has berkheya growing in the wall. Our walls are very dry and hard to get plants
established in. I tried several times to plant it in them with no success. So, I tried
planting it near a wall and then waited until it went to seed. I wetted the wall with
a hose pipe and blasted the seed at the damp wall with a leaf blower. It worked!

GROW This plant needs very little care and thrives in dry soil. It just needs sunshine.

Type
Perennial
Flowering
Summer
Height/spread
75cm x 10cm
Position
Full sun
Soil
Dry
Hardiness
USDA 8b/9a
/ RHS H4

Type
Perennial
Flowering
Winter, spring
Height/spread
50cm x 1m
Position
Part shade, doesn't
like the wind
Soil
Moist, well-drained
Hardiness
USDA 7b/8a / RHS H5

Helleborus argutifolius
Holly-leaved hellebore

All hellebores are gorgeous and, quite frankly, I am pleased to have
anything that flowers in winter. This one has vibrant green flowers, spiky
leaves and looks quite architectural. It has a 'Jurassic' feel about it and
stands a bit more proud than most other hellebores. It also looks good
pretty much all year round and makes a great foliage plant.

GROW Keep the plant looking fresh by pruning out any parts as they go
over. Mulch with homemade compost in winter.

Type
Evergreen shrub
Flowering
Spring, summer
Height/spread
3m x 2m
Position
Full sun, does really well
against warm walls
Soil
Well-drained
Hardiness
USDA 7b/8a / RHS H5

Olearia phlogopappa
Dusty daisy bush

This is one of those plants that we always get asked about at
Hestercombe when it's in flower. It's a shrub that is prolifically
covered in small white daisies and loved by bees and other insects.
It makes a great backdrop to other flowers.

GROW Once established this plant needs very little care. We just prune
it after flowering to help maintain shape. It then produces more of its
pretty grey-green foliage.

Type
Perennial
Flowering
Spring, summer,
autumn
Height/spread
40cm x 1m
Position
Full sun, part shade
Soil
Dry
Hardiness
USDA 7b/8a / RHS H5

Erigeron karvinskianus
Mexican fleabane

Almost every nook and cranny of Hestercombe's formal gardens
is filled with this low-growing white daisy. It's a good gap filler
providing ground cover and growing in cracks in walls. It softens
all of architect Edwin Lutyens' hard landscaping and creates a
romantic feel across the garden.

GROW It is a fabulous self-seeder. If you want to get this plant growing
in your walls, plant a pot full of it next to the wall and let nature take
its course – it likes to decide where it wants to live! To stop the plants
getting too leggy, just cut them back hard after they have gone to seed.

JOE RICHOMME
Botanical horticulturist,
Royal Botanic Gardens,
Kew, UK

Joe Richomme is a botanical horticulturist working with Kew's outdoor temperate collections. These are plants that survive the UK climate, grown outside at the site in west London. He did his early training in the Kitchen Garden at Kew and still has an interest in edible plants. *kew.org*

Lysimachia clethroides
Gooseneck loosestrife

I love this plant's unique flower spike, which is curved like a goose's neck. It makes you wonder how it could have evolved that way – what advantage did this strange shape confer? It looks great too: different enough to catch the eye, but with a real understated elegance.

GROW Cut back to ground level when it starts to flag at the end of the season. Not as vigorous as some other lysimachias, but it still spreads if left unchecked. Spade around the clump after cutting back to make sure it stays in place. Once established it needs little specialist care and even stays nicely upright by itself without staking.

Type
Herbaceous perennial
Flowering
Summer
Height/spread
1m x 1m
Position
Full sun, part shade, sheltered
Soil
Any
Hardiness
USDA 6b/7a / RHS H6

Type
Biennial
Flowering
Spring, summer
Height/spread
4m x 1m
Position
Full sun, sheltered
Soil
Well-drained
Hardiness
USDA 9b/10a
/ RHS H3

Echium pininana
Giant viper's bugloss

These are a common sight on the verges in Jersey where I grew up. Not only do they make me think of home, but they are also a real reminder of how impressive plants can be in their efforts to reproduce – the flower spike can be up to 4m tall and seems to appear out of nowhere. It's such a showstopper.

GROW While possible to grow in milder areas, they are on the edge of being tender. You can try tying up the growing point with fleece for extra protection in cold spells, but these will struggle with any prolonged frost. They tend to rot and collapse at the base if the soil stays too wet, so aim to grow them in a well-drained spot. Make sure to plan for succession – being biennial they only flower a year (or possibly two) after germination and die soon after. Seedlings germinate readily in milder temperatures so leave some of these to mature if you're in the right climate, or make sure you plant new ones each year.

Epimedium alpinum
Barrenwort

This epimedium offers so much for a shady spot, and is good ground cover. It has delicate bronze foliage in spring and red leaves in autumn. The flowers of this particular species are also stunning – they're a cross shape with red on the outside and yellow on the inside, which makes them look like miniature jester hats. They're also small, so it feels like you're in on the secret when you spot them.

GROW The flowers are often held below the leaves. To get the best out of these, cut back the foliage early in the season before the flower stalks start growing. It will feel brutal, but as long as you do it early enough, you'll do no damage and the new foliage and flowers will be much more visible.

Type
Rhizomatous perennial
Flowering
Spring
Height/spread
25cm x 50cm
Position
Full shade, part shade, sheltered
Soil
Moist, well-drained
Hardiness
USDA 6b/7a / RHS H6

Type
Annual grass
Flowering
Summer
Height/spread
1m x 50cm
Position
Full sun, dappled
shade, open
Soil
Moist, well-drained
Hardiness
USDA 6b/7a / RHS H6

Briza maxima

Greater quaking grass

This grass is small but striking. When the specimen that we have at Kew is at its best (which is as it sets seed) I do a double take every time I walk past. The contrast between the spray of deep tan insectoid seedheads and the green of the foliage of new plants at the base is incredibly arresting, and it's a great demonstration of how a plant can bring a lot to the table without being too brightly coloured.

GROW Though annual, these quite happily self-sow if left to their own devices. If you leave seedlings through the winter and the foliage looks sad, don't be tempted to cut it back. It's better to simply comb out any dead material to neaten up the clump. Copes with dappled shade.

Eryngium × zabelii

Sea holly

Sea holly is so impressive for its ability to grow in the most unpromising of places. It can be found wild on sand dunes and in shingle, where its white-veined, spiky leaves and purple globe-like flowers always feel slightly alien in their appeal. It's something fantastically different, a testament to the variety of plant life. Cultivars of this particular hybrid cross (for example 'Jos Eijking' or 'Big Blue') have intense blue flowers and stems, making them even more of a draw.

GROW Too much organic matter around the crown can cause them to collapse so avoid mulching too heavily. Cut back when it begins to look tatty.

Type
Herbaceous
perennial
Flowering
Summer
Height/spread
75cm x 50cm
Position
Full sun, open
Soil
Well-drained
Hardiness
USDA 7b/8a / RHS H5

Paulownia tomentosa

Foxglove tree (SEE ILLUSTRATION PAGE 185)

While it flowers beautifully and prolifically as a specimen tree, coppicing or pollarding the foxglove tree has a different effect altogether – it produces metres-high stems in a matter of months, with oversized leaves up to 60cm across. I love the resilience of its response and the atmosphere created by the enlarged foliage is hard to beat.

GROW Once established, these don't need too much looking after, but keep an eye on them in hot weather for the first few years after planting to make sure they get enough water. Even as coppiced or pollarded specimens they take up a lot of room, so be aware of their surroundings. If coppicing or pollarding, prune in spring, making a clean cut with a saw a healthy distance above a bud roughly where you want your plant to sprout from. If coppicing, cut all the stems down to about 10cm off the ground.

Type
Deciduous tree
Flowering
Spring
Height/spread
12m x 8m (or 3m x 3m
if grown as a plant)
Position
Full sun, part shade
Soil
Well-drained
Hardiness
USDA 7b/8a / RHS H5

DANIEL JONES
Head gardener,
Morton Hall Gardens,
Worcestershire, UK

Daniel Jones undertook work experience at Chatsworth, Great Dixter and the Schynige Platte Botanical Alpine Garden in Switzerland and studied at RHS Wisley. In 2020 he became head gardener at Morton Hall Gardens where he enjoys looking after a complex and highly ornamental public and private garden. *mortonhallgardens.co.uk*

Fritillaria meleagris →
Snake's head fritillary

The flowering of the spring meadow at Morton Hall is one of the most impressive moments in the gardening year; it comes in waves from the early crocus to the camassia in late spring. But it peaks in mid-spring with the blooming of 250,000 naturalised snake's head fritillaries. The sight is made all the more special by a high proportion of the more unusual white-flowering form. En masse, they are an impressive sight, but the detail of the individual plant is just as beautiful. From the unfurling of the flower like a snake out of the grass to the extraordinary detail of the individual flowers. A great addition to the spring garden and particularly for naturalising in grass.

GROW This can be grown in almost any location, but a windy site may damage the flowers. The meadow at Morton Hall stays damp through the year owing to the heavy clay soil. Constant moisture, particularly in summer, is the key to successfully naturalising in grass. Allow the fritillaries to drop their seed before cutting the meadow in summer (late June), to encourage them to spread. Leave the hay for a while to allow the seed to drop.

Type
Bulbous perennial
Flowering
Spring
Height/ spread
25cm x 10cm
Position
Full sun, part shade
Soil
Moist, well-drained
Hardiness
USDA 7b/8a / RHS H5

Gentiana lutea
Great yellow gentian

I enjoy spending time walking in the Alps and I have taken many trips to Switzerland to visit family. It was only a few years ago, while undertaking my horticultural training, that I had the opportunity to look more closely at the plants of the Alps and I have spent many happy days working with the gardeners at the Schynige Platte Botanical Alpine Garden. The garden is reached by a 40-minute train ride and the tall, yellow flower spikes stand out in the meadows at the side of the track. It is very different from the other alpine gentians, emblems of the alpine flora with their small, blue, tubular flowers. It is a clump-forming herbaceous perennial with long fleshy roots and large, ribbed, blueish-green leaves at its base. It is the tallest of all gentian species and in the summer, its clusters of yellow flowers are arranged in rings up the flower spike.

I am also really interested in cultural and medicinal uses of the yellow gentian, and it was probably the first gentian to be cultivated owing to its medicinal uses. The root is known to ease digestion; it is fermented in the sun in a fruit liquor for six weeks to create a very bitter tonic, perfect after a cheese fondue or raclette! Crucially, the leaves are arranged oppositely, which is different to *Veratrum album*, a highly poisonous plant that is often confused with the yellow gentian, with potentially fatal consequences.

GROW Be patient! It can often take many years to produce a flower spike, but it will be worth the wait. *G. lutea* is a robust plant so can be grown in almost any location. However, a particularly windy location could damage the flower spike and shorten the season of flowering interest. It prefers full sun or part shade as it would get in the meadows of the Alps. Seed can be collected from plants that have flowered in the garden, and a cold frame is ideal as the seed requires a cold period for germination to occur. In the Alps, it grows in soils that are rich in calcium but it will tolerate most types of soil that remain moist through the growing season. Over many years it can spread to form large colonies.

Type
Herbaceous perennial
Flowering
Summer
Height/ spread
1.5m x 60cm
Position
Full sun, part shade
Soil
Moist, well-drained, most soil types
Hardiness
USDA 7b/8a / RHS H5

Tulipa 'Black Hero'
Tulip 'Black Hero'

In spring the borders of the kitchen garden and south garden at Morton Hall explode into life with nearly 6,000 tulips blooming together. The double late, peony-flower tulip 'Black Hero' is one of my favourites and very versatile – it works well with the pastel colours of the south garden and the hot colours of the kitchen garden. It is an elegant tulip with its velvety maroon-black flowers.

GROW We plant shallowly and mulch generously. This is so we can retrieve the bulbs easily after flowering and replace them with new bulbs the following year. To deter squirrels, we dust the beds with chilli powder. We feed the beds with a pelleted fertiliser in early spring and keep well watered. A sheltered location is best as strong winds can damage the flowers. Tulips need plenty of sun to produce their best blooms.

Type
Bulbous perennial
Flowering
Spring
Height/ spread
60cm x 50cm
Position
Full sun, sheltered
Soil
Moist, well-drained, fertile
Hardiness
USDA 6b/7a / RHS H6

Aesculus hippocastanum
Horse chestnut

The horse chestnut is widespread in English gardens and countryside, however at Morton Hall we have a particularly beautiful, majestic and elegant example that watches over the garden. It is the largest and oldest tree in the garden, having been planted when the house was built in the 1770s, making it over 250 years old. It is one of the healthiest horse chestnuts I have seen as it appears unaffected by the horse chestnut leaf miner which can cause unsightly foliage damage and premature leaf fall. We are also careful to look after it as best we can, clearing the leaves regularly from underneath the tree in autumn to discourage the leaf miner from overwintering in leaf litter. Carpets of winter aconite, snowdrops and *Cyclamen coum* alongside epimedium and erythronium bloom in spring and light up the base of this grand old tree.

GROW Requires a large, open site to appreciate its grandeur as it matures. Mulch during the winter around the root zone to lock in moisture and improve soil fertility and structure.

Type
Deciduous tree
Flowering
Spring
Height/ spread
25m x 20m
Position
Open
Soil
Moist, well-drained
Hardiness
USDA 6a–1 / RHS H7

Narcissus pseudonarcissus 'Plenus'
Daffodil 'Plenus'

The true sign that the dark winter days are behind us is the emergence of the first daffodils in spring. Narcissus is a fascinating and very diverse group of bulbs that I became interested in while studying at Kew, and this daffodil has a particularly interesting history. It was first described in 1629 by botanist John Parkinson and is a very rare form of the wild daffodil with double flowers, often given the common name Gerard's double daffodil after Parkinson's friend John Gerard. Like all daffodils, it is a bulbous perennial with grey-green narrow leaves. It is a small trumpet daffodil, producing a single, small flower with a paler outside and deeper yellow centre. It was once thought to be wild, but in 1933 botanist Herbert William Pugsley hypothesised that this daffodil, along with several other naturalised double-flowered daffodils, were relics of former cultivated varieties imported from France and the Netherlands. However, most double-flowered daffodils are sterile, meaning they produce no viable seed so spread by producing bulb-offsets underground over many years.

GROW Large clumps can be dug up and divided after flowering and moved to new areas in grass and in borders. To encourage it to produce healthy bulbs and spread by offsets, pinch off the developing seed pods as the flowers fade.

Type
Bulbous perennial
Flowering
Spring
Height/ spread
35cm x 10cm
Position
Full sun, part shade
Soil
Moist, well-drained, fertile
Hardiness
USDA 6b/7a / RHS H6

JOHN CULLEN
Nursery owner,
Lincolnshire, UK

John Cullen is the founder of John Cullen Gardens, which holds the National Collection of *Achillea millefolium* and specialises in plants for pollinators and scented plants. He has won multiple awards, including a gold medal at Blenheim Palace Flower Show. *johncullengardens.com*

Achillea millefolium
Common yarrow

'What is your favourite plant?' It is a question we're asked a lot at the nursery and one we struggle with. For us it is like choosing a favourite dog. We all have one but you really shouldn't say it out loud. But there is a plant I always gravitate towards, so much so that back in 2016 we decided to start assembling a National Collection as there wasn't one in the UK. This ensures that the plants don't disappear from the horticultural landscape because, as with anything, types of plants come in and out of fashion all the time. So now we hold the National Collection of *Achillea millefolium*.

They come in such a wide range of sizes, from the alpine variety 'King Alfred' to short varieties such as 'Moon Dust' and 'Little Moonshine', and all the way up to *A. filipendulina* 'Cloth of Gold'. They also come in a cacophony of colours, ranging from pale white and pale and acid-yellow to burnt orange, pastel, vibrant and fluorescent pink and on into rich and ruby reds and plums. The only colour you won't find is blue. Depending on the variety, the leaves are either pale green, mid-green or a bluish-grey green and have a fern-like appearance.

My all-time favourite is *A. millefolium* 'Pomegranate', which is super floriferous and a lovely warm, rich red. It's a real statement plant that will look equally good planted in a mixed border or in signature pots on the patio. Planting lots of varieties together creates a great melding pot of colours. The other great feature is that the flowers of some varieties change colour as they mature and age, so you often have five different shades of colour on the one bloom. Achilleas are also great for pollinators, in particular short-tongued bees and butterflies. Both of these love the flat landing pad, which allows them to land and drink up the nectar and collect the pollen.

GROW Achilleas need a sunny, open position and do not like to be planted under shrubs or trees – they will lean for the light. They are drought tolerant but need to be watered into their new homes and get established; you don't need to fuss over them. They are easy to divide and the best time to do this is late summer/early autumn. Sink a sharp shade through the middle and you will have two new plants.

Type
Herbaceous perennial
Flowering
Summer, autumn
Height/spread
Up to 2.5m x 1m depending on variety
Position
Full sun, open
Soil
Well-drained
Hardiness
USDA 8a–1 /
RHS H5–H7

JEKKA MCVICAR
Founder, Jekka's,
Gloucestershire, UK

Jekka McVicar is the founder of herb farm Jekka's. She is an organic grower of herbs and a horticultural author, designer and consultant. She is renowned for her knowledge of herbs and for growing and designing sustainable herb gardens. She has been awarded the RHS Victoria Medal of Honour and is the author of several books. *jekkas.com*

Artemisia dracunculus French
French Tarragon

Many years ago a girlfriend was visiting me at home and asked if she could have a bit of my French tarragon. I said, yes of course, help yourself. And then I thought: my gosh, you can't buy that anywhere. It was 1984 and that was the start of the herb farm. I love it and use it a lot in cooking and my mother used it a lot as well, but the fact that it was the start of Jekka's makes it one of my top choices.

GROW Propagate by cuttings or division.

Type
Perennial shrub
Flowering
Summer (rarely flowers)
Height/spread
90cm x 45cm
Position
Full sun
Soil
Well-drained, loam
Hardiness
USDA 8b/9a / RHS H4

Type
Deciduous subshrub
Flowering
Summer
Height/ spread
m x 2.5m
Position
Full sun
Soil
Well-drained, loam
Hardiness
USDA 9b/10a / RHS H3

Aloysia citrodora ↘
Lemon verbena

Lemon verbena casts me back to childhood every time I smell it. It always grew outside my great aunt's house, and when I was a child she used to make me lemon verbena tea, which she used to call *la tisane verveine*, so that's what I knew it as. When we moved here in the early 1980s, this warlock turned up and demanded 'vervain' from my garden, meaning *Verbena officinalis*, but I gave him lemon verbena – that didn't go down too well, and the whole family had a series of accidents after that.
I still love it, of course.

GROW Propagate from cuttings.

Zanthoxylum simulans
Sichuan pepper

My first plant was given to me by Mark Diacono when he started Otter Farm, and I've now cracked germinating it, so I'm really chuffed. I have two forms: a Chinese and Japanese one. Chefs travel miles for them, the flavour is amazing, stunning even. Though I did nearly kill a Michelin-starred chef who tasted one – he had such a sensitive palate! The clusters of yellow-green flowers are followed by the aromatic red fruit, which surrounds the black seeds.

GROW Sow seed in early spring until mid-summer under cover into modules or small pots. Plant outside when the threat of frost has passed.

Type
Shrub or small tree
Flowering
Summer
Height/spread
4m x 4m
Position
Full sun
Soil
Well-drained
Hardiness
USDA 6b/7a / RHS H6

Ferula assa-foetida
Assa-foetida

Again, this is very rare in the UK, and I can't remember how I got my first seed. It's beautifu. Like giant fennel, it's a member of the *Ferula* genus and it's the root that is used in Persian cooking and also in Indian cooking. Kids love that assa-foetida's other common name is 'devil's dung', basically because it smells of shit. Anything with 'foetida' in the name indicates that it smells, and assa means ass. So there you are. But it really is the most graceful plant. Any landscapers who see it here are amazed – Tom Stuart-Smith saw it one day and was wowed by its looks. It's stunning when it flowers: yellow umbels shoot up from this elegant leafy plant. For me, a plant has to be of use too, and I like it because it's culinary and it's medicinal.

GROW Unfortunately you have to kill the plant to extract its roots; it takes about seven years to flower, which you need it to do as it germinates from fresh seed. So you need a couple on the go.

Type
Herbaceous perennial
Flowering
Summer
Height/spread
4m x 1.5m
Position
Full sun
Soil
Well-drained, loam
Hardiness
USDA 8b/9a / RHS H4

Type
Evergreen tree
Flowering
Summer
Height/spread
6m x 5m
Position
Full sun
Soil
Well-drained
Hardiness
USDA 11 / RHS H1c

Bergera koenigii
Curry tree

I'm one of the few English growers of curry leaf, and it took me decades to crack how to grow it with UK material, either from cuttings or seeds. And now my trees are 20 years old. There's nothing like the scent of a curry leaf – it's aromatic, spicy and heady and takes you straight to the tropics.

GROW My number one tip? Grow it from seed... and wait.

KEVIN PRATT
Owner, Village Plants,
Cheshire, UK

Kevin Pratt was a landscape gardener for 35 years and now owns a rare plant nursery. He's a gardener, plantsman and speaker, has held two National Collections (*Fritillaria* and *Eucomis*), was an RHS gold medallist in 2006 and is an RHS Trials Committee member. *kevinpratt.co.uk*

Narcissus 'Cheerfulness'
Daffodil 'Cheerfulness'

My grandparents had a bulb farm growing cut flowers in Norfolk, and I spent all my holidays with them from an early age. Daffodils were their main product, and the principal bulb was *N.* 'Cheerfulness', a double button daffodil with the most powerful scent. Not just a useful cut flower in yellow and white that lasts and lasts in a vase, it is also an outstanding spring garden bulb. I always grow a few in the garden and in a huge pot by the back door. And guess what? They smell like my grandad!

GROW Always look for the largest bulbs. The biggest bulbs have the swelling dormant flowers waiting to push through the soil, so the large bulbs mean you're off to a good start. Plant 15cm deep. There is no need to do anything else, no lifting after flowering, just leave them in the soil to flower every year.

Type
Bulbous perennial
Flowering
Spring
Height/ spread
50cm x 10cm
Position
Any
Soil
Moist, well-drained
Hardiness
USDA 6b/7a / RHS H6

Fritillaria meleagris
Snake's head fritillary (SEE ILLUSTRATION PAGE 279)

When I was a child I would bike to my grandad's flower farm, but oddly enough it wasn't the farm that first inspired my love of plants. Rather, it was along the dykes that I found my first obsession, snake's head fritillary – or as my grandad would say, 'They're weeds, boy!' Still, at the age of ten I was captivated by these flowers, with their perfectly arranged squares of dark and light purple on nodding bells. I remember them shaking in the wind along with the long grass and dandelions. They were probably introduced to the dykes through discarded spent compost, an act practised by bulb growers in the 1950 and 60s, when old or small bulbs were thrown to the dyke edges along with chaff dust from the bottom of the bulb boxes. I actually still have a dozen of my grandad's original bulb boxes, each inscribed with C. H. Pratt. They are in daily use, 60 years after they were made.

GROW Fritillary bulbs don't like being dried out or kept warm. They are native to moist meadows, so wait until spring and buy them 'in the green' (growing with leaves). Buy them with flower buds and you will have a much better success rate. I have grown fritillaries in moist soil and dry sandy soil, but the best results have been in well-drained soil on a sunny site. Grow them in your borders or even free-draining pots and you will see how they appreciate good growing conditions. I often hear people say how they want to grow them in grass meadows – and you can, they look wonderful – but it is a project started for the next generation as you need years of patience.

Type
Bulbous perennial
Flowering
Spring
Height/ spread
30cm x 10cm
Position
Full sun, part shade
Soil
Moist, well-drained
Hardiness
USDA 7b/8a / RHS H5

Stachyurus praecox
Early stachyurus

Before I went to college I was a plant swot. My sister and I would practice plant names, hunting out the longest ones – *Mesembryanthemum* and *Metasequoia glyptostroboides* and, my favourite, *Juniperus × media pfitzeriana aurea*. When I finally arrived at college my plant vocabulary was off to a head start. One day, gazing out of the window, I saw the most outstanding shrub. Standing 2m high and dripping in 10cm-long pendulous spikes swaying in the breeze like they were waving at me. From that moment I was hooked. The tutor said it was a rarely grown shrub called *Stachyurus praecox*. When I tried to buy one from a nurseryman, nothing was available. They would say they aren't hardy, they're hard to grow, or that they die back in spring. Some even said they need a particular acid soil. Yet I continued to find them growing in every large garden from Hampshire to Northumberland. There is even a 50-year-old specimen local to us in Stockport.

GROW Get the site correct from the start, as they really dislike being moved after they have established their roots.

While at college I conducted experiments on 50 stachyurus plants (the results are on my website), thinking there must be a trick to growing these super attractive spring flowering shrubs. I found they have no pH preference but they are best in a moisture-retentive soil that doesn't dry out in summer. They grow really well in shade, but most importantly need shelter from cold spring winds. In 20 years of growing stachyurus, there have been a few late frosts which can damage the new growth, but they have always recovered after a few weeks.

Type
Deciduous shrub
Flowering
Winter
Height/ spread
4m x 2.5m
Position
Shade, sheltered
Soil
Moist, well-drained
Hardiness
USDA 6b/7a / RHS H6

Polygonatum
Solomon's seal

I have met many influential people in my years as a gardener – some have been rather prickly, with closely guarded growing secrets, but in general most gardeners are generous. One of the nicest is nurseryman Bleddyn Wynn-Jones. He introduced me to many plants, none more captivating than polygonatum. I have lost track of how many different species I've grown over the years. If you already grow the common *Polygonatum × hybridum*, which is around 1m tall, then you should consider the smaller growing (60cm) *P. odoratum*. This has distinctive stems that are angled side to side along the growing point. Another is *P. falcatum*, which is hardy with me in the north of the UK, although it only grows 30cm in our cooler climate. This beautiful species has a distinctive central silver stripe and is very eye-catching in our shade garden.

I must mention a few upright polygonatums, which grow vertically and don't exhibit the usual right-angle growth. They add height and structure to any garden design and the easiest to obtain is *P. cirrhifolium*, which has white flowers in summer followed for a short period by blood-red berries – until the blackbirds spot them. *P. zanlanscianense* has huge stems that grow through my shrubs and exhibit green-brown flowers in summer and black berries in autumn, which the birds also love. I don't think I have ever come across such an impressive perennial or one that gets so many comments along the lines of 'Wow, what's that?'.

GROW Polygonatums are shade-loving perennials that grow best with other shrubs as an understorey ground cover, but a few of ours have crept out into the sunshine and seem to grow very well.

Type
Herbaceous perennial
Flowering
Spring
Height/ spread
30cm-4m x 50cm
Position
Sheltered
Soil
Moist, well-drained
Hardiness
USDA 6a–1 / RHS H7

Sorbus
Rowan

From my 35 years of landscaping there are some plants that stand out – plants that are used again and again, reliable plants that are for a particular purpose. With shrubs there are too many to mention here. However, trees for small gardens pose many different problems. The trick is finding a tree with non-invasive roots and a head that allows some light into the understorey. Also, everyone wants a long-flowering, colourful tree.

Commonly called rowan or mountain ash, *Sorbus* is the genus we sell most of at my nursery. In spring, flowers appear, white and strongly scented. The nectar-rich blooms are highly prized by bees and insect life – I have even seen blue tits feeding on them. The loose branches carry fine leaves during the summer, and in autumn they turn the richest red. The wonderful spring flowers slowly develop during the summer and eventually swell into berries of many colours that are a favourite food for waxwings, redwings, thrushes, blackbirds and starlings.

My pick would be *Sorbus sargentiana*, which has large, long leaves that are shiny green in the summer and richly red in autumn, the usual white scented flowers in spring followed by the deepest red berries in autumn. My other favourite is *S. commixta* 'Embley', a tree I first saw in a supermarket car park! The red leaves coupled with the bright orange berries is a once seen, never forgotten moment. This is a much smaller tree and could easily be grown in a small garden. But an even smaller sorbus is the white fruiting *S. cashmiriana*. This has arching branches when laden with fruit. I have one, which after 20 years, is only now putting its head above a six-foot fence.

GROW *S. sargentiana* is a tall tree and perhaps over time a touch too big for the smallest gardens, but it is possible to prune it in winter to give it a smaller shape.

Type
Deciduous tree
Flowering
Spring
Height/ spread
Varies
Position
Full sun, part shade
Soil
Well-drained
Hardiness
USDA 6b/7a / RHS H6

Betula
Birch

Birch trees have some very attractive hazel-like catkins in the spring and the most superb golden yellow autumn foliage, but it is the incredible bark that is so useful in any small garden. There are usually many species available in garden centres – I'm going to completely dismiss the ubiquitous *Betula utilis* subsp. *jacquemontii*, and instead start with *B. u.* subsp. *j.* 'Doorenbos', sometimes called 'Snow Queen', found in the 1930s as a superior form within a batch of *B. j.* seedlings. This has a much clearer white bark that can peel at an early age. Often it is white while still at the garden centres at just two years old.

B. u. var. *prattii* was named after my ancestor, A. E. Pratt, an explorer who went to China at the turn of the last century. This is a tree with dark chocolate-brown bark that peels translucent brown like sweet wrappers in autumn. Sadly, this is not an accepted name any more, but it can still be seen growing in botanical gardens and is offered for sale under this name in many nurseries. Another is called *B. u.* subsp. *utilis* 'Dark-Ness' which has deep brown bark and light silver lenticels.

There are some fine red bark birch trees I have used many times – the bark can be pink or rose-red, always peeling lighter, but in some, such as *B. u.* subsp. *albosinensis* 'China Rose', the bark has the most amazing sunset orange-red bark in winter. 'Red Panda' and 'China Ruby' are also excellent garden subjects.

GROW Buy from a reputable supplier and ask for grafted trees.

Type
Deciduous tree
Flowering
Spring
Height/ spread
12m x 8m
Position
Full sun, part shade
Soil
Moist, well-drained
Hardiness
USDA 6a–1 / RHS H7

SOPHIE WALWIN
Head gardener, Somerville
College, Oxford, UK

Sophie Walwin is passionate about biodiversity enrichment and
sustainable horticulture. She loves to grow ferns and promote their wider
use in gardens. She previously worked as a horticulturist in the Temperate
House at Royal Botanic Gardens, Kew. *some.ox.ac.uk*

Cheilanthes tomentosa
Woolly lip fern

This is a fern I grow in my home garden and it brings me such joy because it
reminds me of a plant study trip to California in 2013. I travelled around the
foothills of the Sierra Nevada mountains with David Schwartz, an American
Fern Society member and amazing horticulturist, and there we found this
species growing on rock ledges.

Ferns are a diverse group of plants – there's a fern for every spot in your
garden! Also, ferns and flowering plants look great together. *C. tomentosa*
has lovely grey-green fronds with dense white hairs on both sides, giving it
a soft, fuzzy appearance. It is a dainty, beautiful plant and, extraordinarily
for a fern, grows happily in full sun and tolerates drought. In the wild it often
goes dormant in dry periods; its fronds curl up and it looks like it has perished,
but rain revives it in hours – the brown fronds unfurl and become green again.

At home I keep my specimens in pots and water regularly, which keeps the
pretty, hairy fronds upright and healthy. They look great among pots of lush,
green herbs or with other dryland plants, such as aloes and cacti. Desert
ferns such as *C. tomentosa* are grown beautifully at the Royal Botanic Garden
Edinburgh where they are planted outside in small raised beds under a rain
shelter, because in areas with high winter rainfall such as Edinburgh, these
ferns would gradually rot and die. In Oxford and southeast England, this isn't
so much of a problem.

GROW I've found *C. tomentosa* easy to grow in pots in sandy, loamy, free-draining
compost with a gravel mulch, but you could grow it in a border with very good
drainage – a rock-garden situation would be perfect. Shelter from rain to prevent wet
roots in winter. This species can form dense colonies after a few years. Feed sparingly
with a balanced fertiliser when growing in pots. Water regularly to maintain green
foliage, but allow to dry out slightly between watering. Prune any brown, curled-up
fronds at the base.

Type
Evergreen
fern
**Height/
spread**
50cm x 50cm
Position
Full sun
Soil
Well-
drained
Hardiness
USDA 8b/9a
/ RHS H4

VICKY CHOWN
Medical herbalist and
permaculture teacher,
London, UK

Vicky Chown is a trained medical herbalist. Together with Kim Walker, she runs the Handmade Apothecary and has co-written two books, *The Handmade Apothecary* and *The Herbal Remedy Handbook*. Vicky teaches food and medicine growing, and helped set up the Seed Saving Network through Omved Gardens. *handmadeapothecary.co.uk*

Achillea millefolium
Common yarrow

Yarrow is both beautiful and useful. A companion plant, it attracts beneficial pollinators and is a food source for many insects. Several cavity-nesting bird species use it to line their nests and studies suggest it has antimicrobial qualities that inhibit the growth of parasites. Humans have utilised these same antimicrobial effects in medicines for millennia.

The first part of yarrow's Latin name, 'achillea', hints to this medicinal use, referring to the Greek warrior Achilles. Achilles' mother, a sea nymph called Thetis, dipped him in the River Styx to make him immortal, leaving only his heel vulnerable to attack. It is said that he was slain on the battlefield by an arrow through the ankle and that yarrow popped out on the spot where his blood dropped. Yarrow is an excellent wound herb, containing many anti-inflammatory, healing and antimicrobial volatile oils, including chamazulene – a beautiful, electric-blue compound that can be added to creams and oils for wound healing and skin problems.

Yarrow is an erect perennial plant with feathery leaves that are evenly distributed along its strong stem. Larger leaves form at the base and can grow to 30cm in length in ideal conditions. But in compacted soil and regularly mown lawns the leaves stay small, only reaching 5cm, and the plant rarely flowers. The white-cream and sometimes pinkish flowers are borne in clusters of ray and disc florets that have a sweet, almost cheesy smell. Yarrow makes great ground cover as it spreads by both rhizome and seed. Allow it to grow in your lawn for a more biodiverse garden.

GROW The best thing about yarrow is that it grows well almost anywhere – many consider it a weed. It has no special requirements. It spreads but is very manageable. Most people already have some growing in their lawns, but with regular mowing it does not flower – even more reason to allow a wild patch to flourish in your garden!

Type
Herbaceous
perennial
Flowering
Summer
**Height/
spread**
50cm x 50cm
Position
Full sun
Soil
Moist, well-
drained,
prefers
a slightly
sandy soil
Hardiness
USDA 6a–1
/ RHS H7

LUCY SKELLORN
Gardener, designer and
researcher, Suffolk, UK

After a career in film and television design, Lucy Skellorn returned to her native Suffolk and retrained in horticulture. She has formed a National Plant Collection of *Iris* bred by her great-great-grandfather, Sir Michael Foster, who is known as 'the father of iris breeding'. *fosteririses.com*

Euphorbia mellifera
Canary spurge

Garden stalwarts, euphorbias are hardworking, adaptable and architectural plants. I have many different types in my garden and each delights with acid-green flowers. Their evergreen foliage demands little attention for maximum reward and their scented flowers are attractive to bees. I have planted this exotic-looking, magnificent euphorbia by the door so I can enjoy its delicious honey scent. It's an impressive plant without being showy and acts as a brilliant backdrop for bright colours – tulips in spring, dahlias in summer and winter bedding.

GROW If it starts to get leggy, prune back hard in spring. As with all euphorbias, handle with care – wear gloves to guard against the milky sap. A sheltered position is best – it can withstand a more exposed position but will lose more leaves during winter. Prune spent flowerheads at base.

Type
Evergreen shrub
Flowering
Spring, summer
Height/spread
2m x 2m
Position
Full sun, part shade
Soil
Well-drained
Hardiness
USDA 9b/10a
/ RHS H3

Eryngium giganteum ↘
Miss Willmott's ghost

I love the story behind this plant's common name – eminent horticulturist Ellen Willmott is said to have surreptitiously spread seeds of it in the gardens of friends and acquaintances. With its ornate leaves and branched, silvery seedheads, it is a great performer throughout the year, adding excitement as it seeds itself in unlikely places. It has architectural, silvery foliage and is attractive to wildlife.

GROW Seed is best sown fresh, tapped out of the seedheads before winter and lightly worked into topsoil or a gravel area. Do not cut back until the following spring.

Type
Biennial
Flowering
Summer
Height/spread
1m x 50cm
Position
Full sun
Soil
Well-drained
Hardiness
USDA 6b/7a
/ RHS H6

Glycyrrhiza yunnanensis
Yunnan liquorice

Closely related to liquorice, this fantastic, clump-forming plant comes into its own during autumn and winter. Gorgeous pinnate leaves give rise to lilac-purple flowers on tall stems, which develop into fluffy brown seedheads that remain throughout winter. Its upright habit also provides autumn colour and it is attractive to wildlife.

GROW This impressive plant is easily grown from seed. The seedheads can be used as winter decorations in the house. Clear dead foliage in spring to make way for new growth.

Type
Herbaceous perennial
Flowering
Summer
Height/spread
1.5m x 80cm
Position
Full sun, part shade, moderately sheltered
Soil
Moist, well-drained
Hardiness
USDA 7b/8a / RHS H5

Type
Rhizomatous perennial
Flowering
Spring
Height/spread
60cm x 30cm
Position
Full sun
Soil
Well-drained
Hardiness
USDA 6a–1 / RHS H7

Iris **'Mrs Horace Darwin'**
Bearded iris 'Mrs Horace Darwin'

Of all the irises in my National Collection, this is my favourite. Bred by my great-great-grandfather Sir Michael Foster in 1888, this delicate-looking white iris with purple veining is a tough little grower with an upright habit and is very floriferous. New leaves emerge tinged with purple at their base and look great among spring-flowering annuals.

The name adds to its delight: Mrs Horace Darwin was the daughter-in-law of the great Charles Darwin, with whom Sir Michael worked and was friends. A beautiful, historic, garden-worthy iris.

GROW It looks great at the front of a border; I mix it with *Cerinthe major* 'Purpurascens' and forget-me-nots. After flowering, remove spent flower stalks at the base and any browning leaves. Don't be too quick to cut back leaves, as their upright sword shape can be valuable in the border. Remove dead and dying leaves throughout the year. Dig up and divide every three years. If the soil isn't free-draining, dig in grit when planting. Always plant the rhizome so it sits above the soil level, allowing it to bake in the sun.

JAMES HORNER
Gardener and designer, East Sussex, UK

James Horner cultivates a space within an old walled garden where he collects and assesses plants for use in his practice and to help further his creative abilities as an artistic gardener. *jameshornergardens.com*

Heuchera sanguinea **'Alba'**
Coral bells 'Alba'

What attracted me to 'Alba' was its simple green foliage, which is quite something for a heuchera, because the masses of rhubarb-and-custard varieties that fill trolleys in garden centres are the norm. After years of growing this North American woodland plant I can strongly recommend using it in gardens in temperate Europe. It is persistently vigorous with a low habit close to the soil. Out of flower, 'Alba' is subtle and keeps foliage throughout winter. A single plant produces hundreds of flower stems, and the masses of dusty cream, bell-like flowers are popular with bees. Definitely a plant to repeat several times through a space, and equally splendid for the front row of the grandest mixed border.

GROW I make many cuttings of this by raiding plants for their basal shoots in early summer after flowering has finished. These go in my propagation box with a gently heated base, and within a year you will have a plant.

Type
Perennial
Flowering
Summer
Height/spread
50cm x 50cm
Position
Full sun, part shade
Soil
Moist, well-drained
Hardiness
USDA 6b/7a / RHS H6

Type
Perennial
Flowering
Spring, summer
Height/spread
30cm x 50cm
Position
Damp shade or cool cracks in sun
Soil
Moist, well-drained
Hardiness
USDA 7b/8a / RHS H5

Corydalis ochroleuca
Pale corydalis

Starting from just a small packet of seed, this has gently self-sown in the gravel and brickwork around the barn where I live. The entire plant (often known as pale fumitory), seems to settle precariously on a hairline anchor root, which can also find niches on vertical stone walls. The stems are brittle but cope with some exposure. What you get with this plant is a discreet and delicate lace of slightly glaucous green foliage, and tiny tubular white flowers with a yellow lip. This falls into a category of plants that, by settling into nooks and crannies, can in just a few years make a garden feel like it has been gardened for many more.

GROW Once you set these in motion, invite other gentle self-sowers such as the *Dianthus armeria* and *Erodium trifolium*. More prolific colonisers such as *Erigeron karvinskianus* and *Centranthus ruber* are beautiful, but be cautious if you have gravel paths nearby that you'd like to keep clean.

Rhinanthus minor
Yellow rattle

Type
Annual
Flowering
Summer
Height/ spread
50cm x 1m
Position
Full sun
Soil
Moist, well-drained
Hardiness
USDA 7b/8a / RHS H5

Cycling to my first gardening job in the Yorkshire countryside, I used to stop along the road verges to search for cowslips in spring. They were splendid and I didn't know anything about them. Later in the year the field scabious would come up in huge numbers, scattered across the thin soils. I later gained first-hand experience of managing meadows while working at Great Dixter in East Sussex. There, the meadows are many and of differing ages. One in particular was formerly a manicured lawn with a fleet of yew topiaries. Today, summer grasses sway in the breeze and thousands of common spotted-orchids set a technicolour stage for the dark solid yew forms.

The romance of wilder landscapes coupled with the collective conversation about gardens aiding wildlife has seen more land given over to meadow cultures in recent years, as well as placed them at the forefront of gardeners' preoccupations. One plant critical to the success of making meadows more diverse is yellow rattle, so much so that it could be regarded as the plant equivalent of a keystone species. Because it is parasitic on native meadow grasses, it physically weakens their growth rate to the point that it creates more space and opportunity for wildflowers – the mild UK winters mean grasses don't go dormant and are therefore quick off the blocks in spring. Yellow rattle's name comes from the days when children followed parents to work in the meadows and would play with its dried stem and rattle its seed pods.

GROW It is best to start yellow rattle's annual life cycle in autumn so it can germinate over winter. Allow the plant to dry fully before mowing, so that you keep perpetuating a good population.

MARK LANE
Principal designer, Mark
Lane Designs, Kent, UK

Mark Lane is the UK's first landscape designer and TV gardening expert/presenter in a wheelchair. Mark is a regular presenter for BBC's *Morning Live* and *Gardeners' World*; he is an ambassador for charities Greenfingers and Groundwork, and a trustee and co-chair of Gardening with Disabilities Trust. *marklanedesigns.com*

Vernonia arkansana 'Mammuth' →
Arkansas ironweed 'Mammuth'

Type
Herbaceous perennial
Flowering
Summer, autumn
Height/ spread
2.5m x 1m
Position
Full sun, part shade, open
Soil
Moist, fertile, but will also do well on poorly-drained
Hardiness
USDA 6a–1 / RHS H7

I love height, colour, texture, shape and form in the garden, and *V. arkansana* has all of these characteristics in abundance. I love it for the late clusters of deep purple, sometimes almost magenta thistle-like flowers that sway in the wind. Where I live we are surrounded by fields on all sides and, being in a small valley, we get quite a bit of wind, but ironweed is strong and robust, and no matter how much force it comes up against, it remains tall and proud. Being such a tall plant, it is great used either towards the back of a border or towards the centre, underplanted with late-flowering symphyotrichum, helenium, rudbeckia and ornamental grasses.

I love naturalistic planting schemes, which I call 'contemporary wild', and this plant looks good all the way through to winter with its fluffy white seedheads that age beautifully to a rusty orange, hence its common name. If you like to attract bees, butterflies and other beneficial pollinators to your garden then you will not be disappointed. Throughout autumn, it is covered in them, and the gorgeous seedheads also become small nesting spots during winter for ladybirds and other insects. The flowers also make great cut flowers.

GROW I have found it to be pest- and disease-free, and mainly grow it in full sun. I also have a white form which grows happily in partial shade. It is the perfect plant for our changing climate. It loves high summer temperatures and very cold winters. It can be found in the midwest of the USA where it grows on open prairies, so it does well across the UK and Europe.

It does have coarse green, toothed leaves, but these are obscured by underplanting it with tall ornamental grasses such as *Miscanthus sinensis* 'Ferner Osten', *M.* 'Kleine Fontäne' and *Molinia caerulea* subsp. *arundinacea* 'Transparent', as well as *Verbena bonariensis*, *Rudbeckia hirta* 'Prairie Glow' or *Perovskia* 'Blue Spire'. In an area of my garden that is particularly dry, I also grow *Vernonia noveboracensis*, which comes from eastern USA, and I find it to be more drought tolerant.

At time of planting, mix in some moss to retain moisture in the soil. No difficult feeding or watering requirements. Leave the faded leaves and seedheads for winter interest. Cut back to ground level in early spring. Mulch in spring with well-rotted homemade compost to deter weeds and retain moisture. Deadhead to prolong flowering. Can be easily propagated by collecting dry seed or by division.

Baptisia australis
Blue false indigo

Type
Herbaceous perennial
Flowering
Summer
Height/ spread
1.2m x 1m
Position
Full sun
Soil
Well-drained
Hardiness
USDA 6a–1 / RHS H7

I love this plant. I grow the blue version, but I'm really tempted to grow the other varieties in gorgeous shades from white to chocolate-purple. The flowers may only last for a couple of months, but when they are out they really catch your eye. They are pea-like, and I have them growing in my blue and yellow borders as well as my long border. I leave the black seed pods on over winter, as well as the stems with whorls of leaves. It looks tender but is fully hardy.

GROW This sits alongside *Amsonia tabernaemontana* in my blue and yellow borders, with its small clusters of light blue star-like flowers. The textures of each plant work really well with each other and both like well-drained soil and sunny positions.

Lupinus arboreus **blue-flowered**
Tree lupin

I have the blue-flowering version of the usually yellow-flowing tree lupin, which is a great shrub that forms soft mounds of grey-green palmate foliage topped with lupin-like spikes. This too grows in my blue and yellow border, and is doing so well that it has self-seeded – so much so, that I need to thin them out. They look amazing when in flower, and the bees and butterflies love them. One year a branch collapsed under some heavy snow and split. I left it until the end of winter/early spring and noticed that it was still growing. For some strange reason I didn't cut it off, but bound the split branch with some electrical tape (the only thing to hand at the time) – incredibly, it survived and looked stunning in summer.

GROW It likes well-drained, slightly acidic soils. Sometimes they can get a little top heavy and will collapse, but I find if I prune back hard in early spring, they remain at around 90cm rather than towering too high. You need to give them space, however, as they do spread out to around a metre.

Type
Evergreen shrub
Flowering
Spring, summer
Height/ spread
2m x 1m
Position
Full sun, part shade, sheltered
Soil
Well-drained, acid
Hardiness
USDA 8b/9a / RHS H4

Digitalis ferruginea **'Gigantea'**
Foxglove 'Gigantea'

I removed an old pond a few years ago and in its place planted up a prairie border using *Molinia caerulea* subsp. *caerulea* 'Poul Petersen', *Persicaria amplexicaulis* 'Firetail', *Aruncus* 'Horatio', *Deschampsia cespitosa* 'Goldtau', *Sesleria autumnalis* and these wonderful towering digitalis, to name just a few of the plants. They have reached 1.6m in this border, with wonderful evergreen foliage. They are often described as short-lived perennials, but they have come back year-on-year for four years and show no signs of slowing down. In fact, they have multiplied wonderfully into large clumps, which I'll divide in the spring. The tubular, rust-orange flowers with red veining are just exquisite, and punctuate the grasses here and there. The bees, hoverflies and other beneficial pollinators love them. They are growing in partial shade, are west-facing and are a delight for mid-summer wonder.

GROW Despite their height they don't take up much room close to the soil, meaning that they can be scattered through a planting scheme with great ease.

Type
Short-lived perennial
Flowering
Summer
Height/ spread
1.6m x 50cm
Position
Full sun, part shade
Soil
Moist, well-drained
Hardiness
USDA 6a–1 / RHS H7

JANE MOORE
Head gardener, author and
broadcaster, Bath, UK

Jane Moore is a speaker at gardening clubs and events. She has
been a guest presenter on *Gardeners' World* and won the Relais
& Chateaux Garden Trophy for her garden at the Bath Priory Hotel.
She is the author of *Planting for Butterflies* and *Planting for Wildlife*.
twitter.com/janethegardener

Nigella damascena
Love-in-a-mist (SEE ILLUSTRATION PAGE 74)

This is such an easy-to-grow,
delicately beautiful annual
that is always early flowering.
It reminds me of gardening
with my dad as a child. It's one
of the first plants I remember
growing – sowing the seeds
with him and loving the wiry,
crown shape of the flowers.

GROW Scatter the seeds from the
shaker seed pod to propagate.

Type
Annual
Flowering
Summer
**Height/
spread**
50cm x 50cm
Position
Full sun
Soil
Well-
drained
Hardiness
USDA 9b/10a
/ RHS H3

Betula pendula
Silver birch

I love silver birch trees,
especially in winter when their
fine, wispy habit makes them
look so graceful. They're one
of those trees that just seem
to go with everything and look
good in any type of planting
scheme, whether it's modern
or naturalistic.

GROW A very tolerant tree suitable
for most aspects and soils.

Type
Deciduous
tree
Flowering
Spring
**Height/
spread**
10m x 5m
Position
Full sun, part
shade
Soil
Moist, well-
drained
Hardiness
USDA 6a–1
/ RHS H7

Fritillaria meleagris
Snake's head fritillary (SEE ILLUSTRATION
PAGE 279)

This is a beautiful and delicate
flower. I have managed to
naturalise some in a 'spring
glade' corner of the garden
where every spring its flowers
always make me smile and wish
longingly that I could paint.

GROW An ideal bulb for
naturalising in grass.

Type
Bulbous
perennial
Flowering
Spring
**Height/
spread**
30cm x 10cm
Position
Full sun, part
shade
Soil
Moist, well-
drained
Hardiness
USDA 7b/8a
/ RHS H5

Hesperis matronalis
Dame's violet

A brilliant plant for butterflies,
this is super for early flowers
and produces lots of them.

GROW The beautiful purple flowers
are long lasting through spring and
summer and feed early-emerging
butterflies such as the orange-tip.

Type
Biennial,
short-lived
perennial
Flowering
Spring,
summer
**Height/
spread**
1m x 50cm
Position
Full sun, part
shade
Soil
Moist, well-
drained
Hardiness
USDA 6b/7a
/ RHS H6

KATY MERRINGTON
Cultural gardener,
Hepworth Wakefield,
West Yorkshire, UK

Katy Merrington is cultural gardener at an award-winning art gallery and public garden. She works closely with the garden's designer Tom Stuart-Smith and is responsible for nurturing the planting with a team of dedicated volunteers. Katy has worked at Royal Botanic Garden Edinburgh and Longwood Gardens in Pennsylvania, USA. *hepworthwakefield.org*

Type
Herbaceous perennial
Flowering
Summer
Height/ spread
1.5m x 50cm
Position
Full sun,
Soil
Moist, well-drained, tolerant of poor soil and drought
Hardiness
USDA 6a–1 / RHS H7

Liatris pycnostachya ↘
Kansas gay feather

This is a herbaceous perennial that shape-shifts through the seasons. It brings height to perennial borders in mid-summer, with a flowering stem that dries and remains into winter as a slender line. It begins with low linear leaves, then puts up a flowering spike nearly as tall as a person. In summer the flower spike changes from green to purple and hundreds of tiny flowers open from the top downwards, creating narrow columns of feathery purple. The flowers are striking in their verticality, standing upright like a cat's tail and occasionally curling at the end with a living eccentricity. Sometimes liatris grows at a curiously comical angle, as its line meanders through the air seeking the vertical. They look like lines drawn in space and remind me of artist Paul Klee's lovely idea of a drawing being 'an active line on a walk'.

GROW Native to central and southeastern North America, *L. pycnostachya* likes full sun and a free-draining soil. As one of the tallest species in the *Liatris* genus, it is narrow and wiry and so grows well among other herbaceous perennials that offer support. This prairie dweller does not enjoy wet soil in winter or being mulched too heavily around its collar. Can cope with windy weather if sited amid densely planted perennials. Cut back old vegetation in late winter/early spring before the new growth emerges.

Echinacea pallida
Pale purple coneflower

E. pallida are coneflowers and as such are true to their name: they begin and end their flowering process with the central cone. Dynamic sun lovers, these echinacea offer rich rewards to pollinating insects and provide interest in the garden from summer through to winter. In mid-summer the linear rays appear from the centre of the flower, pale pink like rose lemonade. They lengthen and lengthen, reflexed back until they eventually fade and fall away. The seedheads remain and withstand the winter weather with an intense darkness – they act as inky silhouettes, looking beautiful against golden grasses.

GROW This pale purple coneflower enjoys free-draining soil and does not like sitting in wet soil in winter. Self-seeds readily when happy. Enjoys an open site and can withstand some breeze as long as planted amid other perennials offering support. Cut back old vegetation in late winter/early spring before the new growth emerges.

Type
Rhizomatous perennial
Flowering
Summer
Height/spread
1.5m x 50cm
Position
Full sun, open
Soil
Moist, well-drained tolerant of poor soil and drought
Hardiness
USDA 7b/8a / RHS H5

Eryngium yuccifolium
Rattlesnake-master

Rattlesnake-master is always elegant and very robust. The leaves are coarse, fibrous and resilient – archaeologists in North America have found ancient shoes made from them. The leaves, stem and flower are duck-egg blue and remain solid and turquoise all summer before they settle into a brown colour for winter. An architectural perennial that brings height and elegance to the border with its refined outline and subtle tones.

GROW It is important to make sure the crown of the plant is kept free of mulch and leaf litter in winter, as the plant resents wet winter weather and can rot at the base if sitting in damp conditions. Enjoys a bright and open site. Cut back old vegetation in late winter/early spring before new growth emerges.

Type
Herbaceous perennial
Flowering
Summer
Height/spread
1.5m x 50cm
Position
Full sun, open
Soil
Tolerant of poor soil
Hardiness
USDA 8b/9a / RHS H4

JAKE HOBSON
Founder, Niwaki, Dorset, UK

Having studied sculpture at the Slade School of Art, Jake Hobson won a travel award to Japan. A trip to see the cherry blossom turned into two years, which included working at a traditional tree nursery in Osaka. Back in the UK, he developed a pruning style inspired by what he'd learned and founded garden tool store Niwaki. *niwaki.com*

Cryptomeria japonica var. *radicans*
Radicans Japanese cedar

I'm not really a gardener. I much prefer climbing up ladders and chopping things down – what you'd call pruning, but quite specifically pruning in Japanese styles. While living in Japan I was introduced to the art of pine pruning (very tricky) and *karikomi* (easier, using shears, much like topiary), but I really fell in love with the way they pruned *Cryptomeria japonica*. In Japanese, it is called *kitayama daisugi*.

Firstly, the tree. As a timber-producing conifer it is planted over much of the country, swathing the mountain sides along with Hinoki cypress and pines. It is everywhere, to the extent that come the spring, its release of pollen is a massive cause of hay fever. Old growth forests and venerable old trees in temples and shrines can grow to be enormous, and the effect of walking through places like the cemetery in the mountaintop town of Koyasan is quite extraordinary, rather like exploring the redwoods of California, but with the added spice of incense and Buddhist chanting in the air.

To recreate a sense of this mountain magic on a smaller scale in gardens, the trees are pruned in a curious way – they're effectively coppiced a couple of feet off the ground, producing multiple stems all rising from one short trunk. As the multi-systems grow, their side branches are removed, leaving only the newest whorls at the top. This technique began in the mountains north of Kyoto where the trunks were, and still are, produced for timber – the tree can be harvested without actually chopping it down and the trunks, because their side branches are removed each year as they grow, are knot-free (highly desirable for certain elements of traditional Japanese buildings).

I love the balance of the fresh new trunks reaching for the sky, sitting atop the heavy squat trunk, and I love the strong verticals the bare trees create – a rare element in many gardens – but most of all I love the technique. Chop the tree at knee height, wait for it to resprout, and then chop the side branches off as the new trunks grow. It's a bit harder than that of course, but it's a lovely process that owes more to woodcraft – coppicing and pollarding – than to topiary.

GROW Try to get a good dense plant that stays green over winter (not one that reddens).

Type
Evergreen conifer
Flowering
Spring
Height/ spread
15m x 6m
Position
Full sun, open
Soil
Moist, well-drained
Hardiness
USDA 6b/7a / RHS H6

MARK ROWE
Assistant park manager,
the Regent's Park,
London, UK

Mark Rowe is responsible for the plant collections and horticulture
in the Regent's Park. He is interested in nurturing soil biology through
organic mulches, bio-stimulants and compost teas. He has worked at
a tree nursery in Germany and Brisbane Botanical Gardens in Australia.
royalparks.org.uk

Nymphaea 'Candidissima'
Waterlily 'Candidissima'

I find it hard to say that I have a favourite plant. Some plants have a meaning
for me by way of association with a person, a place or a time in my life. Often,
when outside, a particular plant in a certain light, or against a certain backdrop,
its scent, colour or foliage, will grab my appreciation. However, when I really think
about it there has always been one plant which, since the age of seven when I
first started to dig a pond with my father, I have rarely lived without. And that's
water lilies. There are not many I dislike, except maybe the dark reds which seem
too unnatural in a pond for me, but 'Candidissima' would be my first choice.
It suits most ponds and has small, sweet-scented white flowers with a yellow
centre surrounded by deep green leaves.

GROW It should be planted 30–60cm deep, so can be planted close to the pond edge.
If planted where growth needs to be restricted or on a clean hard liner, use a 3.5 litre fine
mesh pot and divide and repot every 3–5 years. However, in the lake at Queen Mary's
Garden in the park – which is clay-lined and has several centimetres of silt – I want large,
spreading clumps that look after themselves, so I have taken to splitting the sides of the
aquatic pots so that the root rhizomes can grow out into the lake bed.
  Where possible, deadhead as flowers fade and remove dying leaves, as much for the
pond's health as for aesthetics. Pests and diseases are not really a problem – remove
any leaves eaten by leaf miners and, if water lily beetle is an issue, submerge the leaves
to shake off the beetles.

Type
Aquatic
perennial
Flowering
Summer
**Height/
spread**
60cm x 75cm
Position
Full sun, at
least six
hours per
day
Soil
Medium to
heavy loam
Hardiness
USDA 7b/8a
/ RHS H5

Alchemilla mollis
Lady's mantle (SEE ILLUSTRATION PAGE 190)

A number of plants are described as 'good doers' – no-fuss plants that do well
under varying conditions. This is one of those plants. In my experience, it can put
up with pretty well any conditions, even reasonably dry soils once established.
It takes its name from Arabic meaning 'little magical one'. The fan-shaped,
serrated leaves complement other leaf shapes, especially long, narrow leaves
such as grasses. The lemon-green flowers fit into most flowering schemes. If
you cut it back when it looks tired and untidy, within a few weeks it's back in
leaf looking fresh again. It can be used in any type of garden, even very formal
and minimalist planting schemes, lightening sharp lines and brightening dark
foliage. But for me, the real joy of *A. mollis* are those mornings when conditions
are right and I have woken up early enough to witness the beads of water at the
leaf edges sparkling in the sunlight. Caused by high soil moisture and humidity,
guttation is a process where some plants can rid themselves of excess water
through specialised cells called hydathodes. It reminds me of the wonderful
adaptations plants make to survive environmental conditions, and some of the
plant science I used to know so well.

GROW Best grown in cool, moisture-retentive soil in semi-shade, where the light green
foliage and yellow-green flowers will stand out. Add plenty of compost when planting and
don't be afraid to cut back hard and water well after flowering for a flush of new growth
and possibly a second flush of flowers. Feed with a general fertiliser in spring. Lift and
divide every few years if required. Pest and disease free.

Type
Herbaceous
perennial
Flowering
Summer,
autumn
**Height/
spread**
50cm x 50cm
Position
Full sun, part
shade, full
shade
Soil
Moist, well-
drained
Hardiness
USDA 6a–1
/ RHS H7

Cryptomeria japonica 'Elegans'
Japanese cedar

I have always found conifers difficult to identify and remember, especially during plant identification tests back in my college days. However, when I first saw *C. japonica* 'Elegans' I was amazed by its feathery foliage and autumnal colours, unlike any other conifer I had ever seen before, and so I've never had a problem identifying or spelling it. It is a fantastic plant, permanently in its juvenile foliage form, which gives it a soft feathery texture. In autumn and over winter it turns a purple-bronze, reverting to its blue-green foliage in spring. Suitable as a specimen shrub or at the back of the border as a foil for other plants.

GROW Best established by planting small plants, which will quickly grow to catch up with those at a larger size, however they will be better rooted and more stable. Plant in a sunny but sheltered position that will catch the winter sun for part of the day to illuminate its glorious colours. Prune to maintain a central leader if required, cut back to maintain size. If space is an issue, plant 'Elegans Compacta'.

Type
Evergreen conifer
Height/ spread
8m x 3m
Position
Full sun, part shade
Soil
Slightly acidic, moisture-retentive, deep soil, but it is tolerant
Hardiness
USDA 6b/7a / RHS H6

Delphinium elatum 'Amadeus'
Larkspur 'Amadeus'

Type
Herbaceous perennial
Flowering
Summer
Height/ spread
1.5m x 1m
Position
Full sun
Soil
Moist, well-drained
Hardiness
USDA 7b/8a / RHS H5

My father, a better gardener than I'll ever be, loved his delphiniums. He sowed seed both bought and collected from his own plants, and took cuttings. Apart from the veg seedlings, propagated delphiniums were the only other thing to take up room in the greenhouse and in front of my west-facing bedroom window. I'm not aware of any particular cultivar he enjoyed over others, but 'Amadeus' is my favourite, with deep blue-purple flowers. When I moved to the Regent's Park, I was delighted to find that there was a collection of *D. elatum* cultivars. It's not considered the easiest of plants to grow, but the challenge and reward make them worthwhile.

GROW Deadhead after flowering, cutting back to a healthy leaf. I have found supporting flowering stems with a cage of three stout canes and three or four circles of garden twine better than supporting each individual stem. Feed with a high potassium fertiliser in early spring and after the first flowering. Do whatever you can (and your conscience allows) about slugs and snails. Propagate from basal cuttings in spring; root in perlite to increase stock and to move to new positions every few years to avoid disease.

Trachelospermum jasminoides
Star jasmine

I'm not sure when I first came across this plant, but it wasn't until I had been a professional gardener for some time. For that reason it has always felt to me like a modern plant. I think it is best suited to contemporary landscaping. In my opinion it is by far the best evergreen climber, particularly as a screening plant, but it can also be used for hedging. It has deep, glossy green leaves, which are bronze for a few days when young. Its summer flowers have an almost overpowering jasmine-like scent. It requires little attention apart from cutting back to keep it in shape in early spring. Just make sure you grow it on a good, long-lasting support.

GROW Plant where it's going to get a good six hours of sunlight. I have it near the back door, hiding the fence, where it gets the morning sun for a few hours but doesn't produce much in the way of flowers compared to a neighbour of mine who grows it in her front garden as a hedge that gets the sun from 10am onwards. That said, the leaves of mine are dark green and hers more bleached. I recommend using a liquid feed for acid-loving plants a few times during the growing season. Plant near your entertainment area and the scent and brightness of the flowers at dusk will be memorable.

Type
Evergreen climber
Flowering
Summer
Height/ spread
12m x 6m
Position
Full sun, part shade
Soil
Well-drained loam or sand, prefers slightly acidic
Hardiness
USDA 8b/9a / RHS H4

Lolium perenne
Perennial ryegrass

Wildflower meadows are now being championed, which is great. Over the last 20 years I must have created quite a few hectares of urban meadows and managed and improved many more. However, common grass lawns are still a must, in my view, and much more suitable for smaller areas than wildflower long grass. Of all the types of lawn grass, I think perennial ryegrass is the best, with selected cultivars used for everything from Premier League football clubs to the back garden.

What's not to like about the smell of freshly cut grass? Or about lying down on it or walking barefoot across it and feeling its soft, bouncy texture? A lawn is a place for playing games or sports, a place where many childhood memories are made, a place to entertain friends, a stage for the rest of the garden. As a soakaway for downpours and for its cooling effect, it's much better for the environment than paving. Yes, you must cut it regularly, which helps to keep the pollen count down, but our patches of grass give us so much for so little.

I admit I have always liked cutting grass as a task, and I appreciate a deep green, striped, well-maintained lawn. But it wasn't until I had the responsibility of looking after the 14 hectares of sports turf at the Regent's Park that I really started to appreciate grass as a plant, and particularly perennial ryegrass cultivars. It's been exciting and challenging to learn about their cultivation. Due to the money involved in premier sports, the science behind the breeding of these cultivars has produced finer leaves, seed that germinates at 5°C, and grass that can be cut down to 12mm. The requirements to grow it at its best have been researched to the nth degree.

GROW It's the choice of seed that will give you a good, hard-wearing lawn with relatively low maintenance, although the more maintenance you put in the better the lawn will look. Mow once a week when actively growing. Regular cutting causes the plant to 'tiller', which means producing more leaves from the base, resulting in a thicker, lusher sward of grass. Also by cutting regularly the job is quicker, easier and puts less stress on the plant, as you are not taking away so much of its energy-producing leaf.

The more you put in the better the result. Cut once a week when actively growing, but don't fret if you miss a week. Rake to remove thatch and moss in the spring and apply a high nitrogen fertiliser. Apply a high-potassium fertiliser in the autumn. Fork or spike at varying depths from 20cm down to 30cm two or three times a year. Apply 2.5cm of water a week.

Type
Perennial grass
Flowering
Summer
Height/ spread
10cm x 3cm
Position
Open, full sun, at least 6 hours sun a day
Soil
Moist, well-drained
Hardiness
USDA 6a–1 / RHS H7

JAMES CROSS
Head gardener, Bishop's
Palace, Somerset, UK

James Cross worked at Sissinghurst Castle Gardens, Sheffield Park Gardens and the Courts Garden in Wiltshire before joining Bishop's Palace in 2004, where he and his team have created a diverse 14-acre garden. *bishopspalace.org.uk*

Hydrangea quercifolia
Oak-leaved hydrangea

This is a great plant with unusual, architectural, oak-shaped leaves that are deep green in spring and summer and rich red and purple in autumn. It also has fantastic long-lasting creamy-white conical panicles of flowers. It is simple to grow and easy to propagate – particularly from naturally occurring layering, but also from softwood cuttings. Although fairly tough, it appreciates some protection to form its best shape.

GROW I find it looks best if you thin out older stems back to the base and allow it to grow as tall and wide as it would naturally.

Type
Deciduous shrub
Flowering
Summer, autumn
Height/spread
1.8m x 2.5m
Position
Full sun, part shade, sheltered
Soil
Moist, well-drained
Hardiness
USDA 7b/8a / RHS H5

Persicaria polymorpha
Alpine knotweed

This is such a useful plant and is interesting in bud, in flower and when it has gone to seed. It looks incredible in the Bishop's Palace garden at the foot of the windows of the ruined medieval great hall. A tough plant, it nevertheless benefits from a slightly sheltered location. It has upright stems and masses of frothy spikes of creamy-white flowers that sit above large, pointed persicaria leaves, which form big, strong clumps. The flowers appear in summer, before turning into reddish brown seedheads that can look almost as impressive.

GROW I apply a decent layer of mulch and fertiliser in early spring and it thrives on that. Easy to divide and propagate.

Type
Herbaceous perennial
Flowering
Summer
Height/spread
1.5m x 1m
Position
Full sun, part shade, sheltered
Soil
Any average to moist soil
Hardiness
USDA 6b/7a / RHS H6

Type
Shrub rose
Flowering
Summer, autumn
Height/spread
1m x 1m
Position
Full sun, sheltered
Soil
Moist, well-drained
Hardiness
USDA 6b/7a /
RHS H6

Rosa **Munstead Wood ('Ausbernard')**
Rose Munstead Wood

This rose is amazing not only for its free-flowering nature and colour – the flowers open to deep velvety crimson – but also for its fabulous old-fashioned fruity scent. It is tough and less susceptible to diseases than many roses. We do not use any pesticides; keeping the soil clear of fallen rose leaves and regularly deadheading gives us a long season of generally disease-free roses. It looks great in many of our borders, especially if paired with *Stipa tenuissima*, astrantias or geraniums.

GROW A big handful of fertiliser and a decent mulch in early spring, plus regular deadheading provide great results. Prune back up to two thirds of growth in late winter. Pick up any dead leaves.

Stipa tenuissima
Mexican feather grass

This is my favourite grass as it is so versatile in the garden. It is graceful and soothing in the way it billows and ripples and flows with the summer and autumn breezes, becoming more golden-blonde as the season advances. It forms feathery, arching clumps of almost cotton-thin grass and fluffy plumes of light golden flowers. It lasts well into winter and as other plants die back, its position in the garden becomes more prominent. It does die back later in winter, however, particularly in colder and wetter weather. At Bishop's Palace it has been paired with *Rosa* 'Darcey Bussell' and *Geranium* Rozanne.

GROW It seeds freely but does not like being disturbed or mulched. Where possible leave the swathes undisturbed and spot weed in between. It can be reduced by cold, wet winters. Carefully pull off dead foliage around the base of the plant in spring but avoid cutting it all back.

Type
Deciduous grass
Flowering
Summer, autumn
Height/spread
1m x 50cm
Position
Full sun, sheltered
Soil
Moist, well-drained
Hardiness
USDA 8b/9a / RHS H4

Tetrapanax papyrifer 'Rex'
Chinese rice-paper plant 'Rex'

I love the architectural value of this suckering plant. It's a large shrub or small tree, and it loses its large (up to 1m across) palmately lobed leaves in late winter and looks great with other exotic plants. The tall, bare stems in winter and spring look almost as striking and architectural as the plant in full leaf. Some people are allergic to the fine hairs on the leaves, which can cause coughing and sneezing, but I'm prepared to put up with that for its sheer impressiveness!

GROW It benefits from compost and feeding and prefers a sheltered, sunny aspect. Requires little special attention other than removing dead leaves to get the best architectural value in winter. Remove or propagate from suckers.

Type
Shrub or small tree
Flowering
Autumn
Height/spread
5m x 4m
Position
Full sun, sheltered
Soil
Well-drained
Hardiness
USDA 8b/9a / RHS H4

Type
Herbaceous perennial
Flowering
Summer, autumn
Height/spread
1m x 50cm
Position
Full sun
Soil
Moist, well-drained
Hardiness
USDA 6b/7a / RHS H6

Phlomis russeliana →
Turkish sage

This is a real conversation starter. It looks so unusual with its three or four whorls of yellow, tubular, deadnettle-like flowers up the stems, each sitting on a mat of large, hairy, green-grey, sage-like leaves. Even after it goes to seed the structure remains, so leave the deadheading until late winter. *P. russeliana* looks great when mixed in a hot border, for example with red poppies, *Nepeta sibirica*, anchusas, heucheras and fennel, and gives many weeks of interest. It's also tough and reliable.

GROW It benefits from lifting, splitting and replanting every three or four years as it can become blind after a time. Add a general fertiliser in early spring and a light mulch.

GREG LOADES
Editor, writer and author,
East Yorkshire, UK

Greg Loades is a gardens and gardening writer, and the author of
The Modern Cottage Garden. He was previously deputy editor of
The English Garden and gardening editor at *Gardeners' World*.
instagram.com/hull_urban_gardener

Euphorbia × martini
Martin's spurge

There is something wonderfully contrary about this plant. As summer
turns to autumn and the foliage of many plants declines and decays, this
valuable perennial shows off an abundance of lush, dark green fingers
of foliage that can almost kid you into believing it is spring again. Such
freshness is most welcome at this time of year and the plant is a picture
when placed among late-flowering perennials such as persicarias
and sedums, or an evergreen sedge such as *Carex oshimensis*
'Everillo'. Maintaining its freshness through winter, it then dazzles with
more vibrant colour, its showy lime-green bracts with a deep red centre
give the patio or garden a beautiful boost before most of the spring
bulbs have burst into bloom. It's a plant to savour on those unseasonably
warm days at the end of winter, when the garden gets a glimpse of
spring to come and it's possible to sit comfortably outside.

GROW I have grown this plant in pots of equal parts soil and multipurpose
compost, topped with grit, and also in the garden in clay soil. It has thrived
in both. The only preening I do is to remove the old flowers in summer (take
care when doing this because the cut stems exude a milky sap that can
irritate the skin).

Type
Evergreen subshrub
Flowering
Spring, summer
Height/spread
1m x 1m
Position
Full sun, part shade,
sheltered
Soil
Well-drained
Hardiness
USDA 7b/8a / RHS H5

KATE BRADBURY
Wildlife gardener,
Brighton, UK

Kate Bradbury is a wildlife gardener, broadcaster and author of a number
of books, including *Wildlife Gardening for Everyone and Everything* and
The Tree in My Garden. twitter.com/kate_bradbury

Type
Deciduous tree
Flowering
Spring
Height/spread
6m x 5m
Position
Full sun, part shade
Soil
Moist, well-drained
Hardiness
USDA 6a–1 / RHS H7

Crataegus monogyna
Common hawthorn

Hawthorn is my favourite tree for a small garden. It's a fantastic
wildlife plant, packed with blossom in spring and nutritious haws in
autumn. Its leaves are eaten by the caterpillars of several species
of moth and its gnarled bark provides lots of nooks and crannies
for insects to sneak into. Birds nest in its branches, too. Hawthorn
can be grown as a small tree, a shrub or as a hedging plant – it's
really versatile. I wouldn't have a garden without at least one.

GROW If growing as a tree, stake it properly to ensure it establishes well
and flowers and fruits to its maximum potential. If growing as a hedge,
trim every other year to ensure some species can complete their life
cycle rather than ending up on the pruning pile.

LINDA SMITH
Owner, Waterside Nursery,
Leicestershire, UK

Linda Smith has been growing and selling pond plants and water lilies for over 25 years. She has won seven gold medals at the RHS Chelsea Flower Show for her aquatic plant exhibits. *watersidenursery.co.uk*

Type
Aquatic perennial
Flowering
Summer
Height/spread
30cm x 15cm
Position
Full sun for best flowering and below the depth of any potential ice on the water
Soil
Clay loam compost
Hardiness
USDA 7b/8a / RHS H5

Nymphaea 'Pygmaea Helvola' →
Waterlily 'Pygmaea Helvola'

I love this miniature water lily as it is so tiny yet so exquisitely formed. The leaf is olive-green with maroon markings and is only 3cm wide. The flower is the palest yellow, with a spiked petal, and each flower reaches 3–4cm across. A dainty plant, it grows from a basket placed on a 25cm base so that the leaf grows up to the water surface. The whole plant only covers a width of 15cm when mature so is ideal for providing surface cover in small patio-container ponds, shading the water to help control algae growth.

GROW A miniature water lily should not be placed more than 25cm below the water – making it grow from too deep a position means it will have no energy left to flower. Give it a flowering boost with a feed ball twice a season in spring and early summer, so it has plenty of nutrients in the compost to encourage the formation of buds. Keep all water lilies in still water – they do not like to be sited under waterfalls or fountains where the top surface of the leaf will get splashed.

Aponogeton distachyos
Water hawthorn

This plant is a favourite as it flowers at the opposite time of year to most others in the pond, from spring into summer and sometimes again when the water cools in autumn. The flowers have a lovely vanilla scent I really adore. When we have hundreds of them all flowering at once in the nursery their fragrance completely fills the air. It grows 15cm-long oval leaves that float on the surface of the water. It is a great addition to a pond as it is the first plant to flower in the year. The white flowers have an unusual forked shape with contrasting black anthers that float on the water surface. Stunning.

GROW Place in the same planting zone as a water lily, to complement the water lily season and extend the period of interest of leaf and flower across the water surface. Grow in an aquatic mesh basket and clay soil placed approximately 60cm under the water surface (below any potential ice), and allow the leaf to travel up through the water. Helps control early algae bloom in a pond. Feed with an aquatic feed ball when the plant shows growth early in the season.

Type
Aquatic perennial
Flowering
Spring, summer, autumn
Height/spread
10cm x 1m
Position
Full sun, part shade, full shade; leaf and flower lasts longest in shade where water is cooler
Soil
Clay loam compost
Hardiness
USDA 8b/9a / RHS H4

Anemopsis californica
Apache beads

This plant is unique in its looks and its scent, which reminds me of honey. The perfume comes from the flowers, which are creamy-white and formed from a cone of small flowers with five to eight large white bracts like petals around the base of the cone. You have to get quite close to smell it, but it is worth bending down for. The plant grows with upright oval grey-green leaves that turn red tinted later in the season – another bonus. Good for colonising a pondside, it can screen the edge of a pond and boggy areas as its running rootstock is able to wander between the

Type
Perennial
Flowering
Summer
Height/spread
50cm x 50cm
Position
Full sun, part shade
Soil
Clay loam compost, bog
Hardiness
USDA 6b/7a / RHS H6

two zones. People often ask if this unusual and tropical-looking plant is hardy through the winter – they can't believe their luck when they learn that it can grow outside in a pond or boggy area in the UK!

GROW Grow in an aquatic mesh basket with clay soil with 2–3cm of water over the top of the basket in a pond or permanently waterlogged boggy area of ground. Feed with an aquatic feed ball when the plant shows growth early in the season. Leave any stoloniferous root runners to spread – they will root from the nodes into boggy soil and produce new plants. Or, when each node has rooted into the water of a pond, the rootstock can be cut off and divided into sections to be potted on or transplanted.

Type
Perennial
Flowering
Summer
Height/ spread
8cm x 50cm
Position
Sun, part shade
Soil
Clay loam compost, poorly-drained
Hardiness
USDA 6b/7a / RHS H6

Myosotis scorpioides
Water forget-me-not

This is a favourite of mine because it is a favourite of more than one type of pondlife. It is key in pond ecosystems, enhancing the life cycle of many creatures. In spring the newts wrap their eggs in its leaf foliage and tadpoles and other underwater species hide beneath its stems. Later in summer its blue flowers are visited by airborne insect pollinators such as butterflies and bees. *M. scorpioides* is an easy-to-grow native British pond plant that spreads across the water surface from a basket placed on a shallow shelf. As it grows out into the central area of water or around a shallowing beach area, it softens the harsh edges of the pond and links groups of upright plants to create habitats for wildlife.

GROW Grow in an aquatic mesh basket with clay soil with 4cm of water over the top of the basket. Do not cut back in autumn or you will remove the new growth for next year. In winter leave the black stems that run across the water as these will reshoot all along their length in spring. Easy to reproduce from seed or divide in summer and replant in wet soil.

Cyperus involucratus
Umbrella plant

This evergreen plant, with its interesting leaf structure, is so good at adding upright foliage to the pond. The leaf structures are actually bracts in a spoke arrangement sitting on top of a tall, upright stem of 60–80cm that grows through summer without the need for staking. This stem is used by dragonfly and damselfly larvae when it is time for them to climb up and out of the pond water, becoming adults that fly and mate and complete their life cycle. Later in the year it produces clusters of seedheads on fine stems. Unlike some cyperus of this shape and texture, it is hardy as long as the crown of the plant is kept below water level and out of ice and frost areas. It gives a pond an almost tropical feel.

GROW Grow in an aquatic mesh basket with clay soil with 4cm of water over the top of the basket in a pond. Feed with an aquatic feed ball when the plant shows growth early in the season. Leave stems to stand during winter and only cut back in spring when new shoots have started to grow strongly. Reproduce from seed or cut off the top of a stem with a spoked bract head and plant in wet soil – it will root down to form a new plant. Children can grow the head in water on a windowsill and see the roots grow from the underside of the head. Once it's strongly rooted, they can pot it into a basket.

Type
Perennial
Flowering
Summer
Height/ spread
1m x 1m
Position
Full sun, part shade
Soil
Clay loam compost, poorly-drained
Hardiness
USDA 7b/8a / RHS H5

MIKE NELHAMS
Garden curator,
Tresco Abbey Garden,
Isles of Scilly, UK

Mike Nelhams returned to Tresco Abbey Garden in 1984 as head gardener, having previously trained there in 1976. In 1994 he took up the post of garden curator. He is also a fellow of the Institute of Horticulture and an associate of honour of the RHS. *tresco.co.uk*

Leucadendron argenteum
Silver tree

If I had to choose one plant above all others, it would be the specimen that visitors to Abbey Garden have most asked about over the last 35 years – the silver tree. It is singular and has a striking appearance that invites comment on a daily basis. It also draws a fine line between easily grown and easy to die – the conditions on Tresco perfectly mirror the climate of its native South African Western Cape, so when all is well they flourish, but when any spell of cold weather appears, they do not. Today its natural habitat is limited to the slopes of Table Mountain, Cape Town. Although the tree doesn't occur naturally anywhere else in the world, it grows surprisingly well on Tresco. Atlantic, salt-laden gales, drought-ridden summers and poor-nutrient soil fit it perfectly. Its horticultural appeal, and the 'silver' of its name, comes from its beautiful leaves. The leaves are covered with tiny hairs that give them a soft appearance but do a good job of deflecting sunlight and trapping moisture.

GROW Find the windiest and most open spot you can for planting, avoiding cold winds and areas where moisture and frost may accumulate. The general misconception is that, since they have a tender quality, they need to be sheltered. This would be a mistake. Most plants in the *Proteaceae* family, to which the silver tree belongs, enjoy plenty of air movement. If given a humid, still atmosphere, they tend to sulk. Plenty of drainage helps. To determine if they are growing well, we are not looking for flowers but a silvery leaf that shimmers when presented with any sort of wind. You will not be disappointed. Do not give it any assistance with nutrients, especially phosphate. It thrives on nutrient-poor soils and produces thousands of short-lived rootlets, along with normal roots, that are extremely adept at absorbing water and the required nutrients. If planted in rich soil, they do not produce these rootlets as they would absorb lethal doses of nutrients and perish.

Type
Evergreen tree
Flowering
Spring, summer
Height/ spread
10m x 4m
Position
Full sun, open
Soil
Well-drained, acid, neutral
Hardiness
USDA 9b/10a / RHS H3

PAUL MALGET
Creative director,
La Famille, Surrey, UK

Paul Malget is the creative director at La Famille, a flower business with a passion for seasonality and renowned for its naturalistic approach to design. *lafamille.co.uk*

Lychnis coronaria
Rose campion

I grew up with gardening, following my mother around and grabbing handfuls of annuals along the way. Quite often I would be found lifting plants by the roots and presenting them to visitors. As a professional florist I have never been afraid of colour, but I look for strong transition flowers that knit the tapestry together. I guess I approach gardening in the same way that I do floral design – thinking about focal flowers, textures for shape and form. I have never had a particular favourite plant, but *L. coronaria* is just such a doer. I like to be knocked out by a garden plant, and this one courts favour and catches your eye in any setting. It looks good planted in cottage-style and coastal gardens, as well as in containers, and its self-seeding properties lend it to naturalistic, prairie-style planting.

GROW A good cut-and-come-again flower; if you're not cutting for the vase, deadhead regularly. You can also use the strong silver foliage, which is attractive in arrangements.

Type
Biennial, short-lived perennial
Flowering
Summer
Height/ spread
1m x 50cm
Position
Full sun, part shade
Soil
Well-drained
Hardiness
USDA 6a–1 / RHS H7

JO THOMPSON
Garden designer, East
Sussex, UK

Jo Thompson has won multiple awards, including four RHS Chelsea Flower Show gold medals. She sits on several RHS advisory committees, lectures in the UK and abroad and is a visiting tutor at the London College of Garden Design. Her love of colour is celebrated in her book *The Gardener's Palette*. *jothompson-garden-design.co.uk*

Rosa 'Félicité-Perpétue'
Rose 'Félicité-Perpétue'

Type
Rambler rose
Flowering
Summer
Height/spread
8m x 4m
Position
Full sun, part shade, sheltered
Soil
Moist, well-drained
Hardiness
USDA 6b/7a / RHS H6

I am in love with the rose – I have been referred to as the queen of roses! I feel that a garden without roses is like a sky without stars. Even in the wildest garden, I can find a spot for a rose and make it feel totally at home.

'Félicité-Perpétue' is a wonderful rose with clusters of tiny creamy-white, delicately scented pompoms, flowering later than the other ramblers. I grow it with early-flowering *Clematis alpina* in order to get colour earlier on. It provides sparkles and glimmers in the evening as it climbs over a pergola or against a wall.

Another fabulous rambler is 'Adélaïde d'Orléans'. It has elegant, slightly frilled petals that are creamy-white tinged with pink – the flowers are exquisite drooping down through a rose walkway. I have this on an arch over my garden gate and it provides the prettiest of welcomes in the summer, dropping a carpet of confetti petals as the flowers fade.

GROW For best flowering apply a balanced fertiliser and mulch in late winter or early spring.

Type
Rambler rose
Flowering
Summer, autumn
Height/spread
4m x 4m
Position
Full sun
Soil
Moist, well-drained
Hardiness
USDA 6b/7a / RHS H6

Rosa The Albrighton Rambler ('Ausmobile')
Rose [The Albrighton Rambler]

Such a fabulous rambler, which I prize as much for its repeat flowering as for its elegant blooms. Graceful in habit, in my garden it provides a pretty backdrop to a wilder area. Unusually for a rambler, it has fully double flowers that are small and cup-shaped. They are blush-pink fading to blush-white and are held in large, pretty hanging sprays.

GROW I have it with *Erigeron karvinskianus* at ground level – a really delicate and pretty combination.

Rosa 'Meg'
Rose 'Meg'

Type
Climbing rose
Flowering
Summer, autumn
Height/spread
4m x 2.5m
Position
Full sun, sheltered
Soil
Moist, well-drained
Hardiness
USDA 6b/7a / RHS H6

I first saw this fabulous climber at Sissinghurst and fell in love with it on the spot. Her peachy-pink relaxed flowers have an untidiness about them that makes them appear so delicate and yet confident at the same time. The open nature of the flowers makes them a target for pollinators. Her blooms give way to red hips that continue the colour through the seasons.

GROW Flowers very happily on an east-facing wall.

Rosa 'Blush Noisette'
Rose 'Noisette Carnée'

Type
Climbing rose
Flowering
Summer, autumn
Height/spread
3m x 1.5m
Position
Full sun, sheltered
Soil
Moist, well-drained
Hardiness
USDA 6a–1 / RHS H7

An excellent compact climbing rose for a tighter spot. Beautifully scented, it has flowers that go on and on and on. I have even known it to be flowering on Christmas Day. Tiny, delicate, blush-pink blooms flower in hundreds of clusters all over the plant, giving off a rich, musky clove fragrance.

GROW I match the gorgeous little cupped blooms of 'Blush Noisette' with *Clematis* 'Étoile Violette', whose purple petals show up well against the pale pink.

Type
Shrub rose
Flowering
Summer, autumn
Height/spread
1m x 1m
Position
Full sun, any aspect
Soil
Moist, well-drained
Hardiness
USDA 6a–1 / RHS H7

Rosa 'Tuscany Superb'
Rose 'Tuscany Superb'

A compact, prickly shrub rose that is very fragrant, with velvety dark blooms. I am a huge fan of old roses – I don't find that they are susceptible to disease in my organic garden. I don't spray, and any aphids soon get snapped up by baby blue tits. With 'Tuscany Superb', deep red ruffles of petals are the foil to gold stamens – there's a gentle nobility about these flowers, and their long-lasting nature only adds to the charm of this upright rose.

GROW I team the rich colours of 'Tuscany Superb' with *Salvia nemorosa* 'Caradonna' and *Geranium* Rozanne for an easy, sumptuous display.

Rosa 'Ispahan'
Rose 'Ispahan'

Type
Shrub rose
Flowering
Summer
Height/spread
1.5m x 1.5m
Position
Full sun, sheltered
Soil
Moist, well-drained
Hardiness
USDA 6b/7a / RHS H6

Another old rose I can't do without, a vigorous and bushy medium-sized damask shrub with fragrant, double pink flowers. In my garden, self-seeding *Briza media*, the common quaking grass, ripples along in front of it, creating movement and linking it happily to the clover lawn beyond. It is always one of the first of the summer-flowering old roses to bloom and has a strong, fine fragrance.

GROW Exquisite scent and beautiful blooms made up of unruly petals make this rose perfect by a path or, as in my garden, by a seating area.

Type
Shrub rose
Flowering
Summer, autumn
Height/spread
1.5m x 1.5m
Position
Full sun, sheltered
Soil
Moist, well-drained
Hardiness
USDA 6b/7a / RHS H6

Rosa The Lark Ascending ('Ausursula')
Rose [The Lark Ascending]

There are so many shades, hues and tints within the petals of this glorious rose bred by David Austin. Pinks, apricots, yellows, oranges and peaches all gleam in a manner reminiscent of mother-of-pearl, the petals so fine and delicate that it seems you are handling an object in the finest of fragile porcelain. Named after the much-loved piece of music by Ralph Vaughan Williams.

GROW Repeat-flowering, this rose goes, I say bravely, with any other rose in the garden, with a versatility of colour in its flowers. Easy and recommended.

Rosa Gentle Hermione ('Ausrumba')
Rose [Gentle Hermione]

This is named after the wife of Leontes in Shakespeare's *The Winter's Tale*. A shrub rose with perfectly formed, shallow cups of pure light pink, paling to soft blush on the outer petals. The leaves are tinged red at first, later turning green. Sweetly scented, these shell-like blooms in proper are a mainstay of the borders I create, and their 'gentleness' stops every garden visitor in their tracks. They have a strong, warm myrrh fragrance.

GROW Looks beautiful as a foil to pale blue irises and forms an attractive, quite broad shrub, with slightly arching stems.

Type
Shrub rose
Flowering
Summer, autumn
Height/spread
1.5m x 1.5m
Position
Full sun, sheltered
Soil
Moist, well-drained
Hardiness
USDA 6b/7a / RHS H6

Type
Shrub rose
Flowering
Summer
Height/spread
1.5m x 1m
Position
Full sun, sheltered
Soil
Moist, well-drained
Hardiness
USDA 6b/7a / RHS H6

Rosa Falstaff ('Ausverse')
Rose [Falstaff]

This has a petal-rich full flower and one of the best deep reds I know among the English roses, which changes beautifully into purple. A repeat-flowering medium shrub with a good fragrance.

GROW Its portly yet elegant blooms combine satisfactorily with *Verbena bonariensis* and all shades of violet to mauve.

LEE CONNELLY
Gardening educator, Skinny Jean Gardener, Essex, UK

Lee Connelly, known as the Skinny Jean Gardener, is a gardening podcaster and presenter. He hosts podcast *Teacher/Parent Garden Club* and is author of *How to Get Kids Gardening*. His School Gardening Success Plan supports primary schools in the UK in teaching children how to grow their own. *skinnyjeangardener.co.uk*

Wildflowers

I've chosen UK native wildflowers – a group of plants including yarrow, corncockle, cornflower, common knapweed, foxglove, viper's bugloss, lady's bedstraw, corn marigold, ox-eye daisy, field forget-me-not, common poppy, selfheal, meadow buttercup, red campion, white campion, salad burnet and great mullein – because they are the easiest and most rewarding plants to sow for children, and they're incredible for attracting wildlife to our gardens. This teaches children that wild areas in our gardens are as important as neat lawns, as they create places for our pollinators and other wildlife to make a home.

I remember the first time I sowed wildflower seeds with my daughter when she was small. That first thing we grew together made gardening a magical activity that we have created memories from ever since. A great way to get children involved is to get their hands messy by creating wildflower seed balls. Mix seeds, compost and water, roll the mixture into balls and dry them out on the windowsill. Throw these out into your chosen area of the garden and over time you'll get a mini-wildflower meadow. A sprinkle of red clay and chilli powder in your seed balls helps them better hold together and deters pests from taking them away.

GROW Wildflowers need plenty of water and sun to get started, but once germinated generally need no help to continue growing. A well-weeded area is needed before sowing seeds to stop competition. If left to grow and die off, they will reseed for the next year.

Type
Annual, biennial, perennial
Flowering
Summer
Height/ spread
Various
Position
Full sun, part shade
Soil
Moist, well-drained
Hardiness
Various

TIMOTHY WALKER
Lecturer, botanist and
author, Oxfordshire, UK

Timothy Walker is a lecturer in plant biology at Somerville College, Oxford,
and was formerly director of the University of Oxford Botanic Garden and
Harcourt Arboretum. *timothywalker.org.uk*

Euphorbia × pasteurii
Pasteur spurge

In 1999 a very vigorous euphorbia seedling appeared in my wife's garden in
Oxford. It was growing close to *Euphorbia mellifera* (from Madeira and the
Canary Islands) and *E. stygiana* (from the Azores). The seedling was subsequently
identified as a hybrid between the two by George Pasteur, a third-year biology
undergraduate. In form and structure the hybrid was intermediate between its
parents, but using DNA analysis George showed unequivocally that half of its
genes were from *E. mellifera* (the pollen parent) and half were from *E. stygiana*
(on which the seeds developed). It was formally named in 2003, and is a record
of George's work. It produces fertile seeds that come true if there are no parent
plants in the vicinity. But it is also fully fertile with both of its parents, so there are
many hybrids of unknown parentage in cultivation. The only plants that can be
guaranteed are those in my wife's garden

Like many euphorbias, Pasteur spurge makes a great backdrop to other plants
such as tulips, irises, amsonia, eryngiums, *Geranium phaeum* and agapanthus. It
has flowers typical of euphorbias and a honey scent.

GROW It's happy in any soil from clay to alluvial loam. No maintenance required
whatsoever, but if it gets too big for its situation, it can be cut to the ground at Easter.
It will grow back to 2m in three to four years.

Type
Evergreen
shrub
Flowering
Summer
**Height/
spread**
3m x 6m
Position
Full sun
Soil
Well-
drained
Hardiness
USDA 8b/9a
/ RHS H4

SARAH WYNDHAM LEWIS
Co-founder, Bermondsey
Street Bees, London, UK

Sarah Wyndham Lewis is co-founder of sustainable beekeeping practice
Bermondsey Street Bees. She is a professional honey sommelier, writer
and author of *Planting for Honeybees*. *bermondseystreetbees.co.uk*

Malus sylvestris
Crab apple

This wonderful tree is a stalwart of Britain's ancient woodlands and an ancestor
of most of our eating apples and ornamentals. It's a significant source of pollen
and nectar, serving a wide variety of pollinators. On the bee front, it is a magnet
for both honey bees and their wild cousins, the bumblebees and solitary bees.
As an ancient native species, it is perfectly attuned to our climate and the needs
of our native wildlife. Bats will roost in its branches and the profuse autumn-into-
winter fruits feed foxes, badgers and smaller mammals, as well as many birds.
The fruit is also a pectin-rich treat for human foragers, making a delicious jelly.

With a fretwork of twisty branches and an impressive crown, crab apples are
beautiful trees with enormous character and presence, even in winter. Glossy dark
green leaves turn to a pretty yellow in autumn. Its spring flowers (often scented)
are profuse in white or pink and accompanied by the buzz of happy bees. Its slow
growth rate makes it a good choice for small gardens. There are hundreds of
varieties to choose from – my advice would be to go for one with an RHS 'perfect
for pollinators' designation, such as *M. × zumi* 'Golden Hornet' or *M.* 'John Downie'.

GROW This is an incredibly easy-going tree, perfect for small gardens as it takes such a
long time to reach its full size and can be kept trimmed. Fully hardy, its only real issue is
a dislike of waterlogged soil, so make sure you provide proper drainage. Prune
sensitively in late winter or early spring to maintain the natural shape.

Type
Deciduous
tree
Flowering
Spring
**Height/
spread**
12m x 8m
Position
Full sun,
part shade,
exposed,
sheltered
Soil
Moist, well-
drained
Hardiness
USDA 6b/7a
/ RHS H6

LAWRENCE AND ELIZABETH BANKS
Hergest Croft Gardens, Herefordshire, Wales

Lawrence Banks was treasurer of the RHS, his wife Elizabeth is a landscape architect and former RHS president. In 2017 she was awarded a CBE for services to horticulture. The Banks family's roots on the Hergest estate go back over 200 years, when Richard William Banks inherited it in 1858. It is now in the care of Edward and Julia Banks. It has one of the finest collections of trees in private ownership in the UK. *hergest.co.uk*

Davidia involucrata →
Handkerchief tree

This is a historic tree, grown from a seed collected by Ernest Wilson in China in 1904. Spreading and vase-shaped, it is spectacular when covered in bracts in late spring – they look like paper handkerchiefs, hence its common name. Our specimen is a Tree Register of the British Isles (TROBI) champion.

GROW Water well when young.

Type
Deciduous tree
Flowering
Spring
Height/spread
25m x 25m
Position
Full sun, part shade
Soil
Moist, well-drained
Hardiness
USDA 7b/8a / RHS H5

Type
Deciduous tree
Flowering
Spring
Height/spread
15m x 10m
Position
Full sun, part shade, sheltered
Soil
Moist, well-drained
Hardiness
USDA 6b/7a / RHS H6

Acer palmatum 'Sango-kaku'
Coral-bark maple

This is an easy-to-grow, small deciduous tree that provides colour all year round. It has red twigs in the winter, yellow spring leaves and golden autumn colour. We believe that the plant at Hergest came from Thomas Herman Lowinsky, who spent his wealth gardening at his Georgian home Tittenhurst Park at the turn of the twentieth century. Our specimen is a TROBI champion.

GROW Note that this is one of the larger *A. palmatum* cultivars.

Zelkova serrata
Japanese zelkova

Large deciduous tree with a graceful, wide, spreading habit and colourful flaky bark with leaves spread all the way down the branches. An easy tree to grow, and resistant to elm disease.

GROW Water when young.

Type
Deciduous tree
Flowering
Spring
Height/spread
25m x 25m
Position
Part shade, open woodland
Soil
Moist, well-drained
Hardiness
USDA 6b/7a / RHS H6

Type
Deciduous tree
Flowering
Spring
Height/spread
15m x 5m
Position
Open woodland, not too shady
Soil
Moist, well-drained, acid
Hardiness
USDA 8b/9a / RHS H4

Magnolia campbellii 'Dick Banks'
Magnolia 'Dick Banks'

'Dick Banks' is the first *M. campbellii* that ever flowered at Hergest. It was a gift from horticulturist Harold Hillier to my father. It is a spectacular dark pink form, flowering in spring and offering a wonderful burst of colour.

GROW Do not plant in a frost pocket, and give it plenty of height to grow.

Pseudotsuga menziesii
Douglas fir

The Douglas fir is one of the grandest of conifers, reaching a great height. It is one of the finest forest trees, and probably the tallest tree to grow in Britain since the ice age. The oldest trees at Hergest Croft were planted in 1867 on a steep, north-facing slope.

GROW An easy tree to grow.

Type
Evergreen conifer
Height/spread
65m x 15m
Position
Woodland, part shade
Soil
Well-drained
Hardiness
USDA 6b/7a / RHS H6

Arbutus menziesii
Madrona

Conspicuous panicles of flowers (much like lily of the valley) are followed by orange strawberry-like fruit; the bark peels to reveal orange and green underneath. Our specimen was planted in 1910, a fine introduction by botanist David Douglas from California.

GROW Watering and frost protection are needed when the plant is young.

Type
Evergreen tree
Flowering
Summer
Height/spread
20m x 15m
Position
Full sun, sheltered
Soil
Moist, well-drained
Hardiness
USDA 8b/9a / RHS H4

Abies cephalonica
Greek fir

Our rugged old veteran specimen of *A. cephalonica* has withstood many a storm. It's an easy tree to grow and it's bomb-proof. A large evergreen conifer tolerant of a wide variety of conditions, with a straight trunk and occasional large boughs.

GROW Tolerant of most conditions. Water when young.

Type
Evergreen conifer
Height/spread
30m x 15m
Position
Full sun, part shade
Soil
Moist, well-drained
Hardiness
USDA 6b/7a / RHS H6

Tilia maximowicziana
Lime

A broad, spreading tree, heavy with blooms in summer. This is one of the finest limes for flower and scent. Its leaves are dark green, the undersides are a lighter shade of green with white hairs, which appear when the leaves move in the wind.

GROW An ideal parkland tree.

Type
Deciduous tree
Flowering
Summer
Height/spread
20m x 20m
Position
Full fun
Soil
Moist, well-drained
Hardiness
USDA 6b/7a / RHS H6

Type
Deciduous tree
Flowering
Spring
Height/spread
20m x 10m
Position
Full sun, part shade
Soil
Moist, well-drained
Hardiness
USDA 6a–1 / RHS H7

Betula utilis subsp. *albosinensis* 'Bowling Green'
Chinese red birch 'Bowling Green'

This upright, vase-shaped birch is one of the best seedlings raised from seed collected by plant collector Ernest Wilson. It has very fine pink-to-copper peeling bark, probably the best of all coloured-bark birches.

GROW A medium-sized, quick-growing deciduous tree, it is simple and undemanding, and a good plant for woodland edge.

PHILIPPA STEWART
Flower farmer, Cheshire, UK

Philippa Stewart started dahlia farm Justdahlias in 2016 and now grows over 150 varieties of dahlia for cutting. *justdahlias.co.uk*

Dahlia

Dahlia (SEE ILLUSTRATION PAGE 89)

I first started growing dahlias in my garden many years ago because I was in need of some late summer colour. That first summer I couldn't believe how well the dahlias kept pumping out bloom after fabulous bloom until the frosts came. Once I realised there are thousands of different varieties out there, I was hooked. After contacting florists in my area I discovered there was a market for these flowers, so in 2017 I increased my growing area into a field in the hope of selling flowers to help fund my obsession. My passion started with the large, dinner-plate varieties – how marvellous it was to produce flowers that are 30cm in diameter. Over the years my taste has got smaller and smaller, and last year it was the mini pompoms that had me enthralled. With so many different shapes, sizes and colours, there's a dahlia out there for everyone.

Dahlias are easy to grow and do well in pots, so no matter how big your plot, there's always room for a dahlia... or 10. But be warned, I started with five or six and this year have planted out over 500. I am frequently asked which my favourite varieties are and I have to say this changes on a regular basis. 'Café au Lait' is probably one of the best known and a must-have on my plot. Other favourites include 'Linda's Baby', 'Carolina Wagemans', 'Barbarry d'Amour', 'Le Castel', 'Coral Strand', 'Tam Tam', 'Snowflake', 'Jean Fairs', 'Sourire de Crozon', 'Small World', 'Cornel Brons', 'Rossendale Flamenco', 'Chat Noir', 'Nuland's Josephine', 'Platinum Blonde', 'Silver Years'... I could go on and on. Since 2019 I have also been drying my dahlias and I am finding that many varieties I do not like fresh dry beautifully. This is doing nothing to help me cut down on numbers.

GROW I take my tubers out of winter storage at the end of March (early spring), when I also divide them. They are then potted up and brought on in a greenhous. I start my dahlias in the greenhouse because I find a larger plant is less susceptible to pests and diseases. It is very important not to over water the plants at this stage as dahlia tubers do not like sitting in the wet. Shoots should appear within a few weeks and, after a period of hardening off, they can be planted out once the risk of frost has passed.

Dahlias prefer full sun, although they also do well in light shade. Add fish, blood and bone meal to the planting hole to promote healthy growth. Once they start flowering, a foliar spray of liquid seaweed helps them keep producing gorgeous blooms. The dahlias in my field are staked using sweet pea netting laid horizontally between hedge-laying posts, but in the garden I use canes and twine.

Deadheading is essential to keep your dahlias flowering all the way until the frosts. Plants in the ground should be checked to see if they need watering once a week and those in pots should be checked every day. During the heat of the day, dahlias sometimes appear to wilt, but this is just their way of preserving moisture. If you wait until the evening before watering, you should find that the plant has recovered.

I lift my tubers in the winter as we are on heavy clay and they would rot in the ground. If you are on lighter soil, it is possible to leave them in over winter – it would be advisable to mulch them thickly to protect them from freezing. Dahlias need dividing, otherwise they produce increasing amounts of foliage and poorer quality blooms. If you leave them in the ground, I recommend lifting and dividing every two to three years.

Type
Tuberous
perennial
Flowering
Summer,
autumn
**Height/
spread**
Varies
according
to variety
Position
Full sun,
sheltered
Soil
Moist, well-
drained
Hardiness
USDA 9b/10a
/ RHS H3

JIM GARDINER
Vice president, RHS, UK

Jim Gardiner was formerly director of horticulture at the RHS, having spent over 20 years as curator of RHS Wisley. He has been curator of Sir Harold Hillier Gardens, and worked and trained at the Royal Botanic Garden Edinburgh, Cambridge University Botanic Garden and Windsor Great Park. He is a trustee of the Tree Register of the British Isles. His books include *Magnolias: A Gardener's Guide*. rhs.org.uk

Type
Tree or shrub
Flowering
Spring, summer
Height/ spread
Varies depending on species
Position
Full sun, part shade
Soil
Moist, well-drained, slightly acid loam
Hardiness
USDA 9a–7b / RHS H4–H5

Magnolia ↘
Magnolia

With over 300 species native to the Americas and Asia, as well as thousands of hybrids, the ancient genus *Magnolia* includes great plants for gardens of all sizes and soil types. These aristocrats of the plant world can be used as accent plants or in the border, collectively flowering for eight months of the year and with many scented, deciduous and evergreen options.
They vary from compact or even wall-trained shrubs to columnar and broad spreading trees. There is a wealth of flower colour, size and shape to choose from, from white, pinks, purples and yellows to stars, tulips, cups and saucers and goblets. There is little differentiation between petals and sepals, so magnolia flowers are composed of tepals. With such a glittering array of choices here are my Gardiner's 'dozen', guaranteed to give all-year-round pleasure.

M. × *loebneri* 'Leonard Messel' (illustrated) is one of the best-known magnolias, having been selected by the head gardener at Nymans, James Comber, during the early 1950s. It is a slow-growing deciduous shrub with pink, star-like flowers crowded on to a fine branch network of stems during spring. A similar yet more compact grower is *M.* × *l* 'Mag's Pirouette', with beautiful white gardenia-like flowers – it makes an ideal shrub for the smallest of gardens.

M. × *soulangeana* is one of the most commonly grown magnolias with white, pink and purple flowers that, depending on variety, often grow into large, wide-spreading shrubs. New Zealander Vance Hooper introduced the *M.* 'Genie', which is far more compact with rich burgundy-red flowers.

Spring-flowering and similarly compact, but this time evergreen, are *M. laevifolia* 'Gail's Favourite' and *M.* 'Fairy Blush'. These produce richly scented white or pale pink flowers from mid-spring to summer and are grown either as free-standing or fan-trained wall shrubs.

There are often comments about spring magnolia blooms being frosted, but two upright pyramidal small trees – *M.* 'Galaxy' and 'Spectrum' – both have frost-tolerant pink flowers. American geneticist Dr August Kehr raised yellow-flowering *M.* 'Daphne' and 'Sunsation', as well as 'Daybreak', with its distinctive pink-with-peach flowers. All three are upright-growing, small trees flowering during spring.

The American species *M. grandiflora*, with its distinctive dark green, waxy foliage and scented white flowers that appear from late spring to autumn, is no stranger to gardens. They have been planted in Britain since the early eighteenth century and are often seen growing against the walls of country houses. But there is a huge diversity of flower and leaf size, as well as vigour, with more recent introductions suited to smaller gardens. *M. g.* 'Kay Parris' and 'Little Gem' both have upright habits, growing into compact large shrubs or small trees. Their size can be mitigated by pruning (even into shapes), which should take place before spring growth begins, but this isn't necessary every year.

GROW Ideally, magnolias prefer a moisture-retentive slightly acidic loam but are also tolerant of mildly alkaline soils, which can be either light or heavy. During the first few years of establishment, their root systems dislike drying out so benefit from having an organic mulch applied. Young plants can be pruned during late summer/early autumn while overmature plants can also be pruned in spring. Magnolias are generally free of pests and diseases, though young plants attract slugs, so be prepared!

ROBERT COLE
Retired nurseryman,
Warwickshire, UK

Robert Cole and his wife Diane ran perennial plant nursery Meadow Farm after his retirement as an architect and landscape architect. They both retired in 2020.

Echinacea
Coneflower

We had been growing *E. purpurea* and a few of its cultivars in the garden at Meadow Farm for some time, but I became interested in this plant when the distinctive, orange-flowered variety 'Art's Pride' was introduced. I began researching cultivars and experimenting with breeding my own plants. Over the years I raised thousands of seedlings as I searched for plants with attractive, strong colours that grew reliably well. My experiments have always been carried out on an amateur, hobby basis, and the bees have always done the pollinating – I merely chose what I considered the best results of their work. But raising and assessing these plants has given me so much pleasure over the years, and provided an array of interesting variations. Particularly notable was my first double seedling, a dark orange from seed of *E. purpurea* 'Razzmatazz', itself a double, but pink. I named it *E.* 'Feckenham Flame'.

GROW I sow seeds in late winter and use a 3:2:1 mixture of peat-free compost, John Innes No.2 and horticultural grit, all passed through a 0.5cm sieve to ensure a loose, friable mix, a boon when you come to separating and pricking out the seedlings in spring. Winter wetness can be an issue, so a well-drained soil is important. Deadhead to prolong the flowering season.

Type
Rhizomatous perennial
Flowering
Summer, autumn
Height/spread
1.5m x 50cm
Position
Full sun, part shade, prefers an open position without competition
Soil
Well-drained
Hardiness
USDA 7b/8a / RHS H5

JO MCKERR
Landscape consultant
and planting designer,
Somerset, UK

Jo McKerr is a landscape consultant and planting designer specialising
in biodiversity. She runs workshops and writes about nature-led
gardening in her brownfield meadow garden in Somerset. *jomckerr.com*

Polystichum setiferum 'Pulcherrimum Bevis' →
Soft shield fern 'Pulcherrimum Bevis'

Type
Evergreen
fern
**Height/
spread**
1m x 1m, but
can be more
Position
Full shade,
part shade,
open or
sheltered
woodland
conditions
Soil
Moist,
humus-rich,
but can
tolerate dry
soils when
established
Hardiness
USDA 6b/7a
/ RHS H6

To be honest, especially when I was younger, I didn't always like gardens, and
many I positively hated. I preferred landscapes, predominantly neglected country
lanes, derelict abandoned places and woodlands – particularly Wistman's Wood
in Dartmoor, Devon. A mesmerising fairy-tale landscape of contorted oak trees,
boulders covered in moss and epiphytic ferns and lichens, this wood is thought to
be a leftover from the ancient prehistoric woodlands that once covered Dartmoor.

Naturalistic gardens can only ever hope to be faint echoes of ancient
landscapes such as Wistman's Wood. Nonetheless, when we use plants such as
the soft shield fern in our gardens we can evoke some of the mood and feel of
those inspirational wild places.

The soft shield fern has fine filigree fronds and is one of the UK's native
woodland ferns. 'Pulcherrimum Bevis', which was found growing in a hedgerow in
Devon by one Mr Bevis in 1876, is a particularly handsome upright cultivar that I first
saw in the garden of Derry Watkins in Somerset. It has an archetypal fern shape
and the most beautiful evergreen fronds that look good right through the depths
of winter, particularly after a frost.

GROW This is a plant that can go almost anywhere you want to add foliage and
texture. It is easy to grow in the dark corners that you don't know what to do with.
Its versatility makes it incredibly useful and its evergreen architectural foliage instantly
gives a distinct woodland-edge feel to any planting. I like to use it under deciduous
trees, creating a lush green underplanting once the more ephemeral spring bulbs and
early flowers have died back. This type of interplanting and 'layered' planting covers
ground and helps to create a naturalistic feel in the garden as well as allowing for
'low-maintenance' and more wildlife-friendly ways of gardening.

Keep it happy by adding leaf mould, homemade compost and well-rotted bark.
This fern is classed as evergreen but it grows fresh new fronds every spring. Remove
the dead fronds in spring to allow the new ones to unfurl. It is sterile (doesn't produce
spores) so can only be reproduced by dividing or micro-propagation.

Type
Deciduous
tree
Flowering
Spring
**Height/
spread**
8m x 8m
Position
Full sun,
sheltered
Soil
Moist, well-
drained
Hardiness
USDA 6b/7a
/ RHS H6

Malus domestica 'Bramley's Seedling'
Apple 'Bramley's Seedling'

Much of my childhood was spent in a small, thatched cottage called
Applegarth on the edge of Dartmoor. This cottage and its garden had been
in my family since the 1500s (and probably before that). It had a sprawling
wild garden full of plants and was dominated by two apple trees (hence the
name of the cottage – 'garth' means a clearing in the woods). One of the apple
trees sat outside of my bedroom. It was a 'Bramley's Seedling' – probably a
remnant of an orchard that was once in the garden. It was an ancient tree,
wonderfully gnarled with low-slung branches that were perfect for climbing.
In spring it was full of blossom and bees; in winter it was full of mistletoe and
song thrushes.

Making gardens that connect emotionally with people is about making
landscapes that evoke a sense of belonging. Past associations, archetypes
and histories weave through gardens and give them a narrative that bonds
human stories with those of plants. We humans seem to be attracted to trees.

In large urban parks we are drawn beneath them to munch our sandwiches and rest. I often notice that outside spaces transform into landscapes and locations to relax in as soon as you plant a tree. Planting a tree gives a garden three dimensions, it provides shade and habitat, and it gives it a legacy of hope for the future. My favourite tree for a garden is the apple, but you may have your own tree.

'Bramley's Seedling' is a bushy, gnarly variety with a distinctive 'apple' shape and habit. It has pale pink blossom in spring that is loved by bees and the fruit can be harvested in autumn and stored over winter. The apples are large, very acidic and one of the best varieties of cooking apple.

GROW This is one of the trickier larger and more characterful apple trees to grow. It is a self-sterile triploid in Group D, which means its flowers need to be pollinated by other nearby apple (or crab apple) trees in pollination Groups C, D and E to make any fruit, and it cannot pollinate other trees. It also requires a reasonable amount of pruning to allow air and light through the tree to prevent disease and encourage fruit to ripen. If that sounds impractical, there are other apples that are self-fertile. There are also ornamental crab apples that grow in a similar fashion to apple trees. These need little pruning and don't suffer from so many pests and diseases, but only produce small crab apple fruits.

Type
Short-lived perennial
Flowering
Summer
Height/ spread
1.5m x 1m
Position
Full sun, part shade
Soil
Moist, well-drained, but tolerates most soils apart from waterlogged
Hardiness
USDA 8b/9a / RHS H4

Valeriana officinalis
Common valerian

I have chosen this plant because it is beautiful and its form and elegant, airy, wild manner immediately evokes a romantic meadow feel in a garden. Its silhouette is extremely distinct: a tall, delicate, upright column with small branching stems topped by little pink-white flowers that emit a strong marshmallow scent in early summer. Umbellifers are my favourite go-to flower forms – in my opinion the 'cow parsley' shape is the one that best conjures a sense of wildness. At its base is a dense clump of green, glossy, serrated leaves.

In early summer it produces nectar and pollen for honey bees, bumblebees, solitary bees, butterflies and beetles. And it is an 'officinalis', a medieval Latin epithet meaning that it was used in medicine and herbalism, and its common names (all-heal, cut-finger) clearly point to its medicinal uses – valerian is still used to treat insomnia, anxiety and menopausal symptoms. For me these herbal uses and ecological functions are important. I like to make gardens that are aesthetically pleasing, add to biodiversity and can be used in other ways too. Plants are beautiful not just as ornaments but as building blocks of ecosystems and most of the material we need to live a full life. Celebrating this within a garden helps us to recreate a thoughtful relationship with nature.

GROW This plant is easy to grow and can become too successful in a garden. It is a good idea to cut it back before it goes to seed to stop it spreading too much. Don't worry if it does seed, though, as it's easy to weed and hoe out the extra seedlings. Try to grow it in poor soils in naturalistic planting schemes as in rich 'fertile' soils it can become beefy and less attractive. I like to grow it on the edge of wildlife ponds.

JIM MARSHALL
Trustee and vice chair, Plant
Heritage, Suffolk, UK

Jim Marshall has worked at Hidcote Manor Garden and the Royal Botanic Garden Edinburgh. He has been a gardens advisor for the National Trust and is vice chair of the RHS Herbaceous Committee. He retired in 2003 to make a one-acre garden in Suffolk with his wife, gardener Sarah Cook. He holds two Plant Heritage National Collections: Malmaison carnations and perpetual flowering carnations. *plantheritage.org.uk*

Dianthus 'Souvenir de la Malmaison'
Malmaison carnation 'Old Blush'

I have been involved with the genus *Dianthus* since an early age. On joining the National Trust as a gardens advisor in 1978 I became interested in historic plant cultivars. Malmaison carnation 'Old Blush' was registered in 1857. It flowers once during summer, with flamboyant, highly scented blush-pink flowers. I also love the similarly flamboyant Malmaison carnation 'Princess of Wales' because of my keen interest in history. It was registered in 1875 and named after Alexandra, the wife of the future Edward VII (son of Queen Victoria). She was Danish, and a keen photographer and watercolour painter. This carnation also flowers once during summer, with strong pink flowers.

GROW Grown in pots in a cold glasshouse, these withstand some degree of frost. They need to be disbudded to get the best flowers. Do not over water, especially in winter. Feed with high-potash liquid feed once the flower buds appear but be aware that overfeeding causes all foliage and no flowers. Needs support in the pot.

Type
Perennial
Flowering
Summer
**Height/
spread**
90cm x 20cm
Position
Full sun
Soil
Peat-free
growing
medium
Hardiness
USDA 9b/10a
/ RHS H3

Dianthus 'Marchioness of Headfort'
Perpetual flowering carnation 'Marchioness of Headfort'

Dianthus 'Marchioness of Headfort' is registered as a 'threatened cultivar' by Plant Heritage. It was given to me by a large estate in Suffolk along with a number of other pre-1970 perpetual flowering cultivars. In fact it was registered pre-1930. It flowers from late spring, with flushes of bloom throughout the summer. The scented flowers have salmon-red ground with white edges.

Another fantastic perpetual flowering carnation is *D.* 'Earl Kelso' – the cultivar is a sport from 'Duke of Norfolk', which occured in our glasshouse in 2012. It flowers in a similar way to 'Marchioness of Headfort', but has creamy white, lightly scented flowers.

GROW These plants should be kept growing throughout winter with careful watering. Start feeding in spring. Grow as sprays, or disbud to grow as a single flower per stem, which gives larger, better-quality flowers. Needs support in the pot.

Type
Perennial
Flowering
Spring,
summer
**Height/
spread**
1.1m x 20cm
Position
Grow in
pots in a
frost-free
glasshouse
Soil
Peat-free
growing
medium
Hardiness
USDA 10b
/ RHS H2

Type
Shrub rose
Flowering
Summer, autumn
Height/spread
1m x 1m
Position
Full sun, open
Soil
Good, moist, well-
drained loam
Hardiness
USDA 7b/8a / RHS H5

Rosa Claire Marshall ('Harunite')
Rose [Claire Marshall]

Named for my late daughter, this hardy, repeat-flowering, bushy floribunda rose has highly scented, attractive, magenta pink, large-petalled flowers with shades of mauve and lilac and dark green foliage. In 2013 it was named the Golden Rose of Baden-Baden, one of the most important awards made to rose breeders.

GROW Keep deadheading to encourage repeat blooming. Roses do not like competition from other plants. Prune hard and feed lightly in spring. We use a mix of fertiliser, sulphate of potash and kieserite (which contains magnesium to improve disease resistance).

Rosa 'Fantin-Latour'
Rose 'Fantin-Latour'

I first saw this beautiful rose, named after the French artist, in the rose garden at Sissinghurst Castle. We now grow it in our own garden and it is one of our favourite roses. As a centifolia rose, it flowers once during early summer, with mid-pink, highly scented double blooms.

GROW It needs some form of support. Can be grown against a wall, but in our garden it grows trained along a 'hurdle fence'. We use sheep hurdles to divide our garden; they give several of our roses (and our tender climbers) support with a good flow of air, which discourages diseases. Feed lightly in spring. We use a mix of fertiliser, sulphate of potash and kieserite (which contains magnesium to improve disease resistance).

Type
Shrub rose
Flowering
Summer
Height/spread
2m x 2m
Position
Full sun
Soil
Good loam
Hardiness
USDA 7b/8a / RHS H5

Rosa 'Charles de Mills'
Rose 'Charles de Mills'

This was one of my favourite shrub roses growing at Hidcote Manor, where I worked in the early 1960s to gain experience prior to studying at Royal Botanic Gardens Edinburgh. It's a Gallica shrub rose with flat, open blooms in rich magenta and a delicate, medium scent.

GROW Looks lovely grown as a specimen on a tripod. Flowers well if pruned. Prune autumn or spring; it flowers on growth made the previous year, so when taking out old growth, leave the strongest shoots.

Type
Shrub rose
Flowering
Summer
Height/spread
1.5m x 1.5m
Position
Full sun, open
Soil
Moist, well-drained
Hardiness
USDA 7b/8a / RHS H5

Type
Short-lived perennial
Flowering
Spring, summer
Height/spread
50cm x 50cm
Position
Full sun, open
Soil
Well-drained, neutral to alkaline
Hardiness
USDA 7b/8a / RHS H5

Dianthus 'Gran's Favourite' ↘
Pink 'Gran's Favourite'

I visited Mrs Desmond (AKA Pamela) Underwood's Ramparts Nursery in Colchester, Essex with my parents, near the beginning of my gardening career. Underwood raised and introduced this variety. It is a short-lived perennial with grey foliage and white flowers laced with red. It has a long flowering period, especially if deadheaded. Good for picking.

GROW Can be grown as a garden plant in a border or in a container.

MIRIA HARRIS
Director, Miria Harris Design,
London, UK

Miria Harris set up her garden design practice in 2011, having worked for
ten years as a contemporary art curator and producer, before retraining
in horticulture. Her designs, which include projects for city gardens,
country estates and public spaces, are underpinned by a wild and
romantic aesthetic and a sustainable approach. *miriaharris.com*

Rosa 'Rambling Rector'
Rose 'Rambling Rector'

I adore roses, even though when I worked as a florist they used to tear my
hands to bits. It's hard to choose a clear favourite but 'Rambling Rector' is
a truly 'stop you in your tracks' kind of plant. As I'm the daughter of a rector,
it may seem an obvious choice – and I did plant one in memory of my
father when he passed away a few years ago – but my love of this rose isn't
sentimental. It's rooted in the sensational smell of its blooms and the pops of
bright joy left lingering by the rosehips in the winter. Its abundance of flowers
also means that you never feel guilty for cutting some for a vase, where they
can hold their own for almost a week. I particularly love planting it where it can
clamber freely into the canopy of a large tree, a perfect example of the William
Robinson-inspired ethos of wild gardening that informs my work.

As its name suggests, it is a rambling rose. Ramblers differ from climbing
roses in that they are bigger, have winter hips and flexible stems that shoot
up from the base, and only bloom once – though this one's clusters of musk-
scented sprays of small, wild-rose-like white flowers persist all summer long.
It is well known for attracting birds, bees and other pollinating insects and its
dense structure offers wonderful opportunities for wildlife shelter.

GROW You'll need gloves and long sleeves if you are going to get involved, even this
rose's juvenile thorns are nasty little spikes. And you do need to get a little bit involved,
at least at first – if you allow the rose to completely ramble away, all the flowers end up
high up and the beguiling fragrance escapes you. To prevent this, you need to arch and
curve the stems as much as possible when it is young to encourage lateral growth and
flowering lower down the plant.

A good companion plant is wisteria. Not only is there no clash of fragrance –
'Rambling Rector' flowers from mid- to late summer – but the strong twisting branches
of wisteria provide a good natural framework to support the rose. As well as climbing
through trees, it is good for covering a wall or shed.

Water generously until established and add fertiliser each spring. Mulch in late winter
or early spring. Prune annually to create a good strong framework and to remove any
dead or diseased wood. Routine pruning can happen in late summer once it has finished
flowering. Carry out renovation pruning in autumn or late winter when the plant has
defoliated and it is easier to see what you are doing.

Type
Rambler
rose
Flowering
Summer
**Height/
spread**
8m x 8m
Position
Full sun, part
shade
Soil
Moist, well-
drained
Hardiness
USDA 6b/7a
/ RHS H6

Plants

People